Introduction to Cybersecurity

Introduction to Cybersecurity

Concepts, Principles, Technologies and Practices

Ajay Singh
MSc. Total Quality Management (TQM) and Business Excellence,
PG Diploma in Cyber Law and Cyber Forensics
Fellow, Institute of Directors;
Member, Academic Advisory Board,
Pace University - Seidenberg School of Computer Science and
Information Systems, New York, USA

Universities Press

All rights reserved. No part of this book may be modified, reproduced or utilised in any form, or by any means, electronic or mechanical, including photocopying, recording or by any information storage and retrieval system, in any form of binding or cover other than in which it is published, without permission in writing from the publisher.

INTRODUCTION TO CYBERSECURITY: CONCEPTS, PRINCIPLES, TECHNOLOGIES AND PRACTICES

UNIVERSITIES PRESS (INDIA) PRIVATE LIMITED

Registered office
3-6-747/1/A & 3-6-754/1, Himayatnagar, Hyderabad 500 029, Telangana, India
info@universitiespress.com; www.universitiespress.com

Distributed by
Orient Blackswan Private Limited

Registered office
3-6-752 Himayatnagar, Hyderabad 500 029, Telangana, India

Other offices
Bengaluru / Chennai / Guwahati / Hyderabad / Kolkata
Mumbai / New Delhi / Noida / Patna / Visakhapatnam

© Universities Press (India) Private Ltd 2023
First published 2023

Cover and book design
© Universities Press (India) Private Ltd 2023

ISBN: 978-93-93330-31-4

Typeset in Minion Pro 10 *by*
SRS Publishing Services, Puducherry

Printed in India by
B.B. Press, Noida 201 301

Published by
Universities Press (India) Private Limited
3-6-747/1/A & 3-6-754/1, Himayatnagar, Hyderabad 500 029, Telangana, India

Care has been taken to confirm the accuracy of the information presented in this book. The author and the publisher, however, cannot accept any responsibility for errors or omissions or for consequences from application of the information in this book, and make no warranty, express or implied, with respect to its contents.

Preface

In a digital world, cybersecurity is an essential and critical survival skill. The numerous benefits that information technology has brought have been accompanied by cyber threats and attacks that can cause severe financial loss, reputational damage, harm to wellbeing and disruption to professional and personal lives. Cybersecurity awareness is a critical part of navigating, surviving and thriving in a digital world that offers many opportunities for growth.

Introduction to Cybersecurity: Concepts, Principles, Technologies and Practices aims to provide students with foundational knowledge across the broad range of topics that they need to navigate cybersecurity challenges at the individual and organizational level. The book incorporates the undergraduate level syllabi of a few universities and the model curriculum developed by the All India Council for Technical Education (AICTE) on the subject. The book assumes no prior knowledge of the subject and is suitable for both technically and non-technically oriented students and others interested in developing a foundational understanding of cybersecurity.

The book comprises 12 chapters. Chapter 1 introduces students to information systems, the need for and goals of information security, basic principles and models. It further covers aspects related to the growth of the Internet and its systems of governance, the types of information system development methodologies in use today as well as information security models.

Chapter 2 covers the various forms of cybercrime, its prevention, computer ethics and global efforts to deal with it. This chapter examines the motivations, tools and methods used by cybercriminals to launch diverse types of cyberattacks and their implications on the targeted organizations.

Every system has some security-related vulnerabilities. Hackers are looking to find them and exploit them whereas defenders are keen to identify them in order to implement security controls and mechanisms to protect their information systems and data. Chapter 3 explains the various sources of vulnerabilities in IT systems, covering a wide range of sources such as application and Internet security, cloud computing and security supply chain and third-party vulnerabilities, vulnerabilities in software deployment, network vulnerabilities and more.

Chapter 4 is devoted to cybersecurity management practices, classification of information and other aspects pertaining to cyber risk management. The role of security policies, procedures, organization and incident response along with their impact on business continuity and disaster recovery are also discussed in the context of enterprise cybersecurity. Further, it covers the importance of standards and frameworks for organizations in implementing their security vision into structured security programs as well as for providing ongoing monitoring, evaluation and strengthening of security measures, all of which contribute to effective cybersecurity management.

Chapter 5 explains the challenges and security issues that are important in building secure information systems, covering different elements such as application development, security design, security of hardware, software, devices, data, networks, operating systems, databases, user management and access control.

Chapter 6 further examines issues and challenges involved in information security governance and risk management. It covers cyber risk management approaches and strategies and the role of frameworks such as ISO/IEC 27001 and NIST. The concept and context of cyber resilience and its integration into cybersecurity and risk management programs and the importance of industry-specific frameworks such as HIPAA, PCI DSS and NY CRR 500 in privacy and data protection is elaborated. The human factor in cybersecurity does not always receive the required attention in cyber risk management; the chapter also examines issues and best practices that can help in motivating employees to take an active part in cybersecurity.

Technology plays a key role in implementing cybersecurity. Chapter 7 is designed to develop an understanding of technologies and related concepts that organizations can deploy for enhancing the security of their information assets.

Chapter 8 familiarizes students with the legal regimen for cybersecurity and acquaints them with key aspects such as cyber forensics, cyber evidence, investigations, Internet forensics, steps for investigating Internet crime and the importance of ethics in cybersecurity. The chapter also examines the importance of cyber laws and the role of governments and international bodies in the establishment of a legal and sustainable ecosystem that can be a foundation for future economic growth.

Online safety, privacy intrusions and breaches and personal cybersecurity are increasingly becoming worrisome for those who are a part of the digital world. In Chapter 9, various issues related to personal security, protection of privacy, data protection and related best practices are discussed.

Chapter 10 analyzes how evolution and advances in digital technologies have had a major influence on both cybercrime and cybersecurity. New approaches and concepts required to address future cybersecurity challenges and the use of technology to boost security and resilience and up the defenders' game against cybercriminals are also explored.

Chapter 11 elaborates on cybersecurity issues and challenges that have emerged based on the use of e-commerce platforms and digital payments, including regulatory guidelines and legal concerns such as privacy and data protection.

Social media has become an integral part of an individual's daily life and organizations too are leveraging it for a variety of purposes including marketing and customer engagement. Chapter 12 examines cybersecurity concerns that have arisen from its increasing usage and further lists best practices that can help individuals and organizations in making their social media-related experiences safer.

The book provides contextual case studies, along with multiple choice and other challenging questions at the end of each chapter to enable readers to assess their understanding. Also provided at the end of the book is an annexure about cybercrime and cyberattack reporting in India, a listing of 50 prominent cyberattacks that have taken place from 2011 to 2021, an additional set of self-assessment questions to test the readers' overall understanding of the subject and a list of abbreviations and acronyms used in the book.

Cybersecurity is an attractive and exciting career option which offers the chance to work with different technologies and a variety of systems. It is a critical area for any modern-day enterprise and represents a high growth opportunity for security professionals all over the world. This book is suitable for students, executives and professionals from any discipline who wish to start learning about cybersecurity and provides foundational knowledge for further exploration of the subject or for pursuing a cybersecurity career.

Ajay Singh

Acknowledgements

Writing a textbook is always a daunting challenge. This book has involved having great clarity about cybersecurity trends, events, news, laws and other related topics in order to be able to present it in a manner that makes the book both comprehensive and readable. The fact that cybersecurity is continuously evolving and shrouded in its own concepts and lexicon has made the task even more difficult.

I have been fortunate to have enjoyed the support of many people who have made this book possible. I am grateful to Universities Press and Thomas Mathew Rajesh, Senior Vice President, and would like to acknowledge the contribution of their editorial staff, especially Kallol Das and Madhavi Sethupathi, whose guidance and support through this process has been most invaluable.

Ajay Singh

Contents

Preface . . . . *v*
Acknowledgements . . . . *vii*
List of Tables . . . . *xi*
List of Info Boxes. . . . . *xiii*

Chapter 1: Security in an Interconnected World — 1

Introduction to Information Systems | What is an Information System? | Evolution and Types of Information Systems | Evolution and Growth of the Internet | Information System Development and Maintenance | Cyberspace and Cybersecurity | What is Information Security? | Organization and Governance of the Internet and Cybersecurity | Information Security Models

Chapter 2: Cybercrime, Cyberattack Tools and Methods, Threat Sources and Cyber Offenders — 23

Introduction | What is a Cybercrime? | Classification of Cybercrimes | Forms of Cybercrimes | Cyber Scams and Frauds | Sources of Threats: Threat Actors and their Motivations | Tools and Methods Used in Cyberattacks/Cybercrimes | What is a Cyberattack? | Responding to Cyberattacks and the Cyber Kill Chain | Cyberattacks: Organizational Implications | Cyberattacks Impacting Citizens and Communities | Prevention of Cybercrime | International Efforts to Deal with Cybercrime | National Cybersecurity Policy | Online Code of Conduct and Computer Ethics

Chapter 3: Cybersecurity Vulnerabilities — 55

Introduction | Security Considerations and Challenges | Types of Vulnerabilities | Project OWASP | Vulnerabilities Assessment | Common Vulnerabilities and Exposures (CVE): Institutional Mechanisms

Chapter 4: Cybersecurity Management Practices — 73

Overview of Cybersecurity Management | Information Classification Process | Security Policies | Security Procedures and Guidelines | Security Controls | Security Organization | Incident Response | Business Continuity and Disaster Recovery

Chapter 5: Developing Secure Information Systems — 91

Introduction | Securing Information Assets | Data Security and Protection | Application Security | Security Architecture and Design | Security Issues in Hardware, Mobile Devices and Internet of Things | Network Security | Operating System Security | Database Security | User Management | Physical Security of IT Assets | Techniques/Methods for Data Security and Protection | Issues Related to Digital File Sharing

Chapter 6: Cybersecurity Strategies and Approaches — 121

Introduction | Information Security Governance and Risk Management | Cyber Risk Management | Cybersecurity Frameworks | Cyber Resilience | Industry-specific Cybersecurity Frameworks | The Human Factor in Cybersecurity | Algorithms and Techniques for Cybersecurity

Chapter 7: Cybersecurity Technologies — 145

Introduction | Securing Networks, Web Applications, Services and Servers | Email Security | Antivirus Technologies and Solutions | Identity and Access Management | Authentication | Cryptography | How Do Digital Money, Cryptocurrency and NFTs Work? | Digital Signatures | Advanced Technologies and Approaches in Cybersecurity | Internet Protocols and Ports

Chapter 8: Cyber Laws and Forensics — 191

Need for Cyber Laws and Regulations | Role of International Law and Governments | Challenges for Law-makers and Law Enforcement Agencies | Cybersecurity Regulations | Cyber Forensics | Cybercrime Techniques | Prevention of Cybercrime and Protection | Cybercrime Investigation | Evidence Collection and Analysis | Intellectual Property Issues in Cyberspace

Chapter 9: Personal Cybersecurity, Privacy and Data Protection — 213

Introduction | What is Personal Cybersecurity? | Common Causes of Personal Security Breaches | Personal Cybersecurity Best Practices | Privacy Regulations and Cybersecurity | The Role of Ethics in Cybersecurity

Chapter 10: Cybersecurity in Evolving Technology and Practice — 233

Introduction | Future Challenges in Cybersecurity | Web 3.0 | Harnessing Artificial Intelligence for Cybersecurity | Blockchain for Cybersecurity | Quantum Computing and Cybersecurity | Combating Advanced Persistent Threats | Digital Trust and Identity Management | 5G Networks and Cybersecurity | Adopting a 'Secure-by-Design' Approach | Supply Chain Cybersecurity | Other Evolving Aspects of Cybersecurity

Chapter 11: Cybersecurity in E-commerce and Digital Payments — 259

Introduction | What is E-commerce? | Elements of E-commerce Security | E-commerce Security Best Practices | Digital Payments | RBI Guidelines on Digital Payments and Customer Protection | Laws on Privacy and Data Protection for E-commerce Companies

Chapter 12: Overview of Social Media and Security — 275

Introduction to Social Networks | Types of Social Media and Popular Platforms | Social Media Marketing | Social Media Monitoring | Social Media Privacy | Social Media Privacy Laws and Personal Data Protection | Flagging and Reporting of Inappropriate Content | Laws Regarding Posting of Inappropriate Content | Data Harvesting and Personal Data Protection | Best Practices for the Use of Social Media

Annexure A: Cybercrime and Cyberattack Reporting in India 287
Annexure B: 50 Significant Cyberattacks/Data Breaches: 2011–2021 289
Annexure C: Self-Assessment Questions 293
Annexure D: List of Abbreviations and Acronyms 297
Index 305

List of Tables

Table 1.1: Organizations and stakeholders that constitute the Internet ecosystem 18
Table 2.1: Surface web, deep web and dark web 27
Table 2.2: Various types of scams 28
Table 2.3: Kinds of cyber offenders 31
Table 2.4: Open source/Free/Trial versions of antivirus software 35
Table 2.5: Four methods of phishing 36
Table 2.6: Common tools and methods used by hackers 37
Table 2.7: Open source/Free/Trial versions of anti-phishing software 37
Table 2.8: Passive and active cyberattacks 39
Table 2.9: Seven phases of a cyberattack 45
Table 2.10: National security policy 50
Table 2.11: Security domains 51
Table 3.1: Tools for website audits 61
Table 3.2: Top 10 web application security risks 66
Table 4.1: Classification of information 75
Table 4.2: System-specific and issue-specific policy examples 76
Table 4.3: CIS controls 78
Table 4.4: Important tasks security departments are required to undertake 80
Table 4.5: Activities classified as breaches of security policy 81
Table 4.6: Criteria to trigger an incident response process 82
Table 4.7: CSIRT roles and responsibilities 82
Table 4.8: Key factors for developing incident response plans and processes 83
Table 4.9: Containment action steps 85
Table 4.10: Post-incident activities 86
Table 5.1: Best practices for data protection and data security 94
Table 5.2: Source code analysis tools 96
Table 5.3: Commonly used SDL methodologies 98
Table 5.4: Areas for designing and implementing controls 99
Table 5.5: Network security open-source tools 103
Table 5.6: OSI layers, protocols, cyber threats and security approaches 104
Table 5.7: Prominent Android security apps 109
Table 5.8: Prominent iOS security apps 109
Table 5.9: Models for access control 114
Table 6.1: Risk categorization criteria 124
Table 6.2: Top cybersecurity frameworks 126
Table 6.3: ISO 27000 family of standards 128
Table 6.4: ISO 27001 control set explained 128

Table	Title	Page
Table 6.5:	NIST framework core functions	130
Table 6.6:	Cybersecurity maturity levels	131
Table 6.7:	GDPR vs PDPB lawful bases comparison	138
Table 6.8:	PDPB-sensitive data	138
Table 6.9:	Popular algorithms and techniques used for cybersecurity	141
Table 7.1:	Cybersecurity applications of AI and ML	172
Table 7.2:	Advantages of blockchain for cybersecurity	176
Table 8.1:	Treaties and conventions on cyber laws	193
Table 8.2:	Important cyber laws and regulations, 1970–1990	194
Table 8.3:	Important cyber laws and regulations, 1991–1999	195
Table 8.4:	Important cyber laws and regulations, 2000–2010	195
Table 8.5:	Important cyber laws and regulations, 2011–2020	196
Table 8.6:	CERT-In functions related to cyber incidents	200
Table 8.7:	Cybercrime techniques, examples	203
Table 8.8:	Key measures for the prevention of cybercrime	204
Table 8.9:	Cybercrime investigation tools	205
Table 8.10:	Steps in digital evidence analysis	207
Table 9.1:	Sensitivity level of different types of information	214
Table 9.2:	Types of cyber frauds and scams	217
Table 9.3:	Top 30 most common passwords over the years	220
Table 9.4:	Mobile threat categories	222
Table 9.5:	Common forms of identity theft	223
Table 9.6:	Partial list of technologies/processes related to privacy	224
Table 9.7:	Basic principles OECD	227
Table 10.1:	Future cybersecurity challenges	233
Table 10.2:	Popular identity management and authentication tools and technologies	242
Table 10.3:	Important threat vectors – 5G infrastructure	244
Table 10.4:	Key actions for implementing a 'secure-by-design' approach	246
Table 10.5:	Defence-in-depth security elements	254
Table 11.1:	Threats to e-commerce security	261
Table 11.2:	Digital payment systems in India	265
Table 11.3:	Excerpts from Payment and Settlement Systems Act, 2007 and related guidelines	268
Table 12.1:	Types of social media platforms	276
Table 12.2:	Benefits of social media marketing	277
Table 12.3:	Social media metrics	277
Table 12.4:	Social media privacy threats	278
Table 12.5:	Sections of law related to inappropriate content	281

List of Info Boxes

Info Box 1: Global Cost of Cybercrime 23
Info Box 2: Cybercrime Offending Patterns 24
Info Box 3: Security Threats from Physical Devices. 29
Info Box 4: Cybercrime Statistics 36
Info Box 5: Stages of a Cyberattack 38
Info Box 6: The DYN DDoS Attack 41
Info Box 7: Operation Aurora 43
Info Box 8: Sony Pictures Cyberattack 44
Info Box 9: The Oldsmar, Florida Cyberattack 47
Info Box 10: Budapest Convention on Cybercrime 48
Info Box 11: IoT Growth Estimates 56
Info Box 12: Cloud and Remote Working Statistics 56
Info Box 13: Phishing Attack Middle East 57
Info Box 14: Smart Device Vulnerabilities 58
Info Box 15: Vulnerability Analysis and Evaluation 68
Info Box 16: Cybersecurity Management 73
Info Box 17: Information Classification 74
Info Box 18: Cybersecurity Policies 76
Info Box 19: Security Procedures 76
Info Box 20: Security Operations Centre 80
Info Box 21: Incident Triage 85
Info Box 22: Cybersecurity Regulations: BC and DR 87
Info Box 23: Security Flaws in Applications 95
Info Box 24: OS-level Security Features Comparison 106
Info Box 25: Database Security Statistics 110
Info Box 26: Mirai Botnet Attack 112
Info Box 27: Common Tips for Storing and Sharing Sensitive Information . 116
Info Box 28: Governance and Management 122
Info Box 29: What is a Framework? 126
Info Box 30: Difference between Frameworks and Standards 128
Info Box 31: Criteria for Incident Classification 133
Info Box 32: Schema for Incident Classification 133
Info Box 33: Mission of PCI Standards Council 136
Info Box 34: NYDFS Regulation 137
Info Box 35: GDPR Implementation Challenges 139
Info Box 36: Human Factors 139
Info Box 37: Guards Functionality 148

Info Box 38: Configuring a Firewall 149
Info Box 39: How an IDS Works 151
Info Box 40: How SIEM Works 152
Info Box 41: How Honeypots Work 153
Info Box 42: How WPA Works 154
Info Box 43: How VPNs Work 155
Info Box 44: Implementing Email Security 156
Info Box 45: How Antivirus Solutions Work 157
Info Box 46: How IAM Systems Work 159
Info Box 47: Authentication Factors 160
Info Box 48: Objectives of Cryptography 161
Info Box 49: How Asymmetric Cryptography Works 162
Info Box 50: Cryptographic Keys: Use and Functionality 163
Info Box 51: Components of Bitcoin 166
Info Box 52: Digital Signature Use Case 168
Info Box 53: Block Cipher Modes of Operation 169
Info Box 54: Components of a Blockchain 174
Info Box 55: Blockchain Basics 176
Info Box 56: Cybersecurity Mesh Architecture (CSMA) 178
Info Box 57: Protocols Used in Each Layer of the OSI Model 183
Info Box 58: Port Numbers and Their Assignment 187
Info Box 59: Section 66A 197
Info Box 60: CERT-In Directive under Section 70B of the IT Act, 2000 – Explained . . . 198
Info Box 61: Victims of Cybercrime 203
Info Box 62: Justice Puttaswamy vs Union of India 225
Info Box 63: An Ethical Dilemma 228
Info Box 64: Weaponizing AI 236
Info Box 65: Leveraging Blockchain for Cybersecurity 237
Info Box 66: Quantum Computing 238
Info Box 67: APT Phases 239
Info Box 68: The GhostNet APT Attack 240
Info Box 69: The Aadhaar Platform 242
Info Box 70: The SolarWinds Supply Chain Attack 247
Info Box 71: Log4J Software Supply Chain Attack 248
Info Box 72: What is OSINT? 252
Info Box 73: Importance of Cybersecurity Culture 256
Info Box 74: E-commerce Sales in 2022 260
Info Box 75: Statistics on E-commerce Security 261
Info Box 76: Digital Payments in India 264
Info Box 77: Social Media Threats are Rising 279

To
My late father, Shri Pratap Singh (IPS retd),
who has been a source of inspiration and a role model to me

1 Security in an Interconnected World

> **OBJECTIVES** ....
> *At the end of this chapter, you will be able to:*
>
> - ☑ List various aspects of security in an interconnected world, including the definition, evolution and types of information systems
> - ☑ Recognize the need for information security along with the principles and concepts surrounding it
> - ☑ Describe the common threats to information security and the types of controls that can help mitigate risks arising from them
> - ☑ Describe aspects of the growth of the Internet and its systems of governance
> - ☑ List the development methodologies of the different types of information systems and information security models in use today

1.0 INTRODUCTION TO INFORMATION SYSTEMS

Technology-based information systems and the Internet have become an important part of our daily lives. Whether it is accessing news, banking, education, entertainment, making payments, socializing, searching for jobs or making travel reservations, we depend on information systems that are connected through the Internet.

Business enterprises as well as other organizations use information systems extensively in running their day-to-day operations and to improve the quality of their decision making. Governments use Internet-based information systems to provide speedy and cost-effective public services to citizens and businesses.

Many modern companies are created completely around technology-based information systems. For example, e-commerce companies such as Amazon, online marketplaces like Alibaba and eBay, social media giants like Facebook (now Meta) and LinkedIn and search engines like Google and Yahoo.[1] Organizations across sectors and industries use digital information systems to perform financial accounting and to run their supply chains. The Internet and its related technologies have transformed systems in multiple ways by leveraging capabilities for providing instant availability, access, processing and sharing of information. Organizations around the world are investing billions of dollars to modernize their information systems and use the latest available technologies to automate routine transactions, improve decision making, provide better and faster customer services, reduce cost and gain competitive advantage, while some may do so even to ensure survival in a competitive marketplace. While information systems have long remained the backbone of organizations, the use of modern technology has brought about transformational changes in their performance and outputs.

---

[1] Vladimir Zwass, "Information System - Computer Software," Britannica, last updated August 24, 2022. https://www.britannica.com/topic/information-system/Computer-software

1.1 WHAT IS AN INFORMATION SYSTEM?

Information systems have been described in different ways.

"An integrated set of components for collecting, storing and processing data and for providing information, knowledge and digital products".[2]

The National Institute of Standards and Technology (NIST), USA, describes an information system "as a discrete set of information resources organized for the collection, processing, maintenance, use, sharing, dissemination or disposition of information".[3]

There is often some confusion in understanding the difference between information system and information technology (IT). One reason for this is that we assume that all information systems are computer-based. While this is increasingly the case, information systems can also exist in other forms. Information system is a broad term that pertains to the systems, people and processes intended to create, store, process, distribute and disseminate information.[4] Information technology, on the other hand, is defined "as the technology involving the development, maintenance and use of computer systems, software and networks for the processing and distribution of data".[5] We will be concerned with only computer-based information systems in this book. Like any other system, information systems also consist of an integrated set of components (Fig. 1.1).

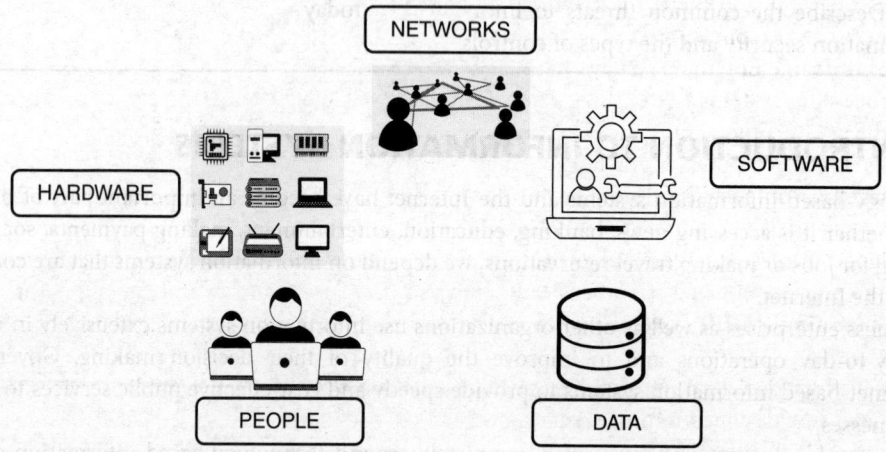

Figure 1.1 Components of an information system

An IT-based information system consists of computer hardware, software, data, people and processes. The purposes range from collection to processing, usage and dissemination of information. Let us examine each of these elements in detail:

- **Hardware and OS:** Consists of any input/output device including computing hardware, operating system (OS), storage, mobile and other peripheral devices.
- **Software:** Consists of various system and application-level programs and procedures.
- **Data:** Consists of data that may be organized as a file, table, database, etc.

---

[2] Vladimir Zwass, "Information System - Computer Software," Britannica, last updated August 24, 2022. https://www.britannica.com/topic/information-system/Computer-software

[3] Barker, WC. "Guideline for Identifying an Information System as a National Security System," National Institute of Standards and Technology (Gaithersburg, MD: 2008).

[4] "SANS Institute: Information Security Resources," accessed April 8, 2021. https://www.sans.org/information-security

[5] Li, B and Zhang, L. "Security Analysis of Cyber-Physical System," *AIP Conference Proceedings* 1839: 020178, (2017).

- **Network:** Consists of hubs, communication media and network devices, including physical devices such as networks cards, routers and cables and associated software such as operating systems, web servers, data servers and application servers.
- **People:** Consist of the users who access the information, device operators, system developers and administrators.
- **Procedures:** Consist of the way information is collected, processed, stored, accessed and distributed.

1.2 EVOLUTION AND TYPES OF INFORMATION SYSTEMS

The mid-twentieth century marked the beginning of the **Information Age**. This period marked a dramatic shift from an economy based on traditional industry, which came about as a result of the Industrial Revolution, to one based on information technology.[6] In this period, information systems also evolved along with the development of information technology and related inventions and innovations. The rise of personal computing, development of computer networks and, most significantly, the advent and growth of the Internet set in motion a series of revolutionary changes.

During the 1950s and 1960s, information systems were mainly used for activities such as transaction processing, record keeping, accounting and scientific research. In this era, which is commonly referred to as the **Mainframe Era,** these systems were called **electronic data processing (EDP) systems** or **transaction processing systems (TPS)**. EDP refers to the electronic or automated form of processing data through the use of computers.

At this time, computers were largely unaffordable and were restricted to large organizations, universities, government agencies and businesses. They could only be programmed, operated and maintained by specialists and required large and specialised data centre facilities. These mainframe computers were designed to serve a large number of users at the same time. To allow authorized access to these systems, the practice of using passwords came into use. The late 1960s saw the rise of **manufacturing resource planning (MRP) systems,** which enabled companies to manage their production processes more efficiently.

The following decade, 1960 to 1970, saw the emergence of **management information systems (MIS)**. These were designed to process data and generate useful informative reports to enable business managers to evaluate their performance and support decision making. MIS reports can be classified into the following types of information:

- **Detailed reports** that provide information related to activities such as weekly sales, inventory and pending orders.
- **Exception reports** that could be obtained by filtering data based on certain conditions such inventory below or above desired levels.

The 1970s marked the development of desktop computing and the introduction of **decision support systems (DSS)**. Computing power could now be distributed across the enterprise and information systems evolved to provide interactive ad-hoc support for the decision-making process to managers and other business professionals. DSS could combine data from multiple sources such as inventory, sales, manufacturing and financial data from an organization's database and process the same to provide insights, trends and forecasts that could be helpful in making better business decisions.

---

[6] Timothy Williamson, "History of Computers: A Brief Timeline," Live Science, published December 01, 2021. https://www.livescience.com/20718-computer-history.html

The personal computer (PC), which was launched in the 1980s, saw computing becoming more accessible and personalised. The managers of big organizations had PCs on their desks and could access information about their businesses on their own without specialist IT help. DSS evolved into **executive information systems (EIS),** enabling executives to access information relevant to meeting the strategic goals of the organization.

In the mid-1980s, local area networks became popular as they allowed computers to be clustered in such a way that they could collaborate and share resources. This led to a new architecture called **'client–server'** as users could connect to a more powerful computer and also gain access to other resources on the network. Soon these evolved further and other systems for communicating like electronic mail came into being and started to grow.

In 1989, Tim Berners-Lee, a British scientist working at CERN, came up with a new means by which researchers could share information over a network. He called the concept the **World Wide Web (WWW).** The open licensing system introduced in 1993 enabled rapid adoption of its offerings and services, making it all-pervasive as it exists today. This also marked a change in the way information was used, stored, shared and consumed across the world. Information systems too evolved to benefit from the changes that were brought about by the Internet and soon websites, search engines and online marketplaces came into being. It was around this time that two prominent online marketplaces of today were created: Amazon and eBay. This period also witnessed the rapid growth of intranets, extranets, Internet and other interconnected global networks, which significantly changed the capabilities of information systems in business and other sectors.[7] It became possible to disseminate information to any part of the world, irrespective of time and space.

Soon a new wave of innovation in the form of knowledge management systems, business automation systems like enterprise resource planning (ERP), globally accessible airline, railway and hotel reservation, business-to-business (B2B), business-to-consumer (B2C), government-to-citizen and many more new systems came into existence.

The first decade of the new millennium became known for the explosive growth of communication through the use of mobile phones and devices. Information systems evolved to incorporate the requirements of mobile computing, which meant anytime and anywhere access to organizational systems. This also led to another new wave where information systems in various spheres of human activity became mobile centric as billions of people around the world became a part of the Internet society. The widespread deployment and use of digital payment systems, which today serves as the basic system for commercial and economic activity, became well established and included the launch of cryptocurrencies. Information systems also incorporated the use of identity management, authentication and artificial intelligence (AI) techniques into business information and e-commerce systems.

Post-2010, information systems evolved to support **Internet of Things (IoT),** where a variety of physical devices equipped with electronic sensors are connected to the Internet and collect and transmit data to their control systems. Cloud-based systems, which refers to the delivery of different applications and services through the Internet, has added a new dimension to the way information systems are owned and operated. Microsoft Office Live and Dropbox are examples of such cloud-based systems. Recent years have seen a convergence of IT and operational technology (OT) systems.

Cyber-physical system (CPS) is a category of systems that is rapidly expanding in various areas like healthcare, power grids, water supply systems and other smart utilities. Newer areas for deployment of CPS are emerging every day as we move into a world of smart systems. CPS comprises an integrated set of multiple digital, analogue, physical and human components that are integrated to perform specific

---

[7] Morris, GD and Dunne, P. "Management Commentary - an Overview," in *Non-Executive Director's Handbook, Second Edition* (CIMA Publishing: 2008), accessed June 7, 2021. https://www.sciencedirect.com/topics/economics-econometrics-and-finance/management-commentary

functions. These systems can provide the basic critical infrastructure for emerging and future smart services and improve our quality of life in many areas.[8]

Information systems are evolving continuously in tandem with information and communications technology to meet the requirements, challenges and opportunities that arise. In the foreseeable future, we can expect fully autonomous robots and vehicles, augmented reality, 3D printing systems, wearable systems, next-generation tracking systems and more.

Throughout this period of evolution of information systems, security issues have existed but have become of greater concern in recent years. Technologies and information systems are seldom fully ready to address the spectrum of security issues that they will face when in use. We have for long been 'bolting-on' security to information systems to meet the security requirements as they arise. A drastic change in approach and current practices in information security is needed to move to an era of information systems where security is 'designed-in' with the flexibility to accommodate new concerns that may emerge during the life cycle of the system.

1.3 EVOLUTION AND GROWTH OF THE INTERNET

The Internet today represents a global information infrastructure. The history and evolution of the Internet involves many aspects such as technological advances, organizational transformations and societal changes. In the early days of the Internet, information security was not of great concern. As new and innovative technologies began to be adapted rapidly by organizations and the use of digital information became more prevalent, security issues started to emerge. Let us examine the milestone developments in the growth of the Internet.

There is ambiguity as to what date should be considered as the birth of the Internet. Some say that it should be 29 October, 1969, when the first message was transferred with the creation of ARPANET, a US military network that had five sites. On this day, a message was successfully sent by a computer science professor from his host computer in the University of California, Los Angeles, to a computer at Stanford. The Internet is widely defined as "a network of networks in which any one computer can send information to other computers". If we go by this definition, then we can agree with this view regarding the date of birth of the Internet.[9]

There are others who link the birth date of the Internet to Tim Berners-Lee's invention of the HTTP protocol in 1989. Lee, who was then a Fellow at the physics laboratory in CERN, Switzerland, found a way to connect pages of information on the Internet, known as 'links.' He called it the HyperText Transfer Protocol or HTTP. Lee and his team also developed uniform resource locators (URLs) and HyperText Markup Language (HTML) to create websites. These inventions became the foundations for the establishment and growth of the Internet.[10]

Over the years, various protocols such as Internet Protocol (IP), Transmission Control Protocol (TCP), domain name system (DNS), Post Office Protocol (POP) and Simple Mail Transfer Protocol (SMTP) came into being, along with the creation of technologies such as browsers, that led to the Internet becoming a fully functional and robust network, thereby boosting its growth and proliferation. It is also important to draw a distinction between the Web and the Internet. The Web is only a type of Internet application, and

---

[8] Griffor, E, Greer, C, Wollman, D and Burns, M. "Framework for Cyber-Physical Systems: Volume 1, Overview", Special Publication (NIST SP), National Institute of Standards and Technology (Gaithersburg, MD: 2017), accessed January 23, 2021. https://www.nist.gov/publications/framework-cyber-physical-systems-volume-1-overview

[9] Ryan Loftus, "The Birth and Evolution of the Internet and Cybersecurity," *Secure Features by Kaspersky* (blog), published on December 25, 2019. https://www.kaspersky.com/blog/secure-futures-magazine/50-years-internet/31957/

[10] Ryan Loftus, "The Birth and Evolution of the Internet and Cybersecurity," *Secure Features by Kaspersky* (blog), published on December 25, 2019. https://www.kaspersky.com/blog/secure-futures-magazine/50-years-internet/31957/

hence, can be said to be a subset of the Internet. Email for instance is not a part of the Web; neither are newsgroups, although Web designers have developed websites through which users the world over access both of these as well as much older forms of Internet media.[11]

Early in the race to use Internet technologies for building new age businesses were companies like Amazon, eBay, AltaVista, Yahoo and Google. Many modern businesses are today built using Internet technologies such as e-commerce (buying and selling goods and services over the Internet using secure connections and electronic payment services), which enable organizations to establish an online presence and be able to reach out to a global audience through websites and social media.

Newer technologies like cloud computing (storing and accessing data and programs over the Internet instead of a local hard disk), the increasing use of mobile devices like mobile phones and laptops, the advent of smart devices (using IoT), to name a few, have made the Internet ubiquitous and all-pervasive in our work and daily lives. Globally, e-commerce is now worth USD 21 trillion, and with 2.14 billion online shoppers expected in 2021, the profits are only going to rise. However, this is not to say that there have not been challenges to security along the way.[12]

The basic characteristics of the Internet such as connectivity, speed, spread and anonymity have also made it a haven for cybercriminals. They can stay invisible and launch attacks from any part of the world that could cause damage to their targets in minutes. They have equipped themselves with all the skills, knowledge, tactics, techniques and procedures to identify vulnerabilities in information systems and then use them to perpetrate cyberattacks. Added to this, the Internet offers them anonymity and it is often difficult to track down cybercriminals and bring them to justice.

Today, it is well established that information systems in organizations around the world are vulnerable to cyberattacks. Experts say that it is not a question of if a cyberattack will happen, but when. The World Economic Forum's (WEF) Global Risks Report 2020 states that cybercrime will be the second most concerning risk for global commerce over the next decade, until 2030. It is interesting to note that if cybercrime were a country, it would soon be the world's third-largest economy.[13]

Internet businesses that started as innovative experiments about 25 years ago have today gone mainstream. Other institutions, both private and public, have leveraged the power of the Internet to exploit the opportunities on offer and reap multiple benefits. But with opportunity comes threats. Any business using the Internet faces the risk of a cyberattack. Information security in the Internet Age is necessary for the existence, survival and growth of any organization or individual who is a part of the digital world. It is important to note that a cyber threat can be perpetrated only through physical access to a computer but also through connectivity. The Internet today is a gigantic network that provides anywhere and anytime access to not only its many users, but also to cybercriminals to pursue their nefarious agenda.

1.4 INFORMATION SYSTEM DEVELOPMENT AND MAINTENANCE

There are many information system development models that can be used by an organization to effectively develop an information system. From an information security point of view, regardless of the model used, security issues and concerns must be incorporated into all stages and phases of system development. The concept of security by design is gaining ground as a means to develop more secure

---

[11] "Internet Technologies/The Internet", Wikibooks, accessed April 9, 2021. https://en.wikibooks.org/wiki/Internet_Technologies/The_Internet

[12] Ryan Loftus, "The Birth and Evolution of the Internet and Cybersecurity," *Secure Features by Kaspersky* (blog), published on December 25, 2019. https://www.kaspersky.com/blog/secure-futures-magazine/50-years-internet/31957/

[13] Marc Wilczek, "Cybercrime May Be the World's Third-Largest Economy by 2021," Dark Reading, published April 13, 2020. https://www.darkreading.com/vulnerabilities---threats/cybercrime-may-be-the-worlds-third-largest-economy-by-2021/a/d-id/1337475

information systems. Bolting on security towards the later stages of the development cycle can be both difficult and ineffective. To develop an understanding of this, we shall first take a look at the different types of information system development processes in use today.

Systems development is a method used for designing, creating, testing and deploying an information system.[14] A software development life cycle (SDLC) consists of several stages of the development process that is used to design, build, test and deploy information systems as per prespecified requirements and cost and time estimates.

We must remember that an information system comprises both hardware and software elements covered in the following stages, namely, planning, analysis, design, development, testing and integration, implementation and maintenance.

1.4.1 Software Development Life Cycle

The SDLC methodology is also called the waterfall methodology to illustrate how each successive step is a distinct part of the process and a succeeding step can be started only after completion of the previous one.[15] While this methodology has been used extensively, there is merit in the argument that it is rigid and does not allow for changes once the development process has begun. Following this methodology means that no software is available until the completion of the programming stage.

The SDLC methodology has variants that could have a different number of stages, but most of them include the following:

- **Preliminary analysis:** The objective of this stage is to analyze the request to determine if a solution is possible and feasible from a technical, legal and economic standpoint and an examination of alternatives.
- **System analysis:** In this stage, analysts work with user groups and other stakeholders to ascertain the specific requirements of the proposed systems. Based on the inputs obtained, procedures and data requirements are documented and validated. The output of this phase is known as the system requirements document (SRD).
- **System design:** In this stage, a systems designer will use the SRD developed in the analysis stage to define the overall system architecture. Typically, two types of design documents are developed:
  - A high-level design (HLD) document, consisting of:
    - An overview and the name of each module
    - An outline of the functionality of each module
    - The interfaces, relationships and dependencies between modules
    - The database tables identified, along with their key elements
    - The proposed system architecture diagrams, along with technology details
  - A low-level design (LLD) document, consisting of:
    - Functional logic of the modules
    - Database tables, which include type and size
    - Complete details of the interface
    - Listing of all types of dependency issues and their addressal
    - Listing of error messages
    - Complete input and output for every module

---

[14] Pendharkar, PC, Rodger, JA and Subramanian, GH. "An Empirical Study of the Cobb–Douglas Production Function Properties of Software Development Effort," *Information and Software Technology* 50, no.12, (2008): 1181–88.

[15] David Bourgeois, "Chapter 10: Information Systems Development" in *Information Systems for Business and Beyond*, (2019), accessed June 7, 2021, https://opentextbook.site/informationsystems2019/chapter/chapter-10-information-systems-development/

These system design documents will contain all the details required by a programmer to commence writing code.

- **Programming:** This is the stage at which coding is undertaken by a programmer or team of programmers. They will use the two system design documents to guide them in developing the program. At the end of this stage, an initial working program that conforms to the requirements gathered at the earlier stages is made available for testing.
- **Testing:** In this stage, trained system testers subject the developed system to various types of tests. The use of automated testing and use case scenarios also forms a part of the overall testing process. Initially, the system is tested for errors or bugs at a programming unit level and is called unit testing. Next comes the system component level test to ensure that each system component is working as it is expected to perform in unison with other components. What follows is a complete user acceptance test, which is conducted by potential users of the system to test if the functionality of the system is as per their requirements and standards. If bugs, errors or issues are observed during the testing stage, they are resolved and then tested again before the system is made available for deployment.
- **Implementation:** The system which is now ready for deployment is implemented in the organization. This stage involves user training, usage guidance documentation and ensuring a smooth transition to system(s) in use prior to the new system.
- **Maintenance:** Once the system has been deployed and is put to use, new bugs may be unearthed and new requirements may emerge. The maintenance phase of the system extends throughout its useful life. In this stage, updates in the form of bug fixes and new features and changes may be regularly provided to the users.

The availability of new software development tools and methodologies and the drawbacks of the SDLC methodology such as its inherent rigidity of approach has led to newer approaches and methodologies coming into use. From an information security point of view, the SDLC process does not offer the desired flexibility to meet new security concerns that emerge after the process has advanced to the later stages. Let us examine the prominent development approaches that have evolved over time.

1.4.2 Rapid Application Development

To provide greater flexibility in the system development process, a rapid application development (RAD) software development methodology was conceived in the 1980s. RAD allows developers to quickly develop a working model to enable them to obtain further user inputs that are then used to update the working model. This is an iterative process, and after multiple development iterations, a final version is ready for implementation. The RAD methodology comprises four phases: requirements planning, user design, construction and cutover (go live).

The RAD methodology represents a compressed form of the SDLC process and differs from it in that user participation, iteration and collaboration is an important part of it. This methodology enables users to actively participate and give their feedback during the different steps of the process. This process is more amenable from a security point of view if users and development teams consciously evaluate security issues in every iteration.

1.4.3 Agile Methodologies

Agile methodologies comprise a set of approaches to product development that is centred around the values and principles enumerated in the 2001 Agile Manifesto for software development. The objective of these methodologies is to eventually deliver the right product through incremental and frequent delivery of small portions of functionality. This methodology is characterised by users and development teams working in small cross-functional teams, having daily status review meetings and completing changes incrementally in short timeframes.

SCRUM is an example of an agile framework that focuses on collaborative development. The name is derived from the game of rugby, where preparation for games involves encouraging teams to learn through experience, self-organize while working on a problem and reflect on their wins and losses to continuously improve.[16] At the heart of this framework is the concept of 'sprints', which emphasizes the breaking up of large and complex development projects into smaller components to make them more manageable, work faster, make more frequent releases and adapt to ongoing changes. These features and the iterative nature of the exercise are useful from a security point of view as changes during the development process can be more easily incorporated before a final version is released.

Another agile framework is the lean software development (LSD) framework, which is based on optimizing time and resources deployed in the development process and strictly delivering a version of the product that can be considered a minimum viable product (MVP). This MVP version is then taken to the market and refined and updated iteratively over time based on market feedback. This approach is particularly useful when a product or information system's requirements are not clearly known, and minimum working versions are created and developed further as the requirements become clear. However, when using such an approach, security issues could take a back seat and get attention only when they arise.

1.4.4 Change Management

Any information system over its life cycle will undergo changes as business requirements may change. More often, security issues and concerns will also need to be addressed through updates to make the systems more secure. Change management in the context of information systems involves any changes to applications, the computing environment, the network, servers and system software. These changes, when made to an information system already in use, could introduce new vulnerabilities and, therefore, involve an element of risk. Hence, a controlled and managed process is necessary for change management. The change management process typically comprises the following steps:

1. Request for change
2. Approval of change
3. Plan for the change
4. Testing the change in a safe environment
5. Communication and implementation of the change
6. Documenting the change and conducting a post-change review

While agile software development methodologies are more flexible in their approach than traditional SDLC waterfall models, when it comes to information security, there may be some issues that must be addressed. Information security is considered a non-functional requirement during the development process, and this could lead to a tendency to leave security issues to be handled later on in the process. This could also lead to design-level issues. Hence, no matter which development methodology is followed, information security must be given due consideration, focus and importance.

Another issue from a security standpoint is the trade-off between user convenience and security. Here, the role of the business users who interact with the development teams is critical and they must ensure that security is not given the go-by simply for user convenience.

---

[16] "Scrum - What It Is, How It Works, and Why It's Awesome," Altassian, accessed June 5, 2021. https://www.atlassian.com/agile/scrum

Incorporating security as a fundamental requirement in the development of information systems is essential for meeting the security challenges that the systems will be subjected to once they are deployed in a hostile threat environment. New approaches to make security an integral part of system requirements not only at an early stage but throughout the life cycle of the information system have emerged in the form of 'DevOps' and lately 'DevSecOps' teams. As the nomenclature suggests, these are combined teams of users, developers and security representatives created so that the respective concerns of each user group are tabled and addressed not only during the development process but also throughout the life cycle of the information system. We will explore this in detail in a later chapter.

1.5 CYBERSPACE AND CYBERSECURITY

The term cyberspace has become a part of the modern-day lexicon. It was coined by William Gibson, who used the term in his science fiction novel *Neuromancer* in 1984. Little did he know that cyberspace would become a reality and an integral part of our existence.[17] The evolution of cyberspace has rapidly engulfed social, economic, cultural, political and even psychological aspects of human activity. Today, there are billions of people and devices who are a part of cyberspace and have distinct digital identities to confirm their existence in this digital world. Cyberspace continues to evolve as more people become a part of it every day (Fig. 1.2).

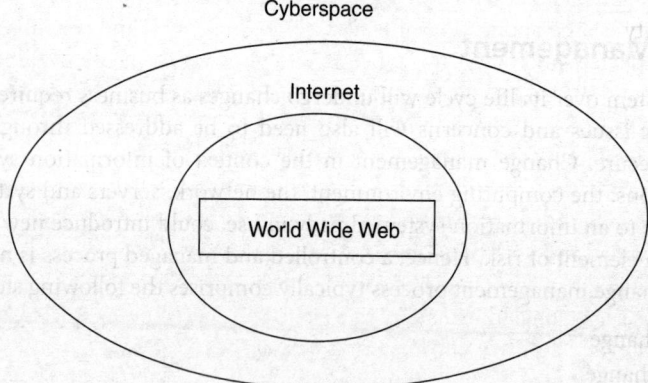

Figure 1.2 Cyberspace

Cyberspace is a concept that can be viewed as a "global virtual domain within the information environment that comprises the interdependent network of information technology (or information systems) infrastructures, which include the Internet, telecommunications networks, computer systems, devices, embedded processors and controllers. Cyberspace can also be perceived as three layers (physical, logical and social) consisting of five components (geographic, physical network, logical network, cyber persona and persona)".[18]

There is often confusion in the usage of the terms cyberspace and Internet. While the Internet is a global interconnected agglomeration of networks, cyberspace is a symbolic and conceptual representation of the virtual space or global domain within the information environment of which the Internet is a part.

---

[17] Heather Holloway, "Evolution of Cyberspace as a Landscape in Cyberpunk Novels," Digital Commons @ Georgia Southern, Electronic Theses and Dissertations. (2004). https://digitalcommons.georgiasouthern.edu/etd/173/

[18] "Cyberspace", AcqNotes, accessed June 11, 2021. https://acqnotes.com/acqnote/careerfields/cyberspace

Another way to look at cyberspace is to consider it as "the non-physical domain of information flow and communication between computer systems and networks".[19] When we talk in terms of information flow, we must be concerned with the security of information across different information domains and systems. The growth of criminal activity in cyberspace is centred around the misuse or unauthorized use of information. The process of securing data and information assets that are contained in cyberspace is known as cybersecurity.[20]

1.5.1 Definition and Importance of Cybersecurity

Our dependence on digital systems has been growing rapidly in recent years and innovations and new technologies like IoT and fifth-generation telecommunication systems are only accelerating this. From manufacturing plants to automobiles and electricity grids, everything is being controlled and managed by digital systems. While this integration between digital and physical activities offers many business opportunities and operating benefits, it also exposes us to risks from digital systems manifesting in the physical world. What is more alarming is that such threats are becoming increasingly common and can be physically dangerous to both people and property. In 2015, hackers launched a cyberattack on the Ukrainian Electricity Grid and isolated seven substations, causing power outages that affected over 200,000 consumers and which lasted several hours.

Cybersecurity comprises the set of practices deployed for defending computers, servers, mobile devices, electronic systems, IT networks/infrastructure and data from malicious attacks. Another way to define cybersecurity is "the application of technologies, processes, and controls to protect systems, networks, programs, devices and data from cyberattacks. It aims to reduce the risk of cyberattacks and protect against the unauthorized exploitation of systems, networks and technologies".[21]

Survival and growth in the cyberworld involves safeguarding data at all times to ensure that we are less exposed and vulnerable to cybercrime. The theft of various categories of data such as an individual's personal data, a corporation's confidential business data, scientific data and intellectual property has existed even in the pre-cyberspace era. However, in the context of cyberspace, data can move around the world in seconds, be traded and used by anonymous cybercriminals to cause various kinds of cyber harm. Cybersecurity is essential for survival in cyberspace as it provides protection to all categories of data from theft and damage, such as personal information, intellectual property, confidential business data, classified government information and industry information systems.[22] This data is held by the information systems that store and process it. The goal of cybersecurity is, therefore, to ensure protection against the criminal or unauthorized use of electronic data through a set of controls and preventive measures.

Consider the following:

- The year 2020 broke all records when it came to data lost in breaches and the sheer number of cyberattacks on companies, governments and individuals.[23]
- The number of users connected to the Internet crossed 60% of the world's population. All these people are now vulnerable to different types of cybercrimes.

---

[19] Ian Carnaghan, "What Exactly Is Cyberspace and Cybersecurity?," accessed June 11, 2021. https://www.carnaghan.com/what-exactly-is-cyberspace-and-cybersecurity/
[20] Ian Carnaghan, "What Exactly Is Cyberspace and Cybersecurity?," accessed June 11, 2021. https://www.carnaghan.com/what-exactly-is-cyberspace-and-cybersecurity/
[21] "What Is Cyber Security? Definition & Best Practices," IT Governance, accessed March 1, 2022. https://www.itgovernance.co.uk/what-is-cybersecurity
[22] Abi Tyas Tunggal, "Why Is Cybersecurity Important?," *UpGuard* (blog), updated September 1, 2022. https://www.upguard.com/blog/cybersecurity-important
[23] Chuck Brooks, "Alarming Cybersecurity Stats: What You Need To Know For 2021," *Forbes*, accessed June 11, 2021. https://www.forbes.com/sites/chuckbrooks/2021/03/02/alarming-cybersecurity-stats-------what-you-need-to-know-for-2021/?sh=775e9a4e58d3

- Our personal lives, work, entertainment, socializing and financial transactions are taking place more often on the Internet than before.
- Starting with the explosive growth of mobile phones and other devices, IoT is increasingly automating various aspects of our lives.
- Cybercrime is the fastest growing form of crime in terms of economic damage and frequency of attacks.
- The movement from a 'walled' environment to a 'perimeter-less' environment with cloud, mobile and remote working represents a paradigm shift in the approach to cybersecurity.
- Cybercriminals have easier access to tools and malware than ever before through organized marketplaces on the dark net.
- Regulations like General Data Protection Regulation (GDPR) enacted by the European Union and other similar privacy protection laws are being passed by countries around the word including specific cybersecurity regulations that specify practices and standards.
- The unprecedented rate of introduction of new technologies has brought new vulnerabilities.
- The proliferation of different forms of frauds and scams has increased.

These are but a few reasons that highlight the importance of cybersecurity to individuals, organizations and governments and for them to undertake the required security measures and programs to safeguard their information as well as protect their organizations from the perils of cybercrime.

1.5.2 Basic Principles of Cybersecurity

Protection of an organization's data, systems and people from any type of external or internal cyber threat is the basic purpose of cybersecurity. To achieve this objective, there are several strategic approaches, technologies, processes, controls, structures and practices.

The Australian Cyber Security Centre suggests the following four cybersecurity basic principles (grouped into four key activities), which provide strategic guidance on how organizations can ensure protection of their systems and data from cyber threats:[24]

- **Governance:** The systems and processes for identifying and managing security risks
- **Protection:** Implementing security controls and mechanisms to reduce security risks
- **Detection:** The ability to detect and understand cybersecurity events
- **Response:** The ability to respond to and recover from cybersecurity incidents

Using these four principles, organizations can assess the degree of confidence that they have in their cybersecurity and the level of maturity that they have attained.

1.6 WHAT IS INFORMATION SECURITY?

Information security comprises a set of practices meant to keep data secure from unauthorized access or alterations when it is stored, transmitted or used by applications. Information security is also sometimes referred to as data security.[25] Statements such as 'data is the new oil' or 'data is the new gold' are often used to emphasize the importance and value of data in today's world. Information is increasingly being considered as one of the most valuable assets today, underlining the importance of focusing on efforts to keep information secure.[26]

---

[24] "The Cyber Security Principles," Australian Cyber Security Centre, accessed March 1, 2022. https://www.cyber.gov.au/acsc/view-all-content/advice/cyber-security-principles

[25] Josh Fruhlinger, "What Is Information Security? Definition, Principles, and Jobs," CSO, accessed June 7, 2021. https://www.csoonline.com/article/3513899/what-is-information-security-definition-principles-and-jobs.html

[26] " Josh Fruhlinger, "What Is Information Security? Definition, Principles, and Jobs," CSO, accessed June 7, 2021. https://www.csoonline.com/article/3513899/what-is-information-security-definition-principles-and-jobs.html

According to SANS Institute, information security refers to "the processes and methodologies which are designed and implemented to protect print, electronic or any other form of confidential, private and sensitive information or data from unauthorized access, use, misuse, disclosure, destruction, modification or disruption".[27]

ISO/IEC 27000: 2009 defines information security as the "preservation of confidentiality, integrity and availability of information. Also, other properties, such as authenticity, accountability, non-repudiation and reliability can also be involved".[28]

In the context of information security, we often use other terms such as computer security, system security and information assurance. While they all refer to securing valuable information assets and are engaged in protecting the confidentiality, integrity and availability of information, they may differ in terms of approaches, methodology and focus. Information security is about data protection irrespective of whether the data is in electronic or other forms.[29]

1.6.1 Information Security versus Cybersecurity

The two terms information security and cybersecurity are often used interchangeably and are overlapping concepts, but it is important to recognize the distinction between them.

While information security comprises the set of processes that maintain the confidentiality, integrity and availability of business data in its various forms, cybersecurity is a broader term that refers to the practice of safeguarding systems, networks and programs from cyberattacks. Other concepts like network security and application security are practices related to information security but are narrowly focused on networks and application code, respectively.

1.6.2 Need for Information Security

Many organizations do not completely understand the value of their own information, what their key information assets are and what harm can come to them if the confidentiality, integrity and availability of their information is compromised. By disregarding information security, the entire organization can be in serious danger and face undesirable consequences, such as damage to the organization's image, financial loss, loss of intellectual property and even legal consequences.

The frequency and sophistication of cyber threats and attacks is only increasing every year and cybercrime has already reached alarming proportions. A cyberattack can cause serious problems and incalculable damage to a business and even derail the achievement of an organization's objectives and mission. More importantly, it can threaten the very existence of an enterprise. In that respect, information security is a survival issue, but it must also be looked at as a foundation for the growth and protection of an organization's value and reputation.

1.6.3 Threats to Information Systems

A cyber threat is a malicious manoeuvre launched by an attacker that exploits a security vulnerability to cause damage and harm to information systems. There are a number of threats to information systems such as malware-driven software attacks, deletion, modification and theft of data, theft of equipment, information extortion and disruption of operations.[30]

---

[27] "Guidance Security Measures for Personal Data Processing," European Data Protection Supervisor, published March 21, 2016.
[28] Cherdantseva, Y and Hilton, J. "Information Security and Information Assurance: Discussion about the Meaning, Scope, and Goals," in *Standards and Standardization: Concepts, Methodologies, Tools, and Applications* (IGI Global: 2015), 167–98.
[29] "SANS Institute: Information Security Resources," accessed April 8, 2021. https://www.sans.org/information-security
[30] "Threats to Information Security," GeeksforGeeks, last updated June 28, 2022. https://www.geeksforgeeks.org/threats-to-information-security/

It is important to know from an information security point of view what kind of information and data cybercriminals are seeking, as well as how and what harm they intend to cause. Given below is a partial list of the ways in which cybercriminals can cause harm.

- Obtaining unauthorized access in order to:
    - Steal or violate intellectual property and related rights such as copyrights, patents, etc.
    - Steal identity information that can enable them to impersonate a person and log-in and access sensitive data.
    - Steal IT equipment and information therein. The dramatic increase in the use of mobile devices to access organizations' information systems has made it easier for cybercriminals.
- Defacing, sabotaging and hijacking a page on a website to compromise legitimate web pages in order to redirect users to a malicious website or harvest credentials.
- Cyber extortion by blocking access to an organization's information systems or stealing data and demanding a ransom for reinstating access or for not exposing that data to interested third parties or the public domain. Ransomware is used by hackers to achieve locking of the victims' data files and render them inaccessible to users, thereby compelling the victims to pay the ransom in return for unlocking file access.
- Hackers deploy attacks to steal information from social media sources and lure users to visit malware-infected websites or unintentionally share personal information.
- Stealing passwords and login credentials through brute force attacks that use a trial-and-error approach to guess login information, encryption keys or find a hidden web page. Hackers work through all possible combinations to guess passwords that they can use to break into an information system.
- Social engineering is widely used by cybercriminals to manipulate users to expose their personal or confidential information such as passwords and bank account details to them or to control their computer by installing malicious software.
- Phishing is a methodology used by cybercriminals in which a target or targets are contacted by email, telephone or text message by someone posing as a legitimate institution to trap unsuspecting individuals into providing sensitive data such as personally identifiable information, banking and credit card details and passwords. The information is then used to access important accounts and can result in identity theft and financial loss.[31]
- Scams and payment frauds such as lottery scams, investment frauds, business email compromise, credit card frauds and Ponzi schemes are among the several types of cybercrimes that are prevalent today.

Threats to information systems can be varied and there are many sources of these threats, including failure of IT and physical infrastructure. It is important to understand that these are directly related to the vulnerabilities in an information system.

Every system is vulnerable in some way. The objective of implementing information security is to identify all the sources of vulnerabilities and implement safeguards and controls to mitigate any damage or harm that can be caused in case security is compromised. The main sources of vulnerabilities in an organizational system context are shown in Fig. 1.3.

The terms cyber threats and vulnerabilities are sometimes used interchangeably, but it is important to understand the distinction between them. In simple terms, an information system vulnerability is a flaw or weakness in a system or network that could be exploited to cause damage or allow an attacker to manipulate the system in some way.[32] Vulnerabilities can be exploited in multiple ways

---

[31] "What Is Phishing?, Phishing.org, accessed April 8, 2021. https://www.phishing.org/what-is-phishing
[32] Eric Dosal, "Top 5 Computer Security Vulnerabilities," Compuquip, accessed April 3, 2022. https://www.compuquip.com/blog/computer-security-vulnerabilities

Application and system software	IT equipment, network and physical infrastructure	Cloud-based cyber threats	Threats from mobile devices and endpoints
Remote working	Threats from the supply chain	Social media	Misconfigured and unpatched systems
Weak user and administration management	Poor password practices and security awareness	The human factor	Weak technical and operational security

Figure 1.3 Common sources of vulnerabilities

depending on the nature of the vulnerability and the motives of the attacker. Vulnerabilities often exist due to unanticipated interactions of different software programs, system components, unpatched or misconfigured systems or are just basic flaws in an individual program. Hence, vulnerabilities can be considered as the gaps or weaknesses in a system that make threats possible and tempt threat actors to exploit them.

Cyber threats are security incidents or circumstances that exploit a vulnerability or weakness and have the potential to create a negative outcome for a network or other data management systems.

Ethical hacking, also known as penetration testing, is increasingly being used by organizations to discover security vulnerabilities and to take suitable measures to strengthen their security implementations. Ethical hackers operate with due permission of the system owners and are often paid by them to successfully penetrate a specific information system by using tactics similar to what cybercriminals might use.

1.6.4 Fundamental Concepts and Principles of Information Security

In the physical world, human beings are predisposed towards protecting anything that they perceive as having value. The modern-day world is driven by data. It is increasingly being recognized that data is a source of value in a digital society and is essential for accomplishing different objectives, but in the wrong hands, it can be a means to cause harm.

The basic objective of information security is to ensure that any data that is valuable (such as confidential, private or sensitive data) is not compromised in any way by unauthorized access or misuse, the disclosure, alteration or destruction of the data or by disruption. Most cyber threats and attacks are aimed at breaching confidentiality, destroying the integrity of data and making data unavailable to users.

Individuals and organizations can take several steps to protect data that is confidential in nature, such as financial transactions, intellectual property information, confidential emails, etc. If this information is breached or put in the public domain, it can cause economic loss and other forms of harm to the owners of this data. In 2017, a failure to update its systems in time by Equifax (a company that provides credit reports and scores) enabled hackers to access over 145 million credit reports. This single data breach compromised confidential information pertaining to nearly half the population of the USA.

The integrity of data in a system is of paramount importance. Cyberattacks that affect data integrity are orchestrated by hackers in multiple ways; for example, by unauthorized access to sensitive data and modification of data to show important information other than what it should be. Imagine the havoc that hackers can cause by accessing a system without authorization and manipulating sensor and control systems operating a power grid or a nuclear installation. The 'Stuxnet' cyberattack on the Iranian nuclear facility at Natanz is an example where malware was used to manipulate the working of the centrifuges, causing a major setback to Iran's nuclear program.

Ransomware and denial-of-service are two types of attacks that prevent access to data and IT systems, respectively. A ransomware attack typically encrypts the data in the target system, thereby preventing an organization from accessing and using its own data. The Colonial Pipeline (one of the largest pipeline operators in the United States) ransomware attack of 2021 caused a major supply shortage of gasoline, diesel, home heating oil, jet fuel and military supplies on the east coast of the United States. Hackers encrypted Colonial Pipeline's data and demanded a ransom, rendering its systems unavailable to carry out regular operations.

An example of a DDoS (distributed denial of service) attack was one carried out by hackers on Dyn (a domain management services company). In 2016, this high-profile DDoS attack resulted in users being denied access to several popular websites such as Amazon, Netflix, PayPal, Visa, The New York Times, GitHub and Reddit for several hours.

The CIA Triad: The three basic principles of information security, namely confidentiality, integrity and availability (also referred to as the CIA triad), are designed to provide protection from different types of cyberattacks.

- **Confidentiality** involves ensuring that only authorized persons can access or use the information.
- **Integrity** involves ensuring that unauthorized users cannot make changes to the data and even changes made by authorized users are tracked.
- **Availability** involves ensuring that the information is accessible when authorized users need it.

Experts have suggested the following expanded definition for the principles of information security:

- Confidentiality
- Privacy
- Quality
- Availability
- Trustworthiness
- Integrity

Additional principles such as maintaining data quality, ensuring privacy and establishing trustworthiness through transparency and accountability are the focus of new regulations such as the General Data Protection Regulation (GDPR) and other privacy and data protection regulations that have been enacted by several countries around the world.

It is essential that every aspect of an information security program (and every security control) should be intended to achieve the objectives enshrined in one or more of these principles.

1.6.5 Types of Information Security Mechanisms and Controls

Based on these higher-level principles, IT security specialists have come up with best practices to help organizations ensure that their information stays safe. These practices involve the design and implementation of administrative, physical and technical controls that are aimed at safeguarding the confidentiality, integrity and/or availability of information.

Administrative controls are those that are designed to address the human factors of information security. They are represented by management directives, policies, guidelines, standards and/or procedures, such as:[33]

---

[33] "What Is InfoSec: The Five Ws of Security," FRSecure, accessed June 2, 2021. https://frsecure.com/blog/the-5-ws-of-information-security/

- Polices for information security
- Plans for incident response
- Programs for training and awareness
- Plans for business continuity and/or disaster recovery
- Procedures for onboarding and termination/de-boarding of users and devices

Physical controls are those that are designed to address the physical factors of information security. Physical controls are generally visible and can be touched and/or seen; they control physical access to information. Physical controls include locks, access control systems and alarm systems.

Technical controls deal with the technical factors of information security. They use technology to prevent and control access. Examples of technical controls are firewalls, antivirus software, access privileges and file level permissions.

The intent of implementing these controls is to strengthen cyber defences and to prevent any unauthorized access, misuse and disclosure of sensitive information.

Information security mechanisms and measures can also be classified as follows:

- Physical
- Personal
- Organizational

Controls and control mechanisms are a very important part of information security programs and must be chosen based on specific requirements and evaluated regularly for their effectiveness and modified, if necessary.

1.7 ORGANIZATION AND GOVERNANCE OF THE INTERNET AND CYBERSECURITY

Internet governance refers to the rules, policies, standards and practices that coordinate and shape cyberspace.[34] The structure, organization and governance of the Internet have a bearing on the way cybersecurity is designed and implemented. The basic technologies and protocols that support the information resources on the Internet such as email, Telnet, World Wide Web (WWW), file transfer protocols and other services and the way they operate must also be factored into cybersecurity approaches. This means that cybersecurity governance and Internet governance models need to be compatible, and the approach we take to one will influence how we approach the other.

When it comes to the Internet, we talk in terms of 'governance' rather than 'government' as the Internet is not created or controlled by a single nation or, for that matter, any single organization. Each constituent network or interest group and other stakeholders (including governments, tech companies, user groups, etc.) create and administer their own sets of policies for access and usage. Let us examine the organizations that govern the Internet.[35]

- Internet Corporation for Assigned Names and Numbers (ICANN) is the organization that maintains the two primary name spaces on the Internet: the Internet Protocol (IP) address and the domain name system (DNS). ICANN carries out the task of assigning numerical Internet addresses to websites and computers.
- Internet Engineering Task Force (IETF), a body of loosely associated international participants, takes care of the support and standardization of core protocols.

---

[34] "What Is Internet Governance?," Internet Governance Project, accessed June 3, 2021. https://www.internetgovernance.org/what-is-internet-governance/
[35] "The Challenges of Internet Governance," Ministry for Europe and Foreign Affairs, accessed April 9, 2021. https://www.diplomatie.gouv.fr/en/french-foreign-policy/digital-diplomacy/the-challenges-of-internet-governance/

- Internet Society was set up by early Internet pioneers and works to promote an open approach to the development and use of the Internet.
- World Wide Web Consortium is concerned with the improvement of Internet technologies and the format of HTML code.
- Private companies in their own way define the conditions that are applicable to Internet users in order to make use of the various services offered by them.
- Internet service providers and telecommunications companies run and manage data flow infrastructure, data centres and international undersea cables through main lines called backbones.[36]

In recent times, there have been increased efforts by the national governments of various countries to regulate activities on the Internet. Civil society also makes its own contributions to the development of regulations by participating in policy making and conducting awareness campaigns. Civil society initiatives such as those for open source and free software that enable community-led enhancement of software platforms, free use and sharing of code have been very successful. Examples of this are Wikipedia, Open Software Foundation, Mozilla Firefox, etc.

It is significant to note that no one organization or body has complete control over the Internet. Instead, various stakeholders such as technical forums and institutions, private companies and organizations, governments, civil society and international organizations all have a part to play. As all these bodies and institutions are also concerned about issues such as protection of privacy and data, security concerns must become an integral part of future policies and governance efforts.

1.7.1 Role of the Internet in Cybersecurity

Making the Internet secure is a key priority and also a huge challenge. While individual and organizational measures are one aspect of this, at a broader level, several challenges need to be addressed. One way is to develop a set of common security values and open, transparent and collaborative processes that contribute to the continued development and adoption of Internet technologies. This calls for greater coordination across the organizations and stakeholders that constitute the Internet ecosystem (Table 1.1).[37]

Table 1.1 Organizations and stakeholders that constitute the Internet ecosystem

Individuals such as technology developers, architects and organizations who coordinate and implement open standards
Organizations that manage resources for global addressing capabilities such as ICANN, domain name registries, etc.
Service providers and vendors
Internet users and user groups
Academicians, governments and multilateral organizations that influence infrastructure building and development and promote the use of Internet technologies
Policy makers who assist in local and global policy development and governance

---

[36] "The Challenges of Internet Governance," Ministry for Europe and Foreign Affairs, accessed April 9, 2021. https://www.diplomatie.gouv.fr/en/french-foreign-policy/digital-diplomacy/the-challenges-of-internet-governance/

[37] "Who Makes the Internet Work: The Internet Ecosystem." Internet Society, last updated March, 2022. https://www.internetsociety.org/internet/who-makes-it-work/

As the Internet represents an open and global information environment, the responsibility for making it secure is a shared one. All stakeholders have a part to play in an environment where adoption of new technologies is often prioritized over security concerns. With the increase in frequency of cyberattacks and the high costs suffered on account of them, there is increased attention on security aspects. However, a coordinated effort among all the constituents that make the Internet work to comprehensively address security challenges still remains elusive.

1.8 INFORMATION SECURITY MODELS

The basic goals of information security are preventing the loss of availability, the loss of integrity and the loss of confidentiality of systems and data. There are a number of information security models that can be applied to specify the rules and policies that are required to meet these goals.

Information security models are expected to deliver a precise set of directions that a computer can follow to implement the vital security processes, procedures and concepts contained in a security program.

An information security model comprises two basic aspects:

- A security blueprint supported by a security architecture
- A security policy on how data is accessed, what level of security is warranted and actions to be taken if security requirements are not met

A diagrammatic representation of an information security model is shown in Fig. 1.4.

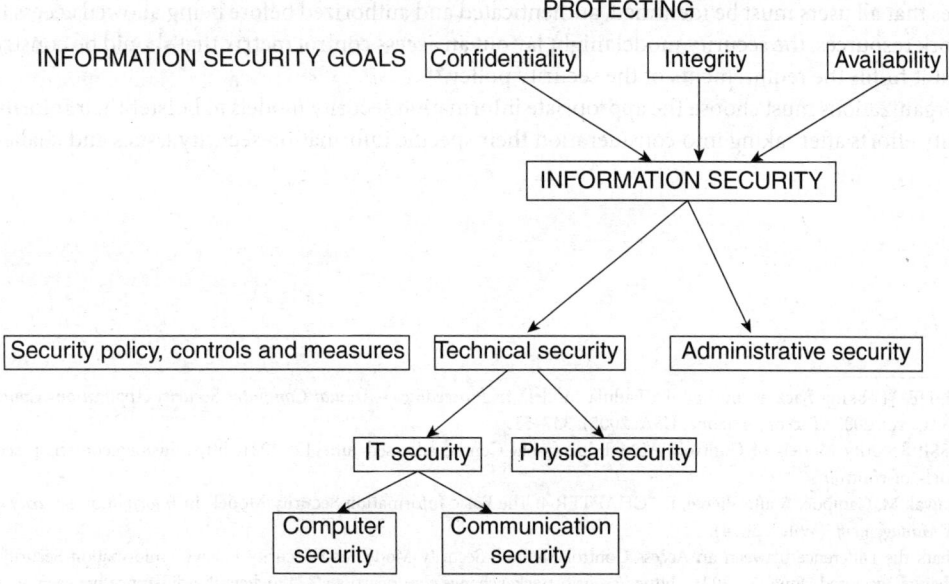

Figure 1.4 Information security model

A security model is required for enforcing rules to protect confidentiality. Some of the well-known models are Bell-La Padula (BLP) and Biba, which are used to enforce rules to protect integrity and provide high security assurance. The BLP model is a state machine model used for applying access control in government and military applications based on security policy and clearances using security labels as objects.[38] The Biba integrity model also defines a set of access control rules to ensure data integrity. Other models such as Clark–Wilson are used more as a framework to describe how security policies should be expressed and executed. Clark–Wilson differs from Biba in that subjects are allowed access to one set of data at one level, while they have access to a different set of data at another level.[39]

Defence-in-depth represents another information security approach wherein a series of security mechanisms and controls are thoughtfully layered throughout a computer network to safeguard the network and ensure data protection even if one of the security layers is breached.

Network security models specify the policies, perimeter security rules as well as privacy and security monitoring protocols to prevent threats to the confidentiality or authenticity of the information that is being transmitted through the network. Such models also involve segmenting networks to prevent infiltration by hackers even if they gain access to one of the constituent network segments. Further evolution of the concept of network segmentation has led to micro-segmentation, which is the implementation of security policies and measures through micro-segmentation based on user groups instead of physical networks.

Zero trust is an information security model developed by John Kindervag over a decade ago. This has gained wide acceptance and has become one of the more popular frameworks in cybersecurity. The concept of zero trust declares that no one (users, devices, applications) can be trusted, not even users inside the firewall, before verification.

The four important components of an information security model are assets, vulnerabilities, threats and controls.[40] There are many models and frameworks that security architects and designers can use to ensure that the security policies envisaged are rigorously enforced. For example, if a security policy prescribes that all users must be identified, authenticated and authorized before being allowed access to any network resources, the security model might lay out an access control matrix that should be constructed so that it fulfils the requirements of the security policy.[41]

Organizations must choose the appropriate information security models to bolster their information security efforts after taking into consideration their specific information security issues and challenges.

---

[38] Bell, DE. "Looking Back at the Bell–La Padula Model," in *Proceedings - Annual Computer Security Applications Conference, ACSAC*, vol. 2005 (Tucson, Arizona, USA: 2005), 337–51.
[39] "CISSP Security Models of Control," ASM Educational Center, accessed June 12, 2021. https://asmed.com/cissp-security-models-of-control/
[40] Agrawal, M, Campoe, A and Pierce, E. "CHAPTER 4: The Basic Information Security Model" in *Information Security and IT Risk Management*, (Wiley: 2014).
[41] "What's the Difference between an Access Control Method, Security Model, and Security Policy?," Information Security Stack Exchange, accessed June 7, 2021. https://security.stackexchange.com/questions/3749/whats-the-difference-between-an-access-control-method-security-model-and-secu

QUICK TEST

1. There is often confusion in the usage of the two terms cyberspace and Internet. While the Internet is a global interconnected agglomeration of networks, cyberspace is a symbolic and conceptual representation of the virtual space or global domain within the information environment of which the Internet is a part.
    a. True
    b. False
2. An information system consists of which components:
    a. Hardware
    b. Software
    c. Data
    d. Network
    e. People
    f. Procedures
    g. All of the above
    h. Only a, b, c
3. The goals of information security are to protect:
    a. Confidentiality of data
    b. Integrity of data
    c. Availability of data
    d. All of the above
    e. None of the above
4. By disregarding information security, the entire organization can be in serious danger and face undesirable consequences, such as damage to the organization's image, financial loss, loss of intellectual property and even legal consequences.
    a. True
    b. False
5. A phishing threat could involve:
    a. Use of email
    b. Use of messaging systems
    c. Use of phone calls
    d. Any of the above
6. Ethical hackers operate with due permission of the system owners:
    a. Sometimes
    b. Often
    c. Always
    d. Not required
7. Security controls can be classified as:
    a. Technical, physical and administrative
    b. Physical, personal and organizational
    c. Both a and b
    d. None of the above

8. The Internet is governed by a central body called ICANN.
   a. True
   b. False
9. An information security model comprises two basic aspects:
   a. A security blueprint supported by a security architecture
   b. A security policy on how data is accessed, what level of security is warranted and the actions to be taken if the security requirements are not met
   c. Both a and b
   d. None of the above
10. The RAD methodology represents a compressed form of the SDLC process and is different from it in that user participation, iteration and collaboration is an important part of it.
    a. True
    b. False

QUESTIONS

1. Cyberspace is a safe haven for cybercriminals. Discuss.
2. Identify five key information security challenges and how the basic principles of information security address them.
3. What are the kinds of controls that can be established for securing information systems? Explain with examples.
4. List and explain five kinds of threats to an information system.
5. Explain the distinction between vulnerabilities and threats.
6. Have the systems of governance of the Internet been effective in meeting the security requirements? Discuss.
7. Who controls and regulates the Internet?
8. How can we ensure that security becomes an integral part of the software development process?
9. What is the CIA model? Does it need to be expanded further? If so, why?
10. What is the need for information security models? Explain the constructs of at least three models.

ANSWER KEYS

Quick Test

1. (a)
2. (g)
3. (d)
4. (a)
5. (d)
6. (c)
7. (c)
8. (b)
9. (c)
10. (a)

2 Cybercrime, Cyberattack Tools and Methods, Threat Sources and Cyber Offenders

> **OBJECTIVES**
>
> *At the end of this chapter, you will be able to:*
>
> - ☑ Define cybercrime
> - ☑ List the various forms of cybercrimes and their prevention, computer ethics and the global efforts to deal with them
> - ☑ Describe cyber scams and frauds, cyber espionage, cyberwarfare and cyber terrorism
> - ☑ Explain the different types of cyber offenders, their motivations, tools and methods and the implications of such attacks on organizations

2.0 INTRODUCTION

Cybercrime today is widely recognised as the fastest growing form of crime in the world. The Internet has brought with it features such as speed of communication, anonymity and a cost-effective way of conducting global operations. These very features are conducive for the growth and spread of cybercrime. Cybercriminals have found numerous tools, methods and operating practices that have made organizations and governments scurry to find methods of control, deterrents and legal remedies for dealing with the menace.

> **Info Box 1: Global Cost of Cybercrime**
>
> There have been various estimates of the global cost of damages inflicted by cybercrimes. According to Cybersecurity Ventures, in 2021, it is expected to be of the magnitude of USD 6 trillion. To put this figure in context, if global cybercrime were to be measured in terms of the economic size of countries, it would rank third after USA and China. They further predict that by 2025, the world will face damages from cybercrime to the tune of USD 10 trillion.[1]

Let us develop our understanding of the various manifestations of cybercrime.

---

[1] Intrusion Inc. "Cybercrime To Cost The World $10.5 Trillion Annually By 2025 Nasdaq:INTZ," GlobeNewswire by notified, accessed February 20, 2021. https://www.globenewswire.com/news-release/2020/11/18/2129432/0/en/Cybercrime-To-Cost-The-World-10-5-Trillion-Annually-By-2025.html

2.1 WHAT IS A CYBERCRIME?

The United Nations Office on Drugs and Crimes states that there is no international definition of cybercrime, nor of cyberattacks. They suggest that offences cluster around the following categories:[2]

- Offences that are against the confidentiality, integrity and availability of computer data and systems
- Offences related to computer systems
- Offences related to content
- Offences related to infringements/violations of copyright and related rights

However, there are a few widely accepted descriptions to understand what cybercrime is.

> **Info Box 2: Cybercrime Offending Patterns**
>
> Cybercrimes include three main offending patterns. The objective of the offence can be the integrity of the system (hacking) or the computer can be used to carry out an offence, else the content of the computer itself can be the purpose of the offending.[3]

Any type of criminal activity that involves the use of a computer, computing device, network device or a network can be called a crime.[4] The U.S. Department of Justice considers the following as cybercrimes:[5]

- Crimes wherein the target is a computer or computing device
- Crimes wherein a computer or computing device is used as an instrument of crime
- Crimes wherein a computer is used as an accessory to a crime

The primary motive of cybercriminals is to generate profits in the form of monetary gains, but over a period of time, several other motives have come into play, such as:

- Pursuing a social or political agenda
- Espionage on competitors or nation states
- To challenge skills and ability – 'white hat' hacking
- Cyberwarfare or terrorism – carrying out disruptive and potentially destructive types of cyberattacks, such as targeting critical national infrastructure (power grids, air traffic control systems, banking networks, etc.)
- To take revenge – employees/insiders, angry users or others having grievances against an individual or organization

---

[2] "Global Programme on Cybercrime," United Nations, accessed June 6, 2021. https://www.unodc.org/unodc/en/cybercrime/global-programme-cybercrime.html

[3] Mshana, JA. "Cybercrime: An Empirical Study of Its Impact in the Society - A Case Study of Tanzania," *Huria: Journal of the Open University of Tanzania* 19, no. 1 (2015): 72–87.

[4] Kate Brush, Linda Rosencrance and Michael Cobb, "What Is Cybercrime? Effects, Examples and Prevention," TechTarget, accessed June 16, 2021. https://searchsecurity.techtarget.com/definition/cybercrime

[5] Hardik, "Cyber Crime," *Legal Service India*, accessed June 6, 2021, http://legalserviceindia.com/legal/article-971-cyber-crime.html

2.2 CLASSIFICATION OF CYBERCRIMES

For gaining a better understanding of the motives and objectives of cybercriminals, the crimes that they attempt/commit are classified based on the target of the crime. Cybercrimes can be broadly classified as crimes against individuals, crimes against property and crimes against governments. For each of these categories, cybercriminals adopt different approaches and use different levels and types of threats.

- **Cybercrimes against individuals** include deceiving an individual or circulating false, malicious or illegal information through the Internet, thereby directly affecting that person. Examples include but are not limited to social engineering, phishing, email harassment, cyberstalking and spreading illegal adult material.
- **Cybercrimes against property** include activities such as breaking in and the unauthorized use of a computer system, vandalising computer resources, spreading harmful programs as well as illegally accessing and taking possession of digital information.
- **Cybercrimes against government** are perpetrated in the form of cyber espionage, propaganda, cyber threats and attacks on government and military agencies, websites and resources.

2.3 FORMS OF CYBERCRIMES

There are many kinds of cybercrimes and numerous ways in which cybercriminals perpetrate them. Cybercriminals use hacking attacks to cause harm and compromise the integrity of any digital device, from smartphones to computers, to entire networks.[6] The first step in understanding the many manifestations of cybercrime is to delve into a cybercriminal's bag of tricks and the modalities used by them. Let us examine various forms of common cybercrimes.

- **Cyberextortion** refers to a cybercrime where money is demanded to either stop a threatened attack or to restore or release stolen data and computing resources that are locked up by the attackers. Ransomware is an example of cyberextortion wherein hackers gain control over organizational systems and data and lock them using encryption and only release the data after a ransom is paid. Ransom is usually demanded in the form of bitcoins.
- **Identity theft** is a very common type of attack, where an attacker gains access to a computer to steal a user's personal and other identity-related information and use this information to access or hijack their email and other online accounts and steal money from bank accounts and credit cards. There is a flourishing market for the sale and purchase of personal information on the dark web and information stolen from instances of large data breaches invariably lands up there.
- **Cryptojacking** is a form of cybercrime where a hacker inserts and run scripts without a user's knowledge or consent with the objective of mining cryptocurrencies.
- **Payment frauds** exist in multiple forms, from fake payment links to credit card fraud. Criminals target credit card information by perpetrating their own attacks or by simply buying credit card information from the dark web, where hacking groups who have harvested (stolen) large quantities of payment card information sell the same to smaller criminal operators who target individual accounts. Sending fake payment links, using fake web pages to collect card information and business email compromise are also common forms of payment frauds.
- **Business email compromise** (BEC) attacks are a form of cybercrime that use email fraud to attack organizations to achieve a specific outcome which negatively impacts the target organization.

---

[6] "Common Types of Cybercrimes and How to Protect Your Business From Them," Embroker, accessed June 17, 2021. https://www.embroker.com/blog/types-of-cybercrimes/

Usually, this is aimed at organizations who conduct wire transfers and have suppliers/business partners abroad. Attackers use previously acquired email account credentials and impersonate people of authority in that organization to direct accountants and people who make payments into sending money or sensitive data to the attacker's account.
- **Theft of intellectual property and software piracy** is a type of cybercrime that involves the unlawful copying, distribution and use of software programs and other forms of intellectual property in violation of copyright, trademark and patent laws.[7]
- **Denial-of-service** attacks are a form of cybercrime wherein attackers seek to surreptitiously establish control over a victim's computer or computing device and use the resource to disrupt the services of a target by flooding the target servers with requests, which makes it unable to provide services requested by genuine users. In a distributed denial-of-service (DDoS) attack, the attacker attempts to disturb the normal flow of traffic between a server and its connected users by initiating a flood of requests such that the server is not able to provide normal services and respond to requests of its legitimate users. DDoS attacks are carried out with networks of bots (botnet) using hijacked computers and other devices (such as Internet of Things or IoT devices) that have been infected with malware, allowing them to be controlled remotely by the attacker.
- **Corporate data theft** is a goldmine for cybercriminals and an omnipresent threat for companies. This involves the theft, sale and misuse of corporate data such as the personal data of clients, financial details, confidential data, in-house data generated during the course of business activity, trade secrets, business plans, software, etc. Data theft includes acts of illegal/unauthorized copying, removal or stealing of confidential, valuable or personal data/information from an organization or business without its knowledge or consent.
- **Cyberespionage** is a type of cybercrime that involves the use of electronic surveillance or hacking systems or networks belonging to governments or other organizations with the objective of gaining access to confidential information. The motives of such activities could vary from making money, selling intelligence information, gaining leverage or in support of their ideology or national purpose.
- **Hacking** refers to various activities that seek to compromise digital devices, such as computers, smartphones, tablets and even entire networks.[8] However, not all hacking is for malicious purposes and only hacking that involves unlawful activity motivated by financial gain, protest, information gathering (spying), etc. or which cause some form of harm can be considered as a criminal activity.
- **Cyberbullying, possession and distribution of child pornography, cyberstalking, illegal gambling and trading in banned items** like drugs and weapons are other common forms of cybercrime.

This list of forms of cybercrime is ever increasing, and law enforcement agencies and legal systems are finding it increasingly difficult to keep pace with the innovative ways and methods of cybercriminals.

The Dark Web: A Flourishing Marketplace: The dark web (Table 2.1), which is a marketplace for cybercriminals, represents the shady underbelly of the Internet. It is a parallel underground digital economy where stolen information, software for launching cyberattacks and other tools used by cybercriminals are bought and sold.

---
[7] Kate Brush, Linda Rosencrance and Michael Cobb, "What Is Cybercrime? Effects, Examples and Prevention," TechTarget, accessed June 16, 2021. https://searchsecurity.techtarget.com/definition/cybercrime
[8] "Hacking," Malwarebytes, accessed June 17, 2021. https://www.malwarebytes.com/hacker

Table 2.1 Surface web, deep web and dark web

Web levels	Characteristics
Surface web	- Accessible to anyone through a commonly used browser - Also called the visible web - Sites can be found using search engines like Google, Yahoo, Bing, etc.

Deep web	- Contents are not indexed by standard web search engines; holds nearly 90% of all websites. Some of the largest parts of the deep web include:
	  - Databases: Protected public and private databases
	  - Intranets: Internal networks for organizations, governments and educational facilities used for internal communication
	  - Financial information
	  - Email and social messaging accounts
	  - Legal information
	  - Protected health information
	- The contents can be located and accessed by a direct URL or IP address but may require authorization credentials such as a password or other security access to get access[9]

Dark web	- The invisible portion of the deep web, as the sites contained therein are not indexed - Holds hidden or invisible content that is only accessible by a specialized anonymizing browser such as TOR (The Onion Router) - Known to be a marketplace for cybercriminals who sell credit card numbers, drugs, guns, counterfeit money, stolen subscription credentials, hacked social media account information, etc.

There are also some cyber experts who believe that there exists a deeper layer to the dark web, called the 'shadow web'. Others say that the shadow web is just a scam site that offers access to more dubious and sinister online spaces and forums often used for criminal activity.

Today, cybercrime has moved from a lone wolf (criminal) activity to an organized ecosystem complete with its own products, services suppliers, markets, buyers and even organized criminal groups.

2.4 CYBER SCAMS AND FRAUDS

Cyber scams and frauds represent yet another growing form of cybercriminal activity. Cybercriminals use a wide range of scam methods to gain access to a device or network, extort money or steal valuable information. A partial list of such cyber scams is shown in Table 2.2.

Regardless of whether the victim of a cybercrime is an individual or an organization, the impact has several negative consequences. For example, in the case of a business organization, it could lead to:

- Financial losses
- Disruption of operations
- Loss of sensitive data that could lead to other consequences
- Loss of reputation and brand value
- Loss of customer and investor trust
- Direct and indirect costs

---

[9] "What is the Deep and Dark Web?," *Kaspersky* (blog), accessed October 4, 2021. https://www.kaspersky.com/resource-center/threats/deep-web

Table 2.2 Various types of scams

Phishing email scams	Lottery scams	Bank loan or credit scams
Fake antivirus software	Economic scams	Spoofing, fake emails and invoices
Travel-related scams	Fake news scams	Fake shopping websites
Fake shopping websites	Payment-related scams	Job-related scams
Tech-support scams	Deep fakes	Impersonation scams

An understanding of cybercrime by individuals and organizations is today essential to fight and develop resistance and deterrence to cybercrime.

2.5 SOURCES OF THREATS: THREAT ACTORS AND THEIR MOTIVATIONS

In order to better understand the dynamics of cybercrime, it is important understand who the threat actors are and their motivations. The Government Accountability Office, Department of Homeland Security of the USA has compiled the following list of threat actors who are potentially a source of cyber threats and attacks.[10] While the context of this study was threats to critical infrastructure, the list is nevertheless universally relevant.

- A **hacker** is someone who uses computer programming, technical and manipulative skills to intentionally violate computer security for a variety of reasons, such as theft, fraud, corporate espionage and even revenge. Sometimes, hackers break into networks just for the thrill of the challenge or for crowing in the hacker community.[11] Over time, the tools to launch an attack have become more accessible and easier to use, enabling hackers to cause serious disruption and damage with minimal knowledge and skill in the domain. Hackers can be divided into three broad categories:[12]
  - **Black hat hackers** are responsible for developing malware and are engaged in launching cyber threats and attacks. Their motivations range from personal or financial gain, political causes or just for fun.
  - **White hat hackers** are also called ethical hackers and are employed or engaged by organizations as security specialists to help them identify security gaps and vulnerabilities.
  - **Grey hat hackers** are individuals who use methods deployed by black hat and white hat hackers, but report their findings on security issues to the system owner and demand a compensation or incentive for their efforts.
- **Botnet operators** are hackers who specialize in taking control over a number of systems not belonging to them and then use the resources to coordinate disruptive cyberattacks.
- **Phishers**, as the name suggests, are individuals or groups who develop expertise in designing and executing phishing schemes, often for monetary gain.

---

[10] "Critical Infrastructure Protection: Department of Homeland Security Faces Challenges in Fulfilling Cybersecurity Responsibilities," U.S. Government Accountability Office, accessed April 15, 2021. https://www.gao.gov/products/gao-05-434

[11] Maliapen, M. "Data Protection" in *Encyclopedia of Applied Ethics, Second Edition*, Ruth Chadwick (ed.), (Academic Press: 2012).

[12] Michael Luciano, "What Are the Three Types of Hackers?," Design World, accessed April 15, 2021. https://www.designworldonline.com/what-are-the-three-types-of-hackers/

- **Spammers** are entities that distribute unsolicited emails or messages, often designed to deceive unsuspecting users into exposing themselves to cyber threats and malware.
- **Spyware/Malware authors** are individuals or entities that produce and distribute malware for the purpose of carrying out attacks.
- **Cybercriminal groups**: Hackers operate individually and also in groups that have specific agendas ranging from profit to pursuing agendas on behalf of nation states. Organized criminal groups have multiple members, each bringing different skills and deploying different tactics and techniques, enabling them to undertake cyberattacks of larger scale and sophistication. These groups are also known to have been hired by national states to carry out cyberattacks.

Info Box 3: Security Threats from Physical Devices

Physical security devices can also be a source of cyber threats. While the focus of threat mitigation is often directed towards protection of information systems, there are other ways in which cyber threats can materialize. A case in point is the 2021 hacking of over 150,000 cloud-based Verkada physical security cameras. It brought to attention the security threat from IoT devices, which have seen an explosion in deployment in recent years and have contributed to the ever-expanding threat surface. The hackers gained access to thousands of cameras installed in hospitals, schools, corporate offices, police stations and jails.[13]

- Finally, the disgruntled or unhappy organization **insider** can also be a source of cybercrime. Insiders include outsourcing vendors, contractors, service providers and their employees who could intentionally or mistakenly introduce malware into organizational systems.

Cyber terrorists and intelligence services of various countries or spies also deploy hacking tools for intelligence gathering, surveillance, launching of cyber terrorism attacks and for other types of espionage activities. Let us examine this in further detail.

2.5.1 Cyber Espionage and Surveillance

Cyber espionage and surveillance are an important part of the intelligence gathering activity conducted by nation states. Cyber espionage entails deliberate actions and the use of cyber tools and techniques to access confidential data resident on computer systems or intercepting such data while it is in transit. The purposes for conducting espionage can range from the military to the economic to the political. The availability of cyber technologies and tools for espionage and surveillance have raised the stakes and rapidly expanded the scope and speed of such operations. Cyber espionage is widely used for economic and military purposes to identify serious vulnerabilities, which can be exploited to disrupt supply, communications and military infrastructure.[14]

2.5.2 Cyberwarfare and Cyber Terrorism

Governments around the world are engaged in perpetrating cyberattacks, often through proxies. Many nation states have allegedly made use of cyberattacks to further their ongoing political, economic and social agendas. Such attacks can be classified as cyberwarfare.

---

[13] Kai Moncino, "Cybersecurity for Physical Security Devices," Security Info Watch, accessed June 15, 2021. https://www.securityinfowatch.com/cybersecurity/article/21224063/cybersecurity-for-physical-security-devices

[14] Banks, WC. Cyber Espionage and Electronic Surveillance: Beyond the Media Coverage, *Emory Law Journal* 66, no. 3 (January 1, 2017).

Cyber terrorism refers to the use of cyber tools to shut down critical national infrastructure (such as energy, transportation, government operations) or to force or intimidate a government or a civilian population. Cyber terrorists usually direct their efforts towards specific targets and objectives. They are adept at cyber incursion, spreading disinformation, indulging in defacement of opponent websites and causing disruption of information systems. Each type of attack they execute may have different objectives and may, therefore, vary in terms of severity of impact.

Today, several nation states are developing their own cybersecurity systems, but are also engaged in developing their cyberwarfare capabilities to pursue their agendas. At last count, as many as 120 countries are ready to conduct cyberwarfare, having developed ways to use the Internet along with other tactics, techniques and malware to target government computer systems, utilities and, of course, the financial markets. Wars between nation states are often conducted through military means over long periods of time, but cyberwars tend to be short skirmishes where there are only allegations of cyberattacks being carried out by adversaries without any concrete proof or further escalation. So far, there has been no official confirmation of a cyberwar between two nation states; what has happened thus far can be referred to as sporadic incidents that have been proactively initiated or that are retaliatory actions. An example is the June 2019 episode where the United States launched a cyberattack against Iranian weapons systems in retaliation to the shooting down of a US drone in the Strait of Hormuz.[15]

2.5.3 Cyber Offenders

Cybercriminals comprise all those people who use digital technology to commit crimes. Cybercriminals could operate as individuals or in teams or groups to undertake malicious activities. All threat actors are not necessary cybercriminals as the question of criminality arises only when their actions are based on malicious or unlawful intent to cause loss or damage.

The act of hacking by itself is not a cybercrime unless it is carried out with some criminal intent or objective. Hence, as such, not all hackers are cybercriminals. Hacking can also be used for positive purposes such as recovering lost information, performing penetration testing to identify vulnerabilities in organizational networks and putting in place preventive mechanisms to thwart cyber threats and security breaches.

The main factors that have contributed to the explosive growth in cybercrime and which help cyber offenders and cybercriminals are:

- A large and growing attack surface boosted by modern technology developments such as IoT devices
- Ignorance and poor cyber practices among users of the way cybercriminals operate and various aspects of cybersecurity, both at individual and organizational level
- Laws that are still evolving and challenges for enforcement agencies in tracing cybercriminals, charging them and proving cybercrimes due to issues like anonymity that the Internet offers, jurisdiction, technology-related issues, evidence gathering and preservation, etc.
- Deep web underground markets that offer not only a market for stolen data but which also provide tools, methodology in the form of specialized products (such as ransomware) and other services required for perpetrating cybercrime. Cybercriminals do not need specialized training or a lot of money to undertake sophisticated exploits as they can use these readymade tools even by renting them.

---

[15] Agarwal, N, Kalambe, P, Ghag, P and Patil, CH. 2020. Study on Cyber Warfare During 2001–2019, *International Journal of Engineering Research and Technology*, ICSITS – 2020 (Volume 8, Issue 05).

- The ease with which hackers can access online information, use social engineering to identify targets and direct their efforts where they have maximum chance of success.
- New contexts such as the pandemic and remote working offer big opportunities for cybercriminals to launch and execute various kinds of cyber scams on unsuspecting victims
- The lack of preparedness of individuals and organizations (such as incident response teams) to deal with cyber threats and cybercrimes

Cybercrime is inherently complex as it is based on the use of technology and deception and is enacted in the borderless sphere of cyberspace by petty cybercriminals to organized crime groups with specific goals and agenda. The possibility of getting away with cyber offences is higher than with traditional crimes as victims are often located in different countries around the world and are hesitant even to report cyber offences.

Like in any field of human activity, specialization not only becomes a requirement due to evolutionary contexts, but also to enhance productivity and the necessary skill and knowledge required to achieve different goals. Over time, cybercriminals too have evolved and developed specialized skills to achieve their goals and objectives. From being solo recreational hackers and amateur cyber vandals, hackers have honed their professional skills to perform different kinds of cyberattacks, and some have become a part of organized and well-resourced cybercriminal groups and syndicates that are even sponsored by nation states for specific activities that could be considered unlawful.

Along with specialization comes division of labour, which can be observed in the organization of a cybercrime gang or group. As in most organizations, there is a team leader who is responsible for meeting goals and monitoring all team activities. He is supported by a network specialist, a coder, an intrusion expert and a data miner – each is responsible for their respective functions and form the core operations team. Then there is the money manager who manages the movement of money, which is the proceeds from cybercriminal exploits.

Table 2.3 lists the profiles of various kinds of cyber offenders.

Table 2.3 Kinds of cyber offenders

Identity thieves	Cybercriminals who steal sensitive personal or financial information related to a person and use their identity information to commit fraud
Data and IP thieves	Cybercriminals focused on stealing confidential organizational data, business-related information and intellectual property
Stalkers, cyber bullies and sextortionists	Cybercriminals who perpetrate crimes related to cyber harassment such as stalking, distribution of child pornography and sextortion
Malicious insiders	Disgruntled employees, contractors or other employees who commit cybercrimes against their employers
Cyber terrorists	Cybercriminals who are engaged in conducting premeditated, politically motivated cyberattacks against the IT infrastructure of nations, causing loss, damage and threats to human safety
Cyber extortionists	Cybercriminals who use ransomware and other methods to extort money from their victims
Cyber scamsters	Cybercriminals who use ingenious schemes to deceive and manipulate victims to steal money or valuable information

(Continued)

Table 2.3 (*Continued*)

Hacktivists	Cybercriminals who carry out cyberattacks in support of political causes; Anonymous is a well-known group of international activists and hacktivists
Cybercrime groups/syndicates	Organized groups of hackers and cybercriminals with other skills who work in concert to commit major crimes by combining their skills and resources; Lazard Group, Cobalt Group and Magecart Group are some examples
State actors	State-owned organizations/sponsored groups that are hired to conduct cyber espionage, steal data, cause economic disruption or undertake cyberattacks against adversaries
Social engineer	A cybercriminal who manipulates a person to take an action to reveal confidential information that can be used against that person
Spear phisher	A cybercriminal who targets specific individuals using phishing techniques
Script kiddies	Inexperienced hackers who generally use existing software to launch hacking attacks
Cryptologists	People with expertise in encryption/decryption of data, not necessarily with criminal intent
Phreakers	Individuals who have specialized capabilities in hacking telephones with or without criminal intent
Advanced persistent threat (APT) agents	Well-resourced cybercrime groups that have strong technical skills to infiltrate IT infrastructure, remain undetected for lengthy periods of time and trigger a full-scale attack at a time of their choosing
Cybercrime market operators	Underground cybercrime market operators who provide tools and services that hackers can buy or rent; they also provide platforms for buying and selling stolen data

2.6 TOOLS AND METHODS USED IN CYBERATTACKS/CYBERCRIMES

Hacking is often not a single-stage activity. Hackers use a variety of tools and methods at different stages of a hacking exploit. Cyberattacks generally follow a pattern wherein hackers first carry out reconnaissance of their targets, then choose/build a cyber weapon or payload consisting of different types of malware, and then execute the attack by selecting a mode of delivery/installation of the exploit to meet their goals. Let us examine the tools that cybercriminals use for accomplishing different objectives.

2.6.1 Reconnaissance

Hackers do their homework in the form of reconnaissance before they commit cybercrimes or cyberattacks. There are two types of reconnaissance. **Passive reconnaissance** is where the hacker attempts to gather information about the target or potential victim system without actively engaging with them. For this activity, they may use tools like WHOIS, social media sites, Shodan, etc. **Active reconnaissance** involves engagement with the target system, including probing a network for open ports and scanning for other vulnerabilities. The tools used for active reconnaissance include Nmap (for network recon), Nessus, OpenVAS and Angry IP, which are vulnerability scanners. The objective of this step is to identify a potential target and find any vulnerabilities associated with it.

2.6.2 Weaponization: Choosing/Building Malware

At the next stage, the hacker uses the information gathered to start exploiting the vulnerabilities by planting malware into the target system to establish control. Several types of malware and methods are available to hackers for this purpose. Malware is essentially a combination of malicious intent and software. Simply put, malware, or malicious software, is any program or file that is harmful to a computer user.[16]

Malware is aimed at causing harm or exploiting a computer system, device, service or network to extract data and/or cause other types of harm. There are several ways in which malware can be classified depending on the intended purpose, the type of harm it can causes, its behaviour, etc. It is important to distinguish malware forms as it leads to better understanding for identification and the types of ways it can infect targeted systems and networks. Even after identifying a certain type of malware, we need to recognize that each malware also has its own variants, and hence, the use of the term malware family.

Malware includes other types of software which can:

- Hinder the normal operation of a computer
- Gather sensitive information
- Secure access to private networks and systems

There are two basic types of malware (Fig. 2.1): malware that is deployed for infecting a system and malware that is defined by its actions.

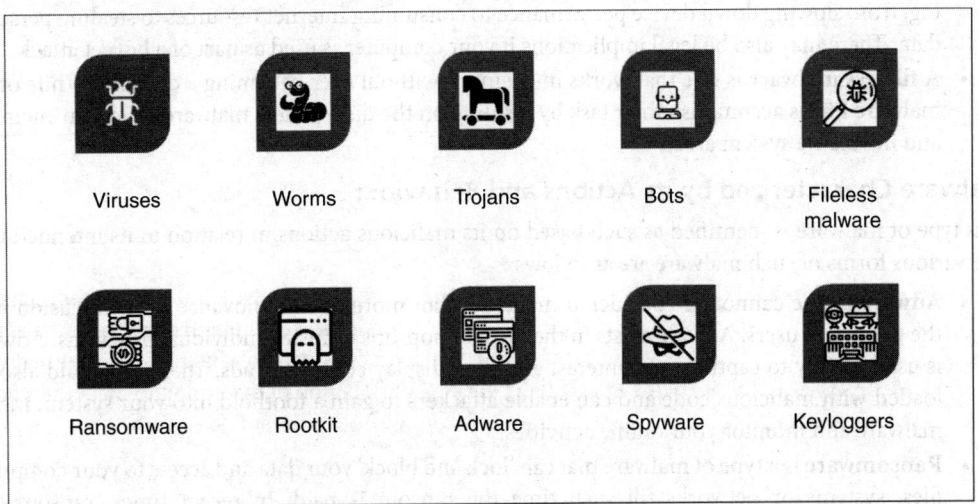

Figure 2.1 Common types of malware

---

[16] Ben Lutkevich, "What Is Malware and How Does It Work?," TechTarget, accessed June 14, 2021. https://searchsecurity.techtarget.com/definition/malware

Malware Used for Infecting a System

Malware that is used for infecting systems are viruses, worms, trojan horses, bots. etc. Let us examine each in turn.

- A **virus** is characterised by its ability to replicate by attaching itself to a program such as files, songs, videos, etc. on the target computer and then inserting its own code and spreading over a network. Viruses can be destructive and can cause damage to files and programs, reformat disk drives or flood a network with traffic, making it impossible to perform any Internet activity.
- A **worm** is a self-replicating form of malware. Fundamentally, the difference between a virus and a worm is that a virus needs to be activated by a host, whereas a worm can autonomously replicate and spread.[17] Many worms are created only to spread and carry 'payloads' and may not aim to change the systems they pass through. At a minimum, a worm can cause major disruption by increasing network traffic and have other unintended effects.
- The concept of **trojans** is based on the famous Trojan horse story in Greek mythology. The Greeks used a big wooden horse, meant to be a gift for the Trojans, to break the security cordon. The Trojans allowed the wooden horse into the city believing it to be a gift, not knowing that soldiers were hiding inside the horse. In the cyber world, a trojan conceals itself inside software that seems genuine, but once the software is run it can perform tasks that the designers want it to execute. This could include activities such as serving as a backdoor gateway for malicious programs or stealing data. Commonly used trojans are remote access, file transfer and proxy.
- A **bot** is an advanced form of a worm. Bots can function autonomously and are programmed to work on their own without any human intervention. A single malicious bot can infect several others by infecting a host server and enable the use of the network's infected bots (botnet). Botnets are used to launch attacks that can paralyze networks by flooding them with Internet traffic in a way that legitimate user requests cannot be served. A botnet attack can be disrupting and devastating, from slowing down device performance to consuming Internet resources to stealing personal data. There may also be legal implications if your computer is used as part of a botnet attack.
- A **fileless malware** is one that works in-memory without ever becoming a disk file. While other malware forms accomplish their task by residing on the disk, fileless malware resides in-memory and in volatile system areas.

Malware Characterized by its Actions and Behaviour

This type of malware is identified as such based on its malicious actions in relation to its intended use. The various forms of such malware are as follows:

- **Adware** per se cannot be considered malicious, but more of an annoyance as an intrusion into the privacy of users. Adware exists in the form of pop-ups or inside individual programs. Adware is used mainly to capture your interest and then display contextual ads. These ads could also be loaded with malicious code and can enable attackers to gain a foothold into your system, install malware and monitor your online activities.
- **Ransomware** is a type of malware that can 'lock and block' your data and access to your computer files, systems or networks till such time the ransom is paid. In recent times, ransomware attacks have become more widespread across sectors and geographies. Ransomware attacks are usually launched using a trojan masquerading as a legitimate file, which the user is tricked into downloading or opening when it arrives as an email attachment.
- **Spyware** is another type of malware that is used to monitor your online activities and expose the information gathered to those who may be interested in it. Trojans, viruses or worms are used to

---

[17] "What is the Difference between a Virus and a Worm?," *Kaspersky* (blog), accessed June 16, 2021. https://www.kaspersky.com/resource-center/threats/computer-viruses-vs-worms

drop spyware, which installs and conceals itself to prevent detection. A keylogger is an example of spyware that records user keystrokes to capture usernames, passwords, card information, etc.
- A **rootkit** is a collection of malware that is aimed at gaining root level access or administrative privileges that would enable the attacker to access, steal, delete or modify any files and data within the system. Rootkit installation can be automated or can be done by an attacker after securing root or administrator access. Rootkit detection is difficult because it often masks its existence.[18]

Hackers also use malware to set up backdoors and trojans as well as to cover their tracks. This allow them more dwell time in target networks by concealing themselves and exfiltrating substantial amounts of data, typically over a long period of time.

While there are several malware protection and detection tools available, tell-tale signs that a system is infected with malware include unusual activity like opening new accounts, an abrupt loss of disk space, slow system responses, recurring crashes or freezes, or an unexpected increase in unwanted Internet activity. Using a well-reputed antivirus software can provide protection and help in detection and removal of malware as well as undertaking regular scans for the same (Table 2.4).

Table 2.4 Open source/Free/Trial versions of antivirus software

Bitdefender	Panda Security	Avira
Kaspersky	AVG Anti-virus	Avast

2.6.3 Execution

We will now examine the common methods used by hackers to execute their attacks, which involves delivery, installation of the exploit and causing further damage by manipulating data, exfiltrating data and other malicious acts.

- **Social engineering**, also referred to as 'human hacking', is an attack vector that relies on manipulation to lure unsuspecting users to gain private information or access to key information assets. Social engineering covers a broad range of malicious activities such as phishing, baiting, tailgating and various other types of scams. Social engineering attacks use some form of psychological manipulation, typically using email or other communication forms, to not only deceive users but also invoke emotions such as urgency, fear or greed or simply play on their desire for getting more information about a subject that they may be interested in. Victims are led to click on a malicious link, open a malicious attachment or trigger a malware download that can lead to compromising the system or exposing sensitive information. Since social engineering involves a human element, preventing these attacks can be challenging for organizations.
- Different types of **phishing** methodologies (Table 2.5) are deployed by hackers. Typically, an attacker may send a link that takes you to a website that then tricks you into downloading malware or giving the attacker your private information. In most cases, the target may not realize they have been compromised, which allows the attacker to go after others in the same organization without anyone suspecting malicious activity. Phishing attacks enable hackers to steal personal and sensitive information including passwords, financial information and other types of sensitive information that they can use to steal money or cause other harm to the victim. Researchers have classified phishing into two types based on the way an attack is carried out:[19]

---

[18] McAfee, "Rootkits, Part 1 of 3: The Growing Threat," Wayback Machine, 2006, accessed June 16, 2021. https://web.archive.org/web/20060823090948/http://www.mcafee.com/us/local_content/white_papers/threat_center/wp_akapoor_rootkits1_en.pdf

[19] Improve Performance and Filter Requests," in *2-Tools and Methods Used in Cybercrime Stages of an Attack on Network*, 1–16. https://docslib.org/doc/4399911/2-tools-and-methods-used-in-cybercrime-stages-of-an-attack-on-network

Table 2.5 Four methods of phishing

Dragnet method	This method involves the use of spammed emails which use fake branding like logos and company names with a view to elicit immediate response.[20]
Rod-and-reel method	This method is used once initial contact with a target victim is established. Here false information is sent to them in a way that they react and disclose their personal and financial data.
Lobsterpot method	This involves the setting up of fake websites that look like legitimate websites to lure users to visit them and part with personal information.
Gillnet phishing	Here the hackers introduce malicious code into emails and websites.[21]

- **Deceptive phishing**: The methodology here is to send persuasive/threatening (giving a deadline or saying if they do not respond, their account will be blocked) messages to unsuspecting users to verify account information, system upgrades/failures that require users to re-enter their information, offering free or discounted services, fake invoices or receipts and many such schemes to a large number of people knowing that at least some of them will click a link or login to a fake web page, enabling the hacker to steal personal information about the user.
- **Malware-based phishing**: The methodology here is to use attachments or downloadable files that can spread malware and infect a system by exploiting known security vulnerabilities.
- **Spear phishing** is a phishing attack that is generally aimed at 'high-value' targets. They are also referred to as whale phishing attacks as they target 'big fish' or the top executives of an organization since they are more likely to possess and have access to information that can be valuable to attackers, such as proprietary information about the business or its operations.

The ways in which you can prevent phishing, spear phishing and whale phishing attacks is to verify with the sender if the content is genuine or hover your mouse over any links (before you click), which would display the uniform resource locator (URL) to confirm if it is legitimate as well as keeping an eye out for suspicious emails, attachments, destinations or parameters.

> **Info Box 4: Cybercrime Statistics**
>
> It is important to note that cybercriminals are sending over three billion emails a day, 94% of malware is delivered by email, and that phishing attacks account for more than 80% of reported security incidents.[22]

- **Smishing** (SMS phishing) is another variant of phishing and a growing threat vector where short message service (SMS) instead of emails is used to launch a phishing exploit.
- **Pharming** is a method that hackers use to tinker with an organization's host files or domain name system in order to direct requests and engage in interaction with a fake website controlled by the hackers.
- **Steganography** is another methodology deployed by hackers that involves concealing a secret message within what seems to be a normal message and then extracting and using it after it has

---

[20] Mohamed Chawki, "Phishing in Cyberspace: Issues and Solutions," Computer Crime Research Centre, accessed June 16, 2021. https://www.crime-research.org/articles/phishing-in-cyberspace-issues-and-solutions/

[21] Mohamed Chawki, "Phishing in Cyberspace: Issues and Solutions," Computer Crime Research Centre, accessed June 16, 2021. https://www.crime-research.org/articles/phishing-in-cyberspace-issues-and-solutions/

[22] Chuck Brooks, "Alarming Cybersecurity Stats: What You Need To Know For 2021," *Forbes*, accessed June 11, 2021. https://www.forbes.com/sites/chuckbrooks/2021/03/02/alarming-cybersecurity-stats------what-you-need-to-know-for-2021/?sh=775e9a4e58d3

recached the recipient. Steganography is a very sophisticated technique that requires hackers to create purpose-specific images, documents, videos and even audio files. While the general objective is to plant hidden messages and malicious payloads into seemingly benign and legitimate digital artefacts, in recent years, it has also been used for exfiltration of data. For example, the famous SolarWinds attack, while being widely known as a supply chain attack, involved the use steganography, which enabled hackers to hide command data during the command-and-control phase of the attack. Cyberattacks involving steganography are hard to detect and require a high degree of user awareness along with strong endpoint detection tools.
- **Code injection** is a methodology where hackers exploit a vulnerability by introducing code that changes the course of execution of a program. If hackers obtain the ability to execute code remotely through a command-and-control server used by them, they can potentially launch a devastating cyberattack.

Table 2.6 provides an assortment of tools and methods deployed by hackers to cause damage, while Table 2.7 lists the commonly used anti-phishing software.

Table 2.6 Common tools and methods used by hackers

Phishing	Ransomware	Rootkits
Pharming	Spyware	Sniffers
Adware	Keyloggers	Spoofing
Social engineering	Trojans	Encryption cracking
Steganography	Backdoors	Bots
Code injection	Vulnerability scanners	Various forms of malware

Table 2.7 Open source/Free/Trial versions of anti-phishing software

Avananan	Brandshield	CoDefense PDR
KnowBe4	Microsoft Defender for Office 365	Valimail

- **Keyloggers** are a form of spyware designed to covertly capture every keystroke, monitor user activity and create a record of anything that is typed on a computer or mobile keyboard. While keyloggers can be used by designers and developers legitimately for capturing user activity and related feedback, it is an important tool in the hackers' arsenal. There are basically two types of keyloggers: hardware and software. Hardware keyloggers are of different types such as keyboard hardware, which is placed in line with the connection cable, or hidden camera loggers placed strategically to record keystrokes or USB disk-loaded keyloggers. Software keyloggers are programs that install on computer disk drives for keystroke logging. Examples are API-based keyloggers, kernel-based keyloggers that bypass system administration permissions and form grabbing keyloggers that record entries made into forms and websites. Form-based keyloggers can compromise personal information of different types, making them potentially more dangerous. Protection from keyloggers is often difficult for a user and requires the use of tools such as LeakInspector, an add-on for the Mozilla Firefox browser.

We must be aware of the fact that new tools and forms of malware are being developed by hacking groups even as existing forms evolve further. The business models to gain access to these tools also keep evolving and malware are available in a software-as-a-service or pay-per-use model in the dark web.

2.7 WHAT IS A CYBERATTACK?

A cyberattack is any bid to obtain unauthorized access to a computer, computing device, system or network with the purpose of disrupting, disabling, destroying, altering, blocking, deleting, manipulating or stealing the data held within these systems. Cyberattacks are generally carried out by hackers (also known as threat actors or cybercriminals) using different strategies, methods and tools.[23] They can operate alone, in groups or owe their affiliation to a crime syndicate. Cyberattacks can be launched using a variety of what are known as tools, techniques and procedures.

> **Info Box 5: Stages of a Cyberattack**
>
> Cyberattacks often take place in stages, starting with hackers surveying or scanning for vulnerabilities or access points, initiating the compromise, and then executing the full attack – whether it is stealing valuable data, disabling computer systems or both.[24]

Cyberattacks can be initiated from inside or outside an organization's security perimeter. Attacks from inside the security perimeter are harder to detect as they are perpetrated by an insider or an outsider who has obtained access to an authorized user's credentials. Here, the role of firewalls and intrusion detection systems is rendered ineffective, as these are safeguards to protect the security perimeter from outside attacks.

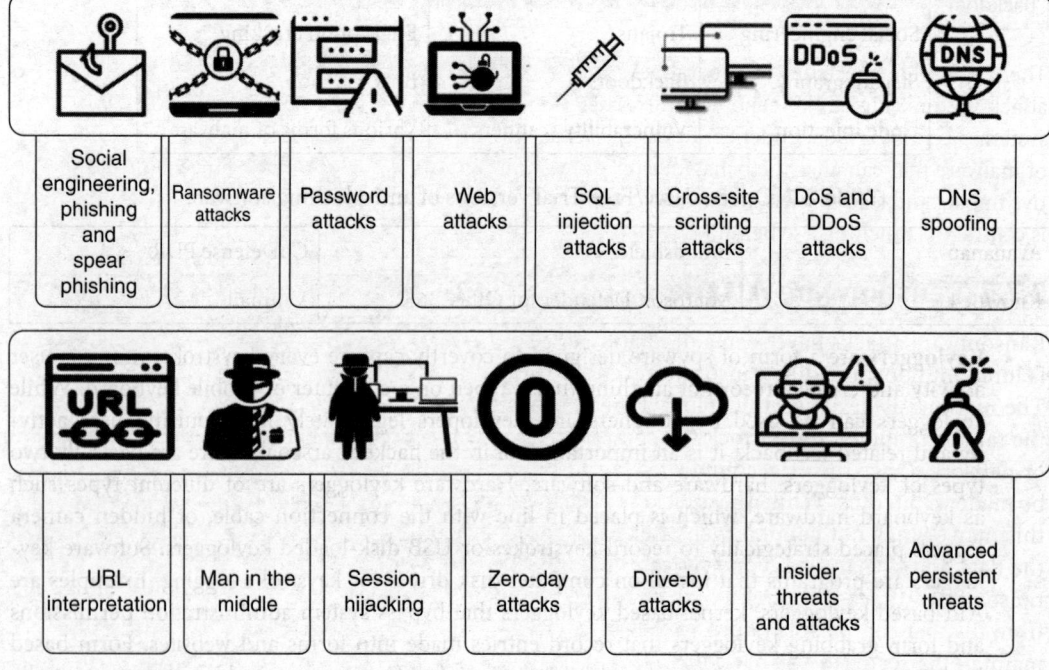

Figure 2.2 Types of cyberattacks

---

[23] Mary K Pratt, "What Is a Cyber Attack? Definition, Types and Examples," TechTarget, accessed June 15, 2021. https://searchsecurity.techtarget.com/definition/cyber-attack

[24] Mary K Pratt, "What Is a Cyber Attack? Definition, Types and Examples," TechTarget, accessed June 15, 2021. https://searchsecurity.techtarget.com/definition/cyber-attack

2.7.1 Types of Cyberattacks

Cyberattacks can be divided into two broad categories. Passive attacks use information from the system without affecting the system resources. Active cyberattacks are attempts that modify a system's behaviour or affect its operation. In other words, passive attacks compromise the confidentiality of information, while active attacks compromise the integrity and availability of information.[25] Table 2.8 lists examples of each.

Table 2.8 Passive and active cyberattacks

Passive cyberattacks	Active cyberattacks
Computer or network surveillance	Brute force attacks
Wire tapping	Cross-site scripting, SQL injection
Fibre tapping	Denial-of-service attacks
Port scanning	Phishing, social engineering and email spoofing
Keystroke logging	Zero-day attacks
Data scraping	Ransomware
Backdoor	Viruses and worms

There is a wide spectrum of cyberattacks that threat actors can launch with the help of a variety of attack vectors (Fig. 2.2). Techopedia describes a cyberattack as "a deliberate exploitation of computer systems, technology-dependent enterprises and networks",[26] and adds that hackers deploy various forms of malware that can alter the behaviour of computer programs and applications that can have a disruptive impact and lead to theft of data and compromise of information systems. Hence, the use of malware is central to launching a cyberattack.

2.7.2 Ransomware Attacks

Ransomware attacks have seen a dramatic increase over the years. In a ransomware attack, a target is lured into downloading ransomware, either from a website or from within an email attachment. The malware is designed to exploit vulnerabilities that exist and proceeds to encrypt the data on the target computer and/or lock the computer, thereby denying access to the compromised system or network. Once this is accomplished, a ransom demand is made, usually asking for payments to be made in bitcoins. While the attackers promise to provide the encryption key and restore access, this may or may not happen even after payment of ransom. Attackers are also known to exfiltrate the data and demand a second ransom for not exposing or selling it on the dark web. Preventing ransomware attacks requires a high degree of vigilance by all users, implementing next-generation firewalls that can perform deep packet inspection, keeping key information assets encrypted and maintaining ready-to-use back-ups.

---

[25] Abi Tyas Tunggal, "What Is a Cyber Attack?," *UpGuard* (blog), accessed June 15, 2021. https://www.upguard.com/blog/cyber-attack

[26] Jenab, K and Moseihpour, S, "Cyber Security Management: A Review," ResearchGate, accessed June 17, 2021. https://www.researchgate.net/publication/305220294_Cyber_Security_Management_A_Review

2.7.3 Password and Phishing Attacks

Passwords are the gateway to IT systems and networks. They are also the most widely used form of access verification tool. For hackers, getting access to a system means laying their hands on a user or administrator password. An attacker may use multiple methods to obtain passwords including shoulder surfing, using social engineering techniques or even by intercepting passwords that are not encrypted as they are transmitted through a network.

Attackers can also resort to using brute force methods to guess passwords. In this form of attack, an attacker uses basic information about the individual or their job title to try to guess their password, such as their name, birth date, anniversary or other personal details that can be used in various combinations.[27]

Hackers similarly try to guess passwords by using the words in a dictionary. This is called a dictionary attack. In this form of attack, common words and phrases, such as those listed in a dictionary, are used to guess the target's password.[28] One of the effective ways of preventing a brute force attack is to encourage the use of passphrases instead of passwords (as they are harder to crack) and implement a lock-out policy, wherein after a certain number of failed attempts, the system will lock out the attacker.

A variant of this form of attack involves the use of bots to crack the credentials. Here, a number of iterations of guessing and trying can be performed quickly. Apart from locking up the system based on failed attempts, not allowing logins from unauthenticated hardware, implementing multi-factor authentication and use of key files (which enable encryption of passwords and provide another level of authentication for their containers) are also useful ways of preventing such attacks.

Phishing attacks are the most common type of cyberattack and involve the use of sending fraudulent communications that appear to come from a reputable source, so that the receiver is duped into revealing sensitive personal information that can be used to cause various types of harm to the individual or the organization he works for. Common phishing attacks use emails, messaging services, smishing and vishing (voice phishing) and other means, which were detailed earlier in this chapter. Hackers also resort to phishing campaigns to capture credentials from popular applications such as Google Chrome, Firefox, Outlook, etc. and to establish control over an infected device, including webcam capturing, clipboard logging, remote desktop control, privilege escalation, keylogging and voice recording using fileless malware such as AveMariaRAT, BitRAT and PandoraHVNC.

2.7.4 Web Attacks

Web attacks are perpetrated by exploiting vulnerabilities in web-based applications. For performing specific functions, web application designers set certain parameters. Attackers indulge in what is called parameter tampering that involves altering the parameters that programmers implement as security measures designed to protect specific operations. Since the execution of the operation is dependent on the parameter that is entered, by modifying the parameters, attackers bypass the security measures that are defined in these parameters. Preventing such attacks involves inspecting web applications to check for and fixing those vulnerabilities. A useful way of patching up these vulnerabilities is to use a cross-site request forgery (CSRF) token or a synchronizer token. In CSRF tokens, an exchange of tokens takes place between the user's browser and the web application.

---

[27] "Top 20 Most Common Types Of Cyber Attacks," Fortinet, accessed June 15, 2021. https://www.fortinet.com/resources/cyberglossary/types-of-cyber-attacks

[28] "Top 20 Most Common Types Of Cyber Attacks," Fortinet, accessed June 15, 2021. https://www.fortinet.com/resources/cyberglossary/types-of-cyber-attacks

2.7.5 SQL Injection Attacks

Another common type of cyberattack is by using a structured query language (SQL) injection on websites that depend on databases to serve their users. The command is inserted using an SQL injection into a data plane instead of a normal input such as a password or login. The server that stores the database then runs the command and the system is penetrated. Hackers use SQL injections to compromise sensitive data or modify or delete other important data. If the hacker is able to gain administrator access, he can inflict additional damage by stopping the functioning of the database. Such attacks can be prevented by following the principle of least privilege, whereby access is restricted to important databases to only those users who need it to perform their job functions. Applying a least-privilege policy can prevent hackers from accessing sensitive information.

2.7.6 Cross-site Scripting Attacks

Using this form of attack, also known as XSS, the attacker transmits malicious scripts using clickable content. On clicking, the script is executed and then transmitted to the target's browser. Since the user is already logged into a web application's session, the input that is entered is accepted as legitimate by the web application but is actually the script that has been altered by the attacker, resulting in unintended program behaviour.[29] XSS attacks can be extremely harmful, especially in the case of financial transactions, where an attacker may change the parameters of a transfer request sent through a payment or banking application. In a fabricated request, the name of the intended recipient of the funds and even the amount of money to be transferred can be replaced with that of the attacker. Prevention of such attacks involves transacting only with whitelisted entities.

2.7.7 DoS and DDoS Attacks

A denial-of-service (DoS) or distributed-denial-of-service (DDoS) attack is intended to overwhelm the resources of a system to the point where it is unable to respond to legitimate service requests. A DDoS attack is executed through the use of several bots (malware-infected host machines or devices) which are controlled by the attacker. In a typical DDoS attack, the victims' servers are flooded with illegitimate requests generated by the bots so that all resources meant to service legitimate users are choked, even leading to the shutting down of the site.

> **Info Box 6: The DYN DDoS Attack**
>
> Dyn is a company that controls much of the Internet's domain name system (DNS) infrastructure. The Dyn cyberattack shut down a large part of America's Internet through the Mirai botnet, which was likely the largest of its kind in history. Dyn's servers were attacked on 21 October, 2016 and remained under sustained assault throughout the day, bringing down sites including Twitter, The Guardian, Netflix, Reddit, CNN and many others in Europe and the US.[30]

---

[29] "Top 20 Most Common Types Of Cyber Attacks," Fortinet, accessed June 15, 2021. https://www.fortinet.com/resources/cyberglossary/types-of-cyber-attacks

[30] "DDoS Attack That Disrupted Internet Was Largest of Its Kind in History, Experts Say," *The Guardian*, accessed April 15, 2021. https://www.theguardian.com/technology/2016/oct/26/ddos-attack-dyn-mirai-botnet

Hackers could also use DDoS attacks to distract defenders while they launch another type of attack. Deploying a firewall that can detect requests that are not from legitimate sources and discarding them is a way to protect systems against such attacks.

2.7.8 Domain Name System (DNS) Spoofing

Hackers make use of domain name system (DNS) spoofing by modifying DNS records to redirect traffic to a fake or 'spoofed' website. Once on the fake site, the victim may enter sensitive information that can be used or sold by the hacker. In a DNS spoofing attack, the attacker deceives the user into believing that the site he is visiting is legitimate and thus unintentionally compromising his sensitive information. Keeping DNS servers up-to-date is a way of ensuring that attackers are not able to exploit this vulnerability.

2.7.9 Uniform Resource Locator (URL) Interpretation

In this form of attack, hackers modify and create certain URL addresses and use them to get access to a victim's personal and professional data. This kind of attack is referred to as URL interpretation since the hacker knows the order in which a webpage's URL information needs to be entered and uses this to determine the path for getting into areas that are not accessible by him.

URL interpretation attacks can be prevented through the use of secure authentication methods for any sensitive areas of the site such as multi-factor authentication (MFA) or secure passwords consisting of seemingly random characters.[31]

2.7.10 Man-in-the-Middle (MITM) Attacks

MITM attacks, as the name suggests, involve an attacker exploiting vulnerabilities in security to eavesdrop on the data being sent back and forth between two people, networks or computers. In MITM attacks, the communicating parties are unaware of the man in the middle and that he could be illicitly modifying or accessing messages/data in transit. Protection from MITM attacks can be obtained by using strong encryption on access points or by using a virtual private network (VPN).

Eavesdropping attacks are a variant of MITM attacks and involve illegal interception of traffic as it is sent through the network. Attackers can intercept sensitive data such as usernames, passwords and other confidential information like credit cards using this method. Eavesdropping attacks can be active or passive. In active attacks, the attacker inserts software to capture data as it moves through the network, whereas in passive attacks he is looking for data that he can steal. Here again, encryption of data in transit and using a VPN can be effective protection.

2.7.11 Session Hijacking

Session hijacking is another variant of MITM attacks. In this form of attack, the attacker 'hijacks' a session between a client and the server and substitutes the Internet Protocol (IP) address of his computer for that of the client computer, and unmindful of this, the server continues the session with the attacker instead of the client. This form of attack works because the server uses the client's IP address to verify its identity. If the attacker's IP address is substituted in an active session, the server may assume that it is engaged in a trusted connection. The use of VPN is recommended as protection against such attacks.

---

[31] "Top 20 Most Common Types Of Cyber Attacks," Fortinet, accessed June 15, 2021. https://www.fortinet.com/resources/cyberglossary/types-of-cyber-attacks

2.7.12 Zero-day Attacks

A zero-day vulnerability is a flaw that is either not known to those who should be concerned (such as vendors) or is recognized and disclosed but is not yet fixed. This provides a window of opportunity for hackers to release malware to exploit this vulnerability in hardware or software and launch attacks known as zero-day attacks.

> **Info Box 7: Operation Aurora**
>
> In 2010, a series of cyberattacks was conducted allegedly by Chinese threat actors using a zero-day vulnerability in Microsoft's Internet Explorer. These attacks were directed at Google, Adobe and several other companies. The attackers were targeting Google's source code in the hope of discovering additional zero-day exploits.[32]

When a patch is released by the developers and applied, the exploit is no longer considered a zero-day exploit and the threat of such an attack diminishes.

Protection against zero-day attacks is difficult, but the following steps can help:

- Timely updating of every software and application, whenever a security patch is released
- Implementing web application firewalls to identify suspicious activity
- Implementing network access control to ward off access attempts from unauthorized machines and devices
- Using IPsec to encrypt and authenticate network traffic, which helps in detecting suspicious activity over the network and serves as a warning to stop such attacks

2.7.13 Drive-by Attacks

In this type of attack, the hacker embeds malicious code into an insecure website. Whenever a user visits the site, the script is automatically executed on their computer system, infecting it. To safeguard against such attacks, users should ensure that they are using the latest versions of software on their systems including applications such as Adobe Acrobat and Flash, which may be used while browsing the Internet. Web-filtering software is also useful in detecting whether a site is safe to visit or not.

2.7.14 Insider Threats and Attacks

When an insider turns rogue and wants to cause harm to a system, he can be a very dangerous adversary. An insider not only knows more about the system and critical data, but he also has insider access and does not have to bypass protection mechanisms like firewalls. Insiders also have a better idea of the organization's cybersecurity architecture, as well as how it is geared up to handle threats. Protection against such threats involves allowing restricted access to sensitive systems, use of multi-factor authentication for access control and implementing zero-trust strategies.

---

[32] Brittany Day. "What Is A Zero-Day Attack & How Can I Prevent Them?," Guardian Digital, accessed October 3, 2021. https://guardiandigital.com/blog/zero-day-attack

2.7.15 Advanced Persistent Threats

Advanced persistent threats is a form of attack which has several phases, including breaking into a network, staying undetected, developing and executing a plan of attack that involves mapping of information resources and important organizational data, and accessing and exfiltrating the data over a period of time. Advanced persistent threats are generally well organized and resourced by hacker groups and have caused several large, costly data breaches and are known for their ability to remain undetectable by traditional security measures.

> **Info Box 8: Sony Pictures Cyberattack**
>
> The Sony Pictures attack of 2014 is an example of an advanced persistent threat attack where hackers penetrated the network and stayed undetected for a long period of time before making a demand to stop the release of an unreleased film 'The Interview' about a plot to assassinate the North Korean leader, Kim Jong-un. The hackers who called themselves 'Guardians of Peace' exfiltrated and then leaked data, including a bounty of information that contained the personal information of employees, internal emails and details of salaries of executives. They also stole copies of films yet to be released, scripts, business contracts and other information.[33] The hackers then employed a variant of the Shamoon wiper malware to erase Sony's computer infrastructure.[34]

In addition to the various forms of cyberattacks, there several other ways in which cybercriminals attempt to compromise organizational information systems. The best way to protect an organization from a cyberattack is to implement layered security or defence-in-depth, as it is called, and make the organization as challenging a target as possible. We will discuss protection strategies and measures in a later chapter.

2.8 RESPONDING TO CYBERATTACKS AND THE CYBER KILL CHAIN

A cyberattack invariably triggers a moment of crisis in an organization. While there is no substitute to having a well-practised playbook to offer the best response to a cyberattack, organizations that do not have structured response processes and systems can still minimize the impact by taking the following actions, including using the cyber kill chain model that can even help them stave off a cyberattack:

1. Inform key stakeholders, report to regulatory authorities and take the assistance of law enforcement, as appropriate.
2. Conduct incident triage to assign a level of importance or urgency to incidents and trigger the incident response team, if available and necessary.
3. Figure out the type of attack and contain the spread of malware.
4. Identify the affected systems, services and data.
5. Evaluate the impact on internal and customer-facing critical business processes.
6. Collate all forensic information regarding the incident.

---

[33] "Sony Pictures Entertainment Notice Letter," State of California Department of Justice Office of the Attorney General, 2014, http://oag.ca.gov/system/files/12 08 14 letter_0.pdf

[34] Nolan Feeney, "Sony Asks Media to Stop Covering Hacked Emails," *Time*, December 16, 2014. http://time.com/3633385/sony-hack-emails-media/

7. Identify additional vulnerabilities that can be exploited.
8. Communicate with internal and external stakeholders with a view to minimizing adverse reputational impact.
9. Start the recovery and restoration processes from back-up systems.
10. Document the lessons learned for the future.

Cyber Kill Chain

The concept of a cyber kill chain was developed from a phase-based model that has its origins in military operations and was adapted by Lockheed Martin to describe the phases of a cyberattack. Each phase not only means that the attacker is establishing his presence in a system, but also represents an opportunity for defenders to detect, respond or thwart the attack and protect organization systems that are under attack.[35] The seven phases of the attack suggested in this model are as listed in Table 2.9.[36]

Table 2.9 Seven phases of a cyberattack

Attack phase	Attacker activities
Reconnaissance	Attacker probes weakness. Try to harvest user credentials.
Weaponization	Build a payload using an exploit and a backdoor.
Delivery	Send the payload to a victim.
Exploit	Execute the exploit on the victim's system.
Installation	Install the malware on the target system.
Command and Control	Set up a channel to control the target system remotely.
Actions	Attacker carries out his intended goal.

While attackers may not adhere to these phases at all times, they need to perform these types of activities. However, the opportunity for defenders to respond/terminate the attack remains throughout the duration of the attack. We will examine incident classification and response in greater detail in a later chapter.

2.9 CYBERATTACKS: ORGANIZATIONAL IMPLICATIONS

Cyberattacks are designed to cause harm. Cybersecurity researchers from the University of Kent's School of Computing and the Computer Science Department of Oxford University set out to define and codify the different ways in which various cyber-incidents take place; they identified a total of at least 57 different ways in which cyberattacks can have a negative impact on individuals, businesses and even nations. These could range from threats to life, causing psychological problems and regulatory fines to disrupting daily activities.[37]

---

[35] Maria Korolov and Lysa Myers, "What Is the Cyber Kill Chain? Why It's Not Always the Right Approach to Cyber Attacks," CSO, accessed June 15, 2021. https://www.csoonline.com/article/2134037/strategic-planning-erm-the-practicality-of-the-cyber-kill-chain-approach-to-security.html

[36] "Cyber Kill Chain®", Lockheed Martin. https://www.lockheedmartin.com/en-us/capabilities/cyber/cyber-kill-chain.html

[37] University of Kent, "At Least 57 Negative Impacts from Cyber-Attacks," ScienceDaily, published October 24, 2018. https://www.sciencedaily.com/releases/2018/10/181024112203.htm

They further classified the types of cyber harm resulting from a cyberattack as follows:[38]

- Physical/Digital
- Economic
- Psychological
- Reputational
- Social/Societal

In the context of a business organization, the direct implications of a cyberattack include the following:

- **Disruption of business:** Given that modern-day enterprises are partially or even totally dependent on the use of information technology in running their operations and achieving the objectives of their organization, a cyberattack can cause sudden disruption in services to customers and internal users. The longer the disruption, the more severe the consequences.
- **Loss or damage to electronic data:** A cyberattack can lead to alternation, modification, deletion and even loss of important organizational data. Such an outcome can lead to other consequences:
  - Loss of customer trust
  - Extra expenses for getting the IT systems up and running again
  - Loss of productivity and income at least until systems are restored
  - If data belongs to your customer or another party, then lawsuits could follow
  - If data is rendered inaccessible by hackers who demand a ransom, then money may have to be paid
  - Costs of notification, where it may be required to notify people whose data has been compromised
- **Reputational damage:** It takes years to build your reputation, but a single cyberattack can potentially damage it. Potential customers may not feel confident enough to do business with you, believing that your internal controls are weak or that an association with you will damage their reputation.
- **Legal and PR costs** in the aftermath of the cyberattack
- **Decreased company valuation:** As financial losses, reputation damage and disruptions that impact productivity following a cyberattack can harm business prospects, it can have an adverse impact on the share value and affect the company's overall valuation.

2.10 CYBERATTACKS IMPACTING CITIZENS AND COMMUNITIES

The threat and potential harm to human safety and societal harm has increased multifold since the advent of smart devices (IoT) and the convergence of IT and OT (operational technology). For example, cyberattacks against power grids can have a devastating impact on millions of people and businesses. The emergence of smart cities where all types of services are provided digitally to citizens and are controlled electronically can result in chaos and havoc in the event of a cyberattack that can even affect the wellbeing or become a threat to human life and safety.

---

[38] Ioannis Agrafiotis et al. "A Taxonomy of Cyber-Harms: Defining the Impacts of Cyber-Attacks and Understanding How They Propagate," *Journal of Cybersecurity* (Oxford University Press: 2018).

> **Info Box 9: The Oldsmar, Florida Cyberattack**
>
> A water treatment plant at Oldsmar, Florida was recently the target of a cyberattack. On February 5, 2021, a plant operator for the city of about 15,000 people situated on Florida's west coast witnessed his cursor being moved around on his computer screen, opening various software functions that controlled the water being treated. The attacker boosted the level of sodium hydroxide or lye in the water supply to a hundred times higher than normal. Sodium hydroxide, which is the main ingredient in liquid drain cleaners, is used to control water acidity and remove metals from drinking water in treatment plants. Lye poisoning can cause burns, vomiting, severe pain and bleeding. As soon as the hacker exited the system, the operator immediately reduced the sodium hydroxide back to its normal level and then notified his supervisor and prevented what could have led to catastrophic consequences.[39]

Similarly, government-to-citizen services, banking, education, military, healthcare and retail, virtually all sectors that play a part in our daily lives, are all vulnerable to cyberattacks. Organizations in these sectors have recognized the importance of cybersecurity and are engaged in the implementation of various best practices that can enhance their cybersecurity and resilience.

Reducing risk from cyberattacks involves the following categories of defensive actions:

- Implementing preventive measures
- Real-time detection of intrusions
- Stopping attacks that are taking place as soon as possible

2.11 PREVENTION OF CYBERCRIME

A world without cybercrime or ensuring total immunity against cyberattacks and complete data protection is a utopian dream, but organizations can reduce their exposure by implementing security controls that can mitigate undesirable consequences and make it difficult for attackers to break into their systems.

Organizations can take the following steps, often called basic cyber hygiene, which can help prevent cybercrime/attacks against them or even mitigate the impact if they are targeted:

- Develop clear security-related policies and procedures.
- Create incident response teams and plans.
- Implement access control measures including authentication measures such as two-factor authentication. Allow only need-based access to information and set privileges accordingly.
- Ensure that all online payment transactions (especially high-value ones) are doubly verified and pass through a maker, a checker and an authorizer system.
- Set up firewalls, antivirus systems and intrusion detection systems (IDS).
- Train employees and enhance security awareness.
- Strictly enforce security policies and procedures.
- Keep all systems updated at all times.
- Maintain up-to-date back-ups.

---

[39] Jenni Bergal, "Florida Hack Exposes Danger to Water Systems," Government Technology, accessed April 15, 2021. https://www.govtech.com/security/Florida-Hack-Exposes-Danger-to-Water-Systems.html

There are many more measures that organizations can consider and deploy to bolster their security and those must be based on a clear understanding of specific risks and part of a structured program for managing them. We will revisit organization security measures again in a later chapter.

At an individual level, the cyber hygiene steps that can make your digital existence more secure and less exposed to cybercriminal threats are:

- Using strong passwords
- Keeping your software and major security patches updated
- Managing your social media settings
- Using a virtual private network
- Taking measures to help protect yourself against identity theft
- Being cybersecurity aware and vigilant and not giving out personal information unless secure
- Not clicking on links in spam emails or untrusted websites
- Knowing what to do if you become a victim
- Carefully examining your bank statements

2.12 INTERNATIONAL EFFORTS TO DEAL WITH CYBERCRIME

With the increasing dependence on information technology, institutions and businesses around the world are more exposed to cyber risks and cybercrimes. The Budapest Convention, which came into force in 2004, was the first international response in the form of a treaty to focus on cybercrime.

The Budapest Convention on Cybercrime serves as a guideline for any country intending to draw up comprehensive legislation to combat cybercrime, and as a framework for co-operation between its state parties. Many countries in Europe and around the world have used it to strengthen their own legislation or as a model law.

> **Info Box 10: Budapest Convention on Cybercrime**
>
> The Budapest Convention defines cybercrime "as a wide range of malicious activities, including the illegal interception of data, system interferences that compromise network integrity and availability, and copyright infringements".[40]

It is important to note that the Convention seeks to define conduct rather than technology, to ensure that laws and procedures remain valid as technology evolves. The Convention also provides a legal basis for international co-operation between signatories to the convention, including information sharing, extradition and mutual assistance.

The Council of Europe is also tackling other aspects of cybercrime and has enacted the following conventions:

- The Convention on the Prevention of Terrorism (2005) includes provisions that make recruiting and training terrorists through the Internet a terrorist offence.
- The Lanzarote Convention (2007) refers to the sexual exploitation and abuse of children, as also the online environment.
- The Data Protection Convention provides protections against the illegal collection and use of personal data.

---

[40] "Kate Brush, Linda Rosencrance and Michael Cobb, "What Is Cybercrime? Effects, Examples and Prevention," TechTarget, accessed June 16, 2021. https://searchsecurity.techtarget.com/definition/cybercrime

Cybercrimes can be carried out by individuals, small-groups and highly organized and well-resourced criminal groups. Hackers could be semi-skilled in terms of technology, but can increasingly access and use tools, techniques and procedures that are available for hire on the dark web. The dark web or dark net is that part of the Internet that is not indexed by conventional search engines. It also represents a marketplace where cybercriminals sell data that they have stolen or buy malware and related services to perpetrate their attacks. Software for carrying out ransomware attacks are even available for hire as a service, as are services for money laundering and other types of cyber frauds.

One of the major factors favouring cybercriminals is that the Internet offers them the anonymity that makes it difficult for law enforcement agencies to identify and attribute crimes to specific persons or groups. To evade detection and prosecution, cybercriminals often choose to operate in countries with weak or non-existent cybercrime laws.

2.13 NATIONAL CYBERSECURITY POLICY

The importance of information security in shaping the national economic and security agenda has led to many countries developing and articulating their national security policy and issuing different guidelines from time to time, not only to secure their IT systems but also to inspire trust in the IT services provided by the government departments and agencies, which can further expand and help in improved e-governance services to different stakeholders. Cybercriminals are today routinely carrying out identity theft and financial fraud; stealing corporate information such as intellectual property, customer data; conducting espionage to access state and military secrets; and disrupting critical infrastructures by exploiting the vulnerabilities in any system connected to the Internet. Governments around the world are rolling out several e-governance-related citizen services and are faced with a multiplicity of threats from cybercriminals, including those acting on behalf of adversary nation states.

In India, the Ministry of Home Affairs (MHA) is the designated lead agency for the protection of "information" in cyberspace. The MHA is tasked with finalizing and issuing guidelines on the codification and classification of information, and keeping it updated in the ever-expanding cyberspace. The aim of national security policies is to protect critical infrastructure across sectors such as public utilities, financial services, nuclear facilities and military institutions, and to sensitize the public and private sectors towards national security concerns and drive their actions for securing information. The MHA published a National Information Security Policy (2013) and issued the National Information Security Policy (Table 2.10) and Guidelines in 2014 (NISPG) to define procedures for handling information and for the security of classified information assets.

The security guidelines issued cover several critical areas and domains of cybersecurity, as shown in Table 2.11.

Focus areas that are covered in the guidelines include the following:

- Managing scale and complexity, emphasizing the need for a more coordinated and collaborative security approach
- Responsibilities of the security function towards observing compliance with laws and regulations
- Alignment of security with processes and functions for each of the ministries, departments, agencies and their subordinate organizations along with the need to distinguish between security-related operational tasks from strategic security tasks
- Best information security practices and functions which integrate security into the strategic and daily operations of an organization
- Adequate provisioning of security budgets based on security assessments
- Availability of security professionals and tools
- Building and fostering a culture of information security; developing a risk averse workforce

Table 2.10 National security policy [41]

National Security Policy 2013
Vision
To build a secure and resilient cyberspace for citizens, businesses and Government.
Mission
To protect information and information infrastructure in cyberspace, build capabilities to prevent and respond to cyber threats, reduce vulnerabilities, and minimize damage from cyber incidents through a combination of institutional structures, people, processes, technology and cooperation.
Objectives <ol><li>To create a secure cyber ecosystem in the country, generate adequate trust and confidence in IT systems and transactions in cyberspace and thereby enhance adoption of IT in all sectors of the economy.</li><li>To create an assurance framework for the design of security policies and for promotion and enabling actions for compliance to global security standards and best practices by way of conformity assessment (product, process, technology and people).</li><li>To strengthen the regulatory framework for ensuring a secure cyberspace ecosystem.</li><li>To enhance and create national and sectoral level 24 × 7 mechanisms for obtaining strategic information regarding threats to ICT infrastructure, creating scenarios for response, resolution and crisis management through effective predictive, preventive, protective, response and recovery actions.</li><li>To enhance the protection and resilience of the nation's critical information infrastructure by operating a 24 × 7 National Critical Information Infrastructure Protection Centre (NCIIPC) and mandating security practices related to the design, acquisition, development, use and operation of information resources.</li><li>To develop suitable indigenous security technologies through frontier technology research, solution-oriented research, proof of concept, pilot development, transition, diffusion and commercialisation leading to widespread deployment of secure ICT products/processes in general and specifically for addressing national security requirements.</li><li>To improve visibility of the integrity of ICT products and services by establishing infrastructure for testing and validation of the security of such products.</li><li>To create a workforce of 500,000 professionals skilled in cyber security in the next five years through capacity building, skill development and training.</li><li>To provide fiscal benefits to businesses for adoption of standard security practices and processes.</li><li>To enable protection of information while in process, handling, storage and transit so as to safeguard the privacy of citizen's data and for reducing economic losses due to cybercrime or data theft.</li><li>To enable effective prevention, investigation and prosecution of cybercrime and enhancement of law enforcement capabilities through appropriate legislative intervention.</li><li>To create a culture of cybersecurity and privacy, enabling responsible user behaviour and actions through an effective communication and promotion strategy.</li><li>To develop effective public–private partnerships and collaborative engagements through technical and operational cooperation and contribution for enhancing the security of cyberspace.</li><li>To enhance global cooperation by promoting shared understanding and leveraging relationships for furthering the cause of security of cyberspace.</li></ol>

---

[41] "About MeitY", Ministry of Electronics and Information Technology, Government of India, accessed October 30, 2022. https://www.meity.gov.in/about-meity

Table 2.11 Security domains

Network and infrastructure security	Threat and visibility management	Security testing
Identity, access and privilege management	Security and incident management	Security auditing
Physical security	Cloud computing	Business continuity
Application security	Mobility and BYOD (bring your own device)	The use of open-source technology
Data security	Virtualization	Establishing visibility over information and its life cycle
Personnel security	Social media	Developing an information-centric security framework

The National Security Policy and related guidelines are subject to regular review and assessment of security scenarios to ensure that they are in line with current security perceptions and realities.

2.14 ONLINE CODE OF CONDUCT AND COMPUTER ETHICS

When we talk about cybercrime and similar transgressions, we must also understand what kind of code of conduct applies to our online activities. A code of conduct sets out the company's principles, standards and the moral and ethical expectations and obligations that individuals and organizations should follow.[42] This is useful in maintaining order and in developing a general understanding of what is expected from us. This 'code of conduct' in the context of the online environment is referred to as computer ethics that govern the professional and social conduct of users. Professor Margaret Anne Pierce has suggested that ethical decisions regarding technology and usage should be subjected to three basic influences:

- An individual's own personal code
- Any informal code of ethical conduct that exists in the workplace
- Exposure to formal codes of ethics

Ethical considerations are also important when it comes to cybercrime, privacy issues, anonymity, freedom of expression, autonomous technology deployment, location tracking systems, usage of intellectual property and many other areas of online activities. Security questions have been raised over the deployment of AI- driven digital assistants such as Siri and Alexa, which could collect personal data and send the same to cloud-based systems for analysis.

Users concerned with sharing their data online can access open-source software to make sure that their consent is taken before any data is stored or used by third parties. Various professional societies around the world have encapsulated code of ethics guidelines for computers professionals and users such as the British Society (BCS Code of Conduct), Institute of Electrical and Electronics Engineers (IEEE) code of ethics, etc.

---

[42] "What Is Code of Conduct?," GAN Integrity, accessed June 16, 2021. https://www.ganintegrity.com/compliance-glossary/code-of-conduct/

Ethical issues that arise in the digital world are unique in many ways. Copying of files without the consent of the owner, unauthorized access and use of computer resources and software, the limits to privacy and freedom of online expression are examples where ethical considerations are involved. While legal ecosystems continue to evolve to meet these challenges, other issues including emerging ones can only be left to the ethical considerations of the stakeholders. However, when it comes to computers and computer-related activities, the scope of ethical considerations and moral responsibility is ever increasing, covering a wide spectrum of issues from cybercrime, protection of IT infrastructure and safeguarding privacy to the responsible use of artificial intelligence.

Over a period of time, we can expect that a number of issues that fall in the realm of morals and ethics today will come under the frameworks of laws and regulations. However, in a rapidly changing technology landscape, new issues will continue to emerge. All computer professionals must be guided by an ethical code of online conduct, whether a programmer or a user, as your actions could cause harm (even if not intended) to others.

QUICK TEST

1. The U.S. Department of Justice considers the following as cybercrimes:
   a. Crimes wherein the target is a computer or computing device.
   b. Crimes wherein a computer or computing device is used as an instrument of crime.
   c. Crimes wherein a computer is used as an accessory to a crime, such as storing illegally obtained data.
   d. All of the above
   e. a and b only
2. Cybercrimes against individuals include activities such as breaking into and the unauthorized use of a computer system, vandalising computer resources, transmission of destructive malware, as well as illegally accessing and taking possession of digital information.
   a. True
   b. False
3. Motives of cybercriminals include:
   a. Financial gains
   b. Pursuing a social or political agenda
   c. Espionage on competitors or nation states
   d. To challenge skills and ability, or 'white hat' hacking
   e. To take revenge
   f. All of the above
   g. Only a, b, c
4. Cyber terrorism is a type of cybercrime wherein attackers seek to surreptitiously establish control over a victim's computer or computing device and use the resource to disrupt the services of a target by flooding the target's servers with requests, which makes it unable to provide services requested by genuine users.
   a. True
   b. False
5. White hat hackers are also called ethical hackers and are employed or engaged by organizations as security specialists to help them identify security gaps and vulnerabilities.
   a. True
   b. False
6. The basic difference between a virus and a worm is that worms must be triggered by the host whereas viruses are standalone programs that can replicate independently.
   a. True
   b. False
7. Dragnet and rod and reel methods are examples of:
   a. Malware
   b. Vulnerability scanning
   c. Phishing
8. Cyberattacks can be initiated from inside or outside of an organization's security perimeter.
   a. True
   b. False
9. Active cyberattacks include:
   a. Computer surveillance
   b. Ransomware attacks
   c. DDoS attacks
   d. a and b
   e. b and c

10. Cyber harm resulting from a cyberattack could be:
    a. Physical/Digital
    b. Economic
    c. Psychological
    d. Reputational
    e. Social/societal
    f. All of the above
    g. a, b and d only

QUESTIONS

1. Explain the reasons for the growth of cybercrime and the efforts required for its containment.
2. Name five types of threat actors and their possible motivations.
3. What is the role of malware in perpetrating a cyberattack? Explain the working of any three types of malware.
4. What is a cyberattack? Describe four types of common cyberattacks and the implications of such attacks.
5. Ransomware attacks are on the rise. How can organizations secure themselves from such attacks? Is it necessary to pay a ransom?
6. What is the cyber kill chain? Explain three strategies to reduce risks from cyberattacks.
7. What is an advanced persistent threat? Explain with an example.
8. Can following a code of ethical computer conduct help in reducing various types of digital harm? Discuss.
9. How far have international conventions helped in controlling cybercrime? Discuss.
10. Given the rapid growth of cybercrime, have prevention measures failed? If so, discuss the reasons.

ANSWER KEYS

Quick Test

1. (d)
2. (b)
3. (f)
4. (b)
5. (a)
6. (b)
7. (c)
8. (a)
9. (e)
10. (f)

3 Cybersecurity Vulnerabilities

> **OBJECTIVES**
>
> *At the end of this chapter, you will be able to:*
>
> - ☑ Describe the vulnerabilities and security gaps that can exist in enterprise systems
> - ☑ List the sources of vulnerabilities
> - ☑ Explain the challenges and areas of vulnerability
> - ☑ Explain how the findings of Project OWASP and vulnerability assessments can help in incorporating better security in organizational systems

3.0 INTRODUCTION

We are in the midst of a technological revolution that is changing the way we live, work and communicate. Human activity has never witnessed such rapid transformation, which is unprecedented in its scope, scale and impact. Dr Klaus Schwab, Founder and Executive Chairman of the World Economic Forum, has called this the Fourth Industrial Revolution, which is building on the Third, the digital revolution, that started in the middle of the 20th century. It is exemplified by a synthesis of technologies that is blurring the lines between the physical, digital and biological spheres. He also observes that today's transformations represent not merely an extension of the Third Industrial Revolution, but rather the advent of a fourth and distinct one in terms of velocity, scope and systems impact.[1]

The breadth and depth of impact of the digital revolution has brought with it numerous benefits but has also posed certain challenges. Organizations have utilized the power of advanced computing, mobile devices, unprecedented processing power, enormous storage capacity and instant access to knowledge in automating various aspects of our existence. However, in our rush to adopt these new technologies, security considerations have been more often than not, an afterthought. We have now suddenly found ourselves vulnerable in terms of security as cyber threats are mounting by the day. The fundamental aspects of speed, global access and processing power are available to cybercriminals as well to carry out threats on a scale that could disrupt and harm businesses, economies and societies. Let us examine the key security considerations and challenges that we face in the digital world today.

3.1 SECURITY CONSIDERATIONS AND CHALLENGES

3.1.1 More Complex Security Challenges

The ever-increasing rate of technology adoption across sectors combined with the increased sophistication and frequency of threats has made the task of security more complex and difficult to manage. Every day, threat actors come up with new types of threats, making the task of the defenders even more challenging. The attacker requires only one vulnerability to exploit, whereas the defender needs to protect thousands of vulnerabilities and security gaps.

---

[1] Klaus Schwab, "The Fourth Industrial Revolution: What It Means and How to Respond," World Economic Forum, accessed April 23, 2021. https://www.weforum.org/agenda/2016/01/the-fourth-industrial-revolution-what-it-means-and-how-to-respond/

3.1.2 Rapid Increase in Attack Surface

The explosive growth of the Internet has meant that more than half the world's population is today connected to it. Further, there are more IoT connections (connected cars, smart home devices, connected industrial equipment) than non-IoT connections (smartphones, laptops and computers).[2]

> **Info Box 11: IoT Growth Estimates**
>
> Of the 21.7 billion active connected devices worldwide, 11.7 billion (or 54%) represent IoT device connections. It is estimated that in the next five years, there will be more than 30 billion IoT connections, almost 4 IoT devices per person on average.[3]

From a security standpoint, all the people and devices connected to the Internet have security vulnerabilities that represent an opportunity for hackers to capitalize on. This is also referred to as the 'attack surface', which comprises the total digital resources that are exposed to threats. Awareness of the attack surface and actively managing it can help reduce exposure to cyber risk.

3.1.3 The Dissolving of the Perimeter

Traditionally, security was built around a 'castle and moat' approach. Information systems were housed in data centres that required greater physical security than digital security measures. Hence, the focus of all security measures revolved around the concept of a 'perimeter.' The advent of cloud-based systems and mobile devices coupled with remote working have completely dissolved the perimeter concept and have given way to the concept of 'boundaryless' security.

> **Info Box 12: Cloud and Remote Working Statistics**
>
> Studies indicate that the average enterprise operates 77% of its workload on the cloud and 70% of global office workers work remotely on a regular basis.[4] This requires an entirely new set of security considerations to be incorporated into security plans and programs.

3.1.4 Safeguarding Credentials and Identities

Stealing of user and administrator credentials like username, password, etc. has been on the cybercriminals' agenda for a long time. Hackers continue to use innovative methods like phishing and other forms of social engineering as well as automated methods to steal login credentials, which then enable them to infiltrate and launch various kinds of cyberattacks. While new approaches like multi-factor authentication, the use of biometrics, context-based and geolocation factors are being used for authentication, safeguarding credentials and identity information remains a major security consideration for organizations as well as individuals.

Management of identities, credentials and access is an especially important part of any security system. The acronym ICAM represents identity, credential and access management, which encompass

---

[2] Knud Lasse Lueth, "State of the IoT 2020," IoT Analytics, accessed April 24, 2021. https://iot-analytics.com/state-of-the-iot-2020-12-billion-iot-connections-surpassing-non-iot-for-the-first-time/

[3] Knud Lasse Lueth, "State of the IoT 2020," IoT Analytics, accessed April 24, 2021. https://iot-analytics.com/state-of-the-iot-2020-12-billion-iot-connections-surpassing-non-iot-for-the-first-time/

[4] "As the Perimeter Dissolves, Block Threats with Zero Trust," CyberTalk.org, accessed April 24, 2021. https://www.cybertalk.org/2019/12/11/as-the-perimeter-dissolves-block-threats-with-zero-trust/

the technologies, tools, policies and systems that enable an organization to administer, monitor and ensure secure access to protected information resources.

> **Info Box 13: Phishing Attack in the Middle East**
>
> An incident where hackers targeted journalists and activists working in the Middle East involved the use of fake Google and Yahoo security alerts to deceive users into connecting to a phishing site for resetting their passwords. Using this technique, they were able to phish out not only the passwords of over a 1000 people, but also obtain their associated additional verification code required for two-factor authentication.[5]

Even as organizations adopt the use of various strategies related to the creation of digital identities and maintenance of linked attributes, issuance of credentials for person/non-person entities, deployment of authentication schemes like multi-factor authentication and zero trust, hackers are looking for ways to find security gaps and vulnerabilities in these processes to gain unauthorized access to pursue other malicious actions.

Apart from their social engineering schemes and phishing exploits to steal passwords and credentials, hackers use more sophisticated techniques for compromising credentials and circumventing authentication protocols and practices. These techniques involve bypassing log-in procedures by exploiting unpatched vulnerabilities, privilege escalation, identifying misconfigured databases and weak authentication practices.

Security problems arise from poor ICAM practices. Ideally, organizations should ensure that entities (person and non-person) are continuously authenticated to keep hackers in check even if they can get through login and basic authentication procedures (using compromised credentials) as that is the only way to prevent hackers who do manage to infiltrate the network from freely moving around the entire network.

Continued reliance on outdated ICAM methods is one of the biggest problems with system security. Over 80% of breaches are the result of weak, default or stolen passwords, which is hardly surprising when you consider that over 60% of people use the same password for multiple websites or services. In a business setting, reusing passwords across platforms makes it easy for hackers to gain access to any application and the data it handles.

3.1.5 Limited Security Awareness and Expertise

Lack of awareness about cybersecurity among users is a common cause for cyberattacks to be successful and hackers exploit this vulnerability in a number of ways. The use of weak passwords, clicking on emails from unknown people and using unsecured devices are just a few ways by which users can compromise security. Cybersecurity specialists are much sought after as there is a global shortage of such professionals. Both lack of awareness and access to specialised skills are key considerations and challenges to cybersecurity and make it difficult for organizations to identify and address security vulnerabilities.

The human element of cybersecurity is a major cause of cyberattacks. Very often, people are responsible for losing their own information or becoming victims or exposing their organizations to cyber threats and attacks. Even the strongest security controls and measures fail if the human interface is vulnerable on account of poor cybersecurity awareness. Hackers prey on vulnerabilities in human nature and their willingness to trust even when they should not. Manipulating users by luring, enticing,

---

[5] "Hackers Love Poor IAM Strategies," Identity Management Institute, accessed March 2, 2022. https://identitymanagementinstitute.org/hackers-love-poor-iam-strategies/

blackmailing, confusing and playing many other psychological tricks to get access to personal and corporate information is something hackers routinely pursue using basic technologies and perpetrating different types of scams.

Poor cybersecurity awareness can be the cause of human errors as well as vulnerabilities that can be exploited by hackers. Security awareness is a survival skill in the digital world and users must be trained in developing a fundamental understanding of imminent and ongoing cyber threats and equipping them with the skills and knowledge required to protect themselves and their organizations from cyberattacks and threats.

3.1.6 Dependence on Third Parties

Dependence on third parties for outsourcing business functions or for meeting other business objectives continues to grow. Yet studies indicate that organizations are unprepared for addressing the associated risk that comes along with it. Generally speaking, smaller organizations that provide a wide variety of services to larger organizations as service providers or that are a part of their supply chain may not have the same security arrangements and organizations as their larger counterparts. Hackers are well aware of these vulnerabilities and are increasingly resorting to launching cyberattacks through the supply chain.

3.1.7 Being Unmindful of Vulnerabilities while Deploying New Technologies

The temptation to deploy the latest technologies to solve problems and automate processes is hard to resist. However, new technologies often come with new vulnerabilities that may expose existing systems to cyberattacks. Technologies such as IoT and 5G are known to have vulnerabilities and yet there is a race to implement them. Any approach to adopt these technologies should, at a minimum, evaluate basic security considerations.

> **Info Box 14: Smart Device Vulnerabilities**
>
> Smart technologies driven by the explosive growth of IoT devices in homes, offices, healthcare, transportation and industrial establishments are omnipresent today and play an important role in our daily lives. The use of these network-connected devices have made us vulnerable to cyberattacks. Mikko Hypponen, the Chief Research Officer of F-Secure, has postulated in what is today known as Hyponnen's Law (in the context of using programable electronic devices) that "if it's smart, it's vulnerable".[6] However, regardless of the threat from vulnerabilities, smart devices continue to be deployed in large numbers in existing and new application areas as factors like fascination, productivity and convenience dominate user preferences.

3.1.8 Still Evolving Cyber Law and Cybersecurity Regulations

While technology development and adoption as well as cyber threats and attacks are happening at an unprecedented rate, the legal systems for bringing cybercriminals to book have been slow and weak. Organizations around the world are subject to different regulations related to guaranteeing a minimum level of cybersecurity and data protection. However, it is of utmost importance to incorporate existing and emerging cybersecurity regulations into organization systems. The challenge to keep up with

---

[6] "Hyponnen's Law: If It's Smart, It's Vulnerable," WaterISAC, accessed March 13, 2022. https://www.waterisac.org/portal/hypponen's-law-if-it's-smart-it's-vulnerable

regulations becomes more difficult if a proactive and committed approach is not adopted. The security considerations outlined in these regulations can often help raise security standards and provide much needed assurance to stakeholders. Non-compliance not only constitutes an offence but may also leave some vulnerabilities unaddressed.

3.1.9 Importance of Threat Prevention, Response and Cyber Resilience

Threat prevention and data protection have always received pride of place in terms of the focus on cybersecurity. As organizations recognize that inevitably a few of the threats will materialize, the focus has broadened to include response systems and achieving greater cyber resilience. These considerations enhance the scope of cybersecurity initiatives and, apart from external threats, organizations can have additional internal vulnerabilities and security holes that must be addressed as an integral part of a security plan or program.

3.2 TYPES OF VULNERABILITIES

Vulnerabilities represent the gaps or weaknesses in a system that make threats possible and enable threat actors to exploit them. Every system, no matter how secure, will have a few vulnerabilities. While some vulnerabilities when exploited by hackers can lead to severe consequences, others may not have much impact or non-serious consequences. ISACA, an international professional association focused on IT governance, in its Risk IT Framework refers to vulnerabilities as "a weakness in design, implementation, operation or internal control".[7]

From a security point of view, it is important to understand that while a vulnerability may be exploitable, there might not be a clear way to exploit it to cause harm. Identifying vulnerabilities that can cause harm and implementing security and mitigation measures is the essence of cybersecurity. Let us now examine the various components of information systems that are the sources of these vulnerabilities.

3.2.1 Software Application Vulnerabilities

Software applications are a major source of vulnerabilities in an IT system. Generally speaking, software applications can be divided into two major categories: general purpose applications, also known as off-the-shelf applications, and custom applications that are developed for a client's specific needs. Both these categories of applications will have various kinds of vulnerabilities, but the processes to fix them may be slightly different.

Software vulnerabilities arise for the following reasons:[8]

- Insecure coding practices
- Shifting threat landscape
- Reuse of vulnerable components and code
- Peculiarities of programming languages

Software development processes are not entirely fool-proof, resulting in application flaws that exist in systems when they become operational. Programmers not only work against stiff deadlines but are also

---

[7] "IT Risk Resources," ISACA, accessed April 25, 2021. https://www.isaca.org/resources/it-risk
[8] Veracode Gbook, "Combating the Top 4 Sources of Software Vulnerabilities," https://www.veracode.com/sites/default/files/Resources/Whitepapers/combating-the-top-4-sources-of-software-vulnerabilities.pdf

often hindered by a lack of full understanding of operating scenarios. Hence, applications are released for deployment and put to use; it often happens that as and when flaws are detected and reported, they are fixed through updates (also called patches). While all flaws may not have security implications, those that do could lead to undesirable consequences.

Hackers are constantly probing applications to find vulnerabilities that they can exploit. Vulnerabilities are also discovered by the software developers themselves, or users or researchers who notify/warn the concerned vendor company that a fix is needed. A software vulnerability that is publicly known to those who should be concerned with its mitigation including the vendor of the target software and for which no fix/patch has been released is called a zero-day vulnerability. Hackers are aware that they have a window of opportunity to launch cyberattacks exploiting these zero-day vulnerabilities until they are fixed by the vendors and patched by the users.

An application security vulnerability can be described as a security bug, flaw, error, fault, hole or weakness in the software architecture, design, code or implementation that can be exploited by attackers.[9]

The most common application vulnerabilities are as follows:[10]

- **SQL injection:** A hacker exploits this type of vulnerability by inserting malicious code using structured query language (SQL) so that he can gain access to and even alter database contents.
- **Broken authentication and session management:** This refers to vulnerabilities that can enable an attacker to circumvent the authentication methods implemented in the application.
- **Cross-site scripting:** This type of vulnerability enables the injection of malicious scripts into the pages of a trusted site.[11]
- **Insecure direct object references:** By exploiting this type of vulnerability, attackers can get data by modifying file names.
- **Security misconfiguration:** This refers to a category of vulnerabilities that emanates from wrongly configuring a server or an application.
- **Sensitive data exposure:** This form of vulnerability exists if data in transit or at rest is not encrypted, which may lead to exposure of sensitive data or authentication credentials.
- **Missing function-level access control:** This type of vulnerability exists when a higher-privilege functionality is visible to an unauthenticated or lower-privilege user or if they are able to access resources that they are not entitled to access/use.
- **Cross-site request forgery:** This is a web security vulnerability that allows an attacker to prompt users to perform unintended actions by partly circumventing the same origin policy that is designed to avoid separate websites from meddling with each other.
- **Third-party code, open-source code and APIs:** Using third-party components having known vulnerabilities allows hackers to exploit them since these vulnerabilities are available in the public domain.
- **Unvalidated redirects and forwards:** This is a form of vulnerability used in phishing attacks to divert users to a malicious site by manipulating the URL.

There are several other vulnerabilities that exist in applications, and application security is the process of making apps more secure by finding, fixing and enhancing the security of apps. While ideally, these vulnerabilities should be fixed in the development and pre-release testing phases, they often get passed

---

[9] Derek Handova, "What Are the Different Types of Security Vulnerabilities?," Synopsys, accessed April 26, 2021. https://www.synopsys.com/blogs/software-security/types-of-security-vulnerabilities/

[10] Jeff Melnick, "Top 10 Most Common Types of Cyber Attacks," Netwrix (blog), accessed June 17, 2021. https://blog.netwrix.com/2018/05/15/top-10-most-common-types-of-cyber-attacks/

[11] Paul Ionescu, "The 10 Most Common Application Attacks in Action," Security Intelligence, accessed June 17, 2021. https://securityintelligence.com/the-10-most-common-application-attacks-in-action/

over and can become the cause of security threats and cyberattacks as hackers increasingly target applications with different types of exploits and attacks.

Conducting a website security audit is a good way of discovering vulnerabilities and security gaps by undertaking an assessment of a web system, including core, extensions, themes and other infrastructure. Using static and dynamic code analysis, a web security audit can reveal weaknesses such as business logic errors, misconfiguration, etc. The free/open-source tools list in Table 3.1 can be used in this regard.

Table 3.1 Tools for website audits

Tool	Purpose
OWASP ZAP	Web application scanner that is useful for penetration testing
Burp Suite	Integrated platform/graphical tool for security testing of web applications
DVWA	A PHP/MySQL web application that provides security personnel a means to test their skills and tools in a legal environment

3.2.2 Hardware and Firmware Vulnerabilities

Organizations are deploying a wide range of devices to derive benefits by automating various areas and systems. Every other day, new smart devices are entering the market and people as well as organizations are quick to deploy them. Vulnerabilities are present in these devices at both operating system and firmware levels.

As far as operating systems are concerned, smart devices use multiple OS types that may not be secure enough. Over time, weaknesses in operating systems are addressed through updates, but vulnerabilities at firmware level exist unknown to the deployers. Protection of firmware in devices is not a priority since vulnerabilities are less visible for organizations and, knowing this, hackers are increasingly exploiting related vulnerabilities. When devices are supplied by vendors, they do not provide a 'bill of materials' to help you understand what is inside.[12] There is also a paucity of tools when it comes to scanning of firmware vulnerabilities. Deployers must, therefore, ensure that they use devices that come from reputed vendors who have a track record of prioritizing security issues.

Conducting a hardware asset security audit periodically is important for vulnerability management, Tools such as WinAudit can help in this process by providing details of inventory of software, licences, security configuration, hardware, network settings, etc.

3.2.3 Cloud System Vulnerabilities

Organizations all over the world are increasingly using the cloud to leverage benefits such as lower costs and speed of deployment. However, cloud systems are not free from vulnerabilities. Cloud infrastructure can increase complexity and reduce visibility and while there are benefits even in terms of security, a new set of issues must be understood and addressed. The common security vulnerabilities in the context of cloud systems are:

- Misconfigured cloud storage
- Insecure application user interfaces
- Loss of visibility and control over end-user actions

---

[12] "Mary Branscombe. "Microsoft's New Security Tool Will Discover Firmware Vulnerabilities, and More, in PCs and IoT Devices," TechRepublic, accessed June 20, 2021. https://www.techrepublic.com/article/microsofts-new-security-tool-will-discover-firmware-vulnerabilities-and-more-in-pcs-and-iot-devices/

- Weak access management
- Account hijacking
- Failure of separation among multiple tenants
- Insider threats
- Data breaches
- Non-compliance with regulations

A careful evaluation and listing of cloud-specific vulnerabilities is necessary before adoption of cloud systems. The vulnerabilities listed above along with other identified vulnerabilities must be addressed and mitigation plans should be developed to help organizations lock down their cloud resources. By adopting a risk-based approach to cloud adoption, organizations can securely gain from the cloud's extensive capabilities.

3.2.4 Supply Chain and Third-Party Vulnerabilities

Just like cloud system vulnerabilities, which are an example of third-party vulnerabilities, there are other types of vulnerabilities emanating from suppliers, vendors, contractors and business partners. Organizations increasingly depend on a network of supply chain partners to meet organizational objectives. These partners have access to organizational information and are also often connected directly with their information systems. Hackers are well aware that organizations do their utmost when it comes to protecting their own information systems, but when it comes to the systems and security practices of their supply chain partners, they are unable to enforce security controls with the same rigour and assurance. While IT system vulnerabilities that are common across organizations apply to supply chain partners as well, certain specific areas of vulnerability in this context that must be considered are:

- Vulnerabilities from software used or provided by third parties
- Vulnerabilities arising from physical or virtual access
- Vulnerabilities arising from poor information security practices
- Compromised hardware or software purchased from suppliers
- Security vulnerabilities in supply chain management systems
- Third-party data storage systems
- Insider threats

Organizations that do not follow strict norms before on-boarding suppliers and providing them access to their systems may expose their systems to all types of cyberattacks that can be launched through the supply chain.

3.2.5 Vulnerabilities in Software Deployment: Misconfiguration, Updating and Patching

More often than not, software vulnerabilities escape the development and testing phases and find their way into systems that are deployed for operational use. While these may represent a variety of vulnerabilities, there are vulnerabilities that emerge from faulty deployment and system maintenance processes as well. Specifically, these are vulnerabilities that are created through misconfiguration of software applications, usage of default settings and passwords, as well as delays in updating systems, even after patches have been made available.

3.2.6 Poor Password Management and System Administration Practices

Many organizations have become victims of cyberattacks due to weak password management and authentication systems, which provide easy entry points for hackers. A password is a key system of entry control and, if not given due consideration, can be a major security hazard. Password management vulnerabilities can emerge from:

- Use of weak unencrypted password practices
- Flaws in system design
- Bugs in the software code
- User inputs that are unverified or authenticated

We shall deal with password practices in greater detail in a later chapter.

System administration refers to the management of one or more hardware and software systems.[13] System administration tasks include installing and de-commissioning new hardware or software, setting up and managing user accounts, maintaining computer systems such as servers and databases, and planning and responding to system failures and other system-related problems. In addition, system administration involves monitoring system health, monitoring and allocating system resources such as disk space, performing back-ups, providing user access, managing user accounts, monitoring system security and performing many other functions.[14] System administrators also play a vital role when it comes to change management as well as granting and removing rights and privileges to users. Any laxity in performing these functions can be a source of vulnerability. Hence, the focus here is on vulnerabilities arising from failures of process and not following best practices.

3.2.7 Weak Authentication and Authorization

Authentication and authorization are critical aspects of security. While authentication is the process of verifying that a user actually is who he/she claims to be, authorization is about verifying whether a user is allowed to do/perform a particular action. Basically, most vulnerabilities in authentication mechanisms can arise in one of two ways:

- If the authentication mechanisms are weak and inadequate to withstand brute force attacks
- Broken authentication that arises from program logic flaws or poor coding, which allow the authentication mechanisms to be bypassed entirely by an attacker

The use of multi-factor authentication is often recommended to enhance authentication systems and reduce related vulnerabilities.

Authorization involves the enforcement of policies in terms of determining what types or qualities of activities, resources or services a user is permitted. Authorization vulnerabilities are exploited through forceful browsing that involves bypassing authentication and gaining access to restricted areas in a web server directory and privilege escalation that involves an attacker gaining the privileges of a peer user with equal or lesser privileges within the application or gaining access to a higher account status or permission level.

---

[13] "System Administration," Australian Cyber Security Centre, accessed June 17, 2021. https://www.cyber.gov.au/acsc/view-all-content/glossary/system-administration

[14] "What Is System Administration?," Techopedia, accessed April 27, 2021. https://www.techopedia.com/definition/22441/system-administration

3.2.8 Network Vulnerabilities

A network vulnerability is any flaw in the design, implementation, construction, operation and maintenance of a network or system that will affect or compromise the overall security policies and management of the network. It could also include vulnerabilities in organizational processes that could result in a security breach of the network. A network vulnerability could arise from any of its components, such as:

- **Hardware vulnerabilities:** Weak security at servers, networking equipment and devices, and endpoints.
- **Software vulnerabilities:** Outdated or unpatched software that exposes the systems running the application and potentially the entire network.
- **Network vulnerabilities:** The vulnerabilities that could arise due to the use of open network connections, unprotected network architecture and public Wi-Fi networks. Misconfigured firewalls/operating systems that allow or have default policies enabled are another source of vulnerabilities.
- **Physical vulnerabilities:** The vulnerabilities that could arise from unauthorized physical access to the network that could be used to plant malware through USB drives.
- **Organization vulnerabilities:** The vulnerabilities that could arise due to the use of weak access controls or default security credentials, inappropriate security tools, audit rules and flaws in administrative actions.

Network security combines various aspects of security policies and controls, which ensure that only authorized users gain access to network resources. Every organization, irrespective of its size and industry, requires a strong level of network security to be in place to protect it from impending cyberattacks as hackers are keenly hunting for network vulnerabilities to exploit.

We have already entered the age of complex network architectures. Reducing complexity requires the conduct of regular audits in order to eliminate redundancies through the following actions:

- Removing incomplete or duplicate information
- Scrapping obsolete or invalid rules
- Getting rid of overly permissive policies that allow easy access, even to those who do not need it
- Undertaking security training to mitigate the possibility of human error that could lead to data leaks and breaches
- Implementing micro-segmentation and security zones

Other methods of managing complex network architectures is through the use of techniques such as attack surface modelling, attack simulation, patch simulation, visual evaluation of entry points and establishing control over endpoints.

3.2.9 Remote Working Vulnerabilities

The concept of working from home or, for that matter, any form of remote working is not new. However, due to the pandemic, a majority of the workforce in many organizations across geographies have been forced to work remotely. The benefits of cost savings, higher productivity and keeping organizations running are obvious; however, remote working employees have exposed several gaps in cybersecurity. The cybersecurity measures and arrangements that were applicable when people were working from the confines of their offices are simply not adequate when it comes to remote working. Remote working calls for a new approach to cybersecurity and consideration of the following vulnerabilities that arise from it:

- Firstly, the employees themselves display a more casual approach to security than they would in an office. When working from home or any other remote location, they need to be more security conscious and strictly adhere to security guidelines.

- Secondly, in a remote working scenario the devices that are used to connect to office systems such as home computers, laptops, tablets and mobile phones are often used for multiple purposes such as entertainment, education, communication, etc. Hence, they may be more exposed as various applications that would not be authorized for use in an office environment are downloaded on personal devices. Installing the required security software, regular and timely patching of the same if not undertaken can create vulnerabilities not only for that particular system, but for the entire network.
- Thirdly, the use of insecure communication networks including public Wi-Fi can bring forth a number of vulnerabilities. Unsecured Wi-Fi networks are often used by cybercriminals to distribute infected software like viruses and malware and even for eavesdropping.
- Fourthly, a new set of administrative controls are required, even for providing IT support, which could often be compromised while offering the same remotely as it may entail exposure of remote administration capabilities.
- Vulnerability from phishing attacks and insider threats has also shown an increase due to remote working and requires special consideration and controls as well as demanding greater awareness of the same among remote users.

Remote working is more than likely to become a permanent feature and new security approaches such as zero trust, making the use of virtual private networks (VPN) mandatory when connecting with organizational systems, strictly following organizational security guidelines and avoiding the use of public networks are some ways to effectively deal with vulnerabilities that arise from remote working scenarios.

3.2.10 Social Media Security Vulnerabilities

Social media has brought many benefits for individuals and organizations such as faster and easier communication, marketing reach and dramatic changes in the way we can engage and share information. However, social media has also made us vulnerable to cyber threats and attacks. Here are six key security-related vulnerabilities that are based on the adoption and use of social media:

- Attackers access personal information about specific individuals to launch phishing and social engineering attacks on them as also the organizations that employ them. Hackers can create fake profiles using stolen identify information to befriend people and, after winning their trust, extract more personal and organizational information that enables them to launch all types of attacks.
- Hackers have also exploited celebrity names and political figures to create fake accounts and spread misinformation, slander and rumours.
- Data breaches have been taking place with increasing regularity, resulting in the compromise of personal information. Popular social media sites like Facebook, LinkedIn and Twitter have all been breached at some point.
- Hackers have also discovered ways to inject malicious code into advertisements and create rogue third-party applications, which infect their computers or gather their personal information.
- Social media is actively used by hackers for spreading spam and malware by using shortened URLs, making it difficult for the user to identify whether it is pointing to a legitimate or malicious site.
- Unused or unattended social media accounts are also a source of vulnerability. This could lead to account misuse or identity theft, leading to undesirable consequences.

Paying attention to social media accounts, using the security settings available on the platforms such as multi-factor authentication and having organizational policies for the use of social media are all steps that can be taken to enhance account security. Attackers often perpetrate social media threats by using social engineering tactics that take advantage of fear and anxiety and play on human vulnerabilities instead of system vulnerabilities. Shutting down social media accounts when not in use for long periods of time can prevent hackers from hijacking or exploiting those accounts.

3.2.11 Cyber-Physical Systems and IoT

Cyber-physical systems and IoT devices are driving a new wave of technology solutions. From IoT devices that are used in building automation systems, automotive and healthcare applications to CPS systems that integrate IT and OT (operational technology) systems in running smart grids, manufacturing plants, oil and gas, water treatment plants, mining and other critical infrastructure, these systems present a new security challenge due to the complexity and heterogeneity of the technology and data.

Common vulnerabilities for this class of systems include, but are not limited to:

- Complexities in system architecture that also involve integration with legacy systems
- Inappropriate security configuration
- Vulnerabilities in physical security
- Insecure firmware or software
- Weak credentials, authentication, access control methods and trust management techniques
- Non-standardization of security protocols across IoT devices

Disruption and damage caused by cyberattacks on cyber-physical systems can have a significant impact on public health and safety and also lead to large economic losses. Given the heterogeneity in these systems, vulnerabilities cannot be generalised and must be identified and addressed at an individual system level.

3.3 PROJECT OWASP

The Open Web Application Security Project® (OWASP) is a not-for-profit organization that is committed to the security of software. The OWASP Top 10 most critical security concerns for web application security is a list of security concerns compiled by a team of security experts based on analysis of data from a number of organizations from around the world.[15] Using the OWASP Top 10 lists of vulnerabilities is an excellent way towards prioritizing the security efforts of software developers and producing more secure code. A recent (2021) list of Top 10 web application security risks is shown in Table 3.2.[16]

Table 3.2 Top 10 web application security risks

1. Broken access control	Refers to weaknesses in enforcing restrictions on what authenticated users are allowed to do
2. Cryptographic failures (previously referred to as sensitive data exposure)	Refers to failures related to cryptography (or lack thereof), which could lead to exposure of sensitive data
3. Injection flaws such as SQL, NoSQL, operating system and lightweight directory access protocol (LDAP injection)	Happen when untrusted data is sent to an interpreter as part of a command or query and enables an attacker to execute unintended commands without proper authorization
4. Insecure design	Refers to risks related to design flaws

(Continued)

---

[15] "The Most Common Web Application Vulnerabilities and Weaknesses," Cyber Risk Countermeasures Education (CRCE), accessed June 17, 2021. https://cyberrisk-countermeasures.info/2020/04/05/the-most-common-web-application-vulnerabilities-and-weaknesses/

[16] "OWASP Top Ten Web Application Security Risks," OWASP, accessed April 29, 2021. https://owasp.org/www-project-top-ten/

Table 3.2 (*Continued*)

5.	Security misconfiguration	Happens due to deployed or incomplete or ad-hoc configurations; timely patching is also necessary to avoid vulnerabilities
6.	Vulnerable and outdated components	Known vulnerabilities in these components can be exploited by hackers
7.	Identification and authentication failures	Results from incorrect implementation of application functions related to authentication and session management
8.	Software and data integrity failures	Focused on making assumptions related to software updates, critical data and CI/CD pipelines without verifying integrity
9.	Security logging and monitoring failures	Previously referred to as insufficient logging and monitoring, this category is now extended to include more types of failures
10.	Server-side request forgery (SSRF)	Refers to flaws in a web application while fetching a remote resource without validating the user-supplied URL; this enables an attacker to force the application to send a crafted request to an unexpected destination, even when protected by a firewall, VPN or another type of network access control list (ACL)

The OWASP Foundation is an important resource for developers and technologists to address key vulnerabilities, thereby preventing cyberattacks and ensuring data protection.[17]

3.4 VULNERABILITIES ASSESSMENT

Broadly speaking, vulnerabilities emanate from the following areas:

- Physical environmental factors
- Human factors
- Procedural and administrative factors
- Hardware, software, networking and connectivity related
- Operations and services

In order to secure any data or information system, an effective vulnerability management process needs to be adopted, the required tools and methods must be used and judgement regarding prioritization must be made based on a quantitative and qualitative evaluation of risks. The purpose of a vulnerability assessment is to enable you to move from a reactive cybersecurity approach to a proactive one, with increased awareness of your vulnerabilities and to prioritize the flaws that most need attention. A structured vulnerability assessment can be carried out by following the steps discussed in this section.

3.4.1 Planning

In this step, it is important to specify the scope and context of the vulnerability assessment exercise, such as determining which systems and networks the assessment will cover (if it includes mobile devices and the cloud) and identifying where sensitive data resides, compliance requirements as well as data and systems that are most critical. It is also important to specify any baselines (risk appetite and tolerance level) and make sure that everyone concerned has the same expectations from the process.

---

[17] "The Most Common Web Application Vulnerabilities and Weaknesses," Cyber Risk Countermeasures Education (CRCE), accessed June 17, 2021. https://cyberrisk-countermeasures.info/2020/04/05/the-most-common-web-application-vulnerabilities-and-weaknesses

Footprinting is an effective way of finding vulnerabilities. Also known as reconnaissance, it involves the collection of as much information as possible about a potential target computer, network or IT environment to identify opportunities that hackers could use to penetrate them. This activity may involve the use of various tools and technologies for both active and passive footprinting. Active footprinting involves the use of techniques like a ping sweep to collect data about a particular target while passive footprinting involves the use of non-intrusive techniques like Google search and WHOIS.

3.4.2 Scanning

The next stage involves the scanning of the system or network to discover vulnerabilities. This can be done using automated and threat intelligence inputs to identify security flaws and weaknesses and filter out false positives. Vulnerability scans and penetration testing are two methods to uncover vulnerabilities and security weaknesses. While vulnerability scans identify known vulnerabilities, penetration testing is used for identifying security weaknesses in IT architecture and ascertaining the degree to which information assets are vulnerable to unauthorized access by a malicious attacker. Vulnerability scans need to be performed more frequently when compared to penetration tests, but both methods are useful in their own way for identifying security vulnerabilities and gaps that are critical to developing a comprehensive security strategy.

Info Box 15: Vulnerability Analysis and Evaluation

Technologies/Methods used for Vulnerability Analysis and Evaluation

Developing an understanding of where the vulnerabilities are is the most important aspect of a cybersecurity program. Without an assessment of vulnerabilities, investments in terms of time, effort and money are all more than likely to be ineffective and leave opportunities for hackers to infiltrate a network and conduct their malicious activities.

Fortunately, there are several technologies and methods that provide the means to undertake a comprehensive scan of systems in a quick, automated and affordable manner. Most of the popular vulnerability scanners in the market enable assessment of where weaknesses exist in an IT environment, help in developing an understanding of the types of risks from each vulnerability as well as provide suggestions with regard to mitigation of risk from the vulnerability. Vulnerabilities largely arise from design flaws, implementation issues and operational issues, which emerge from improper deployment.

Vulnerability scanning tools typically identify and build an inventory of all IT assets within an IT environment (including servers, desktops, laptops, mobile devices, virtual machines, firewalls, switches, printers, etc.) that are connected to a network. The tools also capture information regarding the operating systems, other software installed, user accounts and details of open ports relating to each IT asset. By running these scanning tools, organizations can examine their networks, systems and applications for security vulnerabilities.

Various types of vulnerability scanning tools enable organizations to conduct vulnerability scans on different parts of their network. These are as follows:

- **Network-based vulnerability scanners** are useful in identifying vulnerabilities in wired and wireless networks. Their range of capabilities includes identification of unknown or unauthorized devices and systems on a network, finding unknown perimeter points and rogue access points as well as insecure connections with the networks of other entities.
- **Host-based scanners** assist with detecting and uncovering vulnerabilities that may be present in servers, while also offering specifics linked to patch history and configuration settings.

- A **port scan** helps determine which ports on a network are open and are receiving/sending information as well as the presence of active security devices such as firewalls. Port scanning also helps in obtaining other information such as what services are running, the users who are running them and which network services require authentication. Hackers aggressively search for port-level vulnerabilities that can be exploited by them.
- **Application scanners** are used for testing websites to detect known software vulnerabilities and configuration errors in network or web applications.
- **Database scanners** help in the identification of vulnerabilities such as mistakes in configuration and other weak points in databases.
- **Cloud security scanners** help organizations in locating and fixing security vulnerabilities in their cloud deployment. They are used for security testing of cloud applications, identifying misconfigurations and evaluating cloud resources against specific compliance requirements or standards.

Scanning can be carried out from 'outside-in', also known as external vulnerability scan, to identify weaknesses and security vulnerabilities that hackers could use to gain entry to the network. An internal vulnerability scan can be conducted from inside an enterprise network to detect vulnerabilities that are otherwise missed or omitted by external scans. Some well-known vulnerability scanning and assessment tools are SolarWinds Network Performance Monitor, Acunetix, Angry IP Scanner, Nmap, Intruder, Wireshark, Nikto, Netsparker, w3af, Arachni, Nexpose, Aircrack and Microsoft Baseline Security Analyzer.

3.4.3 Analysis and Evaluation

It often happens that the outcome of the previous step would provide a long list of vulnerabilities that need to be addressed. The list must now be subjected to analysis and evaluation. This step involves categorization based on the criticality of the data at risk and then quantification and ranking in terms of the potential consequences if the risk were to materialize. In order to prioritize further, the ranked list must be subjected to the 'likelihood' test. There may be several risks that could possibly materialize in a given situation, but it may have a low probability of happening. Hence, for addressal, it may be accorded a lower priority.

A good organizational practice is that of maintaining a cyber risk register, which enables tracking and measurement of risks. The register also serves as a basic document for the organization's cyber risk and information security management program. Some of the benefits of maintaining a risk register are:

- Serves as a consolidated repository of various cybersecurity risks and their impact on business
- Recording of ownership of each type of risk, controls and mitigation actions
- Enhancing threat awareness among functional teams and employees
- Demonstrating compliance

3.4.4 Remediation and Repetition

The vulnerability assessments must result in a plan of action where every important (particularly those with high impact and high likelihood) vulnerability has a treatment plan and also an identified person responsible for its implementation and monitoring. There may also be some vulnerabilities that may have minimal impact and where the cost and efforts involved in remediating it may be greater or result in downtime that may not be justified. There may also be some vulnerabilities that you may accept to live with.

Vulnerability assessments are not a one-time exercise and for best results must be performed on a scheduled basis quarterly at least (ideally monthly or weekly), as any single assessment is only a snapshot of that moment in time. Vulnerability assessment reports over a period of time can provide an idea of the progress that you may or may not have made with regard to your overall security mechanisms and position. It must also be remembered that if any additions, modifications or other changes are made to your network or systems, it warrants another round of vulnerability assessment.

A purely technical approach is not enough to protect your information assets. The importance of proper and adequate administrative procedures and controls and users equipped with adequate knowledge of the procedures who are motivated to follow them diligently can be an effective means to address vulnerabilities and mitigate the risks arising from them.

3.5 COMMON VULNERABILITIES AND EXPOSURES (CVE): INSTITUTIONAL MECHANISMS

History

The concept of developing an institutionalised approach to vulnerability exposure listing and cataloguing publicly disclosed cybersecurity vulnerabilities was published in a paper by David E Mann and Steven M Christey of MITRE Corporation in 1999. In the same year, the first set of 321 CVE records was officially launched. The objective of the CVE® Program "is to identify, define and catalogue publicly disclosed cybersecurity vulnerabilities".

Within a year, the program had 29 organizations participating with declarations of compatibility for 43 products. Today, there are over 200 organizations that are a part of the CVE program, with numerous products and services from around the world that are incorporated in CVE Records. Since its inception, over 170,000 software and firmware vulnerabilities have been identified, categorized and catalogued by this program.

Process

The process of creating a CVE Record starts with the discovery of a potential cybersecurity vulnerability. The identified vulnerability is then assigned a CVE ID by a CVE Numbering Authority (CNA). A description of the vulnerability and related references are then added by the CNA. The CVE Record is thereafter posted on the CVE website by the CVE Program Secretariat.

Several operating system and software vendors today include the CVE IDs in security advisories and alerts to ensure that the user/developer community benefits by having them as soon as a problem is announced.

The MITRE Corporation refers to the CVE list as "a dictionary of publicly known information security vulnerabilities and exposures." It further adds that "CVE's common identifiers enable data exchange between security products and provide a baseline index point for evaluating coverage of tools and services."[18]

An example of a CVE is shown below:[19]

> **CVE-2014-0160 (Heartbleed)**
>
> "The (1) TLS and (2) DTLS implementations in OpenSSL 1.0.1 before 1.0.1g do not properly handle Heartbeat Extension packets, which allows remote attackers to obtain sensitive information from process memory via crafted packets that trigger a buffer over-read, as demonstrated by reading private keys, related to d1_both.c and t1_lib.c, aka the Heartbleed bug." [2]

---

[18] "Common Vulnerabilities and Exposures (CVE)," National Institute of Standards and Technology, accessed April 10, 2022. https://samate.nist.gov/BF/Enlightenment/CVE.html

[19] "Common Vulnerabilities and Exposures (CVE)," National Institute of Standards and Technology, accessed April 10, 2022. https://samate.nist.gov/BF/Enlightenment/CVE.html

QUICK TEST

1. From a security standpoint, all the people and devices connected to the Internet have security vulnerabilities that represent an opportunity for hackers to capitalize on.
   a. True
   b. False
2. Software vulnerabilities arise due to the following reasons:
   a. Insecure coding practices
   b. Reuse of vulnerable components and code
   c. Peculiarities of programming languages
   d. a and b
   e. a, b, c
3. By exploiting this type of vulnerability, attackers can obtain data by modifying file names:
   a. SQL injection
   b. Broken authentication
   c. Insecure direct object references
4. This form of vulnerability exists if data in transit or at rest is not encrypted, which may lead to exposure of sensitive data or authentication credentials:
   a. Security misconfiguration
   b. Sensitive data exposure
   c. Cross-site request forgery
5. Security vulnerabilities in the cloud system arise from:
   a. Misconfigured cloud storage
   b. Insecure application user interfaces (APIs)
   c. Loss of visibility and control over end-user actions
   d. All the above
   e. a and c only
6. Organizations that do not follow strict norms before on-boarding suppliers and providing them access to their systems may expose their systems to all types of cyberattacks that can be launched through the supply chain.
   a. True
   b. False
7. Password management vulnerabilities can emerge from:
   a. Use of weak unencrypted password practices
   c. Flaws in system design
   d. Bugs in the software code
   e. User inputs that are unverified or authenticated
   f. All the above
   g. a and e
8. Authentication involves the enforcement of policies in terms of determining what types or qualities of activities, resources or services a user is permitted.
   a. True
   b. False
9. Attackers often perpetrate social media threats by using social engineering tactics that take advantage of fear and anxiety and play on human vulnerabilities instead of system vulnerabilities.
   a. True
   b. False

10. IoT vulnerabilities emanate from:
    a. Insecure firmware or software
    b. Weak credentials, authentication
    c. Non-standardization of security protocols across IoT devices
    d. All of the above
    e. a and b only

QUESTIONS

1. The current cyber threat landscape offers many opportunities to hackers in the form of vulnerabilities. What are the security considerations and challenges that are a reason for this? Discuss.
2. Software applications are a major source of vulnerabilities. Explain the statement.
3. How can poor password management and system administration practices be a source of vulnerabilities and what can be done to fix them?
4. Can reduction in 'attack-surface' reduce vulnerabilities? Explain how.
5. Remote working is more than likely to become permanent. What changes in security approach are required to meet the related security challenges?
6. What is OWASP? How is it useful?
7. What are the areas from which vulnerabilities emanate?
8. Explain the importance and steps in the vulnerability assessment process.
9. What are the tools and methods that can be deployed to discover vulnerabilities?
10. Are current tools, methods and processes adequate to identify security vulnerabilities? Is there a better way?

ANSWER KEYS

Quick Test

1. (a)
2. (e)
3. (c)
4. (b)
5. (d)
6. (a)
7. (f)
8. (b)
9. (a)
10. (d)

4 Cybersecurity Management Practices

> **OBJECTIVES**
> At the end of this chapter, you will be able to:
> - ☑ Describe cybersecurity management practices, classification of information and other aspects pertaining to cyber risk management
> - ☑ State the role of security policy, procedures, organization and incident response and how business continuity and disaster recovery play an important part in the context of cybersecurity
> - ☑ Explain how the use of standards and frameworks can help organizations implement their security vision and translate policies, practices and guidelines into structured security programs

4.0 OVERVIEW OF CYBERSECURITY MANAGEMENT

Information systems today consist of several elements that are interrelated. Each of these elements has its own set of vulnerabilities, which when exploited by hackers can threaten the confidentiality, integrity and availability of information held within them. Cybersecurity management practices comprise the set of policies, procedures, controls and other measures that are designed to protect organizational systems and data from cyber threats and, in the event of a security breach, to trigger response systems that can mitigate any disruption or damage caused by it. Cybersecurity management is of prime importance in a supercharged cyber threat environment to prevent security breaches and cyberattacks from disrupting an organization's functioning, leading to lost revenue and loss of information that could lead to loss of reputation and customer trust.

> **Info Box 16: Cybersecurity Management**
> Cybersecurity management is an organisation's strategic-level capability to protect information resources and competitive advantage in a complex and evolving threat landscape.[1]

The foundation of sustainable enterprise cybersecurity management can only be implemented through a formal set of administrative, technical and procedural measures aimed at the protection of corporate assets and information. A precursor to this activity is to evaluate existing security threats and controls and their effectiveness. There are several IT and cybersecurity frameworks that an organization can adopt to translate their security vision into security measures, coordination of organization-wide efforts and monitoring of their effectiveness. However, there is a lack of unanimity among cybersecurity experts

---

[1] "Cybersecurity Management", School of Computing and Information Systems, The University of Melbourne, accessed June 29, 2021. https://cis.unimelb.edu.au/cyber-security-excellence/research/cybersecurity-management/

and professionals on a single standard cybersecurity framework that is suitable across all countries, industries and geographies.

For a long time, cybersecurity management was focused on prevention. However, organizations have recognised that eventually their cyber defences will be breached, and they need to be prepared with response and recovery processes. With cyber threats and attacks becoming more pervasive, cybersecurity strategies have shifted to incorporate detection and damage control. Cybersecurity management can no longer be approached with piecemeal or ad hoc measures and processes. Effective cybersecurity management involves knowing what information you are protecting, where the vulnerabilities exist and how organization resources can be deployed for the best results. It also involves the optimal use of technical, physical and organizational measures whereby your best defences are deployed in securing your most valuable assets. While this may seem obvious, when it comes down to implementation, organizations often falter by either casting the security net too wide or are narrowly focused on few key vulnerabilities while being oblivious to others. The essence of cybersecurity management comes down to knowing what information is valuable and what is not. For this, it is important to classify information and identify the most valuable information assets.

4.1 INFORMATION CLASSIFICATION PROCESS

Classifying information is among the most important steps in cybersecurity management. It helps you identify your most valuable information as well as to categorize it in a form that enables determination of who needs access to what information as well as devise different levels of controls and security mechanisms to protect the various categories. Clearly, your priority would lie in protecting your most valuable data (often referred to as crown jewels) first and laying out your defences for other categories as per the threat perception and available resources.

> **Info Box 17: Information Classification**
>
> Control Objective A8.2 of the ISO 27001 standard that deals with information classification specifies that organisations must "ensure that information receives an appropriate level of protection in accordance with its importance to the organization".[2]

What is considered as the 'appropriate level of protection' varies with each organization and the way they classify their information. Each organization must determine their own classification model, which should be well understood by all in the organization. A simple classification scheme would be:

- Confidential (access permitted to only specified employees, usually senior management)
- Restricted (access permitted to a restricted number of employees based on job function requirements)
- Internal use only (access permitted to all employees)
- Public domain information (access to everybody)

Such a classification would be overly simplistic for a large organization or a research or military organization where more levels of access and specific authorization may be required. The first step in classification is to list all the information assets and record them in an information asset register along with details of who is required to access it and who is responsible for it. The location (physical or digital)

---

[2] "ISO 27001 Annex A.8 - Asset Management," ISMS.online, accessed July 10, 2021. https://www.isms.online/iso-27001/annex-a-8-asset-management/

of the information asset, its category and the type of handling rules that are applicable (for storage, use and transit such as encryption) must be tagged to each category (Table 4.1).

Table 4.1 Classification of information

Information category	Security level	Examples of types of data	Impact to information if compromised
Top Secret	High	R&D information, formulas, designs, innovations, software algorithms	Extreme damage to organizational interests and business
Confidential	High	Customer and employee data, intellectual property, business plans, financial information, contract data, passwords	Considerable damage to organization and reputation
Restricted	High/ Medium	Internal emails, policy documents, messages	Limited damage
Internal Use	Medium	Training material, organization charts	Routine information, low/ no impact
Public Domain/ Unclassified	Low	Contact information, marketing material, office addresses	No impact

Determining the value of information is a complex task as there is no universal value that can be ascribed to it. The value of an information asset can be determined by the person who uses it, how the information is used and for what purpose it is used. Cybercriminals too understand the value of an information asset based on the damage it can cause and/or the price it can fetch them in the underground markets. While organizations need to protect information that is most valuable to them in the context of their activities, they also need to protect information that is held by them, which can have value for cybercriminals and could cause harm to others if compromised.

Information classification is a useful way of communicating to employees the value of the information they are using and the responsibility they carry for its protection. Apart from establishing protocols for employees for handling different types of information, it also contributes to overall cybersecurity awareness.

Once the information classification is carried out and the vulnerabilities related to each information category have been assessed, it is time to set security policies, controls and procedures directed at prevention, detection and response.

4.2 SECURITY POLICIES

Security policies are an important instrument in the hands of senior management to articulate security expectations from employees as well as the security standards that determine the attitude, approach and behaviour related to security matters. A single cybersecurity policy is not sufficient to define objectives, baselines and guidelines. Cybersecurity polices are directed to support the maintenance of confidentiality, integrity and availability of information. Typically, security policies are prepared for at least three levels: organization level-policies, system-specific policies and issue-specific policies. In terms of content and purpose, they can be regulatory, advisory or informative.

> **Info Box 18: Cybersecurity Policies**
>
> In the context of cybersecurity, the word 'policy' can have different connotations. One meaning is senior management directives to set up a cybersecurity program, defining its scope, establishing goals and guidelines, and assigning responsibilities. 'Policy' could also be used in the context of specific security rules for specific systems. Further, it may refer to specific managerial decisions for setting an organization's email privacy policy or Internet access security policy.[3]

Developing a security policy (Table 4.2) is a complex task and must involve extensive deliberation and consultation. The vulnerability assessment process and the risk assessment process provide the basic inputs for developing a security policy. Along with this, other factors to be considered are the top management's security vision, objectives, scope as well as industry compliance requirements and ethical considerations.

Table 4.2 System-specific and issue-specific policy examples

Email policy	Internet access policy/Acceptable use policy
Physical security policy	Remote working policy
Change management policy	Bring your own device (BYOD) policy
Vendor cyber risk management policy	Back-up policy

In addition to providing employees with operational guidelines, security policies must reflect the security standards and vision of the executive management. The effectiveness of security policies depends largely on management commitment, enforcement, communication and employee understanding and acceptance. Policies must be reviewed and renewed regularly as there are changes such as introduction of new technologies, modifications to existing systems and in overall threat perception in times to come.

Regulations and compliance requirements form an integral part of security policies. While framing security policies, compliance and ethical considerations must be given due weightage and responsibilities for ensuring that these obligations are met should be fixed. To ensure effectiveness, policymakers must make sure that security policies are simple to understand, practical and enforceable.

4.3 SECURITY PROCEDURES AND GUIDELINES

Security procedures and guidelines are required to support and enforce policies. A security procedure is a set of activities that needs to be performed in sequence to perform a particular security task or function. Well-defined security procedures not only function as a guideline for employees but also bring about consistency of performance and help in maintaining security levels. Other benefits of establishing security procedures are that they can be useful for training of existing and new employees, auditing performance and refining the process to accomplish desired outcomes. It is important that security procedures are properly documented and are in alignment and consistent with security policies, standards and compliance requirements.

> **Info Box 19: Security Procedures**
>
> Security procedures aim to answer the 'how,' 'who' and 'when' of the policy.[4]

---

[3] "NIST SP 800-12: Chapter 5 - Computer Security Policy," National Institute of Standards and Technology, accessed June 30, 2021. https://csrc.nist.rip/publications/nistpubs/800-12/800-12-html/chapter5.html#45

[4] "Policy and Procedures - Security Compliance," CCSI, accessed July 1, 2021. https://www.ccsinet.com/blog/policy-procedures/

Information security requires the understanding of both IT and physical security requirements to develop effective security procedures. The adoption of standards like ISO 27001 can help in adopting time-tested best practices and procedures across multiple areas and information domains.

Organizations can also draw on their own experiences and specific requirements to define effective procedures and operating protocols. Information security procedures must encompass all the hardware, software and human elements that support the organization's business processes.

Security procedures must be articulated in sufficient detail, assigning responsibilities to all those who are required to perform task and functions under a given procedure. To understand the relationship between policies and procedures in terms of level of detail, a graphical representation of the same is shown in Fig. 4.1.

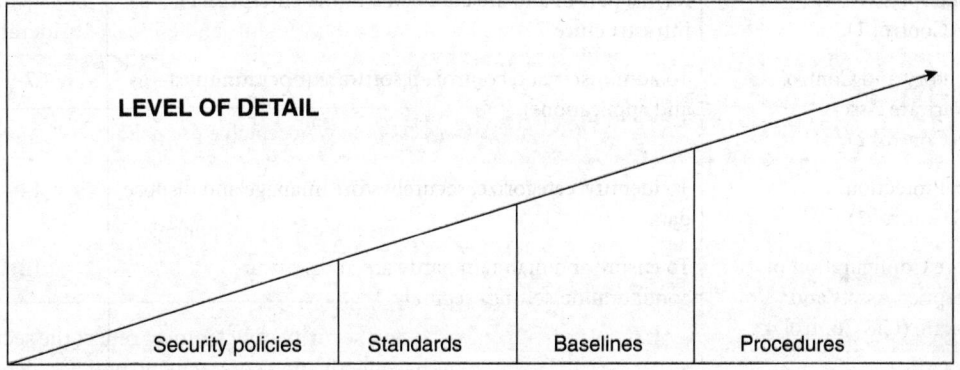

Figure 4.1 Relationship between policies and procedures

Like policies, security procedures must also be reviewed regularly and updated based on changing contexts. These contexts could be in terms of changes in requirements, compliance needs, business process, technology changes and, last but not the least, changes in the threat environment. It must be remembered that procedures are meant not only as a safeguard against external threats, but also employee mistakes, negligence and even wilful misconduct.

4.4 SECURITY CONTROLS

Policies and procedures are in themselves incomplete when it comes to securing information systems. Security controls are a key component of cybersecurity management and need to be put in place to make security stronger and resilient. Security controls can be both automated and manual and must be aligned with the security objectives. They can be used for prevention and detection of cyber threats as well as a part of the response to a cyber security incident.

In order to implement security controls, it is not only important that you choose the most suitable controls and ensure that they meet the purpose for which they are to be deployed, but also that you train employees in using the controls and monitor them for their usefulness and effectiveness. As and when security controls become redundant or ineffective, they must be replaced with newer control mechanisms. Auditing the effectiveness of controls that have been deployed must form an integral part of cybersecurity management.

Typically, security controls are classified into organizational or administrative controls, physical controls and technical.

The Centre for Internet Security (CIS) provides a useful set of guidelines in the form of 18 critical security controls that organizations could deploy to enhance their security and protect themselves from known attack methods. These controls can be automated for enforcement and monitored for their effectiveness. CIS controls have been developed by cybersecurity experts and vendors and provide safeguards against most common cyberattack vectors. Table 4.3 lists the controls and control areas.

Table 4.3 CIS controls[5]

Control area and Control No	Purpose	Number of safeguards
Inventory and Control of Enterprise Assets (CIS Control 1)	To administer and control all hardware devices that form a part of and are connected to the enterprise IT infrastructure	5
Inventory and Control of Software Assets (CIS Control 2)	To administer and control all software (operating systems and applications)	7
Data Protection (CIS Control 3)	To identify, categorize, securely store, manage and dispose data	14
Secure Configuration of Enterprise Assets and Software (CIS Control 4)	To ensure and maintain hardware and software configuration settings securely	12
Account Management (CIS Control 5)	To assign account credentials for system administrator accounts, user accounts and service accounts and provide ongoing account management controls	6
Access Control Management (CIS Control 6)	To set up, assign, administer and remove access privileges for all types of accounts as well as hardware, software and applications	8
Continuous Vulnerability Management (CIS Control 7)	To continuously assess vulnerabilities on hardware, software, applications, information assets and other IT infrastructure	7
Audit Log Management (CIS Control 8)	To collate, maintain and review audit logs that are useful in detecting or recovering from a cyberattack	12
Email and Web Browser Protections (CIS Control 9)	To safeguard cyber threats from web sources and emails	7
Malware Defences (CIS Control 10)	To thwart malicious applications, programs or scripts from being installed, proliferated and executed on enterprise systems	7
Data Recovery (CIS Control 11)	To establish data recovery processes for restoration of systems impacted by a cyber incident to its original state	5

(Continued)

---

[5] "The 18 CIS Controls," Centre for Internet Security, accessed July 10, 2021. https://www.cisecurity.org/controls/cis-controls-list/

Table 4.3 (*Continued*)

Control area and Control No	Purpose	Number of safeguards
Network Infrastructure Management (CIS Control 12)	To manage and control network devices and avert threats emanating from network infrastructure	8
Network Monitoring and Defence (CIS Control 13)	To monitor networks and establish defences against threats from network vulnerabilities and users	11
Security Awareness and Skills Training (CIS Control 14)	To enhance security awareness and influence responsible online behaviour among users	9
Service Provider Management (CIS Control 15)	To establish a process to evaluate and monitor service providers to ensure that they manage and protect sensitive data appropriately	7
Application Software Security (CIS Control 16)	To safeguard from threats emanating through software that is developed in-house, purchased or implemented through cloud-based systems throughout the software life cycle	14
Incident Response and Management (CIS Control 17)	To develop comprehensive response capabilities for responding to severe cyberattacks by setting up incident response processes and systems	9
Penetration Testing (CIS Control 18)	To identify vulnerabilities in technologies, processes and people controls by conducting penetration tests	5

The above list of CIS controls represents high priority areas and a set of recommended controls that can help secure defences and be an important starting point for implementing cybersecurity controls. These controls can also be mapped to cybersecurity frameworks such as ISO 27001 and NIST as and when organizations adopt them.

4.5 SECURITY ORGANIZATION

For security policies, procedures and controls to be effective, they must be supported by a set of people who carry the mandate of implementing and enforcing security across the organization. Traditionally, this task was entrusted to IT departments, but as cyber threats have become more pervasive and frequent, a need for focused security personnel is being increasingly felt. Most modern enterprises that are of medium to large size have created the position of a Chief Information Security Officer who is responsible for designing/proposing security programs and carrying forward the security mandates of the organization. Organizations are also known to entrust security responsibilities to Chief Information Officers (CIO) or Chief Technical Officers (CTO). However, many organizations struggle to meet the present-day security demands in terms of having sufficient workforce resources both in terms of capacity and skills. This gap is often filled by consultants and services providers who work closely with internal security teams.

Every organization, depending on its size, information environment and threat perception (not only of itself, but also the industry it belongs to) and the resources that it can afford must set up its own security organization structure. It is therefore not possible to define a templated security organization structure. Table 4.4 lists some of the important tasks that security departments are required to undertake.

Table 4.4 Important tasks security departments are required to undertake

Develop, define and document security policies and procedures	Coordinate user security training and awareness programs and test the users' knowledge of security requirements
Enforce and monitor compliance with security policies and procedures within the organization as well as service providers	Ensure information security requirements are fully specified in outsourcing contracts and agreements
Plan for and implement all security controls including technical, physical and administrative measures	Monitor the effectiveness of all security related infrastructure and network and application performance to identify any irregular activity
Monitor all operations and infrastructure	Maintain all security tools and technology
Work with different departments in the organization to perform risk assessments and find ways to reduce cyber risk	Actively participate in the implementation of new technology from a security standpoint and undertake security testing of applications
Conduct audits of policies, procedures and controls on an ongoing basis	Ensure physical security for all IT assets and infrastructure
Report to senior management and boards and seek approval for budgets with justification	Set up and manage incident response plans
Make sure that resilience is assured through business continuity and disaster recovery plans	Participate in system development and implementation of security measures like encryption and managing public and private keys
Establish procedures for timely updates for upgrading operating systems and user applications	Perform vulnerability testing, threat detection and intelligence
Set and implement user access controls, identity and access management systems and ensure access to system audit tools and system audit facilities is strictly controlled	Collaborate with user groups and industry forums on cybersecurity

Given the wide range of functions to be performed by security organizations, their operating structure must also keep evolving and changing based on needs, size and the scale of potential threats. Hence, responsibilities within the security organization can be added, removed or modified over time based on changes in technologies adopted, outsourcing programs, skill development, regulatory changes, etc. At a fundamental level, security organizations are required to carry out all activities required to maintain the

Info Box 20: Security Operations Centre

Once the security goals, policies and procedures are in place, organizations, especially large ones, require a team of people to continuously monitor and respond to cybersecurity incidents through a combination of technology and processes. This set of activities, which include detection, analysis and protection from cyber incidents, requires a combination of technology and human skills which are housed in what is known as a security operations centre (SOC). SOC staff include security analysts, investigators, responders and auditors and are led by a manager who is responsible for its functioning and operations. The technology backbone of an SOC is a Security Information and Event Management System (SIEM) that gathers data such as network traffic, telemetry, logs and data flows from IT infrastructure such as firewall, intrusion detection and prevention systems and endpoints for detection and analysis. In the case of serious incidents where incident response teams are activated, the SOC personnel work closely with the incident response team to ensure that security issues are addressed promptly upon discovery.

confidentiality, integrity and availability of data and, while doing so, must provide assurance to all the stakeholders that information is secure and, in the unfortunate event of a security breach, that disruption and damage will be limited.

Issues such as privacy, compliance and related security are not problems for technical specialists to address. As these aspects are closely related to an organization's business area and functions, the involvement of business leaders and functional managers is essential. These issues may have strategic importance for the company and must be led and supported by board-level committees and senior leadership. At a more tactical and operational level, functional managers and those who form part of their teams must also be trained and aligned with the organizational security objectives.

4.6 INCIDENT RESPONSE

No matter how well your defences are organized, the threat of a cyberattack taking place cannot be entirely eliminated. As is often said in the context of cybersecurity, 'hope for the best and plan for the worst.' The adverse consequences of a cyberattack or data breach can range from crippling your business operations to financial losses, loss of reputation and lawsuits. One of the important cybersecurity strategies is being prepared to respond to a security breach. Incident response is a structured approach to responding and handling the aftereffects of a security breach or cyberattack, also known as an IT incident or security incident. The objective of an incident response process is to limit damage and minimize disruption by reducing recovery time and costs.

It is important to note that not all cyber incidents require an incident response team to swing into action. According to the National Cyber Security Centre of the UK, a cyber incident is any breach in a system's security policy that can have an effect on its integrity, confidentiality or availability.[6] It classifies the types of activities shown in Table 4.5 as breaches of security policy.[7]

Table 4.5 Activities classified as breaches of security policy

Any attempt to break into or access a system or data without due authorization.
To utilize the processing power or data storage of systems without due authorization.
Any change to a system's firmware, software or hardware without the system owners' consent.
Malicious disruption and/or denial of service.

There are other types of incidents that can be classified as security concerns such a theft or loss of computing devices, failed access attempts, discovery of malware or unauthorized accounts, sudden

---

[6] "What Is a Cyber Incident," National Cyber Security Centre, accessed July 4, 2021. https://www.ncsc.gov.uk/information/what-cyber-incident

[7] "Cyber Security Glossary at The Eastern Cyber Resilience Centre," The Eastern Cyber Resilience Centre, accessed July 10, 2021. https://www.ecrcentre.co.uk/glossary

increase in network traffic, data exfiltration and many others. All such activities that provide warning to ongoing unauthorized activity, which points to or builds up to a cyber incident, must be identified. Once this is done, then organizations must determine their response strategy. While all such cyber incidents need investigation, analysis and response, the requirements to set in motion a full-fledged incident response process may be determined by each organization based on the severity of the incident, type of threat, potential risk to their critical information resources and compliance requirements. The thresholds for invoking the incident response process must be set in advance and must be known across the organization. A number of organizations use the 'severity test' to fix the triggering of the incident response process based on what are considered moderate to severe cyber security incidents. An example of the criteria used is shown in Table 4.6.

Table 4.6 Criteria to trigger an incident response process

Observing a virus infection that could impact one or more systems
Observing malware infection with data exfiltration capabilities
Observing severe malware database infection/attack that can/or has resulted in significant data exfiltration or destruction

Routine incidents are handled by security and IT teams, while the designated incident response team is deployed in critical situations where the outcomes could range from severe to catastrophic. The incident response team (also known as Cybersecurity Incident Response Team or CSIRT) is an emergency response team that is constituted by bringing together people from different organization functions, with diverse skill sets to address, coordinate and align the key resources and team members during a cybersecurity incident in order to minimize impact and restore operations as quickly as possible. The activation of this multi-skilled response team gives the organization the best chance of minimizing any adverse impact of the cyber incident.

The three important building blocks for setting up the incident response process are:

- Constituting the incident response team
- Planning and preparation
- Incident investigation and response

Constituting the Incident Response Team

The task of the incident response team is to identify, mitigate, review, document and report on the findings of a cyber incident during and after the incident to the management. The first step in the creation of the computer security incident response team (CSIRT) is to identify the roles and responsibilities of each member of the team. Though there is no fixed criterion for the team constitution in terms of roles and number of members, Table 4.7 shows an example.

Table 4.7 CSIRT roles and responsibilities

Role	Responsibility
Team Leader	To lead and coordinate all incident response team activities and direct efforts towards minimizing damage and recovering quickly.
Lead Investigator	To gather and analyze all evidence relating to the incident, undertake a root cause analysis and oversee system restoration and recovery actions.

(Continued)

Table 4.7 (*Continued*)

Role	Responsibility
IT Representative	To coordinate IT-related tasks and activities.
HR Representative	To communicate with employees.
Communications Lead	To ensure proper and timely messaging and communications for all internal and external stakeholders.
Documentation	To document all CSIRT activities along with timelines.

In order to interface with the management and coordinate activities across organization functions and even external agencies, an executive sponsor is recommended.

Planning and Preparation

Planning for incident response involves the definition, documentation and communication of the goals of the process as well as the roles and responsibilities of each member of the team and establishment of operating protocols. This involves the consideration of the key factors listed in Table 4.8 for developing suitable plans and processes that can be adopted.

Table 4.8 Key factors for developing incident response plans and processes

Determine	Nature of cyber threat, attack, security failure or data breach and do a triage to confirm if the cyber incident needs to be addressed by the CSIRT.
Identify	The exact location, sensitiveness and relative value of the information assets that need to be protected.
Ascertain	The capabilities of potential attackers and their motives and methods.
Organize	The incident response activities and workflow among different stakeholders.
Assign	The roles and responsibilities for CSIRT and other relevant stakeholders.
Keep handy	All contact information (email, phone, VOIP, etc.) for all incident response team members, their back-ups and department managers.
Establish	A chain of command for taking decisions in an emergency.
Set up	A separate communication channel that can be operated independent of any compromised system and follow a predefined communication protocol to keep both internal and external stakeholders updated on incidents in a timely, accurate and consistent fashion.
Maintain	A list of cybersecurity regulatory requirements for the organization and set protocols for interaction with law enforcement, media and other regulatory authorities during and after the incident.
Build	An understanding of tactics that cyber criminals use to launch attacks and the types of technologies required for creating a cyber incident response framework including the cyber kill chain.

(*Continued*)

Table 4.8 (*Continued*)

Equip	The team with tools and define the processes for containment, eradication and recovery and make contractual arrangements with service providers wherever internal resources do not have the level of competency and skills required.
Be prepared	With a list of forensic specialists, technology vendors and service providers, legal advisors, customer support teams and public relations consultants who can be operationalised at short notice.
Ensure	That the senior organization leadership are aware of the incident response plan.

The incident response team must have a playbook that specifies their protocols and procedures. The incident response process must be practiced by the team so that when they address a live incident, they are fully prepared. As the incident response team is drawn from different functions and departments, they must meet at least once a quarter to review and prepare.

Incident Investigation and Response

The setting up of the incident response team and the development of incident response processes and plans constitute the preparatory stages of the incident response process. The other activities and phases of the incident response process are as follows:[8]

1. Detection and reporting
2. Triage and analysis
3. Containment, eradication and recovery
4. Post-incident activity

Once the incident response team is activated to handle a cyber incident, the detection phase is set in motion. In this phase, data is gathered regarding the security incident by examining system logs, code samples and other evidence that helps in determining the severity, type of threat and the potential damage that can be caused. Other tools that can help in detection include endpoint detection and response tools, antivirus software and user behaviour analysis tools. It is also important at this stage to determine whether the attack is ongoing and if the attackers have established any persistence.

The golden hour is a concept that is being increasingly recognized as critical to incident response activities. This represents the time window within which incident response teams must make important decisions regarding the incident based on the information available with them at that time. In this phase, triage and analysis of the incident is required to make decisions such as:

- Taking stock of the events in order to determine which events are more serious in terms of business impact for prioritizing responses.
- Determine if any critical or sensitive data has been compromised, exfiltrated or corrupted and, if so, what the potential risk might be to your business.
- Determine actions on changing passwords, isolating infected systems and shutting down access to the systems that are compromised.
- Does the incident warrant informing the organization's senior leadership, regulatory authorities, law enforcement agencies or notifying customers?

---

[8] "Information Security Handbook: Incident Response and Management: NASA Information Security Incident Management," NASA, 2011. https://www.nasa.gov/pdf/589502main_ITS-HBK-2810.09-02%20%5BNASA%20Information%20Security%20Incident%20Management%5D.pdf

> **Info Box 21: Incident Triage**
>
> In incident triage, every minute and every hour is crucial.[9] Important actions that can boost the chances of surviving the attack are to:
> - Bring in the experts
> - Stick to predefined response processes
> - Check the network to see what processes are running
> - Isolate infected systems
> - Test back-ups

The phases of containment and eradication that follow the detection and analysis phases are aimed at eliminating the threat (malicious files, hidden backdoors and artefacts) that led to the security incident. Before executing containment action, it is important to identify and consider the indicators of compromise as well as check the affected systems and verify if back-ups also have been affected. Apart from isolating infected systems, other containment actions could include updating of firewalls, suspension of privileges, changing of system and user passwords and using the cyber kill chain model to stop the attack and to minimize the breadth of the incident and prevent it from causing widespread damage. Other steps for containment could be to stop the attackers from undertaking the actions specified in Table 4.9.[10]

Table 4.9 Containment action steps

Credential dumping from operating system processes that enforce security policy
Cross-process injection
Process hollowing (a security exploit in which an attacker replaces code in an executable file with malicious code)
User account control bypass
Interfering with antivirus (such as disabling it or allowing the malware as exclusion)
Contacting command and control to download payloads
Boot record modification
Installation of root certificate
Exploiting other vulnerabilities

Incident response teams must maintain a log of the incident and response activities, including the time, data, location and extent of damage from the attack. They must document the methods used in the attack as well as preserve and list all the artefacts gathered during the course of the investigation and details for further analysis of the incident.

---

[9] Matt Sherman and Michael Smith, "4 Ways to Ensure You Do Incident Triage Right," Broadcom Software, published July 29, 2019. https://symantec-enterprise-blogs.security.com/blogs/expert-perspectives/4-ways-ensure-you-do-incident-triage-right

[10] "Behavioral Blocking and Containment," Microsoft Ignite, last updated September 16, 2022. https://docs.microsoft.com/en-us/microsoft-365/security/defender-endpoint/behavioral-blocking-containment?view=o365-worldwide

Eradication of infected files, wiping and rebuilding affected systems, patching software, replacing hardware if required, identification of root cause and path of the attack and implementing security controls to prevent further exploitation are steps that follow the containment step. It is also advisable to conduct a fresh vulnerability assessment at this stage to further strengthen defences. Even as the incident response activities are in progress, the legal and communication members of the team must engage in examining compliance and related risks and contact law enforcement agencies if required. Communication about the cyber incident, key findings and response actions must be communicated to all stakeholders appropriately and regularly for the duration of the incident. It is important to note that as much as possible communication should be factual and not driven by subjective assessments, downplaying the incident or any sort of exaggeration. It is therefore suggested that adjectives such as 'major,' 'disastrous' or 'catastrophic' are not used in the communications.

Once the eradication phase has been completed, the recovery processes are set in motion. The objective of the recovery phase is to restore the system back to the pre-incident state. Checking for data loss and verifying the integrity of the data of back-ups is necessary. A coordinated shut down of all systems or affected systems may be required to rebuild the systems and the cooperation of IT and business functions will be necessary to accomplish this. All users may be required to change passwords and additional controls can be deployed to ensure greater protection. It is useful to set up a small team of users and IT personnel to recertify the rebuilt environment before opening it up to all users for normal business operations.

The work of the incident response team is not over with the containment and eradication of the cyber threat. There are several post-incident activities that are required to be carried out with the same rigour and focus as the other response activities (Table 4.10).

Table 4.10 Post-incident activities

Gathering of information related to logs, memory dumps and network traffic data must be continued for a further period.
Completing the incident response report, including root cause analysis and preliminary assessment of impact.
Conducting a review of the incident response process: what went right, what went wrong, what can be improved.
Documenting and sharing lessons learned and updating procedures where required.
Implementing additional security controls wherever required and updating technical security appropriately.

Incident response teams should meet on a regular basis and use playbooks to conduct simulation exercises and dry runs of incident response process. They must also review, test and update security processes, controls and systems based on fresh threats and vulnerability assessments.

4.7 BUSINESS CONTINUITY AND DISASTER RECOVERY

Cyberattacks cause more harm to organizations today than ever before. Organizations have also become more dependent on IT for their business operations and in practical terms are not able to revert to the manual mode of operations, even in an emergency. Resiliency is increasingly being demanded from organizations by customers, partners and regulators as they face threats from natural disasters, climate change, epidemics and cyberattacks. Business continuity (BC) and disaster recovery (DR) are two practices that can help organizations remain operational after an adverse event.

BC and DR are increasingly being considered as an integral part of cybersecurity to boost cyber resilience. The objectives are to ensure that there are no outages or disruptions to business operations and, in the case of such an event, to get back to normal operations in the shortest possible timeframe.

BC and DR, while being closely related, are also different in certain respects. BC typically involves consideration of adverse scenarios that can impact a business and adopting a proactive approach with respect to the processes, technologies and procedures an organization must implement so that its mission-critical functions are unaffected by any adverse event. DR, on the other hand, is a process that comes into play when an adverse incident has occurred and recovery actions are required to restore normal operations.

Another area where BC is different is that it focuses on risks faced by the organization and planning of measures to avoid disruption and sustain operations even in the face of an adverse event. Organizations use a business impact analysis (BIA) to determine and quantify the risks of a disruption in operations and prioritize them based on the likelihood of occurrence. This becomes an input to their BC plans. DR is more focused on technological aspects that can help minimize operational downtime and restore systems to their pre-event state.

Info Box 22: Cybersecurity Regulations: BC and DR

As a part of cybersecurity regulations, organizations are required to develop, document and test BC and DR plans. For example, the Health Insurance Portability and Accessibility Act "requires covered entities such as hospitals to provide an emergency mode operation plan, which includes procedures to enable continuation of critical business process for protection of the security of electronic protected health information".[11]

Building a BC and DR plan requires commitment and buy-in from the organization's board and senior leadership (where not mandated by regulators) as it requires investment of time and resources. A process to develop a BC and DR plan follows the following steps:

1. Risk identification and assessment
2. A review of existing infrastructure
3. A business impact analysis exercise
4. Design, implementation and testing of the plan

Cybersecurity initiatives including incident response are considered by many organizations as distinct from their BC and DR initiatives, which are often driven by IT functions. The cyber threat landscape is, however, forcing organizations to include BC and DR under the cybersecurity and risk management umbrella to bring about better alignment between recovery processes and procedures.

---

[11] John Moore, Stephen J Bigelow and Paul Crocetti. "What Is BCDR? Business Continuity and Disaster Recovery Guide," TechTarget, accessed July 5, 2021. https://searchdisasterrecovery.techtarget.com/definition/Business-Continuity-and-Disaster-Recovery-BCDR

QUICK TEST

1. Information classification is necessary for the following reasons:
   a. Communicating the value of information to employees
   b. Establishing protocols for handling different types of information
   c. For raising cybersecurity awareness
   d. All the above
   e. a and b only
2. A single cybersecurity policy is not sufficient to define objectives, baselines and guidelines.
   a. True
   b. False
3. While framing security policies, compliance and ethical considerations must not be given any weightage.
   a. True
   b. False
4. Arrange the terms Policies (1), Baselines (2), Procedures (3) and Standards (4) with regard to the level of detail to be provided.
   a. 1,2,3,4
   b. 4,3,2,1
   c. 1,4,2,3
   d. 1,3,4,2
5. What type of cyberattack would activate response from an incident response team?
   a. Observing a virus infection that could impact one or more systems.
   b. Observing malware infection with data exfiltration capabilities
   c. Observing severe malware database infection/attack that can/or has resulted in significant data exfiltration or destruction
   d. Critical situations based on defined thresholds set by the organization
   e. All of the above
   f. Only c and d
6. The phases of incident response are:
   a. Detection and reporting
   b. Triage and analysis
   c. Containment, eradication and recovery
   d. Post-incident activity
   e. All of the above
   f. a, c and d
7. Containment actions include:
   a. Verifying logs
   b. Updating firewalls
   c. Changing passwords
   d. All of the above
   e. b and c only
8. The work of the incident response team is not over with the containment and eradication of the cyber threat.
   a. True
   b. False
9. A process for BC and DR should include:
   a. Risk identification and assessment
   b. A review of existing infrastructure

    c. A business impact analysis exercise
    d. All of the above
    e. a and b
10. Business continuity and disaster recovery, while being closely related, are also different in certain respects.
    a. True
    b. False

QUESTIONS

1. Determining the value of information is a complex task as there is no universal value that can be ascribed to it. Discuss this statement.
2. What are the ways of classifying information? Build an information classification and define the categories for a hospital.
3. Develop a remote working security policy for a university college.
4. What are CIS controls? How are they effective in ensuring cybersecurity?
5. What are the activities carried out by a security organization?
6. What is the composition of an incident response team? What are its key activities?
7. Should BC and DR plans and efforts be a part of cybersecurity? If so, why?
8. How should the security organization be designed? What should be the structure and team composition?
9. Explain the differences in structure, composition and objectives of a security operations centre and incident response team.
10. Explain the various activities that are a part of the containment and eradication phase that follows a cyberattack.

ANSWER KEYS

Quick Test
1. (d)
2. (a)
3. (b)
4. (c)
5. (f)
6. (e)
7. (e)
8. (d)
9. (a)
10. (a)

5 Developing Secure Information Systems

OBJECTIVES
At the end of this chapter, you will be able to:
- ☑ Describe the activities involved in securing information systems in a way that is effective, flexible and adaptable to ever changing contexts
- ☑ List the challenges and security issues that are important in building secure information systems

5.0 INTRODUCTION

The rapid rise in cyberattacks and security breaches underscore the need for developing secure information systems as well as ensuring their secure deployment. Developing secure information systems involves integrating security into every phase of the development process. This is usually easier said than done as there are many priorities (often conflicting) that development teams need to address at the same time. There is pressure on developers to ensure that all business requirements are met, that applications are released on schedule and within the set cost parameters. Many a time, in order to meet these requirements, potential security issues are not explored or factored into the applications and left for updates that can be provided later. This leaves the applications open to vulnerabilities being identified and exploited by attackers, exposing organizations to unwanted and unexpected risks.

Organizations wanting to adopt secure approaches to developing information systems must be committed to security and encourage their development teams to prepare themselves for the following:

- Obtain buy-in from management for prioritizing security issues
- Envision probable security concerns and deployment environments: on-premises, cloud, mobile, hybrid, etc.
- Understand the best practices related to secure development and train the team on the same
- 'Design-in' security as much as possible
- Implement security checks at every stage of development
- Make use of static code scanners in the initial stages and use dynamic testing tools when the build reaches a stable stage
- Conduct security reviews and audits during the development phases

To develop secure information systems, development teams must understand all the possible threats to the confidentiality, integrity and availability of information and must include relevant controls and safeguards. Organizations must develop and evolve their own software development and maintenance policy, which emphasizes the need for system design principles to be centred on end user scenarios and overall system security.

5.1 SECURING INFORMATION ASSETS

Approaches to securing information assets have evolved from being computer centric to network centric and now to being information centric. They have also evolved from enhancing generic security to focusing efforts and resources on key information assets. In the context of organizational resilience, secure development must encompass not only vulnerabilities that are exploited by hackers, but also points of failure. For any organization, their key information systems that house their information assets are as follows:

- **Safety critical systems** comprise all those systems that if breached/tampered with by hackers or they fail due to any reason can jeopardize the safety of human beings, cause environmental harm or cause injury/damage to people and property. Examples of such systems are nuclear control systems, railway signalling and control systems, water treatment and other distribution control systems. Software development for safety critical systems is a difficult process that must incorporate rigorous application security standards, compliance requirements, fault tolerance and testing, including simulation of adverse events.
- **Mission critical systems** are those that are essential for the survival of the organization and are critical to its meeting its objectives. The failure or disruption of a mission critical system can significantly impact the organization's systems, processes and operations. Examples of such systems for an electricity company would be its generation, supply and distribution systems. Mission critical applications, if compromised by inadvertent actions and those of malicious actors, can lead to severe adverse consequences for businesses, including the following:
  - Critical business activity of the organization is disrupted or stalled
  - R&D information and intellectual property is compromised
  - Threat to life and wellbeing of people
  - Sensitive data
  - Significant reputational damage
  - Financial losses
  - Remediation, legal and regulatory costs

  Secure software development of these systems and safeguards for ensuring data protection must incorporate the following considerations:
  - Reliability (fault detection and remediation, fault tolerance) and scalability
  - Security and safety
  - Operational error tolerance and reparability
  - Damage limitation measures such as data encryption

  Business leaders must determine which assets to protect and what priority to accord to different assets based on the external and internal threats to information security. They also need to resolve conflicts between business managers, IT and security teams, and risk management functions to bring more clarity and better collaboration in ensuring security. In the absence of this, many organizations attempt to apply the same cyber risk controls everywhere and equally, often not striking the right balance in resource allocation to mitigate risks and optimise security efforts.
- **Business critical systems** comprise application data and processes that are critical to business continuity. Disruption or failure in a business critical application may still allow an organization to conduct its business albeit with decreased productivity, degradation of user experience or interruption of some support services. Approaches to the development of business critical applications must consider implementation of specific controls and provide for quick remediation measures

to ensure a quick recovery. Examples of such systems are financial accounting systems, employee records and messaging systems. Many organizations today use third-party, cloud-based applications for these functions, but security concerns specific to the organization must become a part of their deployment and maintenance cycle.

While the above represents a broad classification of an organization's application environment, they comprise the most critical systems required for an organization's functioning and survival. Equal protection of all assets is not a feasible or effective option. All efforts must be directed towards the critical systems that also have maximum exposure to risks. Application of sectional controls that leave any vital information assets vulnerable can be a recipe for disaster in a hostile cyber threat environment.

5.2 DATA SECURITY AND PROTECTION

Development of secure information systems involves the implementation of strategies and technologies for data security and data protection. On the face of it, both may appear to be the same, but while they are related, understanding the distinction between the two concepts is important.

Data security refers to the process of securing data so that only authorized people can access or modify it; whereas data protection is defined as exercising "legal control over the access to and use of data" and includes the process of protecting data from loss, compromise or corruption. In practice, these terms are used interchangeably as they are connected to each other.

Legal obligations with regard to data protection and privacy laws place the responsibility on organizations to ensure that they not only maintain data securely through the life cycle, but also confer rights on their clients to demand assurance that they (the organizations) are taking adequate measures for safeguarding their data.

The basic principles of data security and data protection revolve around maintaining the confidentiality, integrity and availability of data while the areas of focus and the strategies deployed for addressing them may be different.

The **prime focus** of data protection strategies should include the following:

- Risk assessment
- Consent tracking
- Identity management
- Data sharing policies
- Privacy management
- Compliance
- Audit trails

The focus of data security strategies could also include the following:

- Access control
- Authentication and authorization
- API security
- Encryption of data at rest, in transit and in use
- Key management
- Data base security
- Redundancy and back-up
- Security updates
- Scalability

The importance of data protection and data security has never been as critical as it is today. The increased amount of data that is being created and stored has reached unprecedented levels and continues to grow, tolerance for downtime is very limited and regulatory standards demand a high degree of security and resilience from organizations that handle sensitive data. Table 5.1 lists the best practices for data protection and data security.

Table 5.1 Best practices for data protection and data security

Securing databases	Databases store vast amounts of organizational information. Strategies for securing databases include implementing a multi-tier database model that isolates the end user from the database by using an intermediary server(s) and using a NoSQL database (such as MongoDB) to prevent SQL injection attacks.
Classifying data and creating a data usage policy	Identify the sensitive data, classify and prioritize protection. Develop a data policy for granting access depending on the classification scheme and define rules for data usage.
Implementing access controls	Physical measures: Video surveillance, mobile device security, physical access control systems, network segmentation Technical measures: For example, access permissions and privileges, access control lists, security mechanisms like firewalls, network access controls, data loss prevention systems, proxy server Administrative measures: Procedures and policies that all employees must follow
Encrypting data	Encryption of critical business data, at rest, in transit and in use. Hardware-based encryption can also be used in addition to software-based encryption.
Maintaining data back-ups	The time tested 3:2:1 system of back-ups, which involves maintaining three copies of back-ups of data (production data and two back-up copies) on two different media (tape and disk) with one copy off-site for disaster recovery. These back-ups must be well protected and ready to use in case of an attack where data on production systems is corrupted or not accessible, as in the case of a ransomware attack.
Implementing RAID for fault tolerance	RAID comprises a redundant array of risks that ensures protection from data destruction and system downtime. There are various levels of RAID that help in defining the level of data security required.
Hardening systems	This can be implemented by disabling any services that are not needed by applications. Can be implemented at OS and system software level.
Patch management	Updating systems in a timely manner is an essential component of data security. Having a system in place to ensure that this is done is a recommended practice.
Implementing endpoint security	Implementation of antivirus, firewalls and IDS are traditional approaches. Newer approaches include EDR (endpoint detection and response) and XDR (extended detection and response) systems.
Protection from insider threats	Current approaches suggest the use of zero trust authentication, which works on a first verify then trust principle. In addition, micro-segmentation of networks based on user groups can ensure that access is limited, and hence, any threat can be minimized. Verification of user logs and correlation of contexts is another practice.
Testing security	Perform vulnerability assessments and penetration tests.

Malware Analysis: This is an important component of cybersecurity. It comprises the tools and procedures used to identify and understand the behaviour of suspicious files and software artefacts. By conducting malware analysis, analysts and security personnel can figure out the functions, purposes and potential impact of suspected files. The analysis is carried out within a contained environment called a sandbox and can help in distinguishing legitimate files from suspicious ones. Malware analysis can be conducted in three ways: static, dynamic and a combination of both. Some open-source tools for malware analysis are Yara, Rules, Cuckoo Sandbox, Remnux, Google Rapid Response and Bro.

The analysis of suspicious files can reveal or point to the sources of the threat/attack, evaluate the potential damage, trigger off incident response processes if necessary and overall contribute to developing a strong security posture.

5.3 APPLICATION SECURITY

Application security refers to all the processes and tasks that are involved in making applications more secure throughout the life cycle of the application. While the development stage is important in terms of implementing prevention of security issues, the process of finding vulnerabilities and fixing them as well as enhancing security based on current scenarios is equally crucial.

> **Info Box 23: Security Flaws in Applications**
>
> Veracode, an application security company, in a study of over 85,000 applications, found that 83% of them had at least one security flaw. Furthermore, they found that 20% of all apps had at least one high-severity flaw. While all security flaws do not represent significant risks, the numbers by themselves are quite concerning.[1]

There are several tools available today that enable developers to identify coding threats. These tools can be integrated into any development environment, enabling detection of flaws in the development phases, and thereby making the task of fixing them simpler. Newer development methodologies like agile are extensively used today, which means that development teams work on shorter release cycles and release code even on a daily basis. The use of application security tools becomes all the more important as they work in the form of 'in-line' testing systems.

The MITRE Corporation is an American organization that is, among other things, dedicated to enhancing cybersecurity standards. MITRE has developed a knowledge base and model of cyber adversary behaviour based on their prime target strategies and encapsulated in what is known as the MITRE ATT&CK framework. MITRE maintains a record of common weakness enumerations (CWEs) in a database and common vulnerabilities and exposures (CVEs) and publishes the top software security weaknesses based on the frequency of occurrence, the root cause of a vulnerability and the severity of its exploitation. The following are the top 10 CWEs in MITRE's 2021 list:[2]

1. Out-of-bounds write
2. Improper neutralization of input during web page generation (cross-site scripting)
3. Out-of-bounds read
4. Improper input validation
5. Improper neutralization of special elements used in an OS command (OS command injection)
6. Improper neutralization of special elements used in an SQL command (SQL injection)

---

[1] "State of Software Security V12," Veracode, accessed October 6, 2021. https://www.veracode.com/state-of-software-security-report
[2] "2021 CWE Top 25 Most Dangerous Software Weaknesses," Common Weakness Enumeration, accessed October 6, 2021. https://cwe.mitre.org/top25/archive/2021/2021_cwe_top25.html

7. Use after free, a vulnerability that is triggered by closing a connection while data is still being transmitted
8. Improper limitation of a pathname to a restricted directory (path traversal)
9. Cross-site request forgery (CSRF)
10. Unrestricted upload of file with dangerous type

Application security has become more complex with the introduction of new deployment models such as cloud, mobile, hybrid, etc. New technologies too offer new challenges in terms of undiscovered security vulnerabilities. To anticipate security needs across a variety of devices and IT infrastructure requires knowledge of how these are integrated and secured. Integration also brings the question of how secure application program interfaces (APIs) are as well as the use of open-source code as these can be a threat to application security.

Various types of application security tools can be used during the application development and deployment phases. They can be broadly classified as source code analysis tools and application protection tools (Table 5.2).

Table 5.2 Source code analysis tools

Tool	Purpose	Examples
Static application security testing (SAST)	To enable developers to analyze code during the development process for security flaws and issues	Veracode Static Analysis, Fortify Static Code Analyser, AppScan
Dynamic application security testing (DAST)	To test running code by simulating web application threats and attacks for identifying vulnerabilities	Netsparker, Acutenix, AppScan
Interactive application security testing (IAST)	This combines SAST and DAST capabilities. A few of them also include open-source security analysis	Acunetix AcuSensor, Checkmarx
Mobile application security testing (MAST)	To identify and analyze vulnerabilities in applications used with mobile platforms	Zed Attack Proxy, QARK, not. Micro Focus, Android Debug Bridge

Application self-protection tools provide a combination of testing and application protection. Widely known as runtime application self-protection tools (RASP), their prime objectives are to monitor the behaviour of a running application and provide basic protection against reverse-engineering an application. Mobile application development can use the capabilities of these tools such as generating alerts, terminating dubious processes and even shutting-down the application in case it is compromised.

HTTP, SOAP and REST Security: The HyperText Transfer Protocol (HTTP) is the most basic foundation of the World Wide Web. It is used for loading web pages using hypertext links. It also functions as an application layer protocol that supports the transfer of information between networked devices and runs on top of other layers of the network protocol stack. In usage, HTTP involves a client machine making a request to a server, which responds with a message.

HTTP clients are often privy to a lot of personal information such as the user's name, passwords, location, mail address, encryption keys, etc. and since the data is unencrypted, it is susceptible to a variety of attacks. HyperText Transfer Protocol Secure (HTTPS) an extension of HTTP that represents a secure form of communication that is recommended for transmission of any sensitive information. The fundamental difference between the two protocols is that HTTPS uses TLS (SSL) to encrypt normal HTTP requests and responses.

An application programming interface (API) is an agreed format for exchanging data between web services. SOAP and REST are acronyms for the two most used APIs for web services.

Simple Object Access Protocol (SOAP) is a web communication protocol for exchanging structured information in the implementation of web services in computer networks. It is built with Extensible Markup Language (XML). Securing the SOAP API requires the use of Web Services Security (WS-Security), which comprises a set of principles that manage the confidentiality and authentication procedures for SOAP messaging. WS-Security–compliant controls include passwords, digital signatures, X.509 certificates and XML encryption, among other things.

REST stands for representational state transfer and it is widely used in modern application development. REST uses uniform service locators for implementing web services.

Given the difference in approaches between the two protocols, the security approaches too are different. Both approaches can use Secure Socket Layer or SSL for safeguarding data during an API call request; SOAP, while slower, is considered the more secure option. REST APIs are faster as they use HTTP and support Transport Layer Security (TLS) encryption. REST web services can be secured using one the following methods to support authentication:[3]

- Updating the web.xml deployment descriptor to define security configuration
- Using the javax.ws.rs.core.SecurityContext interface to implement security programmatically
- Applying annotations to the JAX-RS classes
- Using Jersey OAuth libraries to sign and verify requests

5.3.1 DevOps and DevSecOps

The evolution of application security development has not only seen changes in methodologies and testing technology, but also in terms of enhancing communication and coordination between development and operations teams. With the adoption of agile methodologies, development cycles have become shorter and more iterative. From an 'over-the-wall' interaction between development and operations teams, DevOps is a concept that facilitates members of both (Development and Operations) teams to work together collaboratively and iteratively to ensure that aspects of operational issues are adequately addressed.

An extension of the DevOps concept is DevSecOps, where security teams also become an integral part of application development so that all security issues are given due attention during every development iteration and stage. Any organization that is using a DevOps approach should actively consider moving to a DevSecOps approach so that security is 'baked-in' to the application as much as possible and not 'bolted-on' as an afterthought. This approach makes everyone from development to security to operations take ownership of security issues and ensure that organizational security objectives are addressed in a more comprehensive manner.

Key trends in application security include the integration of automated testing tools, using software-defined security and configuration within applications and ensuring that the use of open-source software and APIs is done with due security diligence, but in the end, the onus of application security lies with the development teams.

5.3.2 Secure Development Methodologies

In an earlier chapter, we looked at the different Software Development Life Cycle (SDLC) methodologies. Development teams can also incorporate the use of Security Development Lifecycle (SDL) methodologies to

---

[3] "Securing RESTful Web Services," in *Fusion Middleware Developing RESTful Web Services for Oracle WebLogic Server*, Oracle Help Center, accessed May 19, 2022. https://docs.oracle.com/cd/E24329_01/web.1211/e24983/secure.htm#RESTF113

complement and become a part of their SDLC methodology. SDL methodologies are not platform specific and comprise best practices related to security. The commonly used SDL methodologies include Microsoft SDL, SAMM and BSIMM (Table 5.3).

Table 5.3 Commonly used SDL methodologies

Microsoft SDL	Initially developed for internal use, it was recreated as a product which provides a prescriptive methodology to enhance application security
Software Assurance Maturity Model (SAMM)	SAMM is a prescriptive methodology which is maintained by OWASP and provides roadmap templates for different types of organizations
Building Security in Maturity Model (BSIMM)	BSIMM is a descriptive methodology that can be used to benchmark security development practices in terms of maturity

Organizations can adopt any of these methodologies based on their own requirements in order to prioritize security, reduce costs and ensure regulatory compliance. Such approaches also ensure that secure coding practices become ingrained in software development initiatives and in achieving a consistent approach to building secure applications.

5.4 SECURITY ARCHITECTURE AND DESIGN

Security architecture and design has become an increasingly complex task over the years. Traditional approaches that were designed to implement security controls are no longer valid as organizational systems now need to incorporate new considerations, such as the dissolving of the corporate perimeter, the migration to cloud-based systems and the increasing adoption of mobile devices and IoT. The purpose of security architecture is to set up controls and countermeasures against cyber threats and data breaches. Today, security architects need to look beyond traditional approaches such as implementing security policies, controls, tools and monitoring and even consider threats beyond enterprise IT systems and infrastructure such as attacks emanating from supply chain partners and other third parties. The primary purpose of security architecture remains the same, that is, to maintain the critical system's quality attributes such as confidentiality, integrity and availability.

Essentially, cybersecurity architecture is all about how the three major elements, that is, technology, people and processes, are integrated, organized and aligned to protect an organization's IT resources, data and other critical information. To accomplish this, these elements must be driven by a security architecture that incorporates the organization's security expectations and goals, policies, implementation plans and enforcement mechanisms and processes.

Cybersecurity architecture must address the following objectives in order to be effective:

- To neutralize or mitigate cyber threats
- To ensure that all key information assets are encrypted and well protected
- To detect cyberattacks in the early stages so that countermeasures, including incident response mechanisms, can be activated
- To ensure security of endpoints, networks, network elements and other IT infrastructure
- To be flexible to incorporate new and emerging cyber threats

A good starting point for security architecture and design is to conduct an architecture risk assessment. This helps in evaluation of the existing controls as well as of the influence of key information assets, the associated risks and the effects of vulnerabilities and security threats to an organization. This can be followed by a conceptual architecture and security design that addresses all the key concerns and can then be translated into an implementable one, which defines all the security controls that are required to address the business risks. Key areas that need focus while building a program to design and implement controls are shown in Table 5.4.

Table 5.4 Areas for designing and implementing controls

Governance, policy and domain architecture	Operational risk management architecture
Information architecture	Certificate management architecture
Access control architecture	Incident response architecture
Application security architecture	Web services architecture
Communication security architecture	Security standards
IT infrastructure and network security	Database and file security
Mapping of conceptual architecture with physical architecture	Security products and tools

Security architecture is a broad concept that incorporates the security principles, methods and models that are designed to align business goals and objectives through security architecture roadmaps, building blocks and requirements to stay safe from cyber threats. It is useful in translating business requirements to executable security requirements. The translation of a conceptual security architecture into an operational one involves the preparation of implementation guides, administrative issues such as configuration/patch management, logging, monitoring, access management, change management, testing, etc.

Cybersecurity architecture must be based on a comprehensive understanding of the business objectives of an organization and support them through the implementation of proper and adequate controls. Frameworks such as The Open Group Architecture Framework (TOGAF), Sherwood Applied Business Security Architecture (SABSA) and OSA (Open Security Architecture) provide useful and essential guidance to align security needs with business needs and objectives.

The effectiveness of a security architecture and design can only be assessed once it is implemented and the cybersecurity services and processes are operated, monitored and controlled. The architecture must be flexible to incorporate changes in security policy, standards and security architecture decisions based on ongoing risk assessments over a long period.

5.5 SECURITY ISSUES IN HARDWARE, MOBILE DEVICES AND INTERNET OF THINGS

The general perception in terms of security from cyber threats is often focused on software. However, hardware that provides the infrastructure for software applications to run is also vulnerable to different kinds of attacks. More often than not, hardware security issues are left unaddressed by IT teams as the vulnerabilities are more difficult to discover and can be addressed mainly through updates provided by the hardware vendor.

Hackers are aware that if they are able to bypass security controls at OS and software levels, then they could place malware at the hardware levels. A case in point is when in 2020 it was found that a certain processor from a leading manufacturer had a security issue that could be exploited for malicious purposes. There are several examples of IoT devices and mobile devices where such hardware-level security flaws have been unearthed and exploited by expert hackers to launch different types of attacks such as side-channel attacks, trojan attacks, integrated circuit (IC)/intellectual property (IP) piracy, and printed circuit board tampering.

The explosion of mobile and other IoT devices and their rapidly increasing usage by individuals and organizations is a growing cause for concern from a security point of view. While smart devices provide many benefits, they also introduce new risks into the system. The key reasons for hardware-related vulnerabilities in IoT devices are as follows:

- Vendors are more concerned about functionality and cost as there are, as of now, no global security standards for these devices.
- Devices are constrained by hardware to incorporate security mechanisms.
- Devices use different transmission protocols and methods, making standardization difficult.
- The components used in these devices have their own vulnerabilities.
- IT teams and users have limited understanding of security issues on these devices as well as visibility in the context of an enterprise network.

Organizations, therefore, need to develop security strategies to address threats from hardware, mobile devices and other IoT devices. A good first step is to build an inventory of all these devices that connect to the organization's network and evaluate whether these devices need to be connected to the network or not. The next step is to identify the vendors of these devices and establish links with their sites to download and update security patches and firmware. A best-case scenario is that the process of downloading patches is automated to ensure timely updating.

Security threats from IoT devices are harder to detect as the devices are designed to function autonomously. Automated tools could also be used to identify any abnormal behaviour from a pre-set threshold of what is considered as normal and raising alerts in the case of violations.

Other common security issues related to hardware are:

- Use of default passwords: Passwords must be changed at the time of deployment of hardware as using vendor-provided passwords is fraught with risk and can be easily exploited by hackers.
- Use of outdated devices and firmware: As no new security updates for these will be forthcoming, these devices are extremely vulnerable.
- Lack of control in terms of 'locking down' hardware configurations.

Key approaches that can help address hardware security issues are:

- Ensuring timely firmware updates
- Implementing robust access control in terms of configuration and password management
- Phasing out unsupported legacy hardware
- Implementing endpoint security
- Encryption of data

5.6 NETWORK SECURITY

The growing complexity of IT infrastructure combined with the dissolution or 'flexible extension' of network boundaries makes the challenge of managing network security a difficult one. Traditionally, network security revolved around the security of the perimeter or boundary and the movement to a network perimeter that can go anywhere and everywhere data goes requires a paradigm shift in approach.

An enterprise network comprises networking infrastructure such as hubs, routers, bridges and switches, network services and communication protocols, hardware, software, devices and the users connected to the network. To develop a comprehensive understanding of the network, it must be viewed in its physical, virtual and logical forms in order to design and implement effective security measures. Enterprise systems today, which actually help the business run its operations, are heavily dependent on network security, so any downtime from malicious attacks on networks can lead to even severe adverse consequences. All technology building blocks such as servers, cloud computing, mobile devices and applications rely on the stability and security of the network for uninterrupted operation.

Studies reveal that an average enterprise deploys approximately 500 products and over 1100 APIs as a part of its technology stack.[4] Further, the average number of mobile devices connected to an enterprise network has gone up to nearly five per user from just one or two devices per user in the not-so-distant past.[5] The movement towards work from home and remote working has stretched organizational boundaries and requires new approaches to network security. Overall, network security challenges have multiplied in terms of the sheer number of devices, connections and users as well in terms of complexity of network security management and a new set of approaches and responses is required to secure organization networks from different kinds of threats. Let us examine the current challenges and approaches to network security.

Typically, network security includes prevention of unauthorized access, security breaches, malicious attacks (hacking and virus attacks) and data loss. The main challenges that organizations face in order to accomplish these objectives are:

- **Lack of continuous visibility** of all devices connected to the network. At various points in time, new devices and endpoints join and leave the network. In such a situation, it is hard to ensure that all endpoints are properly secured and protected at a given point in time. Data from past connectivity logs is not of much use as security teams cannot act on the same. Small IT and security teams often struggle to cope with establishing continuous visibility of the entire network in order to work on the potential risks and security aspects. Automation implemented through a security operations centre (SOC) is the way forward for large organizations to ensure visibility and undertake close monitoring of endpoints.
- **Misconfiguration** is among the most prevalent and serious network security threats. Installation of firewalls provides a sense of security to organizations, but misconfigured firewalls represent a major security threat. It is true that firewalls are becoming difficult to manage as networks become increasingly complicated. Large networks can have hundreds of firewalls; while configuration management of firewalls can be automated, it also needs human supervision to ensure secure configurations are maintained.
- **Poor system administration practices** can also be a source of vulnerabilities. Practices such as the use of default passwords, using easily hackable usernames and passwords like 'admin' on devices can be a source of threat to network security. In spite of the obvious risks of such practices, negligence and lack of proper process for onboarding computing devices result in hazards. Poor control over access privileges is another area as breaches often start with privileged access abuse. Effective credentials management practices for authenticating users not just on basic credentials but also contextual details such as geolocation, IP address, time zones, etc. can prevent both unauthorized access as well as misuse of privileges.

---

[4] FireMon, "Top 5 Network Security Challenges in 2020 and Beyond," *Security Boulevard* (blog), accessed July 19, 2021. https://securityboulevard.com/2020/05/top-5-network-security-challenges-in-2020-and-beyond/
[5] Stratix, "The Growing Complexity of Enterprise Mobile: Three Trends Complicating Business Use," Enterprise CIO, accessed July 19, 2021. https://enterprise-cio.com/news/2017/nov/03/growing-complexity-enterprise-mobile-three-trends-complicating-business-use/

- **Network security data collation and analysis** is another challenge that is difficult to surmount. While there are a variety of network security tools that can be deployed, integrating data across tools and interoperability between tools is not seamless. Security analytics platforms can provide data and alerts on anomalies to security teams, but the challenge of too many or too few alerts are issues for them to deal with. Enterprise networks today are not a single zone or domain but could be segmented, which again poses a challenge for security teams to obtain a unified view. However, software like SIEM can help collate data across sub-networks and endpoints and provide insights for more effective management of network security. Current-day solutions allow micro-segmentation of networks, which provides additional security by making it difficult for hackers to break into other networks even if they have penetrated the micro-segments. Furthermore, these micro-segments can be created based on user groups, making them virtual rather than physical, and provide an additional level of security.
- Ensuring that **controls** are in lock step with growing volumes and other changes made in IT infrastructure is another key challenge. Security teams struggle to keep pace with growing volumes and the number of activities such as number of vulnerabilities, security patching, new network devices, lack of standardization, new applications and looking at ways to mitigate emerging threats. Orchestration is one way of dealing with all this as it brings together all the security controls and helps automate change management. Orchestration solutions can help in automating various aspects of network security from policy design to implementation, including elements like real-time monitoring, providing scalability and collecting security data as well as normalizing device security rules and storing them in a single database. This also enables total network visibility through a single console along with the ability to command security controls.
- **Data leakage and protection** is another area which can pose challenges. This underscores the importance of regular network administration and housekeeping and the deployment of encryption technologies and implementing the use of virtual private networks (VPNs) and data loss prevention software.
- **Domain name system (DNS) server attacks** represent another type of network security issue. DNS performs the important function of translating domain names to IP addresses. Since DNS is a part of every network and establishes communication with external networks, it functions as an open protocol and cannot be locked down. Hackers are well aware of this and tamper with it for the malicious purposes of conducting network reconnaissance, introducing malware payloads, establishing communication with their command-and-control servers and exfiltrating data. Protection from DNS attacks requires monitoring of DNS traffic with the use of solutions such as IPFIX and NetFlow, which collate network telemetry data and provide aggregate views of network traffic and bandwidth utilisation.

5.6.1 Network Security Techniques and Tools

Traditionally, network security received a lot of attention in ensuring overall cybersecurity. There are several techniques and tools available that security administrators can use. Some of these are as follows:

- Network administrators can deploy packet sniffing tools to monitor, examine and validate data flowing across the network. Packet sniffing is a technique that involves collecting and monitoring the data pieces (packets) that travel through a network or the Internet and can be used by both defenders and attackers for different purposes.
- Network simulation is a technique that enables the replication of the behaviour of a network through software capturing the interactions between the various network entities such as routers, switches, access points, links, etc.

- Network administrators use network auditing for collating and analyzing information related to various network parameters to glean meaningful insights that point out issues related to overall network health and compliance with industry standards.
- Validating the system integrity of hardware and software configurations is another technique that is useful during testing, deployment and system troubleshooting of a network.
- Analyzing network traffic by monitoring network availability and activity to identify abnormalities, detecting malware, and identifying security and operational issues can be done using network traffic analysis tools.

The common open-source tools available for network security management are listed in Table 5.5.

Table 5.5 Network security open-source tools

Tool name	Purpose
DDoS Deflate	A shell script that is useful for blocking a denial-of-service attack and mitigating its impact
Snort	An intrusion prevention system that helps define malicious network activity through a set of rules
Wireshark	A network protocol analyzer that provides microscopic level visibility of network activity by performing deep inspection of hundreds of protocols
Cain and Abel	Tools for the recovery of various types of passwords using methods such as network packet sniffing as well as breaking into password hashes by using techniques like dictionary attacks, brute force and cryptanalysis attacks
iptables	A command line interface for setting up and maintaining tables for the Netfilter firewall for Internet Protocol Version 4 (IPv4), included in the Linux kernel
Windows Firewall	An application provided by Microsoft for filtering information from the Internet as well as for blocking potentially malicious programs
Suricata	An open-source–based program that is useful for both intrusion detection and intrusion prevention
Fail2ban	An intrusion prevention software framework that safeguards computer servers from brute force attacks

5.6.2 The OSI Model

The open systems interconnection (OSI) model is a conceptual framework that separates a network into seven layers that are used for communication over a network and recommends ways for protecting each one of them. While the Internet works on the simpler TCP/IP model, the multi-layer OSI model is helpful in securing every layer from penetration attempts. The OSI model is today known as the ISO-OSI model after its adoption by ISO as an international standard in 1984. The OSI security architecture is focused on security attacks, mechanisms and services.

The objective of the OSI model is to provide guidance to technology vendors and developers so that their products and software programs can interoperate as well as to promote a composite framework that details the functions of a networking or telecommunications system. Table 5.6 shows the different layers of the OSI model.[6]

---

[6] "OSI Model," Imperva, accessed October 6, 2021. https://www.imperva.com/learn/application-security/osi-model/

Table 5.6 OSI layers, protocols, cyber threats and security approaches

Layer	Protocols	Cyber threat examples	Security approaches
Application	End User Layer HTTP, FTP, IRC, SSH, DNS	Malware attacks, DDoS attacks, HTTP floods, SQL injections, cross-site scripting, parameter tampering, FTP bounce, SMTP attacks	Vulnerability scanning and fixing. Use of firewalls and application-level proxies. Secure by design. Authentication and encryption
Presentation	Syntax Layer SSL, SSH, IMAP, FTP, MPEG, JPEG	Phishing, malformed SSL requests, SSL hijacking or sniffing	Strong encryption and better coding
Session	Sync and send to port APIs, Sockets, Winsock	Session hijacking through cross-site scripting, side jacking, fixation, cookie theft and brute force attempts	Use HTTPS or some other protocol that ensures encryption. Prevent access to cookies from client-side scripts. Configure the system to regenerate the session key after it has established authentication.
Transport	End-to-end connections TCP, UDP	Reconnaissance, SYN floods and Smurf attacks, TCP sequence prediction, UDP and TCP flooding.	Use TLS for all pages. Use the 'secure' cookie flag. Prevent caching of sensitive data. Use HTTP strict transport security. Use client-side certificates.
Network	Packets IP, ICMP, IPSec, IGMP	IP spoofing, hijacking, Smurf, wormhole, blackhole, Sybil and sinkhole, MITM	Proper configuration and regular updating of patches on firewalls, IDS (intrusion detection system), routers and switches. Ensure unused ports are blocked. Unused interfaces and services must be disabled. Logging must be enabled. Packet filtering must be enabled. Switch traffic must be encrypted.
Data Link	Frames Ethernet, PPP, Switch, Bridge	ARP spoofing, MAC flooding, port stealing, DHCP attacks	Disable ports. Enable MAC address filtering.
Physical	Physical structure coaxial, fibre, wireless, hubs, repeaters	Interference, jamming, eavesdropping and traffic analysis	Ensure strong password protection for all devices. Maintain back-ups. Encrypt sensitive data. Be vigilant about physical possession of devices to avoid theft.

The OSI model provides a visual representation of the multiple layers that need to be secured. It is useful for network managers to understand what is happening at each layer and for product and application developers to design security at each level to enable higher levels of network security.

5.7 OPERATING SYSTEM SECURITY

Operating systems (OS) are critical to an IT system. They provide the core functionality required by the system such as process and memory management, file and device input/output system, network management and other core functions. As the operating system functions as the central command system of a computing device, security issues relating to it are critical to the overall protection of the system. Hackers can cause considerable damage to hardware and software by exploiting OS vulnerabilities. The key security issues related to operating systems include the following:

- OS comprises thousands of lines of code. During the development phases, several vulnerabilities exist which, despite debugging and bug fixing, get into the deployment phase as well. OS developers like Microsoft, Apple, Google, etc. regularly release patches, updates and new versions of their OSs to address and fix vulnerabilities. Code-level vulnerabilities manifest in the form of unwanted system behaviour, error messages, data corruption and system crashes. From a user point of view, it is important to install the updates as soon as they become available.
- OSs need to follow an authentication process for identifying each user who seeks access and ensure that the user is actually who he or she claims to be. The most common method is the use of log-in credentials that include a username and password. Hackers use techniques such as authentication spoofing (impersonating an authorized user), which can be a major security issue as OS-level access enables them to launch different types of attacks.
- Remote code execution is another security issue that is a challenge for maintaining the stability and security of the operation system. Hackers can use this capability to launch other attacks in the form of denial-of-service attacks (flood attacks and crash attacks) and escalation of privileges, which gives an attacker authorization permission beyond those initially granted whereby they can perform actions to exploit other vulnerabilities.
- Popular operating systems such as Windows and Android are heavily targeted by hackers using a variety of malware such as trojan, viruses, spyware, etc. It will not come as a surprise that Windows was the target of over 100 million malicious software programs in 2019 alone.[7] OS hardening is a useful technique that can be used by security and IT teams to ensure security at the OS level and reduce OS exposure to threat, thereby mitigating associated risks. Hardening involves activities such as secure configuration, regular updating, setting the rules and policies to enhance system security and removing unnecessary applications and services.
- Physical security also is a key factor in maintaining OS security. Operating system files and code are installed on a systems disk drive and an attacker can take advantage of physical access to tamper with OS files, which can lead to security breaches. Deploying various types of physical controls is a means to prevent physical access and combined with the use of multi-factor authentication can ensure that access to system files is denied even if physical controls are bypassed.
- A lax approach to implementing security patches and OS updates can keep the door open for hackers to exploit. Sometimes these are put off as patching may involve downtime, but security teams must ensure timely updates so that this does not become a security threat and allow hackers who can also track unpatched OS to gain entry.

Microsoft Windows is by far the most extensively used computer (desktop, server, laptop, tablet and console) OS in the world, with a market share of over 70%. For mobile devices, Android has a similar market share. Other OSs for servers, workstations and laptops that are popular in specific market segments are Linux and macOS. Linux is an open-source software and is a derivative of the erstwhile

---

[7] Sara Nguyen, "Windows Was the Target of 83% of All Malware Attacks in Q1 2020," Paubox, accessed July 20, 2021. https://www.paubox.com/blog/windows-target-83-percent-malware-attacks-q1-2020/

popular Unix operating system. Android is a modified version of Linux developed specifically for mobiles devices and tablets.

From a cybersecurity point of view, the operating systems with the highest market share are the most targeted by hackers. OSs have evolved over time to address new security vulnerabilities, requirements and strengthen security wherever required.

Given below is a comparison of the OS-level security features of Windows 10, Linux and macOS across 13 important security areas.[8]

> **Info Box 24: OS-level Security Features Comparison**
>
> **Boot-up Protection**
> - **Windows:** Secure boot, measured boot, also known as trusted boot, are a part of the Windows Defender System Guard Protection. In addition, Configurable Code Integrity (CI) is a feature that allows only previously defined and trusted code to run after the trusted boot process is complete.
> - **Linux:** GRUB 2 and other Linux boot loaders access the Basic Input Output System (BIOS) / Unified Extensible Firmware Interface (UEFI) used to boot the host and ensure integrity of firmware and software running on a platform.
> - **macOS:** Apple has used proprietary protections for boot-level safeguards, details of which are not publicly available.
>
> **Memory Protection**
> - **Windows:** Windows features for memory protections aimed at providing protection against initial exploits, zero-day protection and privilege escalation are gathered under the Windows Defender Exploit Guard.
> - **Linux:** All memory pages are linked with a protection key. Memory protection keys offer a tool for implementing page-based protections but do not require modification of the page tables when an application changes the protection domain.
> - **macOS:** Macs have an XD (execute disable) feature built into Intel's processors that stops the memory utilized for data and memory utilized for executable instructions from accessing each other.
>
> **Logon/Authentication**
> - **Windows:** Windows logon authentication security features include passwords, biometrics, digital certificates and other multi-factor devices, such as smartcards and USB authentication tokens.
> - **Linux:** Pluggable Authentication Modules for Linux is a set of shared libraries that enable the local system administrator to choose how applications authenticate users.
> - **macOS:** Since 2017, Macs have been shipped with the T2 chipset, which along with a new Start-up Security Utility, which provides firmware protection, acts as an additional security layer to prevent unauthorized access.

---

[8] Roger A Grimes and Michael deAgonia, "Microsoft Windows 10 vs. Apple macOS: 18 Security Features Compared," InsiderPro, accessed March 20, 2022. https://www.idginsiderpro.com/article/3267893/microsoft-windows-10-vs-apple-macos-18-security-features-compared.html

Data Protection
- **Windows:** Windows provides file and folder encryption (Encrypting File System). BitLocker Drive Encryption is another feature that enables full-volume encryption to address threats of data theft or exposure from lost, stolen or improperly decommissioned computers.
- **Linux:** As Linux systems are less susceptible to cyberattacks, data residing on them is believed to be more secure and easier to protect.
- **macOS:** FileVault 2 is a utility for encrypting start-up disks to prevent unauthorized access.

Privilege Escalation
- **Windows:** Windows Defender Exploit Guard provides first-line protection from privilege escalation attacks. Features like User Account Control can be also used to de-elevate a privileged user.
- **Linux:** Experts suggest that using defence-in-depth is an effective way to counter Linux privilege escalations in a Linux environment.
- **macOS:** There are a few protections to prevent unfamiliar users from making mistakes related to deleting system folders and similar common mistakes.

Application Protection
- **Windows:** Windows Defender Application Control (WDAC) allows system administrators to set a specific level of application control based on what they think is most appropriate. They can choose from utilities like AppLocker, Device Guard, CI and WDAC.
- **Linux:** Linux provides password authentication, file system discretionary access control and security auditing as a means of application protection.
- **macOS:** Gatekeeper is a security feature that verifies the digital signature of software before apps can be installed. If, for any reason, the checks fail, the apps need to be signed by Apple to run on the system.

Browser Protection
- **Windows:** Windows replaced Internet Explorer with Microsoft Edge, which has much less code and surface area and therefore offers greater security. Edge also places greater restrictions on applications and websites, making it more secure.
- **Linux:** Linux per se does not have a native browser, but Firefox is used as the default browser for most Linux distributions. Firefox offers a safe browsing experience and allows control of personal information shared online, security indicators and malware protection.
- **macOS:** Safari, which is Apple's web browser, provides security features such as anti-phishing technology, settings to prevent cross-site tracking and a strong-password generator with links to the iCloud Keychain.

File Integrity Protections
- **Windows:** Windows provides file protection process through the System File Protection (SFP) utility that helps restore critical files that may have been deleted. Windows allows the assignment of every user, file and process a Mandatory Integrity Control (MIC) level such as high, medium or low in a way such that processes of lower MICs cannot modify objects of higher MICs.

- **Linux:** There are multiple ways to check file integrity on
  (a) Hashbrown
  (b) Checksum
  (c) GtkHash
  (d) KDE Dolphin
  (e) Hasher
  (f) The Linux Command Line
- **macOS:** System Integrity Protection (SIP) is a security feature that is designed to protect content and permissions of system critical files and directories from being tampered with even from the root (if hackers install malware or gain unauthorized access). Other features include protection against code injections, unsigned kernel extensions, code and real-time modifications to code without specific permissions.

Disk/Data Back-up and Restore

- **Windows:** Windows has a back-up and restore feature that enables back up of the most used files such as Configuration Settings, My Documents, Desktop, etc. Users can also include and exclude any files and folders when making the back-up schedule.
- **Linux:** Rsync is a Linux command line tool for files and directories.
- **macOS:** Time Machine is a utility that can be scheduled to maintain daily, weekly and monthly back-ups through consolidation.

Anti-Malware Protection

- **Windows:** Windows Defender Antivirus is an un-intrusive anti-malware utility that works with Smartscreen and Windows Defender Exploit Guard.
- **Linux:** While there are third-party anti-virus tools available for Linux, they are not as widely deployed as Windows versions due to reduced threat perceptions related to Linux malware.
- **macOS:** Apple maintains a blacklist of known malware threats and provides warning if such files are opened by users.

Firewalls

- **Windows:** Windows has an always-on firewall which can be used for defining rules, denying/restricting outgoing connections and incorporating additional rules which can be created by user, group, admins, networks, services or applications.
- **Linux:** Most Linux distributions come with a built-in kernel firewall and one which has to be configured and activated.
- **macOS:** Apple provides a firewall on all Macs, but it is disabled by default and needs to be configured and activated.

Network/Wireless Protection

- **Windows:** Windows maintains and manages different network or wireless elements such as firewall, router and other security settings to be enforced on a per-connection basis.
- **Linux:** Command-line Tools and Utilities for Network Management are available for network security.

- **macOS:** Apple devices feature built-in network security technologies that authorise users and help protect their data during transmission.

Remote Access Protection

- **Windows:** Remote Desktop (RDP) sessions which many consider as vulnerable are protected through an encrypted channel, preventing anyone from viewing a session by listening on the network.
- **Linux:** X2Go is an open-source cross-platform remote desktop software similar to RDP, which offers remote access using a protocol, which is tunnelled through the Secure Shell protocol for better encryption of data.
- **macOS:** Mac supports RDP and other protocols for remote access, including native support for Secure Shell (SSH) and secure file transfer protocol.

Android and iOS Security

The use of Android OS for mobile phones and other devices is widespread in spite of the fact that iOS-based devices are considered more secure. Some of the key vulnerabilities include sideloading of apps, vulnerable storage, weak authentication and insecure inter-process communication attributable to Android Debug Bridge (ABD), a utility that allows anyone to connect to a device, install apps and execute commands without authentication.

Table 5.7 Prominent Android security apps

Avast Mobile Security	VIPRE	Safe Security
Malware Bytes	Bouncer	Firefox Focus
Sophos	Nox	Lookout

Xcode represents Apple's integrated development environment, used to develop software for macOS, iOS, iPadOS, watchOS and tvOS. Hackers have been known to target Xcode with malware like Xcodespy and XcodeGhost.

Table 5.8 Prominent iOS security apps

Norton 360 for iOS	TotalAV	Bitdefender
Mobishield	Avira	Lookout

It must be understood that the above comparison represents only a point-in-time snapshot as OSs are constantly undergoing updates and upgrades, perhaps more than any other software, and hence, all the features listed above are subject to change and enhancements.

5.8 DATABASE SECURITY

Databases hold a lot of critical organizational information, including customer and employee information, transactional data, financial data, supplier information, etc. They are sometimes referred to as the information backbone of an organization. It is therefore critical that databases are adequately protected against threats and that the confidentiality, integrity and availability of data is maintained at all times.

> **Info Box 25: Database Security Statistics**
>
> Two important statistics are useful in understanding the importance of database security:
>
> 1. It can take under ten seconds for an average hacker to get in and out of a database with a treasure of valuable data.[9]
> 2. Databases are the top assets involved in breaches (19.6%), followed by POS terminals (15.8%), POS controllers (15.8%) and Web Apps (13.7%).[10]

A single vulnerability in a database can compromise substantial amounts of sensitive data. Hackers are well aware that if they crack database security, they are in for a bonanza. Here are certain key issues in database security and approaches to mitigating related risks:

- Database injection attacks are one of the oldest, most prevalent and highly dangerous security threats to database security. By exploiting the application vulnerabilities, SQL injection attacks can be launched and, if successful, can provide the hacker with almost unlimited access to a database and help avoid the use of dynamic queries.
- The abuse and mismanagement of user privileges is another security issue related to database security. Allowing privileges beyond a user's job function and not disabling privileges granted to employees who have left the organization can leave room for misuse that can lead to compromise of database security.
- Malware is a constant security issue for all elements of an IT infrastructure and databases are no exception.
- Unmanaged databases containing sensitive data, unprotected back-up databases and human errors are also critical issues related to database security.

Best practices related to database security include the following:

- Regular assessment of database vulnerabilities
- Classifying all sensitive data
- Active management of user rights and privileges
- Monitoring database access activity and usage to detect any data leakages
- Barring malicious web requests
- Encryption of data bases, implementing proper back-up and archival processes
- Employee training in identifying database security threats

5.9 USER MANAGEMENT

User management refers to the performance of administrative functions for the management and control of user access to various parts of the IT infrastructure of an organization, including networks, systems, applications, devices, storage systems, cloud services, and more. Administering and controlling user access to IT infrastructure is a fundamental security requirement for any organization. User

---

[9] Kelly Jackson Higgins, "Hacker's Choice: Top Six Database Attacks", Dark Reading, published May 8, 2008. https://www.darkreading.com/risk/hacker-s-choice-top-six-database-attacks

[10] Sydny Shepard. "Report Finds Over 75 Percent of IT Breaches Are Motivated by Money", Security Today, accessed September 28, 2022. https://securitytoday.com/articles/2018/05/17/report-finds-over-75-percent-of-it-breaches-are-motivated-by-money.aspx

management functions are the core of identity and access management which enable onboarding and offboarding user access to IT infrastructure. In addition, directory services are used for authentication, authorization and audit of user access based on the administrative policies and controls. The important security issues related to identity and access management are as follows:

- One of the basic issues that IT teams need to address is to have complete visibility of which user has access to what applications and data and what they can do with it. While this may sound elementary, it is difficult particularly where cloud applications are being used and they do not offer the facility of generating such reports. Even if a few applications do offer the facility, IT and security teams will need to collate such information across multiple applications and have visibility on an ongoing basis. With the rising number of cloud-based applications, this task becomes more complicated and difficult. Organizations deploy Single Sign-On (SSO) solutions to overcome this challenge as users through a single log-in can access all applications, whether on the cloud or on-premises. Microsoft Active Directory (AD) is perhaps the most popular SSO which provides an active and authoritative user directory that regulates access to key IT services, such as email and file sharing. However, SSO also has its fair share of problems and risks. Hackers can get instant and extensive access by gaining access to an authenticated account. Ways to overcome SSO-related risks is by using multi-factor authentication, enforcing strong security policies, restricting endpoints from where a user can log in and implementing privileged session management.
- Managing access for remote workers brings into play several security vulnerabilities. Prime among them is access control and the management of other user privileges. In a post–Covid-19 world, onboarding and de-boarding need to be performed remotely in consonance with other HR processes. The challenge is that now the organization's perimeter is not at the network level, but at the identity level. If not managed properly and actively, it can pose a threat to an organization's information security. The way to manage this is to provide browser-based SSO to all user applications, which must be further subjected to controls related to the user's context, such as location, device and behaviour.
- Another security issue related to access management stems from the fact that IT teams often struggle to keep pace with integration of new applications. Every time a new vendor application is introduced into the enterprise, a process of integration needs to be set in motion. This is not a one-time activity as IT teams need to track changes and address maintenance requirements of new versions. IT teams need to develop ways for making the addition of new applications and their integration into an SSO and user management functions as easy as adding an app on your phone.

5.10 PHYSICAL SECURITY OF IT ASSETS

When we think of cybersecurity, we often think of all IT-related aspects of security and seem to neglect controls related to physical security. Organizations would do well to integrate physical security practices into their enterprise-wide cybersecurity programs as, in the absence of appropriate protection measures in place, an organization could be left vulnerable to physical threats. Key issues related to physical security are:

- Theft of data files and IT equipment
- Absence of visitor logs and protections to prevent tailgating
- Identification theft
- Lack of access controls to sensitive zones
- Lack of surveillance and vigilance

Issues relating to physical security can be addressed through intelligent and proactive design and layering of security controls as well as raising awareness among employees and encouraging them to take an active stance in defending their workplace against diverse types of physical security threats.

5.10.1 Surveillance Systems

Modern organizations strategically deploy surveillance systems to protect themselves from security breaches. Several security cameras and other security devices use IP protocols and are connected to organization networks. Hacking of security cameras is not limited to using them as bots to launch DDoS attacks, but to 'watch over' whatever is happening within the organization. The security ramifications of web cameras are, by no means, limited to hacking. Hackers can gain a ringside view of internal happenings and steal video footage for their malicious purposes.

> **Info Box 26: Mirai Botnet Attack**
>
> The famous Mirai botnet attack (also known as the Dyn attack), which took place in 2016, was launched by hackers using IP cameras and other surveillance devices like digital video recorders (DVRs) as bots.
>
> The attack was massive, shutting down a big section of the Internet and affecting the operations of a large part of the Internet. Internet users could not access the services of high-profile sites like Airbnb, Amazon, GitHub, HBO, Netflix, PayPal, Reddit and Twitter for several hours.
>
> Part of the blame for devices being compromised can be laid at the doorstep of the manufacturers who did not prioritize cybersecurity while developing their products, but deployment teams were also negligent as they continued to use the default passwords provided by the manufacturers.
>
> The use and reuse of default or insecure passwords can develop into a serious threat. Manufacturers must insist that users and administrators change the passwords after deployment so that the attention of deployers is drawn to associated vulnerabilities.[11]

Managing security issues across all devices can be challenging as it involves ongoing visibility of the devices and their vulnerabilities. Further, handling a mix of legacy and new devices often involves working with suppliers to get a security fix where it is required. IT teams also need to track updates and maintain devices through their life cycle and replace them if no support is forthcoming from their suppliers.

5.11 TECHNIQUES/METHODS FOR DATA SECURITY AND PROTECTION

Data security and protection are increasingly becoming key requirements in several regulations across industry sectors. Organizations are facing twin pressures from regulatory authorities and consumers to ensure that data is safe and well protected throughout the data life cycle. There are several methods and techniques that can be deployed to ensure the confidentiality, integrity and availability of data.

Firstly, it is important to understand what types of the organization's data is at greatest risk. Depending on the level of risk for each category of data, appropriate security controls and protection methods can be deployed. Undertaking a risk assessment is a good first step that can help accomplish

---

[11] Brian Buntz, "5 Cybersecurity Lessons Related to IP Security Cameras," IOT World Today, accessed July 21, 2021. https://www.iotworldtoday.com/2019/08/31/5-cybersecurity-lessons-related-to-ip-security-cameras/

this. Once the data to be protected has been identified and classified based on relative sensitivity of the data and the likelihood of a breach based on existing controls, the following methods can be adopted. Some of the techniques/methods involving data security and data protection are covered in greater detail in Chapter 7 (Cybersecurity Technologies).

5.11.1 Encryption

To ensure data security, any high-risk data must be stored, used and transmitted in encrypted form. While any type of data can be encrypted, it is more important to encrypt sensitive information such as intellectual property, personal data of employees and customers, passwords, databases, emails and any other data that is of value to a hacker. Encryption ensures that data is stored in an incomprehensible format, also known as cypher text, by using an encryption algorithm so that only those authorized to view the information can do so with the use of secret cryptographic keys. A cryptographic key is a set of mathematical values that both the transmitter and the receiver of an encrypted message agree upon.

Two types of cryptographic keys are widely used today: symmetric and asymmetric. In symmetric form of encryption, the same key is used for encryption and decryption. Commonly used algorithms for symmetric keys are Advanced Encryption Standard (AES), Triple Data Encryption Algorithm (3DES) and SNOW word-based synchronous stream ciphers.

In asymmetric encryption, two keys are used. The key used for encryption is called a public key as it is shared publicly, while the private or secret key is kept confidential. While the public key and the private keys are different, they are mathematically linked to each other. Commonly used algorithms for asymmetric keys are Rivest–Shamir–Adleman (RSA) and Elliptic Curve Algorithm, which is based on the algebraic structure of elliptic curves over finite fields.

It is important to note that asymmetric and symmetric encryption is the technology that supports SSL encryption and the more secure TLS encryption, which protect data transmitted over the internet or computer network. SSL/TLS are necessary for securely exchanging sensitive data such as passwords, payment data, etc. More details on encryption techniques and methods are given in Chapter 7.

5.11.2 Access Control

Access control is a critical component of any security program to prevent and protect systems and data from any form of intrusion or unauthorised access. Broadly speaking, access control can be described as the selective restriction of access to systems and data through the processes of authentication and authorization.

While authentication ensures that the person requesting access is who he claims to be, authorization determines whether or not a user should be allowed access. In the absence of these two processes, there really can be no data security. Another reason for implementing robust access control systems is that hackers are on the lookout for harvesting user log-in credentials to sell them in the underground web markets.

Access control in an organizational context is enforced through policies and security controls such as authentication and authorization systems. Most organizations work in hybrid environments (cloud and on-premises), allow employees to work from anywhere (from homes to airports to cafes) and use multiple types of devices (desktops, laptops, tablets and phones), which give rise to different types of security issues. It is also required that access control mechanisms be adaptable to these changing contexts and realities.

Organizations need to choose an appropriate model(s) (Table 5.9) for the access control based on the type of information they are trying to protect for compliance and operational requirements.

Table 5.9 Models for access control

Access control model	Assignment of access rights
Discretionary	Access rights are assigned on the basis of user/data owner requirements
Mandatory	A central authority assigns the access rights
Role-based	Access rights are assigned as deemed necessary for the performance of job function
Attributed-based	This is a dynamic methodology of granting access based on user context and attributes such as geolocation, position, time of day, biometrics, etc.

Organizations who have implemented strong access control policies and mechanisms such as multi-factor authentication (including the use of biometrics), are better off than those who have not, but even for them, authorization still remains an area of concern due to the fact that it requires continuous and perpetual monitoring of who is accessing what data and why. It also requires ongoing assessment of whether existing authorization schemes and controls are required and relevant. The dynamic nature of changing requirements and large number of applications make the task of ensuring that inconsistent or weak authorization protocols, which can create security holes, are identified and fixed quickly, a difficult one.

Access controls must be monitored and regularly audited to make sure that they are in line with organizational security objectives, governance, risk management standards and compliance requirements. They must be treated as active parts of the IT infrastructure that require regular attention and deployment of the latest tools to address challenges arising from changing contexts and threats.

The implementation of a zero trust access model is rapidly gaining ground to ensure continuous protection and provide a strong and durable means for access control. Zero trust models when implemented ensure that only authenticated and authorized users are able to access applications and data, thereby providing them security from advanced cyber threats. (More on Zero Trust in Chapter 7).

5.11.3 Firewalls and Intrusion Detection Systems

The implementation of various security measures and controls to address the challenges arising from following secure application development practices, network, database, OS level security, user management and access control by themselves are not enough to ensure data security without implementing network protection measures like firewalls and intrusion detection systems to ensure that hackers do not break into your defences and access sensitive data.

Firewalls and intrusion detection systems are akin to the erstwhile fort walls, gates and moats that provided protection to inmates from outside threats and intrusions by adversaries. In a boundaryless digital world, these protection mechanisms today have to protect an 'invisible and extendable virtual perimeter.' While we will examine other aspects of firewalls and intrusion detection systems in Chapter 7, here we will look at some of the security issues around these protection mechanisms

Firewalls are a basic threat protection mechanism that monitor inbound and outbound network traffic and block data packets from suspicious and unsecured sources based on a set of predefined rules. Security issues and limitations with firewalls include misconfiguration of firewalls, their ineffectiveness against non-technical security risks such as social engineering and lack of protection from insider threats. Since firewalls work on a collection of pre-set rules for identifying and blocking suspicious data packets, they are only as effective as the rules are. Improper settings or a software conflict may also result in firewalls that prevent all data from entering, making it appear as a network connectivity problem. Hence, while firewalls block access, they do not signal incoming attacks. Next-generation firewalls provide enhanced features like advanced network device filtering functions in the form of application firewalls with inline deep packet inspection along with intrusion prevention.

An intrusion detection system (IDS) is a device or software application that monitors a network or system to detect policy violations or other forms of suspicious and malicious activity. An intrusion detection and prevention system (IDPS) goes beyond detection to pre-emptively prevent application attacks such as blocking remote file inclusions that enable malware injections or SQL injections. Key security issues related to IDS/IDPS are that they require experts to ensure proper adaptation of the sensor to its network, host and application environments and that they have been found to be incapable of analyzing encrypted traffic at the application layer. Sizing an IDPS and balancing between false positives and false negatives can also be difficult.

5.11.4 Pseudonymization

Pseudonymization is a useful method which removes identifiers from data sets and replaces them with randomly generated strings. Since the pseudonymized data cannot be identified to a person, it is safe in the event of a data breach. While undertaking pseudonymization, some of the key decision points are:

- Encryption type for de-identification
- Surrogate annotation for re-identification of unstructured data
- Whether the character set, length or record structure are to be preserved
- Whether it is reversible, that is, re-identifiable using cryptographic key or surrogate annotation
- Whether referential integrity (relationship between records) is to be maintained or not

Several regulations around the world mandate the use of anonymization and pseudo anonymization as a means for protecting sensitive personal information of citizens and consumers.

5.11.5 Back-ups, Snapshots and Replication

Maintaining up-to-date back-ups, snapshots and online replication of data is essential for ensuring data protection, especially against wiper and ransomware attacks. The 3-2-1 back-up rule is a very effective way of keeping data safe from various types of threat scenarios. Here, 3 stands for maintaining at least three copies of back-ups; 2 stands for keeping back-ups on two different storage media such as tapes and CDs and 1 stands for keeping one of them at an off-site location.

5.11.6 Data Loss Prevention Solutions

Data Loss Prevention (DLP) comprises a set of strategies and tools that safeguards data from being stolen, leaked, lost, accessed by unauthorized users or accidentally erased. The most important characteristic of DLP tools is content inspection. The tools work by using policy-based rules and spotting violations. Recent versions also incorporate machine learning to identifying behaviour patterns suggestive of a data breach and stopping it. There are different DLP tools for network, cloud and endpoint security.

5.11.7 Storage with Built-in Data Protection

Current-day storage systems provide features like built-in disk clustering, ransomware protection and redundancy which are useful in implementing data security.

5.11.8 Remote Access Security

There are also new age remote access data protection software applications that provide application-layer cryptographic VPN remote access and advanced data protection by combining other features such as multi-factor authentication, eSigning and crypto consent-based transaction authorization, thereby providing additional layers of data security.

5.12 ISSUES RELATED TO DIGITAL FILE SHARING

The Internet has enabled sharing on an unprecedented scale of all types of information. Digital information is easily and quickly sharable in different file formats and through different means such as emails, messaging, file transfer protocol programs, online file sharing services, peer-to-peer networks, removable storage media and other file transfer methodologies. File sharing is defined as the act of sharing, distributing or providing access to digital media like computer software programs, multimedia files (audios, photos and/or videos), data files and other electronic documents or electronic books/magazines.

In this section, we shall discuss security-related issues and implications related to security, legality and ethics that could arise from file sharing.

It is today an established fact that information held and used in business enterprises, military establishments, financial services organizations and practically every organization is of immense value. Any kind of compromise of sensitive information can cause great harm not only if hackers gain unauthorized access, or accomplish a large-scale data breach, but by the simple act of file sharing either intentionally as a part of regular operations or accidentally or maliciously.

In the organizational context, while cybersecurity personnel are focused on preventing network intrusions and data breaches, file sharing remains a weak point from a security perspective as it is largely in the hands of employees whether to share a particular file. Common security risks in file sharing apart from compromising the content itself can arise from downloading an illegal or copyrighted file, deploying a file sharing application that calls for/requests shutting down of firewall services, downloading files containing malware, accidentally placing sensitive files in the public domain or through theft or loss of computers or portable electronic devices/media. Even at an individual level, the same security risks are applicable when it comes to storage and sharing of personal information.

Info Box 27: Common Tips for Storing and Sharing Sensitive Information

- Lock down computers and laptops when not in use.
- Store sensitive information in encrypted format.
- Use features for securing files such as encryption and password protection while sending them.
- Information that is no longer required should be destroyed or deleted securely.
- Before hardware or media is deployed for other purposes, data must be deleted securely.
- Destroy or securely delete sensitive data prior to re-use or disposal of equipment or media.
- Ensure extra physical security and implement multi-factor authentication for portable devices and media and do not leave them unprotected.
- Make sure that employees are aware of what is within organizational rules and policies when it comes to sharing files with internal and external persons/organizations.
- Be aware of the regulations and contractual obligations (including non-disclosure agreements) that prohibit/restrict the circulation of data being shared.

Due to the ongoing Covid-19 pandemic, the shifting of most companies to the cloud and to remote working has become a necessity. This has made file sharing an even more pertinent issue. Here, the importance of educating employees of the risk involved while sharing files and the need for enhanced awareness as well as focusing on ensuring that security measures and procedures are followed cannot be overstated.

One of the most fundamental and often forgotten aspects is the labeling and ascribing of security levels to each file, the absence of which makes its distribution and sharing discretionary in the hands of the person having access to the file. Updating security policies to reflect these new concerns, programs to sensitize employees regarding secure information sharing and using an active directory for and limiting access to sensitive files can prevent accidental damage or deletion.

The following legal issues with respect to file sharing are also important to consider. Generally speaking, file sharing is not an illegal activity and represents a substantial quantity of overall activity on the Internet. However, if copyrighted and unauthorized or unlicensed files are shared then it constitutes a violation of law and amounts to piracy of content.

In spite of legal regimes around the world being concerned about illegal digital file sharing using various laws and enforcement mechanisms, digital files containing music, movies and software are being illegally shared causing losses of billions of dollars to creators and owners of intellectual property. Legal issues arise when peer-to-peer (P2P networks) and torrent applications are used for sharing/distributing and duplication of copyrighted content.

Users are often confused regarding the legality of downloading or sharing files as access to information and files is often freely available on the Internet. It is vital to realize that when a user downloads pirated content, hotlinks a website, reposts, copies or shares digital works protected under copyright from these websites can be subjected to civil and criminal liabilities.

From a user's viewpoint, one of the defences for copyright violations related to sharing digital content is the concept of 'fair use.' Fair use allows the use of limited portions of copyrighted works without authorization from the copyright owner for the select purposes of scholarship, criticism and research.

QUICK TEST

1. A disruption or failure in a mission critical application may still enable an organization to conduct its business albeit with decreased productivity, degradation of user experience or interruption of some support services.
   a. True
   b. False
2. SAST tools enable application security testing by:
   a. Analyzing running code
   b. Analyzing vulnerabilities in applications used with mobile platforms
   c. Only a
   d. a and b
   e. None of the above
3. DevOps is a concept that promotes members of development and operational teams working together collaboratively and iteratively to ensure that security aspects related to operational issues are adequately addressed.
   a. True
   b. False
4. Software Assurance Maturity Model (SAMM) is a:
   a. Descriptive methodology that can be used to benchmark your security development practices in terms of maturity.
   b. Prescriptive methodology which is maintained by OWASP and provides roadmap templates for different types of organizations.
   c. Both a and b
   d. None of the above
5. Key reasons for hardware-related vulnerabilities in IoT devices are as follows:
   a. Vendors are more concerned about functionality and cost as there are no global security standards for these devices.
   b. Devices are constrained by hardware to incorporate security mechanisms.
   c. Devices use different transmission protocols and methods, making standardization difficult.
   d. Components used in these devices have their own vulnerabilities.
   e. IT teams and users have limited understanding of security issues on these devices as well as visibility in the context of an enterprise network.
   f. All of the above
   g. a, b, c, d
6. Physical security also is a key factor in maintaining OS security.
   a. True
   b. False
7. Key issues in physical security are:
   a. Theft of data files and IT equipment
   b. Absence of visitor logs and protections to prevent tailgating
   c. Identification theft
   d. Lack of access controls to sensitive zones
   e. All of the above
   f. a, b, and d only

8. Access control in an organizational context is enforced through policies and security controls such as authentication and authorization systems.
   a. True
   b. False
9. Firewalls are ineffective in ensuring security against non-technical risks.
   a. True
   b. False
10. Next-generation firewalls provide the following in addition to traditional functions:
    a. Network device filtering functions
    b. Inline deep packet inspection
    c. Intrusion prevention
    d. All of the above
    e. Only a and b

QUESTIONS

1. Development of secure information systems involves the implementation of strategies and technologies for data security and data protection. Explain the distinction between the two concepts.
2. The evolution of application security development has not only seen changes in methodologies and testing technology, but also in terms of enhancing communication and coordination between the development and operations teams. Discuss the emergence of concepts like DevOps and DevSecOps in this context.
3. Discuss the issues involved in developing an effective security design and architecture for an organization.
4. Describe the key challenges and security issues in network security.
5. A single vulnerability in a database can compromise substantial amounts of sensitive data. Explain this statement with examples.
6. Administering and controlling user access to IT infrastructure is a fundamental security requirement for any organization. Discuss the pros and cons of implementing Single Sign-On systems.
7. Describe key challenges in managing security issues related to surveillance systems.
8. Explain the importance and challenges in user management with regard to security issues.
9. How can implementing a zero-trust approach provide more secure access control?
10. Explain the limitations of firewalls and how intrusion detection systems can lead to security breaches.

ANSWER KEYS

Quick Test

1. (b)
2. (e)
3. (a)
4. (b)
5. (f)
6. (a)
7. (e)
8. (a)
9. (a)
10. (d)

6 Cybersecurity Strategies and Approaches

> **OBJECTIVES** ·
>
> *At the end of this chapter, you will be able to:*
>
> - ☑ List the issues and challenges involved in information security governance and risk management
> - ☑ Explain the cyber risk management approaches and strategies and the role of frameworks such as ISO/IEC 27001 and NIST
> - ☑ Describe the concept and context of cyber resilience and its integration into cybersecurity and risk management programs
> - ☑ Explain the role of industry-specific frameworks such as HIPAA, PCI DSS and NY CRR 500 and region-specific regulations such as GDPR
> - ☑ Explain the importance of human issues and list the best practices that can help in getting employees to take an active part in cybersecurity

6.0 INTRODUCTION

With the progressively increasing frequency of cyberattacks, combined with sophisticated techniques used by hackers, managing cyber risks is harder than ever before. Ensuring that security architectures are aligned with business objectives, compliant with regulations and address all kinds of cyber risks is extremely complicated, even for the most skilled security teams. Managing risks from cloud services, third-party vendors and an increasingly remotely operating workforce are added dimensions to present-day cyber risk management.

How much cybersecurity is adequate for an organization? The short answer is that it depends. Also implied in the answer is the fact that no amount of security can make the IT systems of an organization completely immune to cyberattacks and data breaches, and yet, organizations must continue to evaluate business risks, prioritize them in order of impact and likelihood of materializing and commit themselves to implementing a coordinated cybersecurity strategy. The challenge is further exacerbated by a dynamic technology and threat environment. The following are some of the actions that organizations can take to enhance their security posture and mitigate risks:

- Identify existing and emerging cyber risks, including risks from third-party vendors
- Develop robust security policies, control procedures and enforcement mechanisms
- Design and implement control mechanisms
- Incorporate compliance requirements from applicable regulations
- Sensitise and train employees in identifying and responding to cyber threats
- Implement risk mitigation technologies and strategies
- Undertake security audits and take corrective action

Adopting cybersecurity standards and frameworks is an excellent way to implement cybersecurity strategies that include all of the above as they provide the necessary guidance along with a tested collection of best practices from different industry sectors as well as geographies from around the world. In effect, implementing a framework enables a coordinated, disciplined and unified approach to cybersecurity and ensures that organizations go through a structured risk management process to continuously upgrade security, monitoring their overall cybersecurity effectiveness, undertaking regular re-assessment of risks, ongoing appraisal of security controls and evaluating mitigation efforts.

6.1 INFORMATION SECURITY GOVERNANCE AND RISK MANAGEMENT

The goal of information security is to ensure the confidentiality, integrity and availability of an organization's information assets. The path to accomplish this involves information security governance, which is "the development, documentation, implementation and updating of policies, standards, procedures and guidelines for risk management, which necessitates the identification and classification of an organization's information assets, identifying risks and vulnerabilities so that effective security measures and controls can be implemented and monitored. With increasing regulation, this also extends to compliance with all legal and regulatory requirements".

The ever-increasing dependence on information technology (IT) elevates the level of cyber risk to a key business risk. Essentially, an information security GRC (governance, risk and compliance) strategy is important because it ties together all of an organization's cyber risk, compliance and governance functions into one strategy and ideally integrates with the organization's overall enterprise risk management (ERM) strategy.

The nature of cyber risks is such that cybersecurity can never ensure total or perpetual immunity from them. Hence, cyber risk management is not a problem to be solved, but a risk that must be managed.

> **Info Box 28: Governance and Management**
>
> It is important to understand the distinction between governance and management. While governance refers to providing leadership through structure, processes, guidance and direction, management is more to do with execution, operation and control.

The key challenges organizations face in establishing an effective cybersecurity governance program are:[1]

- Articulating a clear definition of its risk management policies, strategy and goals
- Standardizing processes that are repeatable and consistent
- Clear assignment of responsibilities and accountability and its enforcement
- Senior leadership engagement and oversight
- Adequate resource allocation
- Cybersecurity skills and employee training

The origins of cybersecurity management lie in the traditional approach, which was focused on prevention and building an organization's capability to withstand security threats. As newer and more severe forms of threats began to emerge, cybersecurity management evolved into a risk-focused approach, which is now widely known as cyber risk management. However, the two terms are focused on prevention and data protection.

---

[1] Seth Swinton and Stephanie Hedges, "Cybersecurity Governance, Part 1: 5 Fundamental Challenges," Carnegie MellonUniversity, *Software Engineering Institute* (blog), accessed July 24, 2021. https://insights.sei.cmu.edu/blog/cybersecurity-governance-part-1-5-fundamental-challenges/

6.2 CYBER RISK MANAGEMENT

It is often said that there is no silver bullet to address cybersecurity. Organizations have turned to a risk-based approach to ensure that the cyber risks that have the biggest impact on their businesses are focused upon, resources and controls are aligned to prevent those risks from materializing and, in the event that they do, to mitigate the impact.

Cyber risk management is "the process of identifying the risks that your organization is likely to face and then prioritizing and choosing and implementing the security controls, technologies, best practices and policies to reduce or mitigate these risks".[2]

The purpose of developing a cyber risk management plan or program is not only to identify and prioritize risks and implement suitable defences and controls, but also to determine the type of treatment for each risk. Not long ago, the job of managing cyber risks was entrusted to IT departments but given the magnitude of harm cyber risks can cause and the rising frequency of cyberattacks, the issue has escalated to a management and board-level issue. Further, cyber risk management today must be the concern of all employees in an organization and effective mitigation of cyber risks calls for participation of all functions and groups of employees.

Today, every organization, big or small, that has a significant digital footprint needs to practice cyber risk management in order to protect its information systems and data. They can do so by following a structured process as is shown in Fig. 6.1.

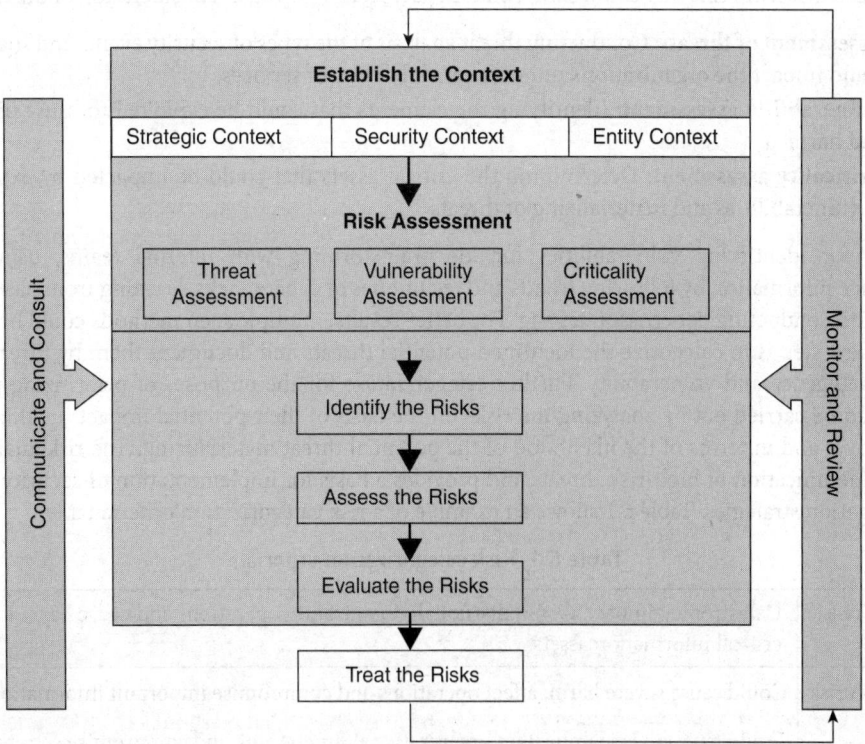

Figure 6.1 Risk management process

---

[2] Sigler, KE and Rainey III, JL. "Cybersecurity Risk Management," in *Securing an IT Organization through Governance, Risk Management, and Audit* (Auerbach Publications: 2015) 32–59.

Cyber risk management revolves around the security risks faced by an organization, which are in the form of loss of confidentiality, integrity and availability of information assets and, with the adoption of IoT technologies as well as convergence of IT and OT systems, could extend to physical harm of people. Hence, assessment of risk becomes a critical activity in the cyber risk management process. In order to undertake a risk assessment exercise, organizations must first establish the context from a strategic, security and entity points of view. This involves defining the scope of the risk management process in terms of the context of the organization's objectives and the criteria against which risks will be assessed.

Each organization, even if it belongs to the same industry sector, may have a different context for its risk assessment depending upon its own objectives, types of internal systems and methods – often referred to as its 'risk profile'. Another factor that is becoming increasingly important is the area of shared risks. These constitute risks shared with supply chain partners, outsourcing partners and service providers. This extends the context of entity for the organization to what is today called the 'extended enterprise'.

The context for the risk assessment must also be established in terms of the organization's own risk tolerance or risk appetite as it has a bearing on the evaluation and treatment of risks. The risk tolerance levels in terms of the expectations from efforts of mitigation and acceptance in dealing with specific types of risk must be articulated along with the boundaries and thresholds for acceptable level of risk taking and the required actions in case of breach of these levels. A methodology for the risk assessment exercise must also be selected at this stage.

Identification of risks that could compromise cybersecurity involves consideration of the following:

- **Assessment of threats**: Conducting threat analysis of the types of security events and sources that could impact the organization's uninterrupted delivery of services.
- **Vulnerability assessment**: Identifying the elements that could be exploited to cause disruption and harm.
- **Criticality assessment**: Determining the critical assets that could be impacted by exploitation of vulnerabilities and materializing of threats.

Methods for identifying vulnerabilities include brainstorming with internal teams, using threat intelligence information by following trends and techniques of cyberattacks, learning from past security failures and conducting penetration testing. For better results, multiple such methods could be used.

The next step is to categorize the identified potential threats and document them by threat source, threat intelligence and vulnerability. Further categorization for the purposes of prioritizing potential threats can be carried out by analyzing the risks on the basis of their potential impact (qualitative and quantitative) and in terms of the likelihood of the potential threat materializing. The risk analysis step helps in identification of high-risk threats and provides a basis for implementation of security controls and mitigation strategies. Table 6.1 shows an example of a risk categorization criteria table.

Table 6.1 Risk categorization criteria

Critical risk	Catastrophic impact. Could disrupt all organization operations and cause harm to critical information assets.
Very high risk	Could cause severe harm, affect operations and compromise important information assets.
High risk	Could have adverse impact on organizational functioning and compromise sensitive information.

(Continued)

Table 6.1 (*Continued*)

Critical risk	Catastrophic impact. Could disrupt all organization operations and cause harm to critical information assets.
Moderate risk	Could cause disruption and operational issues without harming information assets.
Low risk	A threat event that could cause negligible disruption or damage.

Once the potential risks have been identified, listed and subjected to analysis, it is time to apply the criteria regarding risk tolerance, that is, determine whether a risk is acceptable or not. If the risk is acceptable, then the existing controls need to be evaluated for their appropriateness and adequacy. If a risk is unacceptable, then the type of risk treatment that is required to deal with it must be considered.

Organizations have different alternatives to address each risk and due deliberations must be conducted among functional heads and senior leadership to arrive at the **risk treatment** choices. The risk treatment options are:

- To avoid the risk by not undertaking those activities that could cause harm
- To accept the risk and take suitable control measures
- To share the risk with business associates and service providers through contracts
- To transfer the risk through insurance policies

This exercise must be carried out for each risk with responsibilities fixed for follow-up actions and communicated to all concerned. At the end of the exercise, there could be some risks remaining, even after controls have been applied, referred to as residual risks. Organizations must be aware of residual risks and aim to address them with better control or other measures in the future.

The cyber risk management process is not a one-time activity but must be carefully monitored, reviewed and evaluated to confirm if existing controls are still fit for the purpose for which they were originally deployed. The process must be repeated with fixed periodicity (typically at least once a year) or when there are any changes in the cyber threat landscape, technologies, regulations and the organizations systems, objectives and activities.

6.3 CYBERSECURITY FRAMEWORKS

Cyber risk management must become a part of an ERM program for it to be more effective. To enable this to happen, organizations must take the following steps:

1. Align cyber risk management with business objectives.
2. Concentrate the threats and risks unique to the organization.
3. Use a cybersecurity framework such as ISO 27001 and NIST, which are consistent with broader enterprise risk management frameworks such as ISO 31000.

A cybersecurity framework is a comprehensive set of guidelines, best practices and standards that an organization can adopt to make their efforts more structured and effective. The frameworks help in aligning security measures and processes with business objectives. Organizations can use cybersecurity frameworks to lay the foundation of a comprehensive and durable security program that also ensures that all the elements are given due consideration.

> **Info Box 29: What is a Framework?**
>
> Some experts have suggested that a framework would provide a 'table of contents' for a security program, which lists out business requirements, government regulations, best practices, industry standards and requirements as well as other requirements that may be specific to an organization.[3]

Cybersecurity frameworks have been developed based on experiences across industries and geographies to incorporate all the elements required to protect an organization's information assets and provide a structure and methodology for the same. Cybersecurity frameworks and standards have also evolved in the context of regulatory changes and requirements. It is important to understand that the popular frameworks have stood the test of time and provided organizations with much-needed guidance. Cybersecurity frameworks strongly emphasize a risk management approach that forms the basis for the implementation, monitoring and review of security objectives, controls and mechanisms. Cybersecurity frameworks could be regarded as generic (applicable to all industry sectors and geographies), industry-specific or state-mandated (geography-specific). Table 6.2 lists 13 of the top cybersecurity frameworks.

Table 6.2 Top cybersecurity frameworks

Framework/Standard	Applicability	Purpose
International Organization for Standardization (ISO/IEC 27001)	Generic framework used globally	To provide a framework of standards for organizations to protect and manage their information and data
National Institute of Standards and Technology (NIST)	Generic framework used mainly in the USA	To provide guidance for organizations to manage and reduce cybersecurity risk
Control Objectives for Information and Related Technologies (COBIT)	Generic framework	For the development, implementation, monitoring and improvement of IT governance
Center for Information Security (CIS)	Generic framework	To provide a set of information security controls for developing baseline security programs
Health Insurance Portability and Accountability Act (HIPAA) of 1996	Industry-specific (healthcare) and applicable in the USA	To provide guidelines for enabling organizations to implement sufficient controls for securing employee or customer health information
General Data Protection Regulation (GDPR)	Applicable to EU citizens' data	To provide a set of mandatory security requirements for organizations to secure personally identifiable information belonging to European citizens
Federal Information Security Management Act (FISMA)	Specific to US government agencies and vendors	To provide security standards for federal government agencies for implementing adequate measures to protect critical information systems from different types of attacks.

(Continued)

---

[3] "Cyber Security Framework Explained," CISOSHARE Cares, accessed July 7, 2021. https://cisoshare.com/blog/cyber-security-framework-explained/

Table 6.2 (*Continued*)

Framework/Standard	Applicability	Purpose
Service Organization Control (SOC 2)	Generic framework, applicable in the USA	To enable organizations that collect and store personal customer information in cloud services to maintain proper security
New York State Department of Financial Services (NYDFS)	Industry-specific (financial services) in the state of New York	To provide cybersecurity requirements that can enhance financial organizations' security postures and the third parties they work with
Payment Card Industry Data Security Standard (PCI DSS)	Industry-specific (card processing)	To enhance security for consumers by setting guidelines for any company that accepts, stores, processes or transmits credit card information
Information Assurance for Small and Medium Enterprises (IASME)	Generic framework for SMEs, similar to ISO 27001	To provide a basic and affordable framework to help improve the cybersecurity of small and medium-sized enterprises (SMEs)
Committee of Sponsoring Organizations (COSO)	Generic framework, used mainly in the USA	For designing, implementing and evaluating internal control for organizations
Consortium for IT Software Quality (CISQ)	Generic framework	To provide security standards that developers can use when developing software applications

Adopting a cybersecurity framework can help in enhancing the cybersecurity standard of an organization in the following ways:

- Take stock of risks and security standards in the organization.
- Establish a cybersecurity program and a roadmap for the same.
- Implement best practices.
- Identify areas for improving security.
- Incorporate regulatory requirements and monitor compliance.
- Provide a consistent, repeatable, adaptable and cost-effective approach to cybersecurity.
- Ensure security alignment with business objectives.

Of the frameworks listed above, some are mandatory depending upon the industry sector and/or geography where the business operates; some are voluntary such as NIST; and some also allow for third-party certification (ISO standards), which provide assurance and confidence to all stakeholders about the cybersecurity approaches and capability of a particular organization.

We will now examine two of the most widely used frameworks: ISO/IEC 27001 and NIST.

6.3.1 The ISO/IEC Cybersecurity Framework

ISO/IEC 27001 is one the most widely used frameworks for information security management, both in terms of industry sectors and geographical spread. The International Organization for Standardization (ISO) is an international standard-setting institution that has representatives from various national standard bodies. ISO provides a family of standards which comprise the ISO/IEC27000 family. The more prominent among them are listed in Table 6.3.

Table 6.3 ISO 27000 family of standards

ISO/IEC 27000:18	Offers an overview of information security management systems and terms and definitions used in the ISO family of standards.
ISO/IEC 27001	The most well-known standard for information security management, which organizations can deploy to secure their information assets, including financial data, intellectual property, employee data or information entrusted by third parties.
ISO/IEC 27002:2013	Provides guidelines for information security management practices such as selection, implementation and management of controls after taking into account the security risk environment in which the organization operates.

Post implementation of the ISO 27001 standard, an organization can seek certification of its implementation by third-party auditors who are qualified to issue such certifications. Obtaining a certification does not mean that an organization is entirely safe from cyber risks. What it does provide is assurance to stakeholders such as customers, employees, regulators and other third parties that the organization is committed to cybersecurity and that it has adopted a structured and process-driven approach to securing its information assets and those entrusted to it by others. Certification of this standard is recognised around the world and provides the confidence that all required security controls based on threat perception are in place and that there is a process to monitor, review and improve based on performance and new security considerations.

> **Info Box 30: Difference between Frameworks and Standards**
>
> A framework consists of best practices that are usually employed, while standards represent a set of accepted best practices. Also, frameworks provide general guidelines while standards are more specific and represent the best way of doing something. Using frameworks, an organization can also evolve their 'own best way' of doing something.[4]

The ISO/IEC 27001 standard allows an organization the flexibility to choose and implement those controls that are necessary with the caveat that they should provide justification for not implementing particular controls. This helps in ensuring that all controls are given due consideration before selection. A list of controls sets and the number of controls under each of them is given in Table 6.4.

Table 6.4 ISO 27001 control set explained

ISO 27001 control set	Primary purpose	Number of controls
A.5: Information security policies	Managing the direction of information security in consonance with and compliance of organizational requirements.	2
A.6: Organization of information security	Establishing a framework for initiating, controlling and operating information security programs.	7

(*Continued*)

---

[4] Olivia, "Difference Between Standard and Framework," DifferenceBetween.com, accessed July 8, 2021. https://www.differencebetween.com/difference-between-standard-and-vs-framework/

Table 6.4 (*Continued*)

ISO 27001 control set	Primary purpose	Number of controls
A.7: Human resource security	Ensuring that all employees and vendors understand information security and are capable of performing their roles.	6
A.8: Asset management	Identifying assets that form the scope of implementation of information security and protection mechanisms	10
A.9: Access control	Limiting and controlling access to information systems and processing facilities.	14
A.10: Cryptography	Ensuring the effective deployment of cryptographic technology to safeguard the confidentiality, integrity and authenticity of information.	2
A.11: Physical and environmental security	Ensuring protection from unauthorised physical access, tampering or damage to the organisation's information and information processing facilities.	15
A.12: Operations security	Ensuring security of operation of information processing facilities and systems through clear definition of operational procedures and responsibilities.	14
A.13: Communications security	Ensuring protection of communication networks and the information within it and in its information processing infrastructure.	7
A.14: System acquisition, development and maintenance	Making sure that information security is an integral part of information systems through the entire life cycle.	13
A.15: Supplier relationships	Protecting the organisation's valuable assets that are accessible to or affected by suppliers.	5
A.16: Information security incident management	Ensuring a structured and consistent approach to security incidents and following through the life cycle of security incidents.	7
A.17: Business continuity management and information security	Integrating information security continuity into the organisation's business continuity management systems and processes.	4
A.18: Compliance	Ensuring compliance with regulatory, statutory and contractual requirements relating to information security.	8

ISO 27001 mandates that organizations follow a PDCA (Plan, Do, Check, Act) cycle for implementation. The effective implementation of ISO standards requires long-term commitment by the organization's senior leadership, aligning required resources and teams as well as consideration of the following aspects:

1. Defining an information security policy
2. Defining the scope of the implementation
3. Performing a security risk assessment

4. Identifying a risk treatment plan to manage the identified risk
5. Selecting controls to be implemented and applied
6. Undertaking a certification audit
7. Monitoring, reviewing and updating the policy

Implementing the ISO 27001 standard helps organizations meet legal and regulatory requirements, provide audit trails and other evidence of security measures and minimize costs related to data breaches.

6.3.2 NIST Cybersecurity Framework

The National Institute of Standards (NIST) is a non-regulatory US government agency for the enhancement and competitiveness of US organizations through the advancement of measurement science, standards and technology. NIST standards are endorsed by the US government and provide a set of best practices and guidelines, which an organization can use to attain a high standard of cybersecurity. NIST standards are applicable across industries and adoption by organizations is voluntary. NIST guidelines also help organizations comply with specific regulatory requirements. For instance, NIST provides the following guidelines that enable organizations to comply with the Federal Information Security Management Act (FISMA) regulation:[5]

1. Categorize the information assets that you need to protect.
2. Create a baseline for the minimum controls to safeguard the information assets.
3. Perform risk assessments, build and document a security plan.
4. Implement the security controls.
5. Monitor the effectiveness of the implemented controls.
6. Establish your security level based on evaluation of the security controls.
7. Authorize the information system for processing.
8. Keep monitoring the security controls on a continuous basis.

The NIST framework is organized among five core functions. Each of the functions complements the other to represent a security life cycle. Each function consists of multiple categories and sub-categories as shown in Fig. 6.2.

The definitions of the five core functions according to the NIST standard[6] are listed in Table 6.5.

Table 6.5 NIST framework core functions

Identify	Build the organizational context and understanding of managing cybersecurity risks with respect to assets, systems, data and capabilities.
Protect	Determine and implement required safeguards to ensure continued delivery of critical infrastructure services.
Detect	Ascertain and implement the actions required to identify a security event.
Respond	Develop and implement the appropriate activities when facing a detected security event.
Recover	Develop and implement the appropriate activities to ensure resilience and recovery from a security event that impairs systems and/or capabilities.

---

[5] Nate Lord, "What Is NIST Compliance?," Digital Guardian, accessed July 8, 2021. https://digitalguardian.com/blog/what-nist-compliance

[6] "Cybersecurity Framework", National Institute of Standards and Technology, accessed July 9, 2021. https://www.nist.gov/cyberframework

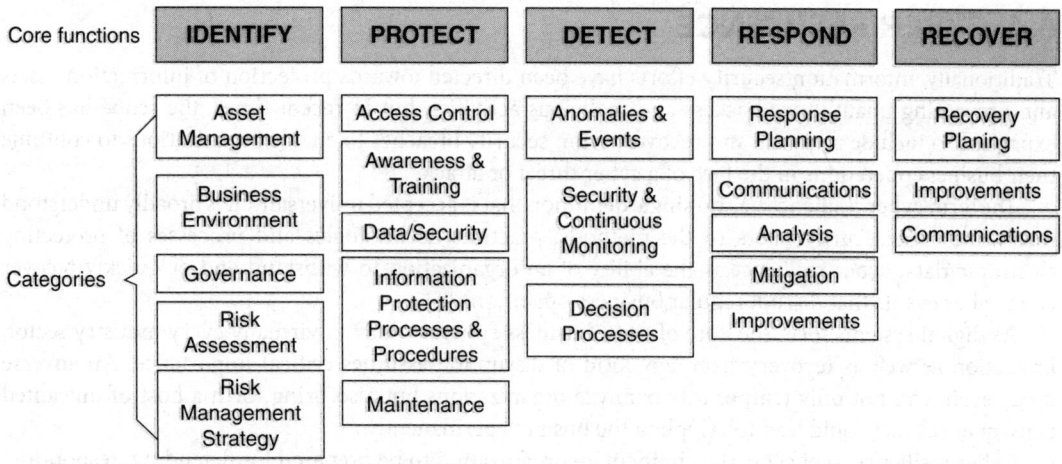

Figure 6.2 NIST cybersecurity framework[7]

The NIST cybersecurity framework also provides organizations with a way to benchmark the cybersecurity maturity level at which they are operating. The four levels[8] listed in Table 6.6 indicate how far the organization has progressed in its cybersecurity journey and how strong their security posture is.

Table 6.6 Cybersecurity maturity levels

Partial	The process of dealing with cyber risk is not formalized and is managed in a reactive and ad hoc manner.
Risk informed	Cybersecurity management is addressed without an over-arching policy and as and when risks emerge.
Repeatable	At this level, formal risk management processes and policies have been implemented.
Adaptable	At this level, the organization is in a position to adapt and evolve its cybersecurity policies and practices based on situations handled, lessons learned and insights gathered through analytics and best practices.

The NIST framework is simple to use as well as implement and focuses on key aspects of cybersecurity. For this reason, organizations outside the US are also using the framework to give shape to their security vision and requirements. Prominent large organizations using the NIST framework include JP Morgan Chase, Bank of England, Intel Corporation, Boeing and Nippon Telegraph.[9]

---

[7] "Cybersecurity Framework", National Institute of Standards and Technology, accessed July 9, 2021. https://www.nist.gov/cyberframework

[8] "What is the NIST Cybersecurity Framework?", Balbix. https://www.balbix.com/insights/nist-cybersecurity-framework/

[9] "Cybersecurity Framework," National Institute of Standards and Technology, accessed July 9, 2021. https://www.nist.gov/industry-impacts/cybersecurity-framework

6.4 CYBER RESILIENCE

Traditionally, information security efforts have been directed towards protection of information assets and preventing unauthorized access and malicious activities, but in recent times, the scope has been expanded to include response and recovery from security breaches to enable organizations to continue their business operations in the face of a cyber threat or attack.

The term cyber resilience has no single definition that is accepted universally. It is broadly understood that while cybersecurity refers to the methods, practices, technologies and processes of protecting electronic data, cyber resilience is the ability of an organization to withstand and or quickly recover from cyber events that disrupt regular business operations.[10]

As digital systems form the core of most business systems today in virtually every industry sector, protection as well as recovery from any kind of disruption assumes critical importance. An adverse cyber event can not only temporarily paralyze organizations but also bring forth a host of unwanted consequences that could lead to crippling the business permanently.

Cyber resilience in effect is the ability of an organization to be prepared for defending, responding to and recovering from cyber incidents that threaten/disrupt business continuity, while limiting their impact and ensuring that activities related to the normal functioning of a business are minimally/not affected as a consequence of the incident. The goal of cyber resilience is to ensure the continued functioning of organization systems and delivery of desired outcomes, even in the face of diverse conditions.

In a competitive environment which is highly dependent on information technology, businesses that focus on being cyber resilient will place themselves in a position of competitive advantage over their rivals who may not have the same approach and ability for cyber resilience. The constantly evolving cyber threat landscape in which a variety of cyber criminals thrive puts added pressure on ensuring cyber resilience on an ongoing basis.

The concept of cyber resilience is still evolving and there is no single approach that can help an organization achieve the same. Rather than limiting risk mitigation approaches to cyber threats and cyberattacks, organizations pursuing the goal of cyber resilience need to broaden the scope to include an assessment of the impact of any incident that could potentially disrupt the most critical organizational processes and essential IT services; and if such an incidents materialize, it must have in place clearly defined standard operating procedures (SOPs) that will minimize disruption, limit any potential damage and ensure quick recovery and restoration of all IT systems as they were before the incident occurred.

Cyber incidents may have different degrees of impact on business continuity and therefore need to be categorized such that critical systems are prioritized. To achieve this, organizations must make an inventory of risks to their IT systems and infrastructure, categorize them based on their potential impact on mission critical systems, business critical systems and safety critical systems and evolve a common lexicon and way to rank the incidents based on their severity of impact.

The National Council of Investigation and Security Services (NCISS), USA, uses a scoring system to determine the severity of impact of a cyber incident. The criteria for arriving at a score to accord priority to a cyber incident are as follows:[11]

---

[10] Rachel Holmes, "Cyber Resilience vs. Cybersecurity: What's the Difference and How to Build a Plan for Both," BitSight, accessed March 21, 2022. https://www.bitsight.com/blog/cyber-resilience-vs-cybersecurity-whats-difference-and-how-build-plan-both

[11] "CISA Cyber Incident Scoring System," Cybersecurty and Infrastructure Security Agency, accessed November 9, 2019. https://www.us-cert.gov/CISA-Cyber-Incident-Scoring-System

Info Box 31: Criteria for Incident Classification

Functional impact
Observed activity
Actor characterization
Information impact
Recoverability
Cross-dependency
Potential impact

Based on the scores obtained, priority levels can be assigned based on the following US national cyber severity schema:

Info Box 32: Schema for Incident Classification

Incident category	Colour code
Emergency	Black
Severe	Red
High	Orange
Medium	Yellow
Low	Green
Baseline	

Organizations can adopt such criteria or develop their own in order to ensure a common, well understood (around the organization) lexicon that denotes the severity and therefore the priority level for remedial actions to begin. Faster and clearer communication can help in better handling a crisis. For example, a ransomware attack on a mission critical or safety critical system may be categorized as an emergency level, while a failed malicious attempt at infiltrating a system may be assigned a low or baseline rating.

Pursuing cyber resilience and integrating it into an organization's overall cybersecurity agenda can provide a number of benefits:

- Cyber resilience is not limited to responding, recovering or surviving from cyberattacks, but helps develop and implement robust security measures that enhance data security and safety from system outages, environmental issues and natural disasters.
- Several industries have stringent requirements for organizations to develop and implement measures to achieve cyber resilience. These are important in various sectors like financial services, public utilities and critical infrastructure services where any downtime can have consequences on

consumers at large. Non-compliance with these regulations can invite increased scrutiny, fines and penalties. Emphasis on cyber resilience brings about closer alignment between business objectives and cybersecurity measures.
- Development of a work culture and processes that support business continuity and disaster recovery along with cybersecurity. Resilience initiatives help raise overall security awareness among employees.
- Cyber resilience helps in mitigating risks and financial losses in case of major security breaches. They also help in assuring all stakeholders that a security breach happened in spite of appropriate measures having been put in place.
- Cyber resilience helps in providing assurance to customers and business associates about security and operating standards as well as data security. Stakeholders also develop confidence that in case of an adverse cyber incident, appropriate systems are in place to ensure resolution and quick recovery.
- Security breaches and prolonged outages of services have an adverse impact of the reputation of an organization. Cyber resilience approaches can help and prevent reputational harm.

The key elements of a cyber resilience strategy include the ability of an organization to handle critical situations that impact business continuity and information security, such as:

- Preparing for adverse incidents and circumstances
- Developing adaptive response systems that can overcome cyber threats and mitigate risks
- Using coordinated systems to withstand an incident/crisis and recover from it as soon as possible
- Ensuring redundancy to provide multiple levels of protection for critical resources
- Implementing a governance system that assures the implementation of a cyber resilience program

Approaches to cyber resilience are built on the premise that adverse incidents that can threaten the fundamental objectives of an organization are inevitable. Cyber resilience approaches involve preparation for business continuity including dealing with not only cyberattacks or data breaches, but other adverse conditions and challenges as well.

The four key actions involved in shaping cyber resilience programs are listed below:[12]

1. Cyber resilience development processes may vary from organization to organization based on their business objectives, industry sector, infrastructure and current capabilities. Using a framework such as NIST, cyber resilience review (CRR) can aid the process of adopting a structured, scalable and cost-effective path to achieve desired levels of cyber resilience.
2. Undertaking a risk assessment from the point of view of sustaining business operations, identifying the related threats and developing appropriate countermeasures. A list of business areas /operations that are based on technology along with other threats to business continuity are a good starting point.
3. Alignment of organizational resources and processes with the objective of cyber resilience is critical. This may also involve time-bound response commitments from service providers and third parties in the face of an adverse event.
4. Robust and tested procedures for incident detection, classification, response and recovery with clearly assigned responsibilities. The consequences of an adverse incident can be minimized by early detection followed by rapid response.

---

[12] "What Is a Cyber Resilience Strategy and How Is It Implemented?," ISSQUARED, accessed August 2, 2021. https://www.issquaredinc.com/what-is-a-cyber-resilience-strategy-and-how- to-implement-it

6.5 INDUSTRY-SPECIFIC CYBERSECURITY FRAMEWORKS

The number of industry specific frameworks for managing cyber risks is growing due to the twin factors of increased cyber threats and regulations. The main purpose of industry-specific cybersecurity frameworks is to address industry-related security challenges that require the implementation of special standards and approaches. Let us examine three examples of industry regulations that have had a significant impact on raising industry standards and awareness.

6.5.1 HIPAA

The Health Insurance Portability and Accountability Act (HIPAA) was enacted in 1996. It is a federal US law that represents an early landmark in setting standards for the privacy, storage, transmission and sharing of personal health information (PHI) of individuals.

HIPAA is applicable to covered entities and includes health plans (health insurance companies, government healthcare programs), healthcare providers and healthcare clearinghouses and their business associates (service providers and subcontractors). It places obligations on both covered entities and business associates to comply with standards and best practices. Non-compliance with the provisions of HIPAA can invite fines and penalties. In 2009, the HITECH Act was enacted to extend HIPAA privacy and security protections for patients.

Organizations covered under HIPAA must ensure that their employees are aware of the following five primary rules:

- **Privacy rule**: This rule prescribes the limits and conditions for the protection and disclosure of PHI that can and cannot be made without patient consent and authorization. It also contains provisions that grant the patient's rights to access, inspect, seek a copy and request corrections to their records.
- **Security rule**: This rule relates to the standards, procedures and practices that must be followed for the protection of PHI. These encompass the storage, accessibility and transmission of PHI as well as the administrative, technical and physical controls that must be implemented.
- **Transactions rule**: This rule defines the formats/codes to be followed for conducting certain electronic transactions to ensure the safety, integrity and security of PHI.
- **Identifiers rule**: This rule specifies the use of three unique identifiers for entities who use HIPAA-regulated administrative and financial transactions.
- **Enforcement rule**: This rule relates to the provisions of the ARRA HITECH Act, which extend the rules of HIPAA privacy and security. It covers the imposition of fines and civil and criminal penalties for the violation of the privacy rule since 2003 and the security and breach notification rules since 2009.

6.5.2 PCI DSS

PCI DSS (Payment Card Industry Data Security Standard) comprises a set of practices that govern the way credit and debit cards are handled to ensure security of transactions and information.

The standard, promoted by payment card industry pioneers such as Visa, MasterCard, American Express, Discover and JCB, has been recognized and adopted by financial regulators around the world. The standard is applicable to any organization engaged in the acceptance, storage, transmission or processing of cardholder information. The standard has become a part of statutory regulation in many countries and is applicable to any organization, irrespective of its size, as long as its activities include card-based processing activities.

> **Info Box 33: Mission of PCI Standards Council**
>
> The PCI SSC mission is to enhance global payment account data security by developing standards and supporting services that drive education, awareness and effective implementation by stakeholders. We achieve this with a strategic framework to guide our decision-making process and ensure that every initiative is aligned with our mission and supports the needs of the global payments industry.[13]

Compliance requirements under PCI DSS include but are not limited to the following:[14]

- Implement and maintain firewalls and antivirus software to safeguard cardholder data.
- Implement data protection measures including encryption while transmitting cardholder data across open, public networks.
- Ensure that vendor-supplied defaults for system passwords and other security parameters are changed.
- Implement physical and technical controls to restrict access to cardholder data.
- Build and maintain secure systems and applications.
- Every person accessing cardholder data must have a unique ID.
- Implement tracking and monitoring of network resources and card data.
- Implement and maintain a security policy and regularly test control mechanisms and processes.

There are four levels of PCI compliance, with the highest level (Level 1) comprising merchants who process over six million card transactions annually and the lowest level (Level 4) comprising merchants who process below 20,000 card transactions annually. Level 1 merchants are required to have annual on-site reviews conducted by an internal auditor and a network scan by an approved scanning vendor, while merchants at levels 2, 3 and 4 are required to complete an annual self-assessment questionnaire and undertake network scans by an approved vendor on a quarterly basis. Organizations that are required to adhere to PCI DSS can implement the following to ensure compliance:

- Educate their employees on PCI DSS requirements.
- Implement security safeguards as prescribed and undertake regular audits to ensure that systems and processes are being followed.
- Regularly test systems and processes.

6.5.3 The NYDFS Cybersecurity Regulation

The financial services industry is one that is heavily targeted by cybercriminals. The reasons for this are quite obvious, such as pay-offs from financial crimes and the potential value of personally identifiable information (PII) of customers to cybercriminals. People entrust their sensitive and personal data with financial services firms such as banks, non-banking financial institutions, credit card companies and investment companies with the expectation that this data will be protected from theft or exploitation. Personally identifiable information includes customer details like home and office address, social security number, phone number, email address, banking data and income information.

The growing number of attacks on financial service providers has prompted legislations such as the New York State Department of Financial Services Cybersecurity Requirements Regulation for Financial Services Companies Part 500 (NYCRR 500) to be enacted and enforced with a view to ensuring that minimum standards of cybersecurity become an integral part of industry ecosystems.

---

[13] "Who We Are," PCI Security Standards Council, accessed October 2, 2022. https://www.pcisecuritystandards.org/about_us/
[14] Owen, "What Is PCI Compliance?," OTAVA, accessed August 4, 2021. https://www.otava.com/reference/what-is-pci-compliance/

> **Info Box 34: NYDFS Regulation**
>
> The NYDFS cybersecurity regulation is aimed at safeguarding sensitive customer data and promoting the integrity of the information technology systems of regulated entities and to ensure the safety and soundness of the institution as well as New York State's financial services industry.[15]

The NYCRR 500 regulation was adopted in March 2017 and is applicable to any entity registered in the state of New York that provides financial services including insurance companies, banks as well as financial services institutions. There are limited exemptions to the NYDFS cybersecurity regulation. Organizations that have less than 10 employees, have revenues of less than USD 5 million in each of the past 3 years, or that hold less than USD 10 million in total assets on their books are exempt from certain regulatory requirements. Key aspects of the NYCRR 500 regulation that covered entities are required to implement are:

- Assessment of their cybersecurity risk profiles, including third-party risks
- Development and implementation of a comprehensive plan that identifies and mitigates cyber risks
- Implementation of data protection measures such as encryption, penetration testing and access controls
- Provision of adequate resources including the appointment of a Chief Information Security Officer (CISO) along with other qualified personnel
- Implementation of incident response plans to respond to data breaches and to notify NYDFS of any material events within 72 hours
- Implementation of audit trails regarding event response
- Implementation of multi-factor authentication for all inward-bound connections to the entity's network
- Ensuring identification and documentation of shortcomings, remediation plans, and providing certifications of compliance on an annual basis
- Ensuring that annual reports include the risks faced, all material events and the impact on protected data

NYDFS CRR demands that minimum cybersecurity standards are maintained by identifying (internal and external) threats and employing suitable defence and detection mechanisms. They also call for having response systems in place for recovery and restoration and for ensuring reporting as per requirements.

6.5.4 GDPR and Other Region-Specific Privacy Regulations

The European Union's General Data Protection Regulation (GDPR) is among the most comprehensive and impactful regulations that address legal issues related to privacy, data protection and cybersecurity. GDPR came into force in May 2018. All 27 countries that comprise the European Union are covered under GDPR. Currently, over 120 countries around the world have some form of privacy laws that deal with data protection and controls over citizens' data.[16] Most countries when developing their own privacy and data protection regulations drew from the GDPR rules and experiences and therefore a wide range of commonalities are found in such laws globally. Table 6.7 shows the six lawful bases for

---

[15] "The NYDFS Cybersecurity Regulation (NYCRR)," Rapid7, accessed August 4, 2021. https://www.rapid7.com/fundamentals/nydfs-cybersecurity-regulation/
[16] "Beyond GDPR: Data Protection Around the World," Thales, accessed March 18, 2022. https://www.thalesgroup.com/en/markets/digital-identity-and-security/government/magazine/beyond-gdpr-data-protection-around-world

the processing of personal data under GDPR and similar provisions can be found in privacy regulations of other countries subject to minor variations. The draft Indian Personal Data Protection Bill (PDPB) has seven bases instead of six, as laid down in GDPR.[17]

Table 6.7 GDPR vs PDPB lawful bases comparison

GDPR lawful bases for personal data processing	Indian PDPB lawful bases for personal data processing
Consent	Consent
Performance of a contract	Legal obligation
Legal obligation	Medical emergency involving a threat to life or severe threat to health
Legitimate interests	Providing medical treatment or health services
Life protection and vital interests	Protecting the safety of individuals during a disaster
Public interest	Employment purposes
	"Reasonable purposes" as may be specified by regulations, including for preventing or detecting unlawful activity, whistleblowing, mergers and acquisitions, network and information security, credit scoring, recovery of debt, the operation of search engines or processing of publicly available personal data

Apart from the above, there are other variations in PDPB when compared with GDPR, such as in the scale of fines and penalties, breach reporting requirements and data storage rules. A significant difference is the proposed broader scope in the definition of sensitive personal data in PDPB, which includes the areas listed in Table 6.8.[18]

Table 6.8 PDPB-sensitive data

Financial data	Health data	Official identifier
Sex life	Sexual orientation	Biometric data
Genetic data	Transgender or intersex status	Caste or tribe
Religious belief	Political belief	Political affiliation

GDPR ushered in a new regime which brought into focus the need to implement privacy and data protection measures as well as fixing penalties and fines for non-compliance. GDPR also called for a need for enhancing cybersecurity and related controls and created awareness for the need for providing greater protection for other organizational information assets. To comply with GDPR and privacy regulations posed several challenges for organizations. While it can be said that the fear of non-compliance and the threat of hefty fines gave organizations the required sense of urgency to address regulatory requirements, it also provided an opportunity to holistically think of protecting their other key information assets as well as upgrade their controls to ward off cyber threats and

---

[17] "Comparison: Indian Personal Data Protection Bill 2019 vs GDPR," Covington and Burling LLP (2019): 1–29. https://www.privacysecurityacademy.com/wp-content/uploads/2020/05/Comparison-Chart-GDPR-vs.-India-PDPB-2019-Jan.-16-2020.pdf
[18] "Comparison: Indian Personal Data Protection Bill 2019 vs GDPR," Covington and Burling LLP (2019): 1–29. https://www.privacysecurityacademy.com/wp-content/uploads/2020/05/Comparison-Chart-GDPR-vs.-India-PDPB-2019-Jan.-16-2020.pdf

cyberattacks. The key challenges in implementing GDPR and other similar privacy regulations are given below:

> **Info Box 35: GDPR Implementation Challenges**
>
> Embedding privacy and data protection requirements into an organization's IT systems and processes
>
> Increase in investments and operating costs to ensure compliance
>
> A long list of regulatory and documentation requirements
>
> Employee training and awareness
>
> Implementing and maintaining updated records and transparency of processes
>
> Keeping track of non-compliances
>
> Re-orienting business systems to give data control to consumers, implementing consumer rights
>
> Enforcing secure access control and physical security
>
> Data protection from external and insider threats
>
> Exponential growth of data

It is important that organizations not limit their cybersecurity programs and controls to meeting regulatory requirements. Instead, they should adopt a wider security posture which includes the protection of their key assets and takes into account their business objectives, threat perceptions and risk appetite.

6.6 THE HUMAN FACTOR IN CYBERSECURITY

The human element is widely regarded as the weakest link in cybersecurity as well as the least predictable. Human behaviour is governed by various factors including skills, knowledge, awareness and intent. Security programs and initiatives are based on the implementation of various technologies to defend against different types of threats; however, when it comes to ensuring 'responsible security behaviour,' the programs often fail to deliver the desired results. Further, changes such as Bring Your Own Device and remote working have obscured the lines between personal and organizational systems to add to the complexity of addressing security issues. While organizations deploy watertight policies and controls, employees tend to follow the easiest path when approaching tasks.

> **Info Box 36: Human Factors**
>
> Hackers are fully aware that they can use employee vulnerabilities to exploit sensitive company data. Therefore, it is not surprising that 95% of security breaches are blamed on human error, proving people to be the weakest link in cybersecurity.[19]

In their relentless pursuit to exploit vulnerabilities to launch cyberattacks, hackers have recognized that the frailties of human behaviour offer many vulnerabilities that they can exploit. Despite this, many organizations focus their cybersecurity efforts mainly on deploying technologies for safeguarding their networks, endpoints and defending themselves from malware attacks. People-centric issues in cybersecurity are often not given the attention they deserve, thereby leading to security and data breaches.

---

[19] Robert Roohparvar, "People - the Weakest Link in Cybersecurity," Infoguard Cyber Security, accessed August 5, 2021. https://www.infoguardsecurity.com/people-the-weakest-link-in-cybersecurity/

It is vitally important for businesses to recognize the need for integrating their technology-driven cybersecurity initiatives with employee education, training and awareness, which can boost their chances of securing themselves against cyberattacks and minimizing risks. In order to prioritize and promote responsible cybersecurity behaviour and a security-oriented culture, organizations need to consider the following aspects:

- Does our cybersecurity program address the human element in cybersecurity?
- Are our employees trained and knowledgeable in order to identify different cyber threats?
- Are our employees aware of their roles and responsibilities with regard to cybersecurity?
- Do employees understand our cybersecurity policies and procedures?
- Are employees exposed to cybersecurity best practices?

Most common human errors that impact cybersecurity include the following:

- Poor password practices
- Opening suspicious links and visiting dubious websites
- Sending important data to unintended/incorrect recipients through email
- Exposing sensitive data on public websites by mistake
- Being deceived by social engineering schemes
- Misconfiguration of devices
- Not following organizational guidelines

Human errors can be classified as skill-based, knowledge-based, carelessness, negligence and following poor cyber hygiene practices. Organizations can focus on the following aspects to enhance cybersecurity and reduce employee errors while developing a comprehensive employee security education, training and awareness (SETA) program:

- Build employee awareness regarding social engineering threats such as avoiding pop-ups, unknown emails and business email compromise and make employees mindful of the scale of the threat.
- Identification and reporting of cyber threats.
- Ensure that employees of service providers and other vendors are aware of security requirements.
- Raising awareness may not be enough; organizations must aim for behavioural change.
- Training in privacy and data protection practices.
- Enforcing the use of strong password protection and authentication.
- Mandate the use of VPNs and avoiding use of insecure Wi-Fi.
- Prohibit the installation of Shadow IT (unsupported/unauthorised hardware and software) on devices used for organizational purposes.
- Ensure firewall and antivirus protection at work and at home.
- Installation of security software updates and backing up of files.
- Assigning responsibilities for compliance requirements.
- Ensure security of physical environments.
- Making sure that employees are not overloaded with work, which can lead to errors.

Cybersecurity cannot be solved only through technology and administrative procedures and controls. It requires the active participation of all employees and organizations must send a strong message that security is everyone's responsibility.

6.7 ALGORITHMS AND TECHNIQUES FOR CYBERSECURITY

The use of computer algorithms for cybersecurity is of great importance. An algorithm comprises a set of clearly defined instructions to solve a specific problem. An algorithm is not limited to a programming language or computer code but is expressed in mathematical terms and, therefore, is portable across programming languages and platforms.

In recent years, cybercrime has become more sophisticated. Hackers have evolved their techniques and make use of various algorithms to defeat cybersecurity systems that are also increasingly dependent on the use of algorithms to identify threats and prevent cyberattacks. Algorithms are an important tool for application developers who want to provide IT and security teams with more sophisticated and automated means to fend off attackers. At one level, it can be said that an algorithm battle is taking place between hackers and defenders who are trying to use them to gain the upper hand. While there are several different algorithms that are being used for cybersecurity, Table 6.9 lists the popularly used algorithms.

Table 6.9 Popular algorithms and techniques used for cybersecurity

Area	Algorithm	Cybersecurity usage
Encryption	• DES Symmetric Encryption Algorithm • 3DES Symmetric Encryption Algorithm • AES Symmetric Encryption Algorithm • RSA • Diffie–Hellman • Elliptic curve Cryptographic hashes • SHA2, SHA3, BLAKE2 MAC algorithms • HMAC, CMAK Key-derivation functions • bcrypt, Scrypt, Argon2	Symmetric encryption Asymmetric encryption Quantum safe algorithms
Artificial Intelligence	Classification algorithms • Naive Bayes • Decision tree • Random forest • Logistic regression • Support vector machines • K Nearest Neighbour	Across multiple cybersecurity areas Intrusion detection, malware detection, spam and phishing detection Threat intelligence
Deep Learning	• Convolutional Neural Networks (CNNs) • Long Short-Term Memory Networks (LSTMs) • Recurrent Neural Networks (RNNs) • Generative Adversarial Networks (GANs) • Radial Basis Function Networks (RBFNs) • Multilayer Perceptrons (MLPs) • Self-Organizing Maps (SOMs) • Deep Belief Networks (DBNs) • Restricted Boltzmann Machines (RBMs) • Autoencoders	Detecting unknown network intrusions Threat intelligence Malware detection
Machine Learning	• Supervised learning • Unsupervised learning • Reinforcement learning • Ensemble learning	User behaviour analytics Threat analysis Task automation

(Continued)

Table 6.9 (*Continued*)

Area	Algorithm	Cybersecurity usage
Data Mining	• Classification	Used for spam and phishing email detection
	• Regression	Used for forecasting trends and cyberattacks
	• Time series analysis	Used for predicting seasonal or time of day attacks
	• Clustering	Used for identifying similarities and differences in data
	• Summarization	Used for reporting and visualization
Anomaly Detection	• Model-based techniques • Proximity-based techniques • Density-based techniques	Network anomaly detection

QUICK TEST

1. Key challenges organizations face in establishing an effective cybersecurity governance program are:
   a. Articulating a clear definition of its risk management policies, strategy and goals.
   b. Standardizing processes that are repeatable and consistent.
   c. Clear assignment of responsibilities and accountability and its enforcement.
   d. Senior leadership engagement and oversight.
   e. All of the above
   f. Only a, b and c
2. Methods for identifying security vulnerabilities include:
   a. Brainstorming with internal teams
   b. Using threat intelligence information
   c. Learning from past security failures
   d. Conducting penetration testing
   e. All of the above
   f. Only a, b and d
3. ISO 27001 is applicable to countries around the world, but NIST is applicable only to US companies.
   a. True
   b. False
4. NIST provides a cybersecurity framework that has the following number of core functions:
   a. Four
   b. Six
   c. Three
   d. Five
5. The HIPAA Act is concerned with:
   a. PII
   b. PHI
   c. Both a and b
   d. None of the above
6. The PCI DSS standard has been adopted by various countries as a regulatory requirement.
   a. True
   b. False
7. The NYDFS CRR 500 is applicable to organizations in New York State that are a part of:
   a. Healthcare Industry
   b. Financial Services Industry
   c. Retail Industry
   d. None of the above
8. Human errors can be classified as:
   a. Skill-based errors
   b. Knowledge-based errors
   c. Carelessness and negligence
   d. All of the above
   e. a and b only
9. The purpose of developing a cyber risk management plan or program is not only to identify and prioritize risks and implement suitable defences and controls, but also to determine the type of treatment for each risk.
   a. True
   b. False

10. ISO 27001 mandates that organizations follow a PDCA (Plan, Do, Check. Act) cycle.
    a. True
    b. False

QUESTIONS

1. The nature of cyber risks is such that cybersecurity can never ensure total or perpetual immunity from them. If so, what is the purpose of cyber risk management?
2. It is often said that there is no silver bullet to address cybersecurity. Why is a risk-based approach regarded as the best way to address cybersecurity?
3. What are the risk treatment options available to an organization? Explain with examples.
4. What are the advantages of implementing cybersecurity frameworks? Explain in detail.
5. What are the considerations for an organization to follow a particular framework?
6. Cyber resilience development processes may vary from organization to organization based on their business objectives, industry sector, infrastructure and current capabilities. Explain the reasons for this.
7. What is the purpose behind industry-specific frameworks?
8. The human element is widely regarded as the weakest link in cybersecurity as well as the least predictable. Discuss this statement.
9. Discuss the importance of regulations in framing a cybersecurity program.
10. What is an algorithm. How is it useful in the context of cybersecurity?

ANSWER KEYS

Quick Test

1. (e)
2. (e)
3. (b)
4. (d)
5. (b)
6. (a)
7. (b)
8. (d)
9. (a)
10. (a)

7 Cybersecurity Technologies

> **OBJECTIVES**
>
> At the end of this chapter, you will be able to:
>
> ☑ Describe the technologies and related concepts that organizations can deploy for enhancing the security of their information assets
>
> ☑ List the functionality and features of the technologies and solutions designed to secure an organization's networks, IT infrastructure, web applications, systems on the cloud and endpoints

7.0 INTRODUCTION

Technology is a key pillar of cybersecurity, the other two being people and processes. Over the past decade, cybersecurity technologies have gone from being important to essential as cyber threats have become more pervasive than before. The consequences of a security breach or cyberattack have also become more potent and devastating. There is no doubt that cyber technologies must be deployed to ensure protection of key information assets and even for the very survival of an enterprise.

Changes in information technology happen at a rapid pace. Microprocessor speeds, storage density and bandwidth all double within 12–18 months. These fundamental changes have an impact on other technologies that also keep evolving over time. Hackers are quick to harness the power and exploit vulnerabilities in new technologies, while cyber defence and cybersecurity technologies often play catch-up.

Information technology infrastructure is built on several layers such as hardware, operating systems, system software, networks, applications, data and endpoint devices. Initially, cyberattacks were targeted at the application and network layers, but over time hackers have become adept at exploiting vulnerabilities at every level of the stack. Modern-day cyberattacks can be lethal in terms of the damage that they can cause. Hackers have learnt to use advanced technologies to carry out varied and sophisticated attacks, which makes the task of ensuring cybersecurity more challenging.

The increasing frequency of cyber threats and attacks has also exacerbated the need for cybersecurity technologies that enable early detection and remediation (to minimize damage), as a manual approach is no longer feasible. Not so long ago, it would take days to detect and respond to cyber threats. From that point, security technologies have evolved along with manual support to accomplish the same within hours. Today, responding to cyber threats is required within seconds or in real-time. Hence, the need for cybersecurity technologies that enable quick detection and response has never been greater.

Cybersecurity technologies have also evolved from being point solutions that could address specific threats into comprehensive platforms that provide protection against a variety of threats. Further, some present-day technologies also help in preventing attacks and neutralizing different kinds of threats.

7.0.1 Considerations for Implementing Cybersecurity Technologies

Every organization has its own unique risk profile, and deployment of cybersecurity technologies and solutions should be based on its risk assessment and aligned with the organizational objectives. Some key considerations for implementing cybersecurity technology would be as follows:

- Prevent unauthorized access
- Prevent network intrusions
- Identify and provide protection against different kinds of malware
- Ensure data protection
- Provide visibility of cyber threats and security breaches
- Enable threat detection and response
- Provide threat analytics
- Integrate with existing systems
- Ensure security, resilience and recovery
- Be cost effective

7.1 SECURING NETWORKS, WEB APPLICATIONS, SERVICES AND SERVERS

As organizations evolve their cybersecurity strategies, the need for more refined and advanced technologies will be felt. A rule of thumb in cybersecurity technologies is that you are more secure by deploying the latest technologies as they often incorporate defences in response to recent trends in cyber threats and forms of attacks.

Further, organizations can choose to adopt 'active defence' strategies that involve the use of offensive actions to outmanoeuvre an attacker and make an attack more challenging to carry out. The goal is to derail the attacker's strategy by impeding potential pathways and exposing their presence or discovering their attack vector. The use of advanced threat intelligence software can also help organizations in adopting a strong security posture.

There is no single piece of software that can provide comprehensive cybersecurity to an organization. Organizations must figure out what technologies can help them execute their cybersecurity plans and programs.

Let us examine a basic set of cybersecurity technologies that form the building blocks and which are deployed to boost cyber defences and enhance cybersecurity and cyber resilience.

7.1.1 Firewalls

Firewalls have been in use for nearly 30 years now and have evolved from just preventing outsider access to enforcing network security policies, maintaining logs of Internet activity and securing network perimeter defences. All traffic from outside a network is routed through the firewall to determine what is allowed into the network and what is not.

Fundamentally, firewalls are a network security device (software or hardware) that filter data packets that attempt to enter a computer or network. Firewalls monitor inbound and outbound network traffic based on a set of defined security rules, which are applied to block or allow entry or exit. Firewalls can also scan packets for malware and other established forms of threats. In case the firewall deems a particular data packet to be a security risk, it then stops it from entering the network.

How Firewalls Work

Firewalls make use of the following primary methodologies for monitoring and controlling network traffic:

- **Packet filtering:** Every packet that crosses the firewall is subjected to inspection and testing based on a set of configurable rules. The packet filtering mechanism is based on the examination of the source and destination IP and port addresses, which are a part of each Transmission Control Protocol/Internet Protocol (TCP/IP) packet. While packet filtering firewalls are fast and efficient, they have limitations as they do not check payloads and can be spoofed. Setting up of access control lists, detailing security policies and ongoing management of the same can also be difficult. Since packet filtering takes place one packet at a time, attackers have learnt to split their scripts into multiple packets, which the packet filtering mechanisms of the firewall are unable to identify.
- **Stateful inspection:** Also called dynamic packet filtering, this examines and evaluates a range of elements from each packet including IP addresses, port information and applications by comparing it to a database of trusted information before barring or allowing access. These types of firewalls not only examine each packet, but also track to determine whether or not that packet is part of an established TCP or other network session. Another variant of stateful inspection is a multilayer inspection firewall, which considers the flow of transactions in process across multiple protocol layers of the seven-layer Open Systems Interconnection (OSI) model.[1] Stateful inspection firewalls are therefore resource intensive, can slow down network traffic and are more expensive to deploy.
- **Circuit-level gateway:** Circuit-level gateways monitor TCP handshakes and other network protocol sessions when they are initiated across the network to determine if the session is legitimate or not and if the system can be trusted. As these do not inspect packets, they only process requested transactions while blocking all other traffic. While they are inexpensive, they have to be deployed along with other security technologies and do not provide any application layer monitoring.
- **Proxy or application firewalls:** Proxy firewalls offer the best security as they work as a gateway or intermediary to monitor and control inbound and outbound data. The proxy service prevents direct connection between customer servers/devices and incoming data, protecting networks against unauthorized entry and malicious packets. An application layer gateway (ALG) is a proxy firewall that acts as a single entry and exit point to a network. It acts on behalf of the application servers on a network, protecting the servers and applications from traffic that is potentially malicious. It also allows the implementation of fine-grained security controls. Application gateways can consume more network resources, may require greater deployment efforts, and may cost more than other firewall alternatives. However, application-layer firewalls are most effective when it comes to protecting IT infrastructure from web application threats as they can block access to unsafe sites as well as prevent sensitive information from being leaked from within the firewall.[2]

---

[1] Amy Larsen DeCario and Robert G Ferrell, "The 5 Different Types of Firewalls Explained," TechTarget, accessed October 27, 2021. https://searchsecurity.techtarget.com/feature/The-five-different-types-of-firewalls
[2] Amy Larsen DeCario and Robert G Ferrell, "The 5 Different Types of Firewalls Explained," TechTarget, accessed October 27, 2021. https://searchsecurity.techtarget.com/feature/The-five-different-types-of-firewalls

- **Guards as firewalls:** Guard firewalls are more advanced and work like proxy firewalls placed within a Demilitarised Zone (DMZ) network. It has the ability to receive protocol data units, interpret them and protect the integrity of information and availability of services in the protected network. Guards can be designed to deliver a range of functionality, as shown below.

Info Box 37: Guards Functionality

Authentication	Source and destination address
Whitelisting	Source and destination address, data formats
Scanning	Data for known malware
Validation	Digital signatures, data formats
Inspection	Encrypted content
Checking	Text against blacklisted phases, consistency of data formats
Removal	Redundant data
Logging	Security-related incidents
Self-testing	Mechanisms

Guards were originally designed to control the release of information from systems holding sensitive data in order to protect its confidentiality, but later on controls that could protect integrity of that data and availability of services were introduced.

- **Next-generation firewall (NGFW):** NGFW provides a range of functionality that includes deep packet inspection features, stateful inspection as well as capabilities like intrusion detection, intrusion prevention, malware filtering and antivirus. NGFW is ideally suited for heavily regulated sectors like financial services and healthcare and other high-threat environments. Deployment of NGFW and their integration with other security systems require some expertise and are more expensive given the multi-functionality.

Firewall Deployment and User Management

There are multiple models for the deployment of firewalls:

- Hardware-based firewalls
- Network-based firewalls
- Software-based firewalls
- Cloud/Hosted-based firewalls

Configuring a Firewall

This is a key factor in preventing cyberattacks. Firewall configuration involves configuring domain names and IP addresses and completing several other actions to keep firewalls secure.

Firewall policy configuration is based on network types called 'profiles' which enable setting up of security rules that can provide protection against cyberattacks. The following steps are generally used to configure a firewall:

Info Box 38: Configuring a Firewall

Step One	Provide basic configuration settings	Change default passwords, restrict privileges, disabling or securely configuring simple network management protocol (SNMP)
Step Two	Configure the firewall zones and IP addresses	Identify the assets that need to be protected, place into networks (or DMZs) based on similar sensitivity level and function
Step Three	Configure access control lists	Provide access control lists that specify what traffic will be permitted into which zones
Step Four	Configure your other firewall services and logging	Disable all the services that will not be put to use
Step Five	Test and monitor the firewall	Test, monitor, conduct vulnerability scans, update policies periodically and firmware as required

Avoiding the following mistakes will ensure that the firewall works in the desired fashion:

- Failure to meet configuration requirements in cloud-centric security environments
- Issues with maintaining whitelists and access control lists
- Inability to apply proper port forwarding rules for remote access
- Failure to implement timely updates
- Failure to upgrade security policies

Firewalls are among the most widely deployed cybersecurity technologies as they protect networks against the following types of attack vectors:

- Backdoors
- Denial of service attacks
- Macros
- Spam
- Remote logins
- Virus infiltration

Firewalls are also useful in supporting user authentication, enforcing networks security policies and logging Internet-related activity. The concept of a firewall is built on the traditional approach of securing the network perimeter in order to protect systems, information and users within the perimeter. Hence, they are ineffective when it comes to cyber threats emanating from inside the perimeter (insider threats).

Further, when it comes to protection from malware such as trojans, firewalls have limited utility and need to be deployed along with antivirus software to be more effective. The dissolving of the 'traditional network perimeter' in recent times into a 'virtual network perimeter' calls for new approaches in the deployment of firewalls. Firewalls continue to evolve and expand their range of capabilities and functions.

Installing a well-configured firewall by itself does not ensure complete security and as such must be seen as one of the security mechanisms that form a part of the overall security architecture. Conducting a periodic firewall configuration review can help in identifying gaps and strengthening the security of the organization.

7.1.2 Intrusion Detection and Prevention

Securing networks involves the deployment a host of strategies and technologies including firewalls, encryption and virtual private networks to maintain the confidentiality and integrity of information. Another technology that is commonly deployed is the use of intrusion detection systems (IDS) to ensure protection from malicious actions and threats from external sources that seek to penetrate the network.

Conceptually, modern-day IDS technology has its roots in a model (intrusion detection expert system) that was prototyped by Dorothy Denning and Peter Neumann as far back as 1984 to 1986. Current-day IDS technology aims to cover all the processes used in the detection of unauthorized uses of network devices or computers through software specially designed to detect unusual or irregular activities.

IDS can not only help analyze the nature and scale of an attack but also help in identifying bugs or issues in configuring network devices. This information can be valuable for organizations to refine and implement better and more effective controls.

IDS has also evolved to incorporate prevention of possible attacks as a part of its offerings and work as an intrusion detection and prevention systems (IDPS). While the IDS part automates the detection function, the IDPS part helps in prevention and reduction of risk to the entire infrastructure.

IDSs are designed to work in different ways:

- **Knowledge-based IDSs** identify intrusion attempts by referencing a database comprising known system vulnerability profiles.
- **Behaviour-based IDSs** analyze traffic behaviour by looking for anomalies or deviations from standard behaviour patterns, temporarily block suspicious traffic, raise alerts to security personnel or a network operations centre (NOC) allowing for investigation and blocking/unblocking as necessary.

Another way to look at IDSs is if they are active or passive. An active IDS is set up to automatically block suspicious activity or an attack, while a passive IDS generates alerts if it identifies abnormal activity but does not undertake any further action.

IDS and IDPS systems can also be categorized based on the way they are designed to function:

- **Host-based IDS** runs on a host system and monitors activities for signs of suspicious behaviour.
- **Network-based IDS** monitors and evaluates network traffic for specific network segments or devices to identify dubious activity. They can also evaluate activity at the transport (TCP, User Datagram Protocol or UDP) and network (IPv4) layers to identify suspicious activity.
- **Signature-based IDS** identifies attack attempts by analyzing specific patterns like byte sequences in network traffic or known malware instruction sequences.
- **Anomaly-based IDS** is capable of detecting both network and computer intrusions and exploitation by monitoring system activity and categorizing it as either normal or anomalous.

Info Box 39: How an IDS Works

It is important to note that IDS and IDPS work in similar ways, but with the distinction that while an IDPS can perform both automated detection and prevention, an IDS is capable of only detection. In the case of an intrusion being detected, the IDPS will respond based upon pre-set rules, which could include actions such as blocking incoming network traffic, killing a malicious process, quarantining a file, etc. An IDS is a more suitable option when an organization would like to determine and control the course of action when a threat is detected, while an IDPS has the benefit of faster response to detected threats.

IDPS systems can also combine the dual capabilities of signature and anomaly detection in order to enhance detection capabilities. This provides protection from known threats through signature-based detection and zero-day threats using anomaly-based detection. Hence, a combination of the two approaches can give better results than using either of the two approaches individually.

IDS and IDPS can be installed on the premises or be cloud-based. In the case of cloud-based implementation, all requests are routed through a remote location for examination and filtering and are blocked or allowed into the network.

IDS plays a very important role in cybersecurity as it monitors incoming and outgoing traffic, continuously analyzes patterns and raises alerts on spotting suspicious or unusual activities within the network. The common shadow learning algorithms used in IDSs are:

- **Decision tree:** Uses a tree-like model of decision making and possible outcomes, including chance event outcomes, resource costs and utility
- **K-nearest neighbour:** This is a simple, supervised machine learning algorithm that can be used to solve both classification and regression problems.
- **Artificial neural network:** This is based on a collection of connected units or nodes called artificial neurons, which loosely model the neurons in the human brain.
- **Support vector machine:** This is one of the most used supervised learning algorithms, deployed for classification and regression problems.
- **K-means clustering:** This is a method of vector quantization, originally from signal processing, which aims to partition 'n' observations into 'k' clusters in which each observation belongs to the cluster with the nearest mean, serving as a prototype of the cluster.
- **Fast learning network:** This is used to compute network weights between output and hidden layers in a single iteration, and thus, can dramatically reduce learning time while producing accurate results with minimal training data.
- **Ensemble methods:** These are techniques that create multiple models and then combine them to produce improved results.

There are some challenges in ensuring the best performance from IDS such as false alarm rate, low detection rate, unbalanced datasets and response time. In addition, it must be noted that IDS cannot detect attacks where a malicious actor uses legitimate credentials to enter a network and those attacks that prey on weak authentication.

7.1.3 Security Information and Event Monitoring

A security information and event management (SIEM) solution provides an organization with the means for threat detection, compliance and security incident management through the collation and analysis of security events. SIEM enables organizations to detect security incidents and manage security by filtering large amounts of security data from across different systems and by raising security alerts.

> **Info Box 40: How SIEM Works**
> SIEM solutions work by collating security logs and event-related data produced from different applications, devices, networks, domain controllers and other IT infrastructure. They use the data to store, normalize, aggregate and apply analytics to that data to discover trends, detect threats and enable organizations to investigate any alerts. The SIEM system can be deployed on-premises or in a cloud environment.

SIEM solutions are not a replacement for firewalls, IDS and IDPS or antivirus software but work in consonance with these systems to collate and corelate threat information and event logs. The power of SIEM lies in the fact that they aggregate security data from across the entire IT infrastructure to provide enterprise-wide threat visibility.

7.1.4 Network Segmentation

Network segmentation is an architectural approach that splits a network into several segments or subnets, with each acting as its own micro network. This enables network administrators to impose restrictions and control the flow of traffic between subnetworks by defining and implementing granular policies. Network segmentation establishes network boundaries between subnetworks and also allows the implementation of security policies and controls; it can be used as a stepping stone for implementing zero-trust approaches.

The key steps in implementing network segmentation are as follows:

1. Determining the key information assets, assigning levels of importance and establishing appropriate segmentation policies and protective zones based on the sensitivity of data
2. Defining asset groups and mapping data flow
3. Defining segment boundaries and enforcing access controls in such a way that all inbound and outbound traffic must pass through a segment gateway
4. Setting up access control policies based on the principle of least privilege
5. Undertaking regular audits and reviews to evaluate effectiveness and identify the required changes

Demilitarized Zones (DMZ)

Organizations can also set up a DMZ to protect internal local area networks (LANs) from untrusted traffic. A DMZ is a kind of subnetwork that is placed between private networks and the public Internet and provides an extra layer of security for data stored on internal networks. The purpose of DMZ is to permit access to external untrusted networks like the Internet, while making sure that its internal network or LAN remains secure.

The DMZ houses external-facing services and other resources such as servers for the DNS, File Transfer Protocol (FTP), email proxy, Voice over Internet Protocol (VoIP) and web servers. Hence, it works as a security buffer between the internal and external systems.

The DMZ has multiple layers of firewalls, one which filters traffic coming in from external sources and another that filters traffic between the DMZ and internal networks. The implementation of a DMZ makes it difficult for an attacker to get past multiple layers of defences without alerting security administrators of their activities.

The DMZ also offers additional protection in the form of preventing network reconnaissance, blocking IP spoofing attempts and setting up additional security controls for different network segments.

Honeypots

They are a form of deceptive technology designed to trick attackers or unauthorized intruders into accessing what appears to be a legitimate part of the network so that they can be distracted, giving security teams time to examine information such as their IP address, email address and other site addresses to determine their true intentions.

> ### Info Box 41: How Honeypots Work
>
> A honeypot is a useful security mechanism to lure and trap attackers. It is designed to appear vulnerable and unprotected and therefore an exploitable part of a network to potential attackers. It is often strategically positioned in the DMZ along with web services, email services and various other public-facing services. As they are placed on decoy servers inside the DMZ, they can be mistaken for real servers by an attacker. The data that these decoy servers hold is real-looking files with dummy data.
>
> Once defenders spot an attacker entering the honeypot arena, they must determine how long they want to allow them to move around in the honeypot gathering data.
>
> Honeypots provide useful information about the methods and behaviours of an unsuspecting attacker who does not know that he/she is under surveillance. Other network monitoring tools, such as IDSs, cannot provide information that can help understand the attack patterns as effectively as a honeypot.
>
> Badly set up honeypots can be hijacked by smart hackers to feed misinformation to administrators and distract them while they undertake malicious actions. Hackers also use honeypots to set up fake Wi-Fi networks and other websites to lure unsuspecting users to give away valuable sensitive information. The three types of honeypots are:
>
> - **Pure honeypots:** These are designed to detect an attack through a 'listening device' such as a bug tap.
> - **Low-interaction honeypots:** These mimic the functions of a real service or system and enable collection of attacker methods like the use of worms, malware, botnets, etc.
> - **High-interaction honeypots:** This is a comprehensive set-up that is similar to production environments and enables attackers to interact with the system more extensively, keeping the attacker busy and away from the real production system.[3]

Honeypots may be expensive to set up and cannot replace traditional security mechanisms like firewalls, IDS, etc. They are, however, useful in capturing information regarding the tools, techniques and methods used by cybercriminals and provide advance warning and time to respond to their overtures. They can also help in testing an organization's incident response capabilities and procedures and examine their effectiveness in real cyber threat scenarios.

---

[3] Guru, "What Is a Honeypot? How Does It Improve Network Security?," Cyber Security News, accessed September 6, 2021. https://cybersecuritynews-com.cdn.ampproject.org/c/s/cybersecuritynews.com/what-is-a-honeypot/?amp

7.1.5 Wireless Security and VPNs

Wireless security involves the prevention of unauthorized access or harm to computers or data by using wireless networks, including Wi-Fi networks. Generally, wireless security is implemented by deploying wireless devices (routers/switches) that encrypt all wireless traffic by default. Hackers use various techniques to break Wi-Fi security:

- **Man in the middle (MITM)** is a form of attack wherein the attacker infiltrates a private network by stealing log-in credentials. Typically, the attacker will impersonate a legitimate Wi-Fi network to deceive an unsuspecting victim into parting with log-in credentials.
- **Cracking and decrypting passwords** by launching a brute force attack is another way for attackers to guess their way through to obtain log-in credentials. Attackers can also use software like Nessus and John the Ripper to make their job of cracking passwords easier. The same software can be used for testing the strength of passwords.
- **Packet sniffers** are often deployed to monitor network traffic, intercept data packets and access their contents. These can be used by attackers to introduce errors and even bring down a network.
- **Passive capturing** poses another type of threat to wireless security. The attacker sets up listening devices that can capture information transiting through the network and use the information to cause other types of damage.
- **Denial of service** is another form of attack that can exploit weaknesses in Wi-Fi security to enable attackers to disturb signals on the network and cause high level of interference to cause disruption of normal services.

In order to develop wireless security defences, it is important to understand the following underlying protocols:

- **Wireless Equivalent Privacy (WEP)** is the oldest wireless security protocol to be deployed. It was designed in 1997 and is still in use on some of the older devices. The encryption scheme used in WEP (a combination of user- and system-generated keys) is no longer effective as hackers have found ways to break the encryption.
- **Wi-Fi Protected Access (WPA)** was designed to overcome the weaknesses in the WEP and uses a Temporal Key Integrity Protocol (TKIP), which is a dynamic 128-bit key unlike the static key used in WEP. It further provides a message integrity check to scan and verify any packets sent by hackers.

> **Info Box 42: How WPA Works**
>
> Wi-Fi Protected Access (WPA) security offers several enhancements to the earlier WEP protocol in the way it handles security keys and the way users are authorized. This is accomplished using a four-way handshake to authenticate the Wi-Fi client and encrypt all communications with the access point.
>
> When any type of device successfully connects to a WPA network, keys are generated using a four-way handshake that takes place with the access point (usually a router) and device.[4] Where Temporal Key Integrity Protocol (TKIP), an encryption protocol, is used, a message integrity code is included to ensure that the data is not spoofed.

---

[4] Bradley Mitchell, "What Is Wi-Fi Protected Access (WPA)?," Lifewire, accessed March 29, 2022. https://www.lifewire.com/definition-of-wifi-protected-access-816576

- **Wi-Fi Protected Access 2 (WPA2)** was introduced in 2004 and became an industry standard. The Wi-Fi Alliance that has been responsible for the creation and setting up of this protocol announced in 2006 that all future devices with the Wi-Fi trademark must use WPA2. WPA2 uses the Counter Mode Cipher Block Chaining Message Authentication Code Protocol in place of TKIP to provide stronger encryption.
- **Wi-Fi Protected Access 3 (WPA3)** was introduced by the Wi-Fi Alliance after a gap of 14 years and provides several advancements when compared to WPA2, such as:
    - Better general Wi-Fi encryption based on Simultaneous Authentication of Equals (SAE). This enables the use passphrases when compared to other passwords that can be cracked through brute force attacks.
    - WPA-3 Personal provides more personalized encryption, making it difficult for hackers to snoop or passively observe network traffic or ascertain the session keys.
    - Another important development is a new feature to connect display-less and IoT devices to Wi-Fi networks.
    - Greater security for enterprise Wi-Fi through optional 192-bit security for greater protection.

The key points to be noted for ensuring security while using Wi-Fi systems from your home are:

- Change the default Wi-Fi password and the service set identifier (SSID). The SSID, also known as Network ID, is the name of your wireless network. It is used to connect to your network and is visible to anyone having a wireless device within the range of the network.
- Use long and strong alphanumeric passwords.
- Enable the router's firewall.
- Enable media access control (MAC) address filtering. The MAC address is the physical address, which uniquely identifies each device on a given network.
- Disable the remote administration function.
- Use a VPN connection. VPN tools authenticate communication using IPsec or Secure Sockets Layer (SSL) between secure networks and an endpoint device and create an encrypted tunnel for secure communication.

Info Box 43: How VPNs Work

VPN technology is used to provide a secure connection by encrypting all traffic between a user and the Internet. Organizations deploy VPN solutions to safeguard data since it ensures that all the data traffic is routed through an encrypted virtual tunnel. VPNs also mask the user's IP address by disguising it and making its location invisible to everyone.

7.2 EMAIL SECURITY

Emails and other messaging systems constitute a very important channel of work or personal communication. There is, however, growing concern with regard to the security and privacy issues that surround them. Hackers have become adept at sending mails/messages with malicious content with the intention to steal confidential data and cause various kinds of harm. Emails are also used by hackers as a means of infiltrating networks and spreading malware.

There is no single solution that can be used to bolster email security. By deploying the following technologies, individuals and organizations can enhance email security:

- **Spam filters:** Spamming is a common practice used by marketers to send information about their products and services to potential customers. Hackers also deploy the same technique to send malicious links and payloads that can compromise information security. By installing a spam filter, such spamming attempts can be identified and blocked by sending them into a separate folder. These emails can be deleted automatically after a specified time period or on manual inspection. Hackers often use email attachments that contain files, links and images. Images require advanced spam filters that use reputation-based filtering, behaviour-based filtering and content analysis. The area of content analysis is still to be fully mastered by software vendors. The use of a multi-layered spam filter is considered a good option for filtering image spam.
- **Antivirus protection:** In order to identify malware hidden in attachments or those which are downloaded requires the installation of antivirus software. This software can be used to scan each incoming and outgoing email for malicious content and block their entry or exit, as required.
- **Data encryption:** Email data is normally transmitted in an open format. This makes it vulnerable to interception by cybercriminals. Encrypting email data when in transit along with advanced cryptographic features such as encryption of recipient data and email message headers can significantly enhance email security.
- **Sender policy framework (SPF):** This is a method of authenticating an email by detecting the forgery of an email address during delivery of the email.
- **Domain-based message authentication, reporting and conformance (DMARC):** This is an email authentication method that enables mail administrators to prevent hackers from spoofing their organization and domain.
- **DomainKeys Identified Mail (DKIM):** This is another form of authentication that enables an organization to establish that an email claiming to have come from a specific domain was indeed authorized by the owner of that domain.
- **Closed-loop inspection:** This is a useful method for identifying malicious emails and documents by sandboxing suspicious emails and analyzing them. Every link in an email can potentially represent a phishing attempt. Using deep link inspection, the email system can open the suspicious link in its own sandbox so that it does not impact the system. If the links are found to be malicious, they are blocked or removed.

All of the above strategies help in addressing multiple email security challenges in the form of spam, spoofing and phishing attempts.

> **Info Box 44: Implementing Email Security**
>
> Securing email is about the use of end-to-end encryption. The person sending the email encrypts mails/messages using the recipient's public key. The recipient decrypts the message using a private key.[5]

---

[5] Joel Witts, "What Is Email Encryption, How Does It Work, and How Can It Protect Your Organization?," Expert Insights, accessed March 29, 2022. https://expertinsights.com/insights/what-is-email-encryption-how-does-it-work-and-how-can-it-protect-your-organization/

The following are two techniques that organizations can choose from to implement end-to-end encryption:

- **Pretty good privacy (PGP)** is an encryption program used for signing, encrypting and decrypting emails, texts files, directories and even whole disk partitions to enhance the security of email communications.
- **Secure/Multipurpose Internet Mail Extension (S/MIME)** is another email encryption and signing industry standard widely used by organizations to enhance email security.

7.3 ANTIVIRUS TECHNOLOGIES AND SOLUTIONS

Malware is among the most harmful attack vectors used by hackers. It includes a plethora of viruses, ransomware, spyware, trojans, rootkits, and more. Basically, it refers to any form of harmful software.

Antivirus software is a category of cybersecurity application that protects computers and other IT infrastructure by identifying and removing any malicious software or code designed to cause damage.

New forms of malware are being developed and released for use virtually every hour (some say every second); therefore, it is very difficult for antivirus software to match this kind of speed and introduce protection systems to counter new threats.

In order to protect their information assets, organizations combine the use of antivirus software with other threat intelligence systems, cloud integration and alerts to deal with the volume and diversity of threats.

Info Box 45: How Antivirus Solutions Work

Antivirus software tools are designed to search, detect, quarantine and remove viruses and other kinds of malware. They work by scanning files and programs on devices to identify any suspicious behaviour.

Scanning is done both before the files or programs enter the devices and also for those files already on the devices. Scanning for malware can be set up to offer real-time protection or be run on-demand at any time. Users can also perform smart scans on files selected by them, which are more suspect.

In addition to scanning, they also use methods like checking, interception and heuristic detection to detect malware. Antivirus solutions use the following techniques for malware detection:

- **Signature-based detection** involves identifying malware by comparing scan results with a predefined repository of static signatures that are unique patterns in coding that represent known network threats.
- **Heuristic-based detection** is a popular form of detection that uses an algorithm to compare the signature of known viruses against a potential threat.
- **Behaviour-based detection:** It is possible that a virus may escape the above detection methods, in which case the antivirus solution then analyzes the behaviour of programs running on the computer. Some of the indicators of malicious activity are changed settings in a program, modified or deleted files and remote connectivity.
- **Cloud-based detection** identifies malware by gathering data from protected devices and analysing it on the cloud as opposed to performing the analysis locally.

Other techniques like sandbox analysis, host intrusion prevention system, web filtering and application control, custom DNS servers, web browser extensions/add-ons and firewalls (as a part of security suites) are also deployed for antivirus detection.

A new generation of antivirus solutions is emerging that does not limit itself to signature-based virus detection, but aims to prevent all types of attacks, known and unknown, by monitoring and responding to attacker tactics, techniques and procedures (TTPs).

Next-generation antivirus (NGAV) takes the conventional antivirus software to an advanced level of endpoint security protection. These new age solutions use AI-predictive analytics driven by machine learning and threat intelligence to enable the following:[6]

- Detection and prevention of malware attacks (including file-less attacks)
- Spotting of suspicious/malicious behaviour and TTPs from unknown sources
- Gathering and analysis of endpoint data to ascertain root causes
- Identifying and responding to hitherto unknown threats

NGAV can also be deployed through the cloud so that all inbound and outbound communication with endpoints can be monitored and turned into predictive analytics that proactively protects organizations from malware attacks.

7.4 IDENTITY AND ACCESS MANAGEMENT

Identity and access management (IAM) enables organizations to manage the identities of individuals, devices and software and control access to tools and systems that they are required to use as part of their job functions. IAM encompasses the framework of policies and technologies that are employed for ensuring that authorized users have the appropriate access to technology resources. Key reasons for deploying IAM solutions are increased security through enforcement of administrative controls and activity tracking which enables auditability and regulatory compliance.

Broadly, IAM solutions address two important tasks:

- Authenticating a user, software and hardware by referencing a database
- Authorizing specific pre-approved levels of access and allowing only permitted actions

To accomplish these tasks, IAM systems must integrate with a number of organization systems. IAM systems are required to meet certain standards or technologies to enable this:

- **Security Access Markup Language (SAML)** is an open standard for the exchange of information between the IAM and any service or application for the purpose of authentication and authorization.
- **OpenID Connect (OIDC)** is also an open standard built on OAuth 2.0 standards. The OAuth 2.0 authorization framework is a protocol that allows a user to grant a third-party website or application access to the user's protected resources, without necessarily revealing their long-term credentials or even their identity.[7] The OAuth (open authorization) protocol was developed by the Internet Engineering Task Force and uses tokens (issued by the resource owner) which represent delegated right of access. While SAML uses Extensible Markup Language (XML) for transmitting data, OAuth 2.0 uses JavaScript Object Notation (JSON).
- **System for Cross-domain Identity Management (SCIM)** was first conceived to simplify cloud identity management but has become more pervasive today because its ability to create a single master account of user credentials like user ID and password that could be added to other systems. SCIM is useful in communicating user identity data between identity providers (such as companies with multiple individual users) and service providers requiring user identity information (such as enterprise SaaS apps).

---

[6] "What Is Next-Generation Antivirus (NGAV)?," VMware, accessed April 6, 2022. https://www.vmware.com/topics/glossary/content/next-generation-antivirus-ngav.html

[7] "OAuth 2.0 Authorization Framework," AuthO, accessed August 17, 2021. https://auth0.com/docs/protocols/protocol-oauth2

IAM systems help IT and security administrators obtain full visibility in a single directory to create, delete and modify users or they may integrate with other directories and synchronize them. Provisioning of users is an important aspect of IAM tools that entails granting user access levels such as viewer, editor and administrator based on the roles that they perform in an organization. Deprovisioning is also important from a security point of view to remove access rights when a person leaves the organization or changes his/her role.

Other deployment aspects of IAM solutions are their ability to support functions such as multi-factor authentication (MFA) and single sign-on (SSO). IAM solutions are also useful in laying the foundation for the implementation of zero-trust architecture principles such as least privilege access and identity-based security policies.

Info Box 46: How IAM Systems Work

IAM solutions provide system administrators the ability to set and control access of users such as employees, customers, supply chain partners and service providers. Other than defining a user's role, access permissions and enforcing security policies, IAM tools enable tracking of user activities, logging and reporting as well as modifying or changing user access.

In the context of identity management, devices such as computers, servers, smart phones routers, sensors, etc. can also be managed and administered in a similar way. Traditionally, IAM tools comprised the following elements:[8]

- A directory or identity repository of the personnel data which the system uses to define individual users
- A set of tools for adding, modifying and deleting that data (related to access life cycle management)
- A system that regulates and enforces user access
- An auditing and reporting system

Additional features and functionality are now available in IAM solutions such as multi-factor authentication, credential verification, biometrics, risk-based authentication, SSO and the use of AI and ML.

Risk-based authentication is an approach that assesses the likelihood of account compromise for each login. This dynamic authentication system is designed to consider factors like IP address, user-agent HTTP header, time of access, etc. as a part of a user profile and the risk profile associated with that transaction.

SSO enables users to securely authenticate multiple applications and websites by using just one set of credentials. SSO tokens, which represent a collection of data or information, are transmitted from one system to another during the SSO process. While SSO offers great advantages in terms of centralised identity management, they are more complex when it comes to allowing different levels of access freedoms across different applications.

---

[8] David Strom, "What Is IAM? Identity and Access Management Explained," CSO, accessed March 30, 2022. https://www.csoonline.com/article/2120384/what-is-iam-identity-and-access-management-explained.html

7.5 AUTHENTICATION

Authentication refers to the process of verifying that a person, entity, application, device or website is who it claims to be. It is a way of checking credentials and providing assurance that an incoming request for connectivity or access is real and genuine. There are four authentication factors that are commonly in use today. These are as follows:

Info Box 47: Authentication Factors

Knowledge factors	Authentication credentials consisting of information that the user possesses, such as a personal identification number (PIN), a username, a password, etc.
Inheritance factors	Authentication such as biometrics (fingerprint, facial recognition, retina pattern, voiceprint) or tangible objects such as a SIM card or three-digit credit card code
Location factors	Using the geo-location of an identity as a means of authentication
Behaviour factors	Authentication by continuously analyzing user behaviour and using patterns to identify and authenticate

Organizations can choose from a variety of authentication methods depending on their security assessment and needs. The different types of authentication methods are as follows:

Single-Factor/ Primary Authentication	This simple authentication procedure has been in use for a long time now. It involves the process of securing access to a given system, such as a network, application, device or website, through the use of only a single factor or category of credentials, usually in the form of a username and password.
Two-Factor Authentication (2FA)	2FA provides an additional layer of protection while authenticating by evaluating two factors such a PIN along with a username and password.
Single Sign-On (SSO)	SSO is a session and user authentication service that permits a user to use one set of log-in credentials to log into multiple applications and systems without having to enter it multiple times.
Multi-Factor Authentication (MFA)	MFA requires the user to provide more than two authentication factors for verification such as user ID and password, PIN and a fingerprint.
Password Authentication Protocol (PAP)	This is a dying protocol where a user sends the password and username to the authentication server as plain text. Nowadays, it is seldom used due to it being highly vulnerable. The use of encrypted passwords and user IDs is more in use today.
Challenge Handshake Authentication Protocol (CHAP)	CHAP is designed on the basis of what is known as a shared secret. To authenticate, the authenticator sends a challenge message to the access-requesting party, which responds with a value calculated using a one-way hash function that takes as inputs the challenge and the shared secret.
Extensible Authentication Protocol (EAP)	EAP is more of an authentication framework, which provides some common functions that are often used in wireless networks and point-to-point connections. EAP supports several authentication mechanisms without having to pre-negotiate any particular one.

IT systems are built around the concept of a user or device identity. The process of authentication in the context of computer systems is one of the most critical aspects which is used to ensure that the confidentiality, integrity and availability of data or systems is not compromised on account of any unauthorized access or activity. Authentication provides the means of assurance and confirmation of a user's identity, making it imperative for a user to prove his/her identity and entitlement before gaining access to a system or data.

7.6 CRYPTOGRAPHY

Cryptography is of great importance when it comes to cybersecurity and data protection. Its primary objective is to provide methods to secure and protect information and communications using encryption and related techniques.[9] In simple terms, cryptography refers to the process of converting normal plain text into incomprehensible text and vice-versa. Using cryptography, data at rest and in transit can be protected so that only legitimate users can read and process it. Further, cryptography is used for user authentication and also provides data protection from theft or alteration.

A common question is whether cryptography is the same as encryption. Cryptography is a broader term that refers to the study of methods/techniques such as encryption for secure communication in the presence of third parties.[10] It not only provides methods like encryption that can protect information and communication, but also other techniques like message authentication code (MAC) and digital signatures to safeguard information against spoofing and forgeries.

Encryption is the practice of encoding messages and information through the use of mathematical techniques and algorithms in order to preserve their confidentiality, integrity and availability.

Cryptography is used today in several applications such as chip-based card payments, computer passwords, digital currencies, time stamping, military communications and e-commerce transactions.

> **Info Box 48: Objectives of Cryptography**
>
> The primary objectives of using cryptography are to:
>
> - Maintain confidentiality; unauthorised persons cannot read/use the information
> - Maintain integrity; ensure that information cannot be altered or modified
> - Ensure non-repudiation; the author/sender of information cannot deny the authenticity such as signing or sending a document
> - Authentication: to verify the identity of whoever created the information, such as the user or system
> - Cryptographic availability: to ensure that information is accessible to authorized users
>
> The concept of a key is an integral part of cryptography. Just as in the physical world, a key is used to lock/unlock a safe to protect valuables, in the digital world, a cryptographic key is used to lock (encrypt) and unlock (decrypt) data. A cryptographic key is a string of characters applied within an encryption algorithm to protect information.
>
> **Encryption and the CIA Triad**
>
> Cryptography plays an important role in achieving the three most fundamental objectives of information security, which is to maintain confidentiality, integrity and availability (see Chapter 1 for more information).

---

[9] "Cryptography and Its Types," GeeksforGeeks, accessed April 6, 2022. https://www.geeksforgeeks.org/cryptography-and-its-types
[10] "Cryptography and Its Types," GeeksforGeeks, accessed April 6, 2022. https://www.geeksforgeeks.org/cryptography-and-its-types

Maintaining the confidentiality of information is about preventing unauthorized access to sensitive information. Unauthorized access could be deliberate, malicious or even accidental. Apart from access control mechanisms, cryptography is an important tool to ensure that sensitive information is kept confidential and prevents it from being compromised in any way, even when a hacker gains unauthorized access.

Information while being transmitted is vulnerable to being tampered with and modified. If this were to happen, it could lead to severe consequences since the information would no longer be accurate or reliable as its integrity would be questionable. The use of encryption methods ensures that the integrity of files in transmission is maintained and no alteration, tampering or corruption of the information takes place. The integrity of files can also be verified and validated by checking that the hash values calculated by the receiver matches with that which was generated and appended to the file by the sender.

Cryptography also maintains the availability of data by ensuring reliability and allowing access only to users with necessary permissions to use systems and retrieve data in a dependable and timely manner.

Encrypting all sensitive and regulated data is considered a good practice and encouraged under various regulations and frameworks.

Cryptographic Techniques

The following are cryptographic techniques that are widely used today:

- **Symmetric-key cryptography:** In this case, both the sender and the receiver use a single key for encryption and decryption, respectively. Two kinds of symmetric key algorithms are block cipher algorithms (bits are encrypted in fixed-size blocks of electronic data with the use of a specific secret key) and stream algorithms (data is encrypted while streaming instead of being retained in the system's memory). Examples of symmetric encryption algorithms are AES (Advanced Encryption Standard), DES (Data Encryption Standard), 3DES or 3 key (widely used in EMV chip cards), RC4, 5, 6 and Blowfish.
- **Asymmetric or public-key cryptography:** In this case, two distinct but mathematically related keys are used. While the public key is used for encryption, the private key is paired with it and used for decryption. Hence, while anyone can encrypt data using a public key, only the holder of the paired private key can decrypt such data. The key pairs are generated using cryptographic algorithms which are based on mathematical problems.

Info Box 49: How Asymmetric Cryptography Works

Asymmetric cryptography, also known as public key cryptography, provides the foundation for digital signatures. The process works on the basis of generating and matching two mutually mathematically linked keys as a means of authentication. The person who is signing and sending document generates a set of random string of numbers (could be the public or private key) which are used to convert it into an encoded format known as cipher text. Once it is received by the recipient, the same can be decrypted using the other key so that he can not only read the original contents but also verify that the document and the identity of the sender is genuine.

> The public key, as the name suggests, is in the public domain and is generated by using one of the following algorithms:
>
> - Rivest–Shamir–Adleman (RSA)
> - Elliptic curve cryptography (ECC)
> - Digital signature algorithm (DSA)
>
> The private key is a secret key that is kept confidential by the owner. Private keys are generated using the same algorithms as above. The basic difference between a public key and a private key is that one encrypts while the other decrypts. Among the benefits of asymmetric cryptography is its ability to handle large data volumes, timestamping, verifiability and ability to scale.
>
> **What is the use of an HSM?**
>
> A hardware security module is a security device that protects and manages digital keys and performs encryption as well as decryption functions for digital signatures, strong authentication and other cryptographic functions.

- **Hash functions:** In this case, a hash function is used that converts a numerical input value into another compressed numerical value. The hash function takes an input as a key, which is associated with a record and uses to identify it to the data storage and retrieval application. These keys could be fixed length, like an integer, or variable length, like a name. The output which is a hash code is then used to index a hash table holding the data or records, or pointers to them.[11] Hash functions are commonly used by operating systems to encrypt passwords.

7.6.1 Types and Uses of Cryptography Keys

Cryptographic keys are used for several purposes and functions. Based on its use, the properties of the associated key such as type, length and crypto period will vary.

> **Info Box 50: Cryptographic Keys: Use and Functionality**
>
> | | |
> |---|---|
> | Data Encryption Key | A data encryption key is typically a random string of bits generated with the use of algorithms such as AES and 3DES (symmetric keys) which have a key length between 128 and 256 bits and RSA (asymmetric keys) with a key length of 1024 and 4096 bits, which are used to encrypt and decrypt data. Each key is unique and unpredictable keys take longer and are harder to break. Symmetric encryption keys are generally ephemeral, where the crypto period ranges from a day to a year, while asymmetric key pairs usually have a lifespan of one to five years. |
> | Authentication Key | Authentication is used to provide assurance about the integrity and/or originator of the associated data. It is generally used together with symmetric encryption by generating a hash message authentication code (HMAC). |

---

[11] "Hash Function," Wikipedia, accessed October 27, 2021. https://en.wikipedia.org/wiki/Hash_function

Digital Signature Key	In much the same way as authentication keys, digital signatures also provide assurance about the integrity and originator of the associated data, and in addition, include the concept of non-repudiation, whereby the person signing cannot deny that the signature was false.
Key Encryption Key (aka Key Wrapping Key or Key Transport Key)	Transporting a secret key securely is vital and to implement this, a wrapping mechanism is used which ensures that confidentiality, integrity and authenticity is maintained. The key used for this encryption is a static, long-term key depending on the algorithm that is used.
Master Key	A master key is typically a symmetric key that is used to encrypt several subordinate keys. Depending on the algorithm used, it will be 128–256 bits in length, will have a very long lifespan and should therefore be well protected by using an HSM.
Root Key	In a public key infrastructure (PKI) hierarchy, a root key is at the topmost level and is used to authenticate and sign digital certificates. It is essentially an asymmetric key-pair with a length typically between 256 and 4,096 bits depending on the digital signature algorithm used. The root key often has a lifetime of several years, and the private key will often be protected using an HSM.

7.6.2 Applications of Cryptography

Cryptography is among the most important technologies for building secure systems. Cryptography can protect the confidentiality of data, prevent its unauthorized modification and also authenticate the source of data. Cryptography can help in meeting other cybersecurity challenges as well and is therefore being used in several ways in order to enhance cybersecurity, such as the following:

- **Encrypting computers, laptops, and other devices:** Full-disk encryption is a type of cryptography that can prevent information from falling into the wrong hands when devices are stolen or unattended. By encrypting hard drives, particularly in mobile systems, including pen drives and other removable media, many data breaches or security incidents can be avoided. This is even more important in industries such as healthcare and financial services where loss of data could lead to regulatory action and even financial and reputational loss.
- **Storing passwords and authenticating users:** The perils of storing passwords in plain text is well known by now and is not an option anymore. Cryptography (hashing) is now widely in use. However, hashing alone does not offer adequate security and adding a salt to the hashing process is considered the best option for password storing and authentication. A cryptographic salt consists of random bits added to each password instance before hashing is done. These random bits ensure that even if two passwords are the same, they are unique due to the random element that is added. Salts can prevent damage from hash table attacks by ensuring that attackers are forced to compute them again using the salts for each user. Cryptographic secure hash algorithms like SHA2 and SHA3 have evolved from the MD5 message-digest algorithm, a cryptographically broken but still widely used hash function producing a 128-bit hash value. Currently, bcrypt is increasingly being used for password hashing as it uses both hashing and salting.
- **Encrypting sensitive data and databases:** With the increasing frequency of cyberattacks, it is good practice for organizations to encrypt sensitive data such as IP information or databases

that hold a variety of important information such as customer data, employee data, financial information, etc. Implementing file-level encryption for protecting specific folders or files along with other access and security controls is a useful way to maximize data security.
- **Encrypting email and messaging communications:** A lot of organizational information is shared by email and messaging platforms every day. Not securing these communications can lead to leakage of sensitive information and compromise security. The use of an encryption program like PGP can enable end-to-end encryption of texts, emails and other files to significantly enhance the security of email communications.
- **Website security:** The use of the HTTPS protocol to make website communication more secure is often mandated for websites that transact using sensitive data. The communication port number 443 that is used by the HTTPS protocol is secured by an encrypted algorithm.
- **Smart contracts:** Cryptography is one of the underlying techniques used by blockchain applications such as smart contracts or cryptocurrencies. Smart contracts consist of a set of programmed rules that can be run by nodes within a blockchain network, typically through the use of a virtual machine. Cryptography not only enables implementation of the consensus mechanism used by the blockchain, but is also used for affixing digital signatures, which are used to prove that an individual has the right to perform a given action. Similarly, cryptocurrencies that represent a transfer of value also use cryptography techniques that enforce and ensure trust and safety in each transaction.

7.7 HOW DO DIGITAL MONEY, CRYPTOCURRENCY AND NFTS WORK?

Digital financial transactions using payment systems such as credit and debit cards have existed for a long time. The use of credit cards goes all the way back to the 1920s when oil companies and hotel chains in the United States issued cards as an alternative way for their customers to make payments for their purchases. The proliferation of the Internet and e-commerce brought in new forms of payments such as Internet payments and mobile wallets. For businesses, they improved the speed of the transaction at the point of sale, solved the problem of giving back change and reduced costs associated with the use of physical currency forms. However, they also opened avenues for hackers to steal money by gaining unauthorized access to a victim's account, set up online payment scams, commit frauds and use technology to make illegal payments.

Digital money, or digital currency, is a form of money or payment that exists only in electronic form. It is a natural progression from traditional fiat currency, given its overwhelming advantages as we are moving towards a digital society. Digital money is used, transferred and accounted by electronic codes and technologies and is widely believed to be the future of money, with the use of physical currency becoming minimal if not non-existent.[12]

Cryptocurrencies today have come a long way in a relatively short period of time. While conceptually all cryptocurrencies need not be based on blockchain technologies, the first successful cryptocurrency called Bitcoin was created based on the innovations by Satoshi Nakamoto in 2009. Reports suggest that there are now more than 12,000 cryptocurrencies. Their growth from 2021 to 2022 is nothing short of spectacular as the number of cryptocurrencies more than doubled in this period. At the end of 2021, the

---

[12] Mitchell Grant and Jefreda R Brown, "Digital Money Definition," Investopedia, accessed March 24, 2022. https://www.investopedia.com/terms/d/digital-money.asp

market was adding about 1,000 new cryptocurrencies every month.[13] Popular among them are Bitcoin, Ethereum, Tether, Cardano, Binance Coin and XRP, to name a few. The rising popularity of cryptocurrencies is not just because of the fact that it improves on aspects of traditional fiat currency, but that even though they are not backed by any sovereign governments, they process transactions securely on their own. This also becomes a means of moving money around the world in seconds without regulatory oversight and legal considerations.

Cryptocurrencies are largely based on the use of blockchain technology to record and secure every transaction. They can be freely used as a form of digital cash for products and services in many countries of the world. They can also be bought using digital wallet applications or through exchanges and also reconverted into traditional fiat currency. While governments around the world are cagey about the growing use of cryptocurrencies and want to regulate or introduce their own version of them, the popularity of cryptocurrencies is rising because security concerns of users are well-addressed through the recording of transactions in a public ledger, secured using cryptography, maintaining an irrefutable, timestamped and secure record of every payment.

A cryptocurrency like Bitcoin has the following four basic components:

Info Box 51: Components of Bitcoin

Software	Bitcoin is a software application that defines what a bitcoin is, what it does and how it is transmitted. The software has its own management features such as identity management, authorization and authentication, blockchain management, distributed ledger management, etc.
Cryptography	Cryptography plays a key role in bitcoin. It is used to regulate not only the transfer of bitcoin between transacting parties and the production of new bitcoin units using encryption, but also the safeguarding of data within the system. The bitcoin network supports various kinds of smart contracts created using its powerful scripting language, called Script.
Hardware	Cryptography requires a lot of hardware compute power to manage the activity of the blockchain as well as for mining new bitcoins. Hardware wallets are considered highly secure when it comes to storing the private keys needed to sign bitcoin transactions as well as to transfer, send and receive bitcoins.
Mining	Apart from buying bitcoins, you can also earn them through mining. Miners receive bitcoin as a reward for completing 'blocks' of verified transactions, which are added to the blockchain.[14]

Non-fungible tokens or NFTs are a new asset class that store digital media (music, art, videos, collectibles, etc.) using which creators can sell their creations. Each NFT can be verified and authenticated by accessing its history and ownership. These NFTs are created using technology similar to that of cryptocurrencies. Since cryptocurrencies can be traded or exchanged for one another, they are called fungible. They are also equal in value, that is, one bitcoin and another bitcoin have the same value, but this is not the case in

---

[13] Lyle Daly, "How Many Cryptocurrencies Are There?," The Motley Fool, accessed March 24, 2022. https://www.fool.com/investing/stock-market/market-sectors/financials/cryptocurrency-stocks/how-many-cryptocurrencies-are-there/

[14] Mitchell Grant and Jefreda R Brown, "Digital Money Definition," Investopedia, accessed March 24, 2022. https://www.investopedia.com/terms/d/digital-money.asp

NFTs, each of which have a different value. Cryptocurrency wallets enable the storage of NFTs and they are therefore often bought using cryptocurrencies.

7.8 DIGITAL SIGNATURES

At the outset, it is important to understand the difference between an electronic signature, a digital signature and a digital certificate. An electronic or e-signature comprises any symbol, sound or process that demonstrates the intent to sign something. A scan of a handwritten signature or stamp or just your written name can be considered as an e-signature. A digital signature is a cryptographic technique that validates the authenticity and integrity of a digital document, software or message. In the physical world, a common phrase is 'signed, sealed and delivered' – a digital signature performs the same function in the digital world without the need for a handwritten signature or stamped seal. A digital signature is non-repudiable and uses asymmetric cryptography to make the signature tamper proof while providing evidence of origin, identity and the status of the digital documents. Many countries around the world have recognized digital signatures as legally binding.

A digital certificate is a file or electronic password that proves the authenticity of a device, server or user through the use of cryptography and the public key infrastructure (PKI).[15]

Digital certificates serve a number of purposes:

- They help organizations to make sure that only trusted devices and users are connected to their network by using digital certificates as a means of authentication
- A Security Sockets Layer (SSL) certificate is a type of digital certificate that authenticates a website's identity and creates an encrypted connection between a web server and a web browser.
- Digital certificates are the credentials that enable the confirmation and verification of identities between users in a transaction. They function in a manner similar to a passport, which certifies one's identity as a citizen of a country; the purpose of a digital certificate is to establish the identity of users within the ecosystem.[16]

A digital certificate holds identifiable information, like a user's name, organization and a device's Internet Protocol (IP) address or serial number. It also holds a copy of a public key from the certificate holder, which is required to be paired to a corresponding private key to verify that it is real. A public key certificate is issued by certificate authorities (CAs) that sign certificates to verify the identity of the requesting device or user.[17]

It is important for the person creating the signature to keep the private key secure as if the same is compromised it could lead to the fraudulent use of the digital signature and its associated consequences. There are several features and methods that enhance the security and usability of digital signatures:

- Use of passwords, codes and PINs for purposes of authentication of a signer's identity
- Use of asymmetric cryptography to implement a public key algorithm for encryption of keys
- Time stamping
- Traceability and auditability
- Check sum and cyclic redundancy check (CRC)

---

[15] "What Is a Digital Certificate?," Fortinet, accessed August 21, 2021. https://www.fortinet.com/resources/cyberglossary/digital-certificates

[16] "What Is a Digital Certificate?," Thales, accessed August 21, 2021. https://cpl.thalesgroup.com/faq/signing-certificates-and-stamping/what-digital-certificate

[17] "What Is a Digital Certificate?," Fortinet, accessed August 21, 2021. https://www.fortinet.com/resources/cyberglossary/digital-certificates

- Certificate authority validation
- Third-party validation by a trust services provider (TSP)

The three classes of digital signatures are given below:

- Class 1: Provide a rudimentary level of security as they use only an email and username for validation.
- Class 2: Authenticate signatures based on a signer's identity against a pre-verified database. These are generally used for electronic filing of documents and tax returns.
- Class 3: Mandate the signer to be physically present before a certifying authority and establish their identity before signing. These are used for e-auctions, e-tendering and court filings.

> **Info Box 52: Digital Signature Use Case**
>
> Mr X is the sender and he wants to send a secure, digitally-signed document file to  Ms Y, the receiver and verifier.
>
> Mr X chooses a file that needs to be digitally signed in the document platform or application.
>
> Mr X generates the unique hash value of the file content.
>
> The generated hash value is encrypted with Mr X's private key to create the digital signature.
>
> The digitally signed file is ready for transmission and is sent to Ms Y.
>
> Ms Y decrypts the file using the digitally signed file using Mr X's public key and calculates its hash value and proceeds to verify the validity by comparing it with the hash value of Mr X's file.
>
> The signature is valid if the two hash values are equal.

7.8.1 Block Ciphers and Stream Ciphers

In cryptography, symmetric encryption comprises two main categories: block ciphers and stream ciphers.

Block Cipher

A block cipher is used to convert plain text into cipher text by encrypting data using an algorithm and a cryptographic key. A block cipher produces blocks of equal size, while a stream cipher encrypts one bit at a time.

Data Encryption Standard (DES) and Advanced Encryption Standard (AES) are examples of the use of block ciphers. DES comprises 64-bit blocks along with a 56-bit key, whereas AES uses a 128-bit block with a 128-bit, 192-bit or 256-bit key.

Block ciphers use an initialization vector (IV), which is a random or arbitrary number that is used along with a secret key for data encryption. IVs are used to prevent hackers from cracking the encryption code as the numbers derived from a random number generator change continuously.

Block ciphers are generally difficult to tamper with and need high levels of expertise to break them. The following are five different block cipher modes of operation that define how these blocks are encrypted:

Info Box 53: Block Cipher Modes of Operation

Electronic codebook (ECB) mode	This mode breaks the input plain text into a number of blocks that are sequentially processed. Plain text blocks are encrypted independent of other blocks.
Cipher block chaining (CBC) mode	In this mode, every block of plain text is linked with the preceding cipher text block before being encrypted. Hence, by virtue of being linked, each block of the cipher text is dependent on all the plain text blocks processed before it in a data stream. Popular protocols like SSL and TLS use this mode to encrypt data so that eavesdroppers and hackers are unable to see what is being transmitted over the Internet.
Cipher text feedback (CFB) mode	This stream mode uses an initial chaining vector (ICV) in its processing; each block of plain text is XORed (a Boolean logic operation) with the encrypted version of the preceding cipher text to generate the current cipher text block. The XOR operation is used to conserve randomness, since a random bit XORed with a non-random bit will result in a random bit.
Output feedback (OFB) mode	This mode uses a feedback mechanism, but instead of XORing the preceding block of cipher text with the plain text before encryption, it does so after it is encrypted.
Counter (CTR) mode	This mode is a block chaining mode that uses a counter-based block cipher implementation such that each time a counter-initiated value is encrypted and provided as input to XOR with plain text, it results in a cipher text block. This mode is independent of feedback use and can be implemented in parallel.

Stream Cipher

This is a symmetric key cipher where plain text digits are combined with a pseudorandom cipher digit stream. It uses bitwise XOR operators on binary data as part of their encryption and decryption processes. An XOR operation follows the logic that *if* input bits are the same, *then* the output will be false (0), *else* true.

The basic difference between block ciphers and stream ciphers is that while a block cipher breaks down plain text messages into fixed-size blocks before converting them into cipher text using a key, a stream cipher breaks a plain text message down into single bits, which then are converted individually into cipher text using key bits.[18]

---

[18] Casey Crane, "Block Cipher vs Stream Cipher: What They Are and How They Work," Hashed Out, accessed April 6, 2022. https://www.thesslstore.com/blog/block-cipher-vs-stream-cipher/

Stream ciphers are widely used for the following:

- SSL/TLS connections
- Cellular and 4G connections
- Bluetooth connections

The two main types of stream ciphers are as follows:

- **Synchronous stream ciphers**, where a secret key generates keystreams which are made independently of both the plain text and the cipher text.
- **Self-synchronizing stream ciphers**, where a secret key is used but they contain another form of randomization to make hacking harder.

Some of the benefits associated with stream ciphers are speed of encryption, low level of complexity and ease of use.

7.8.2 Public Key Infrastructure

Public key infrastructure (PKI) plays a key role in modern-day enterprise cybersecurity. It serves as an effective way of managing public key encryption and using digital certificates through a set of roles, policies, hardware, software and procedures that enable the creation, management, distribution, storage and use of the same. Keys and certificates generated by PKI are used by people, devices and applications to enhance security and trust. The basic components of a PKI are:

- Public key
- Private key
- Hardware security module

In order to support the use of digital certificates, the following elements are required as part of the system:

- **Certificate authority (CA):** To issue digital certificates, sign them with its own public key and store them for reference.
- **Registration authority:** To verify the identities of those requesting digital certificates. A CA can function as its own registration authority or employ a third party to do so.
- **Certificate database:** To store the certificates and metadata about them till such time the certificate is valid.
- **Certificate revocation list:** To block invalid certificates. This is used by various endpoints, including web browsers, to ensure a certificate is valid and trustworthy.
- **Certificate policy:** To articulate the PKI procedures followed, which will enable us to judge the trustworthiness of the PKI.

Digital certificates have gained in importance in recent times as a means to ensure data security. Some of the key benefits of using digital certificates include:

- Enhanced security through the encryption of internal and external communications
- Scalability and reliability through speed of operation and standardization of processes
- Ensuring authenticity of communications
- Establishing public trust in digital systems by enhancing security and upholding privacy

7.9 ADVANCED TECHNOLOGIES AND APPROACHES IN CYBERSECURITY

To combat attackers who stage sophisticated attack strategies and ramp up the scale of disruption and damage they can cause is almost impossible using only basic cybersecurity tools. From petty attacks, cybercriminals have moved to targeting critical economic and public utility infrastructures. Any of these attacks, if successful, leave behind severe and grave consequences like public inconvenience, financial losses, reputational damage, regulatory penalties and huge expense in restoring operations. The impacts of attacks such as ransomware and on public utilities are no longer limited to individuals but span across global economic and political systems. To counter modern-day cyberattacks, organizations are turning to advanced technologies to boost cybersecurity. Let us examine some advanced technologies that are increasingly gaining acceptance.

7.9.1 Artificial Intelligence, Machine Learning and Deep Learning

Artificial intelligence (AI) refers to the ability to create computer programs that can perform intelligent functions by mimicking the human brain. AI-based systems can perform repeatable tasks and operate autonomously, thereby boosting productivity. AI is increasingly being deployed in building smart machines/devices/appliances/automobiles (basically smart everything) capable of performing tasks that typically require human intelligence.

Machine learning (ML) is an extension to the science of AI. Systems that support ML are capable of 'learning' from data and with the help of algorithms can adapt to and apply learning to accomplish tasks. Algorithms used for ML can be categorised as supervised learning (parameters are defined for comparing data inputs), unsupervised or self-learning (the system finds the data relationships on its own) and even semi-supervised. The advantages of ML include identification of trends and patterns, continuously improving, handling different data sets and working autonomously. Programming languages like Python and C++ are popular choices for use in conjunction with ML.

Deep learning (DL) is a category of ML based on neural networks and has the ability to correct itself. This capability of DL also enables predictive modelling and analytics. While conventional ML algorithms are linear, DL algorithms are capable of handling greater complexity and abstraction. DL algorithms work iteratively and apply learnings from each iteration on its input to create a statistical model as output.

In the context of cybersecurity, the use of ML is the most commonly deployed approach. While ML offers great potential in boosting security, by itself it cannot handle the myriad issues that are associated with cybersecurity. Integrating AI and ML in cybersecurity systems can provide the following benefits:[19]

- AI-based systems can be trained to identify malware and other forms of threats, generate alerts and protect sensitive data. ML systems can 'learn' a network's typical behaviour and report outliers and anomalies. The ability to learn continuously and adapt makes ML systems more effective in identifying potential threats to enable early blocking.
- AI systems can handle large data volumes. Given the ever-increasing volumes of data traffic, manual approaches to detect threats are no longer viable. AI-based systems are highly scalable and can handle large traffic volumes, analyze them and generate alerts in real time.
- When it comes to identifying vulnerabilities, AI-based cybersecurity systems can increase effectiveness multi-fold, which can help in better vulnerability management and risk reduction.

---

[19] "8 Benefits of Using AI for Cybersecurity," Cyber Management Alliance, accessed August 22, 2021. https://www.cm-alliance.com/cybersecurity-blog/8-benefits-of-using-ai-for-cybersecurity

- Using AI-based systems, repetitive security practices can be automated.
- AI-based cybersecurity systems enable early threat detection and can support quick response, which is key to preventing cyberattacks and minimizing damage.
- Authentication is another major security area where AI plays a key role through the use of tools that enable facial recognition, implementing CAPTCHA codes, and the use of other biometrics like fingerprint and retina-based identification.

To get the best out of AI and ML systems, organizations must focus on data governance. The organization, classification and management of data throughout its life cycle is vital for them to be more effective. In more ways than one, AI and ML have become an integral part of cybersecurity and will continue to be in future. Table 7.1 lists the cybersecurity applications where AI and ML are used.

Table 7.1 Cybersecurity applications of AI and ML

Vulnerability management
Threat hunting/malware detection
Network security
Data centres and cloud security
Security screening
Security and crime prevention
Analyze mobile endpoints
IoT security

7.9.2 Behavioural Analytics

User and entity behaviour analytics (UEBA) is a class of software that enables organizations to understand and monitor the actions of users to determine deviations from 'normal behaviour' such as oddities, outliers and anomalies. This is performed by developing and employing analytics that capture what is considered 'normal behaviour' and using the same as a baseline to determine what is abnormal and what is not. In the context of cybersecurity, these abnormal behaviours can be used as a forewarning of security incidents and breaches.

To be effective, UEBA implementations should cover all types of users and user groups to enable detection of intrusions that find their way past preventive technologies such as firewalls, intrusion-prevention systems and antivirus software. UEBA helps to:

- Automate user behaviour monitoring
- Enable better security monitoring
- Provide cues and alerts for further investigation
- Enable correlation of behavioural data across systems
- Enable the use of powerful analytical tools and ML that can be used in conjunction with UEBA

Behavioural analytics is very useful in determining patterns in user activities in relation to systems and networks as well as offering a consolidated view of any abnormal activity that can help detect potential and real-time cyber threats. For example a sudden increase in data transmission from a particular user device can be detected and flagged to enable cybersecurity teams to investigate if this is indicative of a possible cybersecurity issue or threat. In the race to stay a step ahead or even be equal to the task of identifying any type of malicious user activity that could jeopardize enterprise cybersecurity, UEBA is a useful and, may even be considered, an essential tool in the cyber defence armoury.

7.9.3 Embedded Hardware Security and Authentication

There is ongoing debate on whether hardware components, given their limited functions, can offer greater security than software elements that have a wide variety of functions and, therefore, are more vulnerable from a security perspective. However, hardware devices, while providing a better security option, have their own constraints such as limited memory when it comes to implementing security controls and features.

Embedded hardware-based security can ideally provide greater security for IoT devices by enabling the following:

- Protection of application protocols
- Hardening of embedded devices
- Reporting and blocking of cyber threats
- Detection and reporting of hardware authentication failures

For implementing security in IoT devices, developers can choose from the following hardware security elements.

- **Trusted Platform Module (TPM)** is a hardware component that is designed specifically to perform crypto calculations. A TPM is a separate chip that is physically isolated from the rest of the processing system.
- **Trusted Execution Environment (TEE)** is a high-trust environment for executing code and is capable of ignoring threats from the rest of the device. Examples of the use of TEE technologies that incorporate hybrid approaches (using both hardware and software mechanisms) for implementing security by creating a trust zone are ARM TrustZone and Intel SGX.
- **Secure Element** is a secret store, like a SIM card or a smart card, that can prevent tampering using cryptography. An example of this technology in major use is the EMV chip on payment cards.

Making an IoT device secure and authentic without making it complicated and expensive is very challenging. Experts suggest that both these objectives can be achieved by embedding security through a chip-based implementation of elliptic curve cryptography. Intel Corporation has introduced a range of sixth-generation vPro chips that provide user authentication, which can be embedded into system hardware. The chips support and enable 'authentication security' through multiple levels and methods of authentication working together.

7.9.4 Blockchain

The use of blockchain technology for cybersecurity holds a lot of promise. The distributed ledger technology concept for creating and maintaining trust across the ecosystem combined with features such as recording of encrypted transactional data by all nodes makes for a very secure operating environment. Because of its distributed architecture, lack of centralised control over data and encryption techniques, hackers find it difficult to break into and steal data from blockchain systems.

Blockchain works on the principle of each member (node) being responsible for verifying the authenticity of the data added. Blockchain technology can be deployed along with AI to boost verification and authentication and provide greater security and data protection. Blockchain systems have the capacity to withstand many types of cyberattacks due to its security-oriented architecture and provide greater data protection.

How Blockchain Technology Works

Database as a concept existed even before the use of computer systems. Starting in the 1980s, relational databases have grown in popularity and are still used across sectors in a variety of applications. Relational databases are often centralized repositories of different types of data, which are indexed and supported by powerful query tools that help generate useful insights by slicing and dicing information in many ways. Hackers who understood the value of information stored in relational databases started attacking them using a variety of tools and techniques including SQL injections, privilege escalation and brute force attacks, thereby stealing the data stored therein or, at the very least, compromising the integrity of the stored data.

At a broad level, a blockchain is an open distributed database that records the provenance of an information asset with no single entity exercising control over the blockchain, unlike centralized databases which are administered and controlled by a centralized authority. IBM defines a blockchain as 'a shared, immutable ledger that facilitates the process of recording transactions and tracking assets in a business network'.[20]

The components of a blockchain are as shown below:

Info Box 54: Components of a Blockchain

Asset	An asset in a blockchain is a digital representation of a physical asset (such as a house, land, cash, etc.) or an intangible asset (cryptocurrency, intellectual property, patents, copyrights, etc.). Everything that has a value attached to it can be tracked and traded on a blockchain network, with lowered risk and costs for everyone involved.
Node	A node can be any kind of device (such as computers, laptops or servers) that stores, spreads and maintains blockchain data. Nodes are of two types: a full node that maintains a full copy of the database and a partial node that does not store the full copy of the database, but only the hash value of a transaction.
Blocks and immutable records, nonce and hash	Information or transactions in a blockchain are stored in blocks that are immutable, meaning that no participant can modify or tamper with a transaction once it has been recorded in the shared ledger. If a transaction record is entered erroneously, then a new transaction record must be created to correct the error; as such the original transaction remains immutable. Each block is connected to the ones before and after it, creating a chain. A chain comprises multiple blocks, each containing the following: • The data in the block • A nonce, which is a 32-bit whole number that is randomly generated and used only once when a block is created, which then generates a block header hash[21] • A hash, which is a 256-bit number that is linked to the nonce
Peer network or blockchain network	Blockchain networks operate in a way where participants validate transactions among each other. There is no centralized authority. A blockchain documents transactions as an immutable time-stamped digital block that indicates senders and receivers.

---

[20] "What Is Blockchain Technology?," IBM, accessed March 23, 2022. https://www.ibm.com/topics/what-is-blockchain
[21] "What Is BlockChain Technology? How Does It Work?," QASoft Solution, accessed April 6, 2022. https://www.qasoftsolution.com/what-is-blockchain-technology-how-does-it-work/

Ledger	A ledger in a blockchain is a database of information. Blockchain ledgers can be of three types: public ledgers that are open and accessible to all blockchain participants to perform read/write operations; distributed ledgers, where all the nodes maintain a copy of the database; and decentralized ledgers, where every node participates in the execution of a task. A distributed ledger can therefore be considered as a database that is consensually shared and synchronized across multiple sites, institutions or geographies, accessible by multiple people.[22]
Smart contracts	Transactions in a blockchain are enabled through a set of business rules. For example, a smart contract can be an agreement between a contract creator and the recipient of an asset which is embedded as a set of business rules converted into code that executes automatically based on a trigger. It is like a stored procedure (a group of SQL statements that are stored together in a database) used in normal databases to perform predefined functions.
Membership	The members of a members-only network are unique identities in the blockchain network who receive accurate and timely data, enabling them to view what is generally called a single version of the truth. It also means that data is confidential and cannot be viewed by non-members.
Events	An event is emitted by a smart contract when it wants to communicate with a decentralized application and other smart contracts based on an internal trigger.
Wallet	Conceptually, a wallet is like a keychain in the sense that it holds many pairs of private and public keys. These keys are used to sign transactions, allowing a user to prove that they own the transaction outputs on the blockchain.

It is a fact that both databases and blockchains can be hacked as both have vulnerabilities that can be exploited. However, while hacking a database is relatively easier, breaking into blockchain networks is far more challenging and requires specialized knowledge of how blockchains work. Kelly Jackson Higgins, editor-in-chief of Dark Reading, wrote in 2008 that it does not require a database expert to break into a database and that an average hacker could hack in and out of a database in less than 10 seconds.[23] This is also possible because a hacker needs to attack only one central database. In the case of a blockchain, one of the methods is for miners to obtain control of over 50% of the hashing rate in a blockchain. This then gives them the ability to tamper with the recording of new blocks and start changing the records. This, while possible, is by no means an easy task.

Blockchain applications are almost synonymous with cryptocurrencies, but are growing across different sectors like supply chain, government, financial services, healthcare, insurance and transportation. An uncomplicated way to understand how blockchain technology works is to compare it with the way applications like Google Docs or Microsoft SharePoint work. Thus, a decentralized distribution chain is created that gives authorized users access to the document at the same time. No one is required

---

[22] Christina Majaski, "Distributed Ledgers Definition," Investopedia, accessed March 24, 2022. https://www.investopedia.com/terms/d/distributed-ledgers.asp

[23] Kelly Jackson Higgins, "Hacker's Choice: Top Six Database Attacks," DarkReading, accessed March 24, 2022. https://www.darkreading.com/risk/hacker-s-choice-top-six-database-attacks

to wait while changes are being made by another user, while all changes to the said document are being recorded in real-time, making the changes completely transparent.[24]

> **Info Box 55: Blockchain Basics**
>
> As the name suggests, blockchain is a chain of blocks. Each block consists of a cryptographic hash (which contains information linking it to a previous block) and the transaction data with a time stamp. As and when data is added, new blocks are built on previous ones. The hashes perform the function of holding the blocks together and linking the chain.[25]

The obvious question then is why is it not widely deployed? Firstly, blockchains also have their weaknesses such as node communication (eclipse attacks where an attacker creates an artificial environment around one node or user, which enables him to manipulate the node for malicious purposes), consensus mechanisms (attackers can compromise this by controlling a majority of the nodes) and code vulnerabilities. By exploiting any of these vulnerabilities, attackers can cause serious harm.

Secondly, while blockchain technology can be deployed across several industries and applications, there are some inherent constraints such as slow processing speed, scalability and high cost.

The blockchain concept developed by Satoshi Nakamoto, who implemented it in a Bitcoin system offers several advantages that can be leveraged in the context of cybersecurity (Table 7.2).

Table 7.2 Advantages of blockchain for cybersecurity

Decentralisation and distributed data processing and storage	Transactions are stored in distributed ledgers and there is no need for third-party verification.
Transaction tracking and tracing	All transactions in blockchains are digitally signed and time-stamped, enabling tracking and tracing.
Confidentiality	The confidentiality of network members is maintained through public key cryptography to authenticate users and encrypt their transactions.
Protection from fraud	It is possible to define malicious behaviour through peer-to-peer connections and distributed consensus.
Business continuity	As it is a decentralised system, there is no single point of failure, making the system more reliable and resilient.
Immutability	Protection of data against modification or destruction due to the concept of distributed ledgers and immutability.
Data quality	Once encrypted, blockchain can ensure the accuracy and quality of data.
Protected network access	Remme, an open-source protocol based on blockchain technology, provides each user and each device with a specific SSL certificate that removes the need for passwords. This makes unauthorized access impossible.

(Continued)

---

[24] Sam Daley, "What Is Blockchain Technology? How Does It Work?," Built In, accessed March 24, 2022. https://builtin.com/blockchain

[25] Rishabh Mansur, "What Is Blockchain? Blocks, Distributed Ledgers and Nodes Explained in Simple Terms," The Decrypting Story, accessed September 6, 2021. https://yourstory.com/2021/09/what-is-blockchain-technology-blocks-distributed-ledgers-nodes/amp

Table 7.2 (*Continued*)

Protected communication	Blockchain networks can provide security for business communications through encryption and decentralised storage, reducing opportunities for surveillance.
Smart contract functionality	Blockchain technology is useful in implementing smart contracts and to maintain high security standards for the same.
Availability	The decentralised ledger architecture not only ensures that sensitive data is secure but that it is available to users at all times.

Blockchain technology addresses several cybersecurity challenges including ensuring the highest level of data confidentiality, availability and security. However, the complexity of the technology and deployment challenges has thus far prevented it from being more widely used. Like all technologies, blockchain will continue to evolve and given its inherent strengths in relation to cybersecurity, still holds a lot of promise for the future.

7.9.5 Zero Trust Model

Zero trust is a powerful security concept created in 2010 by John Kindervag when he was working at Forrester Research. In recent years, the concept has rapidly gained ground and several technologies have enabled its implementation. The basic premise of zero trust models or architectures require all users, whether in or outside the organization's network, to be authenticated, authorized and continuously validated for security configuration and posture before being allowed or to retain access to applications and data. Moreover, zero trust works on the assumption that there is no traditional network edge and that networks can be local, in the cloud or a combination or hybrid, with resources anywhere as well as employees in any location.[26] The mantra for zero trust is 'always verify, then trust' which stands in stark contrast to traditional approaches of 'trust by default' and then impose controls and security mechanisms to prevent malicious activity.

Zero trust architecture should ideally be designed to continuously monitor and validate a user as well as their device and grant access only if they have the appropriate privileges and attributes. Implementing zero trust involves developing a deep understanding of service and privileged accounts so that they can establish appropriate controls about what and where they connect. This also means that systems enable continuous validation of user access requests before they are able to access any enterprise or cloud resource. Enforcement of zero trust policies requires online referencing of user credentials and attributes, such as:[27]

- Identity of the user and credential type (human or program based)
- The total number and privileges of each credential on each device
- Information and typical behaviour of normal connections for the credential and device
- Endpoint hardware type and function and applications installed on endpoints
- Authentication protocol and risk
- Geo-location information
- Firmware versions, operating system versions and patch levels

---

[26] Kapil Raina, "Zero Trust Security Explained: Principles of the Zero Trust Model," Crowd Strike, accessed October 27, 2021. https://www.crowdstrike.com/cybersecurity-101/zero-trust-security/

[27] Kapil Raina, "Zero Trust Security Explained: Principles of the Zero Trust Model," Crowd Strike, accessed October 27, 2021. https://www.crowdstrike.com/cybersecurity-101/zero-trust-security/

The key principles of a zero trust approach are:

- Presume all networks are untrusted
- Verify every access request regardless of where it originates from
- Apply least privilege access; restrict access based on the minimum permissions required to carry out a task
- Assume breaches; reduce risk by inspecting and monitoring everything

Implementation of a zero trust model must take into account the following aspects:

- Re-examination of all pre-existing default access controls
- Deployment of preventive measures for identity management, endpoints, data and application access
- Ensuring continuous monitoring and controls to detect and stop malicious activity
- Alignment with the broader cybersecurity strategy

No single piece of software or technology is sufficient to implement a zero trust approach. Technologies that support the adoption of zero trust include multi-factor authentication, IAM, micro-segmentation, orchestration, analytics, encryption, scoring and file system permissions. Zero trust models also need support from other governance and administrative processes such as following the principle of least privilege.

The power of a zero trust security model lies in the fact that no device, user, system or application is trusted by default, regardless of the location it is operating from. Security challenges can be identified and responded to prevent unauthorized incursion attempts in real-time as they occur. Yet another important aspect is that this approach works on the premise that both internal and external networks are susceptible to a compromise and need equal protection. Hence, it not only guarantees protection from external sources but also from insider threats.

> **Info Box 56: Cybersecurity Mesh Architecture (CSMA)**
>
> A cybersecurity mesh represents the design and implementation of IT security infrastructure that goes beyond a single perimeter and establishes smaller, individual perimeters around each device or access point.
>
> The focus of this architecture is to secure the perimeter around each device and access point and help in the implementation of zero-trust architecture by ensuring all data and systems are accessed securely, regardless of their location.
>
> CSMA is a concept that is catching on, but maximum effectiveness lies in being able to integrate various cybersecurity tools, centralize policy management across them and implement and monitor the right metrics. This is easier said than done, as large organizations can have as many as 50 different cybersecurity tools.

As with other approaches, zero trust is not without its challenges:

- Integrating legacy applications and other tools
- Visibility and control within the network
- Complete and unified execution
- Time and resource requirements

As organizations undertake digital transformation, migrate to cloud technologies, and deal with the challenge of an increasingly remote workforce, zero trust models offer a comprehensive approach to cybersecurity challenges that can provide security benefits including simplifying security management, implementing security across on-premises and cloud-based systems, streamlining user access and authentication, securing the remote workforce and enhancing data protection.

7.9.6 Data Loss Prevention

The loss of sensitive data and other forms of confidential organizational information such as intellectual property, financial data, and employee or customer details can lead to significant financial losses and reputational damage. Data loss prevention (DLP) is a set of technologies and solutions that provide protection against loss of sensitive data from organizational systems.

DLP and data leakage prevention may appear to be similar, but in the context of cybersecurity, refer to two distinct issues. DLP refers to the methods and techniques for preventing loss of data while in use, while data leakage prevention refers to using methods to prevent data being transmitted to someone outside the organization.[28] DLP tools and processes can help to:

- Ensure that sensitive data is not lost, misused or accessed by unauthorized users through email or instant messaging, website forms, file transfers or other means
- Provide IT teams and security staff with a comprehensive view of the location, flow and usage of data across the enterprise
- Provide protection against mistakes and deliberate misuse that could lead to data leaks
- Provide data protection against external attacks on the information infrastructure
- Enable reporting to meet compliance and auditing requirements
- Identify areas of weakness and anomalies for forensics and incident response

DLP solutions are basically of three types: network, endpoint and cloud. These solutions can help provide organizations with another line of defence by monitoring, detecting and blocking the unauthorized flow of information. DLP solutions use a set of rules to identify sensitive information that forms a part of electronic communications as well as to detect abnormal data transfers outside the corporate network.

DLP solutions are available in all three states, such as:

- Data in motion or in transit between two locations
- Data at rest, in storage systems, computers and mobile devices
- Data in use, that is, being actively processed by an application or an endpoint by authenticating users and controlling their access to resources

DLP solutions are also capable of deep content inspection and conducting a contextual security analysis of transactions as well as of enforcing data security policies. In addition, they enable centralised management for detection and prevention of the unauthorized use and transmission of confidential information.

With stringent privacy and data protection laws coming into force in many countries, organizations are increasingly concerned about the fines and penalties, liability and negative publicity associated with data breaches. Factors like remote working, bring your own device (BYOD), uncertainty about the protection of sensitive data on the cloud and extensive use of IoT devices has further accentuated the need for DLP systems to not only prevent data loss through malicious intent but also against accidental loss or exposure of sensitive data.

---

[28] Lithmee, "What is the Difference Between Data Loss Prevention and Data Leakage Prevention", Pediaa, published August 5, 2019. https://pediaa.com/what-is-the-difference-between-data-loss-prevention-and-data-leakage-prevention/

7.9.7 Cybersecurity Platforms

From point solutions that were designed to address specific security issues to platforms that combine many security functions in a single integrated piece of software, cybersecurity technologies have undergone many changes, some even transformational in nature. The increasing complexity of organizational systems such as hybrid systems that include on-premises systems, cloud, mobile devices and IoT systems, growing sophistication of cyberattacks which use multiple attack vectors and techniques, the dissolution of the corporate perimeter and other factors have virtually brought to an end the era of point solutions.

The fact that point solutions are still in use is mainly because over a period of time organizations have built their own patchwork of point solutions, often to address specific security problems that they encountered at a given point in time. While these solutions were effective in resolving particular security issues, it is quite difficult to integrate multiple tools and security systems and requires investment of time and effort.

We must recognize that platforms are not only about offering a single point solution to deal with a variety of security issues, but also have a business context, an economic angle as well as deployment options.

Some of the common features of present-day cybersecurity platforms include:

- Coverage from endpoints to data centres to cloud-based systems
- Advanced threat prevention, detection and response capabilities
- Multiple deployment options: cloud and hybrid, modular
- Open standards based with ability to integrate third party functions
- Centralized visibility and reporting

Cybersecurity platforms can help organizations enhance their security posture and mechanisms significantly, reduce operational costs, simplify security management, and help maintain business continuity.

7.9.8 Attack Surface Monitoring

An attack surface is representative of the sum of all possible entry points for unauthorized access into any system (see Chapter 3). It can also be described as the aggregate of all known, unknown and potential vulnerabilities, and controls across all hardware, software and network components. A smaller attack surface provides fewer opportunities for hackers to enter protected systems. By actively monitoring the attack surface, the overall security posture of an organization can be strengthened.

Attack surface monitoring tools are useful for continuous monitoring of an organization's dynamic attack surfaces and work in tandem with threat intelligence tools in evaluating the effectiveness of existing security controls to help the security team in prioritization and implementation of potential security improvements.

The field of attack surface monitoring is relatively new. Attack surface monitoring tools generally offer the following functionality:

- Check for vulnerabilities
- Identify out-of-date software versions
- Log data access by software

- Differentiate between authorized user activity and suspicious account activity
- Reduce the risk of sensitive data loss or disclosure

7.9.9 CASB and SASE

Two recent advances in cybersecurity platform technology have been the introduction of cloud access security broker (CASB) and secure access service edge (SASE). Both are built on the recognition that the perimeter-based cyber defences that were traditionally deployed to protect data centres and local area networks now need to undergo a paradigm shift in approach as well as protect a flexible, invisible and everchanging perimeter since a large percentage of organizational resources lie beyond local networks.

CASB functions as an intermediary between users, devices and cloud-hosted software or on-premises software. CASB solutions are fast becoming an important part of enterprise security as they provide visibility and enforcement of security policies, enabling businesses to address security gaps and protecting corporate information across various type of deployment models such as cloud, on-premises or hybrid.

CASB functions as the hub of security policy enforcement by enforcing them on any device which is attempting to access it, including unmanaged computers, smartphones or IoT devices. This becomes all the more important in a situation where organizations need to support a remote workforce that accesses organizational systems through a variety of personal devices which also host unsanctioned applications (Shadow IT).

CASB solutions are useful in implementing the same level of security controls regardless of whether the systems are on the cloud, on-premises or company-owned or personal systems and devices accessing the corporate network. While being strong on the policy enforcement front, CASB may not have the same capabilities when it comes to inline threat protection capabilities and needs to be combined with other solutions to provide greater protection. Another challenge for deploying CASB solutions is the difficulty in integrating it with legacy and point solutions.

SASE is an emerging cybersecurity concept that was first described by Gartner in 2019. It essentially builds on all the functions of CASB and extends its zero trust capabilities to software-defined wide area network (SD-WAN) to cover remote users and branch offices. SD-WAN is a networking solution that aggregates multiple transport links across systems and locations while providing better performance and reliability. By integrating SD-WAN, SASE enables organizations to gain full visibility to implement total security inspection on traffic flows across the corporate network.

CASB and SASE offer comprehensive approaches to organizational information security, but the choice of which is more relevant will depend on the organization and its security goals and objectives. While CASB is more oriented towards addressing the challenges of protecting an organization's cloud applications, SASE goes beyond and offers other security functions like optimised SD-WAN routing and next-generation firewall functionality.

7.9.10 EDR and XDR

The complexion of workplaces has undergone a number of changes in recent years. From the confines of walled offices and secure data centres to an environment where a variety of devices connect into organization systems from just about anywhere and at any time. Recognition of this new reality in cybersecurity terms involves moving security controls to devices that function as entry points (desktops, laptops, mobile and IoT) to the corporate network.

Endpoint security involves providing protection to these endpoints on a network or in the cloud. Technologies for endpoint detection and response (EDR) are focused on preventing malicious threat actors and exploits from targeting endpoints or entry points. EDR security solutions enable organizations to enhance cybersecurity by:

- Monitoring endpoints and collecting activity data that could suggest a threat
- Using the collected data to identify suspicious threats and threat patterns
- Automatically responding to identified threats by removing, containing or alerting security teams
- Providing greater visibility of endpoints and faster response time
- Offering protection against advanced forms of malware, phishing attempts, etc.

EDR solutions also use AI and ML algorithms which can help detect yet unknown types of malware. EDR solutions are also capable of providing additional features that basic antivirus systems do not provide and can be used to implement multiple security layers to detect and block attacks.

The benefits delivered by EDR solutions with respect to entry point protection has led to the development of a broader solution, extended detection and response (XDR), which integrates security visibility that covers an organization's entire IT infrastructure, including endpoints, cloud infrastructure and networks, email, servers, IoT and mobile devices. In addition, XDR helps security teams in the enforcement of consistent security policies across the enterprise. XDR systems can also apply data analytics and threat intelligence to this aggregated data to identify trends and known threats. Finally, security information aggregation decreases the workload for security analysts, enabling them to better focus their efforts.[29]

XDR solutions integrate threat information across systems which can then be analyzed, prioritized, tracked and remediated to prevent data loss and security breaches. The ability to respond automatically to identified threats and block malicious content from entry into organizational systems not only prevents attacks but also takes the overall threat management capability of the organization to another level.

7.10 INTERNET PROTOCOLS AND PORTS

Internet Protocol (IP) is a set of rules that defines the formats of digital messages exchanged between interconnected computers across a single network or multiple interconnected networks using the IP suite (often referred to as TCP/IP). Various layers of protocols are used in the Open System Interconnection (OSI) model to effectively describe computer packet transfers.

The OSI model is a conceptual framework that describes the functions of a networking system. Developed and supported by the International Organization for Standardization, these protocols are used as a set of rules and requirements which support the interoperability between different products and software.

Cybersecurity threats can occur at all layers of the OSI model. A layer-by-layer approach to cybersecurity enables implementation of a defence-in-depth strategy. Gaining an understanding of the underlying protocols at each layer of the OSI model can help in the following ways:

- Develop an understanding of communication over a network
- Use of diagnostics, which becomes easier by separating functions into different layers
- Enable an understanding of new technologies as they are being developed
- Enable comparison of primary functional relationships between network layers

---

[29] "EDR VS XDR, Check Point, accessed October 27, 2021. https://www.checkpoint.com/cyber-hub/threat-prevention/what-is-endpoint-detection-and-response/edr-vs-xdr/.

The protocols used at each layer of the OSI model are given below.

Info Box 57: Protocols Used in Each Layer of the OSI Model

OSI layer	Major protocols used	Description of the protocol
Layer 1: Physical Layer	Bluetooth	Bluetooth is a standardized secure protocol for sending and receiving data through a 2.4-GHz wireless link over a short range.
	PON	Passive optical network is used by telecommunications network providers to bring fibre optic cabling and signals all or most of the way to the end user. Based on where the PON terminates, the system can be described as fibre-to-the-curb, fibre-to-the-building or fibre-to-the-home.
	OTN	Optical transport networking is an industry standard protocol that offers a way to multiplex different services onto optical light paths.
	DSL	The DSL modem sends data bits over the local loop of the PSTN telephone network.
	IEEE 802.11	The IEEE 802.11 standard is popularly known as Wi-Fi. It defines the architecture and specification protocols for wireless LANs (WLANs).
	IEEE 802.3	This is a protocol for ethernet connectivity that defines the physical layer and media access control (MAC) of the data link layer for wired ethernet networks, usually as a local area network (LAN) technology.
	TIA	Telecommunications Industry Association (TIA) protocol defines signals connecting between data terminals and data communications equipment, such as a modem.
Layer 2: Data Link Layer	ARP	Address Resolution Protocol (ARP) is the protocol used to associate the IP address to a MAC address.
	SLIP	Serial Line Internet Protocol (SLIP) works with TCP/IP for communication over serial ports and routers.
	CSLIP	Compressed SLIP is a version of SLIP that works for improving TCP/IP performance over low speeds of up to 19.2 kbps.
	HDLC	High-level data link control is a bit-oriented, synchronous data link layer protocol for transmitting data between network points (sometimes called nodes).
	IEEE 802.3	This is a protocol for ethernet connectivity that defines the physical layer and media access control (MAC) of the data link layer for wired ethernet networks, usually as a local area network (LAN) technology.

OSI layer	Major protocols used	Description of the protocol
	PPP	Point-to-Point Protocol is a TCP/IP protocol used to connect one computer system to another to communicate over the telephone network or the Internet.
	X-25	This is a protocol suite for packet-switched communications over a WAN. It is mostly used for networks for ATMs and credit card verification.
	ATM	Asynchronous transfer mode is a telecommunications standard for digital transmission of multiple types of traffic, including telephony (voice), data and video signals in one network without the use of separate overlay networks.
	SDLS	Synchronous data link control is a protocol that is used for transferring synchronous, code-transparent, serial-by-bit information over a communications line.
	PLIP	The Parallel Line Internet Protocol is a networking protocol for direct computer-to-computer communications using the parallel port.
Layer 3: Network Layer	IPv4	This is the fourth version of the Internet Protocol. It defines how addressing works and how network hosts can be identified.
	IPv6	This was developed by Internet Engineering Task Force (IETF) to deal with the issue of IPv4 exhaustion.
	AppleTalk	This is a proprietary suite of networking protocols developed for Mac computers, now discontinued.
	ICMP	Internet Control Message Protocol is a network layer protocol used by network devices to diagnose network communication issues such as whether or not data is reaching its intended destination in a timely manner.
	IPSec	This is a security protocol that provides data authentication, integrity and confidentiality across two communication points across the IP network.
	IGMP	Internet Group Management Protocol is a protocol that enables several devices to share one IP address so they can all receive the same data.
Layer 4: Transport Layer	UDP, UDP Lite CUDP, RUDP	User Datagram Protocol is an alternative communication protocol to TCP. UDP Lite, cyclic UDP (CUDP) and reliable UDP (RUDP) are variants of the same protocol.

OSI layer	Major protocols used	Description of the protocol
	ATP	AppleTalk Transaction Protocol is a part of a set of networking protocols that enables the transfer of small amounts of data across a network.
	MTCP	Multipath TCP enables simultaneous use of several IP-addresses/interfaces by a modification of TCP that presents a regular TCP interface to applications, while in fact spreading data across several sub flows.
	TCP	Transmission Control Protocol is one of the most widely used protocols for two hosts to connect and exchange data streams. TCP ensures the delivery of data and packets in the same order as they were sent.
	SPX	Sequenced Packet Exchange is a networking protocol primarily used by Novell Netware, but is also supported by other operating systems.
Layer 5: Session Layer	ASP	AppleTalk Session Protocol allows one or more ASP workstation application or process to set up a session with the same server at the same time.
	PPTP	Point-to-Point Tunnelling Protocol is a now-obsolete protocol for implementing virtual private networks.
	ADSP	AppleTalk Data Stream Protocol is a protocol used to set up a session for exchanging data between various networking devices.
	ITU X.225	Also known as ISO 8327, this provides services for coordinating communication between local and remote applications, and establishing, managing and terminating connections.
	NetBIOS	Network Basic Input/Output System is a network service that enables applications on separate computers to communicate with each other within a LAN.
	PAP	Password Authentication Protocol is a password-based authentication protocol used by PPP to validate users.
	RPC	Remote Procedure Call is a communication protocol that used between one program and another one which is on a separate computer without understanding the networks details.
Layer 6: Presentation Layer	XDR	This uses a standard representation of different data types to ensure that data is interpreted correctly, even if the source data is in a different format.
	TLS	Transport Layer Security is a security protocol which succeeded the SSL protocol and is designed to facilitate privacy and data security for communications over the Internet.

OSI layer	Major protocols used	Description of the protocol
Layer 7: Application Layer	SSL	This provides security to the data that is transferred between a web browser and server through encryption.
	MIME	Multi-purpose Internet Mail Extensions protocol enables users to communicate many forms of digital information through email, such as images, audio, video and other types of documents and files.
	HTTP	HyperText Transfer Protocol is a method for encoding and transporting information between a client (such as a web browser) and a web server. HTTPS is a secure version of the same protocol.
	SMTP	Simple Mail Transfer Protocol is a set of communication guidelines that allow software to transmit an electronic mail over the Internet.
	DHCP	Dynamic Host Configuration Protocol is a client/server protocol that automatically provides an Internet Protocol host with its IP address and other related configuration information such as the subnet mask and default gateway.
	FTP	The File Transfer Protocol is a standard communication protocol used for the transfer of computer files from a server to a client on a computer network.
	Telnet	Terminal Network is a client-server protocol that enables one computer to connect to a local computer.
	SNMP	Simple Network Management Protocol is used for managing and monitoring connected devices in IP networks.
	SMPP	Short Message Peer-to-Peer in the telecommunications industry is an open, industry standard protocol designed to provide a flexible data communication interface for the transfer of short message data between external short messaging entities.

7.10.1 Ports

A port is a virtual point that represents the starting point and termination point of a network connection. Ports are numbered and fall under three ranges:

- Well-known ports are numbered 0–1023
- Registered ports are numbered 1024–49151
- Dynamic or private ports are numbered 49152–65535

These ports are software based and are managed through the OS. The Internet Assigned Numbers Authority (IANA) maintains an official list of well-known and registered port ranges and is also responsible for coordination of IP addressing, DNS root and various other protocol resources.

Notable well-known port numbers and their assignment is shown below:

Info Box 58: Port Numbers and Their Assignment

Port number	Assignment
20	FTP data transfer
21	FTP command control
22	Secure Shell (SSH) secure login
23	Telnet remote login service, unencrypted text messages
25	SMTP email delivery
53	DNS service
67, 68	Dynamic Host Configuration Protocol (DHCP)
80	HTTP, used in the World Wide Web
110	Post Office Protocol (POP3)
119	Network News Transfer Protocol (NNTP)
123	Network Time Protocol (NTP)
143	Internet Message Access Protocol (IMAP); management of digital mail
161	Simple Network Management Protocol (SNMP)
194	Internet Relay Chat (IRC)
443	HTTPS; HTTP over TLS/SSL
546, 547	DHCPv6; the IPv6 version of DHCP

Managing port security involves configuring a security policy for the selected port and identifying the MAC addresses of all devices authorized to access the port.

QUICK TEST

1. Firewalls are among the most widely deployed cybersecurity technologies as they protect networks against the following types of attack vectors:
   a. Backdoors
   b. Denial of service attacks
   c. Macros and spam
   d. Remote logins
   e. All of the above
   f. Only a and d
2. Intrusion detection systems can not only help analyze the nature and scale of an attack, but also help identify bugs or issues in configuring network devices.
   a. True
   b. False
3. Can SIEM systems replace IDS/IDPS and firewalls?
   a. Yes
   b. No
4. Wireless Equivalent Privacy (WEP):
   a. Is the oldest wireless security protocol to be deployed
   b. Is the best security protocol for wireless security
   c. The encryption used in WEP is no longer effective as hackers have learnt to break it
   d. a and b
   e. a and c
5. IAM solutions address:
   a. Authenticating a user, software and hardware by referencing a database
   b. Authorizing specific pre-approved levels of access and allowing only permitted actions
   c. Both a and b
6. Algorithms used for ML can be based on:
   a. Supervised learning
   b. Unsupervised learning
   c. Semi-supervised
   d. All of the above
   e. Only b
7. Zero trust enables organizations to understand and monitor the actions of users to determine deviations from 'normal behaviour' such as oddities, outliers and anomalies.
   a. True
   b. False
8. DLP solutions can help protect:
   a. Data at rest
   b. Data in motion
   c. Data in use
   d. All of the above
   e. Only a and b
9. CASB and SASE offer comprehensive approaches to organizational information security, but the choice of which is more relevant will depend on the organization and its security goals and objectives.
   a. True
   b. False

10. IDS/IDPS and Event Managers (SIEM) have been using techniques similar to EDR for years in that they record, correlate and analyze. The key difference is that EDR has a data set more focused towards endpoints and different metadata.
    a. True
    b. False

QUESTIONS

1. Explain the difference between firewalls, IDS and IDPS.
2. What are the benefits of network segmentation?
3. Discuss ways of implementing email security.
4. What is cryptography? How is it useful in the context of cybersecurity?
5. What is the difference between a digital signature and a digital certificate?
6. The use of blockchain technology for cybersecurity holds a lot of promise. Discuss this statement.
7. What are the key principles of zero trust? How can they help in enhancing enterprise cybersecurity?
8. Explain the reasons for the growth of cybersecurity platforms.
9. What are the protocols used in each layer of the OSI model?
10. Discuss the terms CASB, SASE, XDR and EDR. What role do they play in cybersecurity?

ANSWER KEYS

Quick Test

1. (e)	3. (b)	5. (c)	7. (b)	9. (a)
2. (a)	4. (e)	6. (d)	8. (d)	10. (a)

8 Cyber Laws and Forensics

> **OBJECTIVES**
>
> At the end of this chapter, you will be able to:
>
> - ☑ Explain the importance of cyber laws and the role of governments and international bodies in the establishment of a legal and sustainable cyber ecosystem
> - ☑ List the important cyber laws and treaties and the challenges for law makers and law enforcement agencies
> - ☑ Describe cyber forensics, cybercrime techniques, prevention of and protection from cybercrime and the investigation of cybercrimes

8.0 NEED FOR CYBER LAWS AND REGULATIONS

Laws and regulations play a key role in our lives in matters related to social conduct, business, education, politics or any other aspect of human activity. It is necessary for the smooth conduct and growth and development of societies and countries.

The earliest comprehensive written legal codes were created during the reign of the Babylonian king Hammurabi (1792–1750 BCE). Throughout human history, laws have evolved to incorporate changing contexts with the primary objective of general safety and protecting the rights of citizens and institutions against abuses by other people, organizations and by the government itself.

Digital transactions and the Internet have largely been an unregulated space and the current laws and regulations related to it are mostly of relatively recent origin. Even today, the laws relating to the Internet and cyberspace are still in an early stage of evolution and are being enacted at local, state and national levels. Given the rapid growth of cybercrime, e-commerce, payment systems, e-governance, digital banking and other digital ecosystems, the need for laws and regulations is being increasingly felt around the world.

Cyber laws and regulations that have come into existence are already an important part of the overall legal system to deal with cybercrime, privacy, data protection and other related issues. Cyber laws also address areas such as violation of intellectual property rights, identity theft as well as the freedom of online expression. The rise in the number of Internet users and its increased usage makes the need for cyber laws, their application and enforcement an important imperative in the world of today. A majority of people today are a part of the new digitized world and are affected by any criminal and legal aspects related to it. Consider this:

- Citizens around the world today access and use a wide range of digital services.
- Basic systems like digital payments, banking, e-commerce and healthcare are increasingly becoming a part of the daily lives of people.
- Companies use digital systems for submission of returns, payment of taxes and electronic contracts and deploy information technology to run their operations.

- Governments find the use of e-governance systems both efficient and effective in providing citizen services.
- Communications in the form of emails, messaging platforms, social media and video conferencing have transformed the way we live and work.

We are moving rapidly towards a completely digitized society, and we cannot today imagine a life without digital systems. However, even as we have embraced digital systems, cybercrime has emerged in many forms such as online banking frauds, online scams, theft of Intellectual Property (IP), credit card fraud, tax evasion, virus attacks, cyber sabotage, phishing attacks, email hijacking, denial of service, hacking, pornography, cyber terrorism, cyber espionage and cyberwarfare. Some of these crimes even threaten our survival and faith and trust in electronic systems. All this has paved the way for a new set of laws that are required for a digital society to grow and flourish with strong deterrents for wrongdoers and adequate safeguards for the parties that could be adversely affected by cybercrime.

The terms law and regulation are often used interchangeably, and while their effect is the same, it is important to understand how the two are different. Laws are written statutes, passed by either the central or state legislatures through voting by public representatives and become statutory law. Regulations are rules that are created by the executive branch of governments to provide guidance and operating details that specify how the laws will be enforced by the administrative agencies. Just like laws, regulations are also codified and published so that parties are aware of what is legal and what is not. Without the associated regulations, it would not be possible for regulatory authorities to enforce laws.

Cyber laws and cybersecurity regulations are continuously evolving but are still not able to keep pace with all the complexities and emerging legal issues. Cyber laws today cover a number of cyberspace-related issues such as various forms of cybercrime, IP theft and misuse, contracts, jurisdiction, data protection laws, privacy, e-commerce, online security and freedom of expression. Cyber law also provides legal recognition to electronic transactions and e-documents as well aspects of gathering, storing and presenting electronic evidence in a court of law. We will discuss specific cybersecurity-linked regulations in a subsequent section.

The purpose of cyber laws includes, but is not limited to, the following:

- Provide recognition and an overarching legal framework for electronic transactions, systems and contracts.
- Provide security protection for computer and Internet users.
- Provide protection of a user's personal information.
- Provide protection against computer-related crimes and frauds.
- Provide protection for digital intellectual property.

8.1 ROLE OF INTERNATIONAL LAW AND GOVERNMENTS

An overwhelming majority of countries around the world have enacted cybercrime legislation and more are on their way to doing so. The adoption of these laws is necessary for the development of digital systems and overall economic growth. Cyber laws can be categorized under four major categories:

- E-transaction laws
- Cybercrime laws
- Consumer protection laws
- Privacy laws

A fifth category of recent origin (industry/critical infrastructure-specifc laws) is where cybersecurity laws are increasingly being enacted, especially for vulnerable sectors like financial services and critical infrastructure. The World Economic Forum has suggested that cybersecurity is "too big a job for governments or business to handle alone" based on their findings that business and government are exposing each other to an increasing spectrum of cyber risks. They have also encouraged pooling of cybersecurity resources and sharing of intelligence as a means to enhance overall security efforts.

Through their various enforcement and intelligence agencies, governments have a broader view of potential threats, but they have a tendency to see things through a national security lens rather than commercial risk. Companies on the other hand have firm- and sector-specific threat information, but they cannot easily take an economy-wide view and may find themselves overwhelmed by state-sponsored attackers. As society increases its use and dependence on technology, cybersecurity will become an ever-greater challenge. Governments and the private sector have a common interest and responsibility to face that threat together.[1] The evolution and creation of laws and enforcement mechanisms is an important part of that responsibility.

Governments have different means of creating a legal ecosystem to enforce laws. At the national and state levels, laws and regulations are typically developed within the respective country's constitutional framework and legal regime. Given that the Internet is a global platform, there are several cross-border issues that come into play in a legal context. Here, countries and governments who want to establish cross-border institutional arrangements or procedures can become signatories to bilateral and multi-lateral treaties.

8.1.1 International Treaties and Conventions

A convention is a set of rules for parties agreeing to the convention to solve an issue that affects larger parts of the world. These conventions are drafted by agencies like the United Nations and European Union and are ratified and adopted by member countries.

Table 8.1 shows examples of treaties and conventions on cyber laws.

Table 8.1 Treaties and conventions on cyber laws

Treaties and conventions	Purpose	Date enacted/adopted	Regions/Countries
Convention for the Protection of Individuals with regard to Automatic Processing of Personal Data (CETS No. 108)	The first legally binding international instrument in the data protection field.	1981	Council of Europe (an international organization to which all EU countries belong)
United Nations Commission on International Trade Law (UNCITRAL), Model Law on Electronic Commerce	To enable and facilitate e-commerce, providing national legislators with a set of globally standard regulations intended to reduce legal ambiguity and remove legal barriers for the same.	1996	Adopted by 76 member countries so far
Budapest Convention on Cybercrime	The Convention on Cybercrime, also known as the Budapest Convention on Cybercrime or the Budapest Convention, was the first international treaty seeking to address Internet and computer crime by standardizing state laws, enhancing investigative methods and improving collaboration between countries.	2004	Sixty-five countries have ratified the convention so far

(*Continued*)

[1] Paul Mee and Chaitra Chandrasekhar, "Cybersecurity Is Too Big a Job for Governments or Firms to Handle Alone," World Economic Forum, accessed May 8, 2021. https://www.weforum.org/agenda/2021/05/cybersecurity-governments-business/

Table 8.1 (*Continued*)

Treaties and conventions	Purpose	Date enacted/adopted	Regions/Countries
The Directive on Security of Network and Information Systems (NIS Directive)	The first piece of EU-wide legislation on cybersecurity. It offers legal procedures to enhance cybersecurity in the EU.	2016	European Union (EU) member states
EU Cybersecurity Act	The EU Cybersecurity Act established an EU-wide cybersecurity certification framework for digital products, services and processes. It supplements the NIS Directive of 2016.	2019	European Union (EU) member states

8.1.2 Important Cyber Laws and Regulations: 1970–1990

Technological changes have been both rapid and radical, often changing the way societies live and function as well redefining the ways cybercriminals operate. Cyber laws have been evolving over the decades and focusing on aspects that were most relevant for those times. Table 8.2 shows examples of important cyber laws that were framed in 1970–1990.

Table 8.2 Important cyber laws and regulations, 1970–1990

Laws and regulations	Purpose
Privacy Act, 1974, USA	To establish a Code of Fair Information Practice that governs the collection, maintenance, use and dissemination of personally identifiable information about individuals that is maintained in systems of records by federal agencies.
Electronic Communication Privacy Act, 1986, USA	To modernize federal wiretap laws.
The Computer Fraud and Abuse Act, 1986, USA	This was passed as an amendment to existing computer fraud law, which had been incorporated in the Comprehensive Crime Control Act of 1984. The law forbids gaining access to a computer without consent or without enough authorization.
Privacy Act, 1988, Australia	This was introduced to promote and protect the privacy of individuals and to regulate how Australian Government agencies and organisations with an annual turnover of more than $3 million, and some other organisations, manage personal information.
The Computer Misuse Act, 1980, UK	This safeguards personal data taken by organisations from unlawful entry and alteration. This involves altering or scrubbing data and the insertion of malware or spyware onto a computer and data theft.

8.1.3 Important Cyber Laws and Regulations: 1991–1999

Cyber laws in the decade of the 90s were focused on data protection and the beginning of granting of legal recognition of electronic transactions and acceptance of electronic methods. The important cyber laws and regulations enacted in the 90s are shown in Table 8.3.

Table 8.3 Important cyber laws and regulations, 1991–1999

Laws and Regulations	Purpose
Health Insurance Portability and Accountability Act, 1996, USA (HIPAA)	This is a federal law that required the creation of national standards to protect sensitive patient health information from being disclosed without the patient's consent or knowledge.
The Data Protection Act, 1998, UK	To protect personal data stored on computers or in an organised paper filing system.
Gramm–Leach–Bliley Act, 1999, USA	This act allows extensive sharing of private data by financial institutions such as banks, insurers and investment companies.
Electronic Transactions Act, 1999, Australia	To provide a more secure environment for e-commerce. There were three crucial components: justifying the legality of electronic transactions, guaranteeing non-discrimination in the treatment and approval of numerous types of automated processes, and adding up party autonomy when authorizing alternative provisions and terms. This Act has given vital protections to companies and individuals alike.

8.1.4 Important Cyber Laws and Regulations: 2000–2010

The turn of the century found greater focus of law-making regarding operating aspects of electronic transactions, providing validity and legal effect to electronic contracts and methods. Important legislations enacted in this period are shown in Table 8.4.

Table 8.4 Important cyber laws and regulations, 2000–2010

Laws and Regulations	Purpose
Electronic Signatures in Global and National Commerce Act, 2000, USA	To facilitate the use of electronic records and electronic signatures in interstate and foreign commerce by ensuring validity and giving legal effect to electronically executed contracts.
Federal Information Security Management Act, 2002, USA	The Act requires each federal agency to develop, document and implement an agency-wide program to provide information security for operations and assets of the agency, including those provided by their vendors and business partners.
The Information Technology Act, 2000, India	The Act provides legal recognition to electronic records, transactions and digital signatures. It also prescribes penalties for cybercrimes.
The Information Technology (Amendment) Act, 2008, India	The Amendment was created to address issues that the original bill failed to cover and to accommodate further development of IT and related security concerns as well as issues related to pornography, voyeurism, child porn and cyber terrorism.

8.1.5 Important Cyber Laws and Regulations: 2011–2020

Most recent laws and regulations have focused on privacy and data protection and on sector-specific and cybersecurity-specific legislations. Table 8.5 lists the important legislations in this regard.

Table 8.5 Important cyber laws and regulations, 2011–2020

Laws and Regulations	Purpose
General Data Protection Regulation or GDPR, 2018	Targeted at regulating the way organizations across the world handle their customers' personal information and creating strengthened and unified data protection for all individuals within the EU.
The California Consumer Privacy Act, 2018, State of California, USA	This is a state statute intended to enhance privacy rights and consumer protection for the residents of California, United States.
Cybersecurity and Infrastructure Security Agency Act of 2018, USA	This legislation established the Cybersecurity and Infrastructure Security Agency (CISA), whose objective is to build the national capacity to defend against cyberattacks and work with the federal government to provide cybersecurity tools, incident response services and assessment capabilities to the essential operations of government departments and agencies.
Personal Data Protection Bill, 2019, India – Awaiting Parliamentary approval	First, the Bill seeks to apply the data protection regime to both government and private entities across all sectors. Second, the Bill seeks to emphasise data security and data privacy.

From the various laws and regulations listed above, we can assimilate that the focus has been on different forms of e-commerce, digital signatures and contracts, data protection, electronic communications and freedom of expression, and various aspects of data security and cybercrime.

8.1.6 The Indian Information Technology Act

India introduced cyber laws in the form of the Information Technology Act, 2000, amended substantially in 2008, and is on the verge of passing the Personal Data Protection Bill. While this has provided basic legal frameworks for e-governance, e-commerce and financial transactions, much needs to be done in matching international standards.

The key objectives of the IT Act, 2000 are:

- Provide legal validity for electronic contracts made through secure electronic channels.
- Provide legal recognition for digital signatures along with defining security measures for the same.
- Provisions for establishment of cyber regulatory bodies and certifying authorities.
- To give applicability to offences or contraventions committed outside India.
- To enable e-filing and e-storage of documents with government departments and agencies
- Legal recognition for e-transfer of funds among banks and financial institutions
- Legal recognition for maintaining financial accounting books in electronic form. Further, this is granted under the Evidence Act, 1891 and the Reserve Bank of India Act, 1934.[2]

The subsequent amendments to the IT Act, 2000 were warranted on account of the following:

- The expansion and widespread use of information technology–enabled services such as e-governance, e-commerce and e-transactions.
- The need for protection of personal data and information and implementation of security practices and procedures relating to these applications.

---

[2] "Cyber Laws and IT Act," in *Legal Environment of Business*, IFCAI Business School, accessed June 21, 2021. https://ebooks.ibsindia.org/leb/chapter/cyber-laws-2/

- The need for protection of critical information infrastructure, which forms the backbone of government services, citizen services, businesses and national security.
- Emergence of new forms of crimes like publishing sexually explicit materials in electronic form, video voyeurism, e-commerce frauds and defamatory or offensive posts on social media.
- To harmonize laws relating to digital signatures in accordance with the United Nations Commission on International Trade Law.

Noteworthy provisions of the Indian IT Act are as follows:

- **Section 43:** This section deals with unauthorized access and causing damage to computer systems and entitles the owner to compensation for the damage caused.
- **Section 43A:** Stipulates that a body that processes sensitive personal data or information in a computer resource under its ownership or control must maintain reasonable security practices and procedures and if it is negligent in doing so, causing wrongful loss to any person on account of such negligence, the body corporate shall be liable to pay damages by way of compensation to the person so affected.[3]
- **Section 66:** Applies to any fraudulent committed act referred to under section 43. The imprisonment term for an offence under this section can be up to three years with a fine of up to five lakhs.

> **Info Box 59: Section 66A**
>
> The Supreme Court of India struck down the controversial Section 66A of the Information Technology Act, 2000 that made posting 'offensive' comments online a crime punishable by jail, after a long campaign by defenders of free speech.[4]
> *Shreya Singhal vs. Union of India*

- **Section 66B**: Incorporates the sentences for fraudulently receiving stolen communication devices or computers.
- **Section 66C**: This section covers identity thefts and offences related to password hacking, distinctive identification, digital signatures, etc.
- **Section 66D**: This section relates to fraudsters carrying out impersonations using computer resources.
- **Section 69A**: This empowers the Central Government to block public access to an intermediary (such as telecom companies, social media platforms) in matters which are in the interest of the sovereignty and integrity of India, defence of India, security of the State, friendly relations with foreign States or public order or for preventing incitement to the commission of any cognisable offence relating to the above.[5]

There are also provisions in the Indian Penal Code (IPC) that can be invoked for cybercrimes such as identity theft, cheating and forgery.

---

[3] Rohan Bagai and Shagun Bhadwar, "Cybersecurity 2021 - India Chapter," AZB & Partners, accessed June 24, 2021. https://www.azbpartners.com/bank/cybersecurity-2021-india-chapter/

[4] "Sec 66A of IT Act Scrapped: 5 Points Observed by Supreme Court," *Hindustan Times*, accessed June 23, 2021. https://www.hindustantimes.com/india/sec-66a-of-it-act-scrapped-5-points-observed-by-supreme-court/story-EtZnxzRGrfsutSk5fjML4H.html

[5] "DoT Seeks Industry Views on Blocking Mobile Apps like FB, Whatsapp, Instagram in Specific Situations," *Outlook India*, accessed June 24, 2021. https://www.outlookindia.com/newsscroll/dot-seeks-industry-views-on-blocking-mobile-apps-like-fb-whatsapp-instagram-in-specific-situations/1363789

The Central and State Governments can, by notification in the Official Gazette and in the Electronic Gazette, make rules to carry out the provisions of this Act. In addition, the Central Government can through a notification designate any organization/agency of the government as the national nodal agency for the protection of critical information infrastructure. The Indian Computer Emergency Response Team (ICERT or CERT-In) is such a designated nodal agency that deals with cyber security threats and is responsible for strengthening the security-related defence of the Indian Internet domain.[6]

> **Info Box 60: CERT-IN Directive under Section 70B of the IT Act, 2000 – Explained**
>
> This was issued on 28 April 2022, under subsection (6) of Section 70B of the Information Technology Act, 2000, which relates to information security practices, procedures, prevention, response and reporting of cyber incidents for safe and trusted Internet.
>
> This directive introduces some mandatory provisions on companies such as:
>
> - Mandatory reporting of cybersecurity-related events within six hours of noticing a cyber incident.
> - Mandatory reporting of 20 specified cybersecurity harms. These also include targeted scanning/probing of critical network/systems, compromise of critical systems, unauthorised access of IT systems, etc.
> - Alignment of time servers of service providers, intermediaries and data centres with those of the National Physical Laboratory and National Informatics Centre (NIC).
> - All service providers, intermediaries, data centres, body corporates and government organisations must enable logs of all their ICT systems. They are also required to maintain them securely for a rolling period of 180 days and the same shall be maintained within the Indian jurisdiction.
> - Data centres, virtual private server (VPS) providers, cloud service providers, VPN service providers, KYC norms and practices by virtual asset service providers, virtual asset exchange providers and custodian wallet providers must register details such as names of subscribers/customers, period of hire, IPs allotted to the members, email address and IP addresses used at the time of registration.
>
> Any failure by a company to comply with the new directives could result in imprisonment of up to one year for the concerned officials.

8.2 CHALLENGES FOR LAW-MAKERS AND LAW ENFORCEMENT AGENCIES

Even though there has been an increase in the number of cyber laws and regulations, there are still several challenges faced by law-makers and law enforcement agencies:[7]

- The word 'cybercrime' is widely used and is accepted as a menace that affects individuals, corporates and organizations, whether national, multinational or international, and therefore society in general. However, in a legal context, there is still no single definition of the term.

---

[6] "India Officials Confirm Cyber-Attack on Nuclear Power Plant Network," Industrial Cyber, accessed June 21, 2021. https://industrialcyber.co/threats-attacks/industrial-cyber-attacks/india-officials-confirm-cyber-attack-on-nuclear-power-plant-network/

[7] Ajayi, EFG, "Challenges to Enforcement of Cyber-Crimes Laws and Policy," *Journal of Internet and Information Systems*, 6, no. 1 (2016): 1–12.

- Internet-related crimes are global in nature, but each country enacts laws that are binding and enforceable within geographic boundaries. Jurisdictional challenges relate to the power of a court to judge to entertain an action, petition or proceedings. In the case of cross-border cybercrimes, it becomes difficult to bring criminals to justice due to conflict of laws that may exist between two nation states.
- A vast majority of cybercrimes go unreported as organizations fail to disclose breaches because of the negative impact and loss of trust that would occur.
- Evidence gathering and presentation of the same in a court of law must follow a different set of strict procedures and requires the application of forensic science. Attribution of a crime and maintaining a proper chain of custody of evidence also require special care. Cybercriminals often use advanced methods to cover their tracks, making it more challenging to identify, track and apprehend them.
- Cost, time and lack of expertise required in conducting investigations and prosecution represents yet another challenge.
- The lack of adequate legislation and case laws and non-enforceability of international laws.
- There is a dearth of trained professionals to conduct investigations and conduct prosecutions.
- Finally, there is an absence of a universal law governing cybercrimes.

Other challenges that law enforcement agencies face are non-cooperation from technology platforms, difficulty in establishing the physical location of perpetrators and impediments in international co-operation.

8.3 CYBERSECURITY REGULATIONS

With cyberattacks on businesses and other organizations increasing rapidly, the need for specific measures to protect systems and information from different kinds of cyberattacks and implement prescribed controls gave birth to cybersecurity-specific regulations. The objective of these regulations is to force companies and organizations to maintain minimum standards of cybersecurity by implementing the directives contained in them. Examples of cybersecurity regulations are HIPAA (1996), Gramm–Leach–Bliley Act (1999), FISMA (2002), PCI DSS and GDPR (2018).

Countries across the world are concerned with enhancing standards for online safety, privacy and data protection and minimizing the impact of cyberattacks. The cybersecurity executive order issued in May 2021 by the US Government aims to chart a "new course to improve the nation's cybersecurity and protect federal government networks".[8] The UK Government is also bringing in a new regulatory framework, in the form of the Online Safety Bill (OSB), which will make companies take responsibility for the safety of their users. The Indian Personal Data Protection Bill is awaiting parliamentary approval and is aimed at providing protection of privacy to individuals relating to their personal data, to establish a Data Protection Authority of India for the said purposes and for other related matters.

We are in the midst of a smart device revolution that is popularly known as the Internet of Things (IoT). These devices are all-pervasive today and are deployed in a wide spectrum of applications from automotive, smart homes and cities to healthcare. However, the security for these devices did not need to conform to standards or regulation (as none existed). In their quest for growth and profits, vendors of smart devices neither had any legal obligation nor incentive to incorporate better security into their products, leading to a dangerous security scenario.[9] Hence, it can be said that cyberspace has been

---

[8] Cynthia Brumfield, "Biden Administration Releases Ambitious Cybersecurity Executive Order," CSO, accessed May 15, 2021. https://www.csoonline.com/article/3618730/biden-administration-releases-ambitious-cybersecurity-executive-order.html
[9] "EU Introduces a Cyber Security IoT Standard to Protect Its Citizens," Mender, accessed June 21, 2021. https://mender.io/blog/eu-introduces-a-cyber-security-iot-standard-to-protect-its-citizens

invaded by a large number of highly insecure and fragile connected devices.[10] The European Union was among the first to set a standard as a means to deal with cyber threats from IoT devices, but experts say that this may not be enough, and it will take one big cyber incident to enact a full-fledged GDPR-like regulation. The US on the other hand passed the IoT Cybersecurity Act in December 2020, which not only prescribes standards but also places accountability and imposes legal obligations on the device vendor community.

The Government of India has also set up CERT-In, which serves as the national agency for performing the functions listed in Table 8.6 related to cyber incidents and cybersecurity.

Table 8.6 CERT-In functions related to cyber incidents

Collection, analysis and dissemination of information	Forecasting and alerts	Undertake emergency measures
Co-ordination and response	Issue guidelines and advisories	Publish white papers regarding best practices

CERT-IN can in the course of carrying out its functions seek information and give direction to service providers, intermediaries, data centres and corporate bodies and any failure to provide the information called for or to comply with such direction can invite punishment in the form of imprisonment and fines.[11]

Cyber laws and cybersecurity regulations are a vast, ever-evolving field and, with technological innovations and new forms of cybercrime emerging all the time, the cyber-legal ecosystem has a lot of catching up to do. No single law or strategy is sufficient in itself to address all the legal challenges of cyberspace. What is required is a multipronged approach that integrates legal directives with effective enforcement. It cannot be left to governments and international agencies but requires active public–private participation as well as increased corporate accountability and responsibility in maintaining security practices that can assist in improved enforcement of cyber laws. Harmonizing laws across countries can also play an important role in removing lacunae in existing legal systems across jurisdictions.

8.4 CYBER FORENSICS

With the increasing frequency of cyberattacks and the cost of the damage caused by them to organizations around the world running into billions of dollars, the need for a scientific approach to investigation, attribution and prosecution has never been greater. Cyber forensics refers to the gathering, preserving, analyzing and investigating of data from a computer or mobile device, which is then used as evidence to be presented in court. In other words, the primary goal of cyber forensics is to establish who is responsible for a cyberattack or cybercrime as well as documenting the evidence and subsequently performing a thorough investigation. Cyber forensics is essential for the investigation of crime and law enforcement.

Different types of cyber forensics help in investigating cybercrimes. A few of them are as follows:

- **Network forensics** deals with monitoring and analyzing computer network traffic to collect legal evidence and related information that can help with the investigation process.
- **Database forensics** refers to the study and analysis of databases and related metadata.

---

[10] "EU Introduces a Cyber Security IoT Standard to Protect Its Citizens," Mender, accessed June 21, 2021. https://mender.io/blog/eu-introduces-a-cyber-security-iot-standard-to-protect-its-citizens

[11] Rohan Bagai and Shagun Bhadwar, "Cybersecurity 2021 - India Chapter," AZB & Partners, accessed June 24, 2021. https://www.azbpartners.com/bank/cybersecurity-2021-india-chapter/

- **Email forensics** is concerned with the recovery and analysis of emails, including recovering deleted emails, contacts and information from calendars.
- **Mobile phone forensics** deals with analyzing and investigating mobile devices. It commonly involves recovering SIM and phone contacts, incoming and outgoing SMS, audio, videos, call logs and messages.
- **Malware forensics** is used for identifying malicious code and involves the study of their viruses, payload and worms, among other things.
- **Incident response forensics** are used for examination of the data related to a cyber incident or breach so as to gain insights which can help remediate the attack and prevent a recurrence. This could also involve the use of computer forensics, disk forensics and memory forensics apart from other incident related data.
- **Internet forensics** enables the extraction, analysis, identification and examination of evidence in the form of artefacts such as logs, browser history and cookies relating to a user's online activities.

Cyber forensics plays an important role in the identification and attribution of cybercrime. It is essential for tracking the electronic footprints of criminals, gathering electronic evidence using different types of forensic methods and systematically preserving and presenting the evidence in a court of law to bring cybercriminals to book. Digital evidence is fragile and volatile and requires the observance of strict protocols for collection and preservation to ensure that data is not modified during its access, collection, packaging, transfer and storage.[12]

Experts suggest that "volatile evidence should be collected based on the order of volatility; that is, the most volatile evidence should be collected first and the least volatile should be collected last".[13] The order of evidence collection should be as follows:

- Registers and cache
- Routing table, memory contents, kernel data, process table
- Temporary files
- Data on disk
- System logs and monitoring data
- Network topology, physical configuration
- Back-ups and archival media
- Security software

Digital evidence must be handled in a structured manner following strict protocols covering the five phases of identification, collection, acquisition, preservation and analysis and reporting.

The **identification phase** involves getting acquainted with the facts of the cybercrime before commencing the job of collecting evidence. Questions regarding when, what, who, where and how the cybercrime occurred are the focus of this step. The investigator must focus attention on the types of evidence that is sought and direct efforts to collect the same from different digital devices, activity logs, emails, messages, business transaction records and private as well as public sources of information.

Collection is the next phase and must be conducted with the utmost care, without in anyway altering the data or metadata contained on the digital devices. It must be remembered that collection is not

---

[12] "Module 6: Key Issues: Handling of Digital Evidence," United Nations Office on Drugs and Crime, accessed June 23, 2021. https://www.unodc.org/e4j/en/cybercrime/module-6/key-issues/handling-of-digital-evidence.html

[13] "Module 6: Key Issues: Handling of Digital Evidence," United Nations Office on Drugs and Crime, accessed June 23, 2021. https://www.unodc.org/e4j/en/cybercrime/module-6/key-issues/handling-of-digital-evidence.html

limited to the scene or location of the crime as digital devices used in the commission of the cybercrime and/or that were the target of the cybercrime can exist anywhere.[14] Collection processes that are used for evidence will be different based on the type of devices and sources such as computers, mobile phones, social media and cloud. Collection may also involve the use of experts and a forensic toolkit. Once collected, digital evidence must be listed, recorded and stored in a secure location in conditions that are conducive for its preservation such as temperature-controlled environments that are free from humidity, dust and other possible contaminants. Maintaining documentation is an important part of the investigative process and must be done before, during and after the evidence has been acquired.[15]

The **acquisition phase** is best conducted in a laboratory where evidence is obtained from the devices through the use of tools and techniques that ensure that the integrity of data is preserved. The devices that are seized constitute the primary source of evidence and the analyst makes a duplicate copy of the data from that system referred to as 'image'. The data is then write-protected and encrypted using a hash value to ensure that, if needed, it can be verified that the image is indeed a mirror image of the original file.

Preservation of digital evidence from any modification or contamination is the essence of the entire handling process. To ensure this, a chain of custody must be maintained. Chain of custody refers to the order and manner in which physical or electronic evidence in criminal and civil investigations has been handled. When evidence is presented in court, the prosecution must prove that all evidence was handled according to a properly documented and unbroken chain of custody. Therefore, every handover between initial responders, investigators and forensic experts must be recorded and documented to establish that the evidence has not been tampered in any phase of the investigation.[16]

The **analysis phase** consists of examining the digital evidence and reconstructing the events for further analysis. Different types of analysis can be carried out depending on the type of digital evidence sought such as time-frame analysis, ownership and possession analysis, application and file analysis and data obscuring analysis. A **report** of the analysis with illustrative material, supporting material specifying the methods used, steps taken for data extraction and examination as well as details of chain of custody must be produced.

Cybersecurity and cyber forensics are closely related. Cyber forensics comes into play when cybersecurity fails. While cybersecurity is focused on cybercrime prevention, cyber forensics is focused on cybercrime response. Cybersecurity often draws from what cyber forensics has uncovered through various cases and investigations to enhance security and protection.

8.5 CYBERCRIME TECHNIQUES

In an earlier chapter, we looked at some of the tools and methodologies used by cybercriminals. At a fundamental level, traditional crime and cybercrime are similar. There is a criminal, a means of perpetrating the crime and a target or a victim. However, the biggest difference between the two lies in the proof of the crime. Criminals perpetrating traditional crimes leave behind physical proof of crime such as fingerprints or the weapon which was used for the crime, whereas cybercriminals use virtual tools and techniques which offer a degree of anonymity and leave only digital traces that need specialized methods to track and preserve the evidence. Hence, it can also be said that the extent of examination of proof is far more stringent. Another difference is that traditional crimes can be perpetrated by petty illiterate criminals, whereas cybercrime requires at least basic education and familiarity with online

---

[14] "Module 6: Key Issues: Handling of Digital Evidence," United Nations Office on Drugs and Crime, accessed June 23, 2021. https://www.unodc.org/e4j/en/cybercrime/module-6/key-issues/handling-of-digital-evidence.html

[15] "Module 6: Key Issues: Handling of Digital Evidence," United Nations Office on Drugs and Crime, accessed June 23, 2021. https://www.unodc.org/e4j/en/cybercrime/module-6/key-issues/handling-of-digital-evidence.html

[16] "Module 6: Key Issues: Handling of Digital Evidence," United Nations Office on Drugs and Crime, accessed June 23, 2021. https://www.unodc.org/e4j/en/cybercrime/module-6/key-issues/handling-of-digital-evidence.html

systems. Cybercrimes do not require the use of physical force, whereas traditional crimes like murder may require the use of extreme physical force.[17]

> **Info Box 61: Victims of Cybercrime**
>
> In 2018, nearly 700 million people around the world were victims of some type of cybercrime.[18]

In order to understand the techniques used by cybercriminals, we need to revisit the three categories of cybercrime: where the computer is the target of the cybercrime, where the computer is the instrument of the cybercrime, and where the computer is incidental to the cybercrime.[19]

Tools and techniques used for cybercrime can also be classified based on the categories of cybercrime they are being used for. Cybercriminals use various types of tools and techniques to exploit weakness, defeat security protocols, launch cyberattacks as well as other criminal activities and remove evidence of their crimes. These tools also help hackers automate tasks and enable them to make their attempts at cybercrime more effective. Table 8.7 shows examples of the techniques deployed by cybercriminals to accomplish tasks that enable them to commit cybercrimes.

Table 8.7 Cybercrime techniques, examples

Where the computer is a target of the cybercrime	
Packet sniffers/analysers	Used for passively listening to network traffic, recording traffic data and analysing the same.
Keyloggers and spyware	Used for recording the user's every keystroke and monitoring user activities.
Rootkits, trojans, ransomware	Enables cybercriminals to intrude into target systems and conceal themselves and then be used to cause damage.
Botnets	Compromising the computer to become a part of a botnet.
Where the computer is an instrument of the cybercrime	
Scanners	Used to ping a range of IP addresses, identify the OS and services being used on target servers, listing open ports, probing firewalls for configuration errors and look for open shared resources. Kali Linux is also used by hackers since it is free and has a large number of tools for penetration testing and security analytics.
Password crackers	Used for copying usernames, cracking passwords and bypassing related protections.
Denial of service (DoS)	Used for rendering a network service such as email or HTTP unavailable to others.

(Continued)

---

[17] Antariksh Anant, "Distinction Between Conventional Crime And Cyber Crime," Legal Bites, accessed June 20, 2021. https://www.legalbites.in/conventional-crime-and-cyber-crime/

[18] "Terrifying Cybercrime Statistics - Protect Yourself in 2022," SafeAtLast.Co, last updated February 14, 2022. https://safeatlast.co/blog/cybercrime-statistics/#gref

[19] Gordon, GR, Hosmer, CD, Siedsma, C and Rebovich, D, "Assessing Technology, Methods, and Information for Committing and Combating Cyber Crime," *National Institute of Justice*, 2002, 114. https://www.ojp.gov/pdffiles1/nij/grants/198421.pdf.

Table 8.7 (*Continued*)

Spoofing IP and emails	Used for deliberately misconfiguring IP addresses to hide the source or redirect responses and provide anonymity.
Surveillance software	Used for undertaking unauthorised surveillance.
Virus generating programs	Gives the cybercriminal an opportunity to create custom virus code.
Data extraction tools	Used for exporting large data from target computers.
Where the computer is incidental to the cybercrime	
Steganography	Used to hide information or messages within different forms of information.
Encryption	Used by criminals to hide evidence from storage.
Secure file deletion	Used by cybercriminals to permanently delete all files and traces to defeat all types of forensic software.

There have been several instances around the world of cybercriminals resorting to automated teller machine (ATM) frauds and cryptocurrency crimes. Common techniques deployed in the case of ATM frauds are card cloning (debit and credit), use of skimmers and hidden cameras at ATM locations. Cryptocurrency crimes are hacking attempts using phishing and social engineering to gain access to a victim's bitcoin account private keys to steal bitcoins.

8.6 PREVENTION OF CYBERCRIME AND PROTECTION

A moot question is who is responsible for the prevention of and protection from cybercrime. The simple answer is everyone. All stakeholders including individuals, developers and cyber professionals, organizations, government and law enforcement agencies must play their part in cybercrime prevention and protection. Table 8.8 lists five key measures that each of these stakeholders can undertake to prevent cybercrime.

Table 8.8 Key measures for the prevention of cybercrime

Individuals	Use strong passwords. Use security and privacy settings.	Use secure networks and secure mobile devices.	Update software regularly.	Use an antivirus. When in doubt, do not click.	Be vigilant when sharing personal and financial data.
Developers	Prioritize security.	Adopt security standards and best practices.	Test security scenarios.	Plan for security patching.	Use a code signing certificate.
Organizations	Implement multi-factor authentication.	Train employees to identify and respond to cyber threats.	Identify and protect information assets.	Develop, implement and enforce security policies. Deploy appropriate technical controls.	Regularly assess and test your systems. Adopt security best practices and standards

(*Continued*)

Table 8.8 (Continued)

Governments	Create security awareness. Enact laws and cybercrime regulations.	Prescribe stringent punishments to the offenders.	Define privacy and security policies. Issue alerts regarding cybercrimes.	Train law enforcement personnel/ prosecutors/ judicial officers, and improve cyber forensics facilities.	Participate in international cybercrime prevention efforts.
Law enforcement	Track down and punish offenders and cybercrime syndicates.	Encourage reporting of cybercrime.	Enhance cybersecurity and close the skill gap between cybercriminals and law enforcers.	Keep pace with technology changes and deploy the latest crime prevention and detection tools.	Deploy more resources for cybercrime prevention.

Unfortunately, it must be noted that at this point in time, all the stakeholders are playing catch-up with cybercriminals who have greater expertise and competence in perpetrating cybercrime as compared to those who are trying to prevent cybercrime and protect their data.

8.7 CYBERCRIME INVESTIGATION

Cybercrime investigation refers to the process of investigating the crime by recovering, analyzing, extracting and preserving forensic digital data from computers networks or other digital devices involved in the offence in order to find the culprits who perpetrated the cybercrime, leading to prosecuting them in a court of law. Cybercrime investigations involve the use of a wide variety of tools and processes for evidence extraction, examination, organization and preservation, network forensic tools, attack analysis tools, honeypots, time stamping tools and logs. Investigators who typically belong to law enforcement agencies or private agencies need to be well versed in the use of these tools and processes, not only from an evidence gathering point of view but also from the perspective of preservation and presentation of evidence which is acceptable in a court of law. Popular tools used in cybercrime investigation and the purpose of each tool are shown in Table 8.9.

Table 8.9 Cybercrime investigation tools

Type of tool	Purpose/Function	Popular tools, examples
Disk and data capture tools	Used by investigators and incident response teams to extract and examine digital forensic data from various devices.	The Sleuth Kit, Bulk Extractor, Paraben Suite, SIFT Workstation
	To extract EXIF (exchangeable image file format), which is a standard that specifies the formats for images, sound and ancillary tags used by digital cameras, global positioning system (GPS) data, etc.	ExifTool, EnCase
	Encrypted Disk Detector can be useful for checking encrypted physical drives.	Encrypted Disk Detector

(Continued)

Table 8.9 (*Continued*)

Type of tool	Purpose/Function	Popular tools, examples
Discovery and saving of system activity	To investigate system activity.	Digital forensics framework, Oxygen Forensic Detective
File viewers and analysis tools	To analyze, index, search, track and report on file metadata and file content on disk and in memory.	Varonis, Mandiant Redline
Infrastructure analysis	To map the IT infrastructure of an organization and access DNS information, WHOIS records, SSL certificates, etc.	SurfaceBrowser
Registry analysis tools	The Windows registry holds configuration information for the OS and the applications running on it, which is useful for forensic analysis.	Registry Recon, memory forensics
Internet analysis tools	To track a user's online activities through log files, cookies, browsing history, etc.	Belkasoft
Email analysis tools	To study the source (header details), format, transport protocol and content of emails,	MailXaminer, Digital forensics framework
Mobile devices analysis tools	To track recent chats, call logs, location data, pictures, etc.	OpenSource Android forensics, WhatsApp Xtract, Cellebrite
Network forensics tools	To track communications and establish timelines based on network events logged by network control systems.	Wireshark, Metasploit
Database forensics tools	To use metadata to navigate file system information and reconstruct event timelines.	The Sleuth Kit, FTK

Several other tools can help cybercrime investigators for evidence examination and organization, but specialised tools by themselves are not enough. They need to be combined with generic crime investigations skills to be able to evaluate a digital crime scene effectively. Cybercrime investigation tools and techniques continue to evolve, but the conviction rates of digital crimes are still very low. Cybercrime investigation is a difficult science and investigators need to be able to gather and analyze digital data to track down cybercriminals and bring them to book. Cybercrime investigators need to develop a very specialized skill set, which includes technical aptitude and skills, analytical capabilities, understanding of cybercrimes and cybersecurity and knowledge of cyber forensics, laws and investigation techniques.

8.8 EVIDENCE COLLECTION AND ANALYSIS

Evidence collection and analysis requires strict adherence to the principles of forensic evidence, systematic addressal and correct sequencing. To start, forensic investigators need to identify the different types of information that they need to collect such as computer files, documents, emails, text and instant messages, location data, transaction data, images, logs and browsing histories. The sources of this information could be computers, servers, cloud systems, back-up systems, surveillance systems, access systems, mobile phones, USBs and any other electronic devices that could have been used.

As there are several intricacies involved in the collection of forensic data including documentation and establishing the chain of custody at the time of presentation of the evidence, this activity is best carried out by trained digital forensic professionals. These professionals have the required competencies in pre-examination procedures and legal issues, media assessment and analysis, data recovery, analysis of recovered data, documentation and reporting, as well as presentation of findings.

The people who are the first investigators to reach the scene of offence are known as first responders. Their responsibility is to secure the crime scene and make arrangements for seizing information sources such as computers, mobile phones, other devices, passwords and codes from the people involved and even peripherals, USBs, chargers, cables and manuals. Some of these devices can be examined only with the help of different tools and techniques in a specialized laboratory environment. Due care must be taken to ensure that digital devices are prevented from any exposure to extreme temperatures, static electricity and moisture. When seizing computers and other equipment, care must be taken to avoid any alteration of digital evidence during collection. In case the computer is running a program to delete or destroy information, an image of the RAM memory must be made and the computer should be disconnected immediately to retain whatever is left on the machine. It is the duty of first responders to first document any activity on the computer, components or devices by taking a photograph and recording any information on the screen before they are packed. Mobile devices when seized should be turned off and batteries removed so that cell tower location and call logs are preserved.

While packing the devices, plastic should be avoided as it can convey static electricity and trap humidity. All digital devices must be packed using antistatic packaging such as paper bags or cardboard boxes. While sending the devices to a laboratory for further analysis, investigators need to specify the information that they are seeking from them.

At the laboratory, before conducting any analysis, the first step is to make an image of make an image of the RAM memory and store it on the evidence hard drive/USB. It is necessary to make an MD5/SHA1 hash of the image and save it. To retrieve and analyze data, analysts can also use command line utilities such as 'dd' and 'RAMdump'. The steps to be followed in conducting forensic analysis are listed in Table 8.10.

Table 8.10 Steps in digital evidence analysis

Identification	This step involves finding the evidence and where it is stored.
Preservation	The purpose of this step is to isolate, secure and preserve data as well as ensuring that no contamination or alteration can take place.
Analysis	This step entails undertaking forensic analysis by examining common areas on the disk image for possible malware, evidence, violating company policy, etc. If probable evidence is identified, then further analysis must be conducted to determine the cause and establish the timeline of the event(s). Different types of digital forensics that can be used are disk forensics, malware forensics, network forensics, email forensics, wireless forensics, database forensics and memory forensics. Fragments of information are reconstructed and inferences and conclusions drawn based on the evidence found.
Documentation	In this step, documentation regarding seizure, chain of custody, control, transfer, analysis and disposition of digital evidence must be completed.
Presentation	The final step involves drawing conclusions from digital evidence and presentation to a court of law.

8.9 INTELLECTUAL PROPERTY ISSUES IN CYBERSPACE

The cyberspace domain has brought forth several issues related to the protection of Intellectual Property (IP) and violation of associated rights. The growth of the Internet and e-commerce also has a dark side that represents the creation of an illegitimate ecosystem which is based on unauthorized distribution of IP without permission or payment to the owners of the IP.

The Internet and its infrastructure have provided cybercriminals a perfect platform for building a big business and profit from violation and infringement of patents, copyrights and trademarks, stealing trade secrets like business plans and industrial designs, and using/selling content and software without license or authorization.

IP infringement in cyberspace constitutes any unauthorized or unlicensed use/sale of trade names, trademarks, images, software, music, videos or other forms of online content. There exist several types of infringements which are unique to cyberspace such as unauthorized linking, downloading, hyperlinking, framing, meta-tagging and violation of digital copyrights. Violations can also be in the form of encroachment, transgression or trespass on a right or privilege.

Copyright infringement in cyberspace is a multi-billion-dollar business globally which thrives on the sale of stolen intellectual property. This not only means huge losses for the legitimate IP owners of the copyright but could also lead to security issues. The protection of IP involves cybersecurity and cyber laws to deal with issues arising from the theft, duplication, sale and use or free distribution of IP.

From a legal standpoint, copyright protection is available to the owner/creator of any published artistic, literary, dramatic or scientific work, thus preventing everyone else from using that work and gaining profit from it unless duly authorized by the owner to do so. One of the most famous cases related to copyright infringement was that of Napster, a peer-to-peer file sharing network that was launched in 1999. Music lovers were drawn to it as it allowed free sharing of music in MP3 format. Several record companies who were losing money on account of music piracy through Napster filed a joint lawsuit for infringement of IP. The court noted in its ruling that Napster had benefitted financially from large-scale distribution of free music and imposed damages of USD 26 million, which resulted in the closure of the company.

The legal position is the same whether in cyberspace or in the physical world. However, the incidences of infringements of intellectual property are more frequently observed on the Internet than in the physical world. This can be attributed to factors such as ease of access and making copies and transmission at the click of a button. Cyberspace also allows the perpetrators of IP-related crimes anonymity and the advantage of operating legal regimes and laws that are country specific.

Today, piracy of software, music and other entertainment and other content is rampant in cyberspace. Efforts to control it through laws and other means have so far been largely unsuccessful and over the years the problem of piracy has assumed alarming proportions, causing huge losses to content creators and owners. The following are three categories or modes of piracy in cyberspace:

- **Soft lifting** is the most prevalent type of piracy that involves the sharing a program with someone who is not authorized by the licence agreement to use it.
- **Software counterfeiting** is the unauthorized copying of software and reselling it to unsuspecting buyers. This is a big source of profits for cybercriminals and a cause of major losses to software companies and producers.
- **Uploading and downloading of any software** can also lead to another form of piracy. This is a tricky area as its legality or otherwise determines whether it amounts to piracy or not. File sharing/downloading by itself is perfectly legal, unless the file/content is copyright protected; in which case, permission/authorization is required from the owner of the file/content.

A question that users often contend with in cyberspace is can they download music, movies, images software programs, video games, books and other content as they are available on popular websites and peer-to-peer platforms? It is particularly important for users to be well informed about IP regulations before they download Internet content. WIPO (World Intellectual Property Organization) cautions users against the notion that content published on the Internet, including on social media platforms, are in the public domain and can therefore be used by anybody without due authorization of the right owner' in each case you should, generally, seek the authorization of the right owner prior to use. Most users on the Internet have downloaded copyrighted content at some time or the other, willfully or otherwise. The US Copyright law prescribes punishment of payment of up to USD 150,0000 for 'willful infringement' by illegally reproducing or distributing copyrighted material.

Users must also consider that under some legal systems, a clear list of limitations and exceptions to copyright is available that allows what is known as 'fair use'. Also, where the work is in the public domain and the copyright on the work has expired, it can be used and shared freely.

From a cybersecurity point of view, the protection of IP is of paramount importance. As IP represents one of the most valuable and important classes of assets, it must be secured from any threats, compromise or theft. The following are some basic steps that can be taken for the protection of IP assets:

1. Identify and categorize IP assets based on sensitivity.
2. Implement appropriate policies and procedures tailored to the organization's security needs.
3. Encrypt all sensitive IP assets.
4. Limit access and number of copies and make those who have access aware of how to handle IP assets in a secure manner.
5. As IP is shared at times with vendors and partners, contracts/non-disclosure agreements with them should reflect security requirements and mechanisms for IP protection.
6. Deploy effective security measures against internal and external threats.
7. Make reporting of any IP breaches mandatory.
8. Resort to legal remedies in case of IP compromise/breach.

Cyberspace has now become a fertile ground for violation of intellectual property rights. Cyber criminals have found various ways to profit from the unlawful use of software and other Internet content infringement making it increasingly difficult for organizations and governments to protect IP and prevent its unauthorised use. It is important to understand that there is no single international copyright law that is applicable throughout the world. Every country has its own laws and, since cyberspace is a borderless medium, it becomes difficult to enforce a uniform IP regime.

The US Digital Millennium Copyright Act (DMCA), 1998, is a landmark legislation that addresses specific issues relating to IP violations and protection and goes to the extent of making the act of circumventing an access control a crime, even if there was no actual copyright infringement. It criminalizes the production and dissemination of technology, devices or services intended to circumvent measures that control access to copyrighted work and enhances penalties related to copyright infringement. However, what the DMCA has not been able to do is keep up with the changing times and the birth of several new platforms for content sharing and creation, respectively. The DMCA specifically allows 'safe harbour' provisions for online intermediaries, limiting their liability with respect to any content shared or uploaded by their users. This particular provision has been echoed across the world in a variety of legislations, giving the likes of Google, Facebook and other intermediaries blanket immunity in the sharing of copyrighted material on their various platforms. These safe harbours were a necessity initially to limit the liability of Internet platforms to enable the unimpeded growth of cyberspace. However, now, they are looked at as largely exploitative of content creators, especially those who are independent and without the backing of large media corporations. More legislations and enforcement mechanisms are required around the world which can help in the protection and prevention of crimes related to IP.

IP is at the heart of an organization's activities and, apart from normal security control mechanisms that apply to all categories of information assets, it is important to sensitise users on the procedures for handling IP-related data and employ specific safeguards such as encryption, digital watermarking and implementation of data leak prevention solutions.

QUICK TEST

1. The purpose of cyber laws includes the following:
   a. Provide recognition and an overarching legal framework for electronic transactions and systems and contracts.
   b. Provide security protection for computer and Internet users.
   c. Provide protection of a user's personal information.
   d. Provide protection against computer-related crimes and frauds.
   e. Provide protection for digital intellectual property.
   f. All of the above
   g. a, b, c, d
2. Treaties are one of the foremost sources of international law.
   a. True
   b. False
3. GDPR regulations apply to:
   a. Member states of the European Union
   b. United States of America
   c. UN members
4. The Computer Fraud and Abuse Act, USA was introduced to promote and protect the privacy of individuals.
   a. True
   b. False
5. This US federal law required the creation of national standards to protect sensitive patient health information from being disclosed without the patient's consent or knowledge.
   a. CCPA
   b. Gramm–Leach–Bliley Act
   c. HIPAA
6. The word 'cybercrime' is widely used and is accepted as a menace that affects individuals, corporates and organizations, whether national, multinational or international, and therefore society in general. However, in a legal context, there is still no single definition of the term.
   a. True
   b. False
7. The phases involved in the initial handling of digital evidence are:
   a. Identification
   b. Collection
   c. Acquisition
   d. Preservation
   e. Analysis and reporting
   f. All of the above
   g. a, b, c, d
8. Cybersecurity and cyber forensics are closely related. Cyber forensics comes into play when cybersecurity fails.
   a. True
   b. False
9. Categories of cybercrime include:
   a. Crimes where the computer is the target of the cybercrime.
   b. Crimes where the computer is the instrument of the cybercrime.
   c. Crimes where the computer is incidental to the cybercrime.

d. All of the above
e. a, b
10. Volatile evidence should be collected based on the order of volatility; that is, the most volatile evidence should be collected first and the least volatile should be collected last.
   a. True
   b. False

QUESTIONS

1. Digital transactions and the Internet have largely been an unregulated space and laws and regulations that exist today are of relatively recent origin. Discuss.
2. Explain the need for and role of cyber laws in cybercrime prevention.
3. An overwhelming majority of countries around the world have enacted cybercrime legislation and more are on their way to doing so. The adoption of these laws is necessary for the development of digital systems and overall economic growth. What is the role of governments in framing cyber laws?
4. Cyber laws and cybersecurity regulations are continuously evolving, but are not able to keep pace with all the complexities and emerging legal issues. What are the key challenges faced by law-makers and law enforcement agencies?
5. Why is there a need for specific cybersecurity regulation? Discuss.
6. What are the different types of tools and techniques used in investigating cybercrime?
7. Explain the five phases of handling digital evidence.
8. Discuss the different IP issues in cyberspace. What are the laws that govern the same?
9. How can software piracy be controlled? Discuss.
10. What are the steps that an organization can take to protect Intellectual Property?

ANSWER KEYS

Quick Test

1. (f)
2. (a)
3. (a)
4. (b)
5. (c)
6. (b)
7. (f)
8. (a)
9. (d)
10. (a)

9 Personal Cybersecurity, Privacy and Data Protection

> **OBJECTIVES**
>
> *At the end of this chapter, you will be able to:*
>
> - ☑ List the issues related to personal security, protection of privacy and data protection
> - ☑ Explain the common causes that lead to breaches and the best practices that can enhance your personal cybersecurity
> - ☑ Describe privacy regulations and the role of ethics in cybersecurity

9.0 INTRODUCTION

Personal cybersecurity or online safety is a matter of growing concern for all those who are connected to the Internet. As we move towards a digital society that determines the way we live, work and play in the digital world, our digital identities have to be proactively managed in order to stay safe. Online safety, also called cyber safety or e-safety, involves protecting ourselves and others from online harms and risks which may endanger our personal information, lead to unsafe communications or even effect our mental health and wellbeing.[1]

All the devices that we use to connect to the Internet including personal computers, laptops, tablets and mobile phones along with their applications could be a source of threat to our personal security. As a user, it is imperative that awareness of online safety and security risks to personal information be developed to ensure protection from cybercrime.[2] Lack of awareness of issues pertaining to online safety can lead to many undesirable consequences; even children, teenagers and the elderly are not spared by cybercriminals.

9.1 WHAT IS PERSONAL CYBERSECURITY?

Personal cybersecurity is concerned with security requirements at an individual level. It is applicable to anyone connected to the Internet and using its various applications and services. Regardless of whether you are working from home, office or anywhere else, a high degree of security awareness and vigilance is essential. Online security involves securing all devices, network connections and personal information; being aware of the cyber threat environment; and implementing a minimum basic set of cybersecurity hygiene measures.

---

[1] "What Is Online Safety?," National Online Safety, accessed June 25, 2021. https://nationalonlinesafety.com/wakeupwednesday/what-is-online-safety

[2] "What Is Online Safety?," National Online Safety, accessed June 25, 2021. https://nationalonlinesafety.com/wakeupwednesday/what-is-online-safety

9.1.1 Personal Identifiable Information (PII)

PII or personal identifiable information refers to any data that can be used to contact, locate or identify a specific individual, either by itself or combined with other sources that are easily accessed.[3] Personal information is made of data elements that can be used to identify a particular person such as name, biometric data, telephone number, email address or social security number. PII is often contained in an individual's financial, educational, employment or medical records.

What is the personal information that hackers seek to steal and use against individuals to cause harm?[4] Table 9.1 provides a listing and categorization of personal information.

Table 9.1 Sensitivity level of different types of information

Sensitivity level	Type of information
Low	Full name, residential/work address, telephone numbers
Medium	Date/Place of birth, educational qualifications
High	Passwords, credit card, driver's licence, bank account, social security number, passport details, geolocation data, tax information
Other personal information	Genetic or biometric data. Medical records, employment/residential history, children's names and birthdays

9.1.2 Protected or Personal Health Information (PHI)

Information about the health of an individual is also considered as information to be protected by organizations that generate and use the information in several countries. HIPAA was a landmark legislation enacted in the US for the protection of health information. Typically, PHI is considered to be any health information that is individually identifiable and created or received by a provider of health care, a health plan operator or health clearing house. The information could be connected to an individual's present, past or future health, either in physical or mental terms, as well as the current condition of a person.

Even though the importance of protecting personal information has been known for quite some time, it is only now that advances in technology have made the acquisition, usage, and storage of PII and PHI much easier. However, increased incidences of misuse of data collected by agencies and organizations and frequent hacking incidents have exacerbated the need for proper cyber protections as well as legal frameworks that are targeted at misuse and the criminal use of personal information. Laws that are associated to different forms of PII include HIPAA, Privacy Act, GDPR, GLBA CCPA and various data protection regulations enacted by countries around the world.

9.2 COMMON CAUSES OF PERSONAL SECURITY BREACHES

Individuals, unlike corporations that have access to specialist IT skills and resources, have to depend on their own understanding of security issues and the threats that they face. Often, they are unable to even conceive the various ways in which their personal sensitive information can be compromised and

---

[3] "What Is PII and PHI Security? Why Is It Important?," *FileCloud* (blog), accessed June 25, 2021. https://www.getfilecloud.com/blog/2015/03/what-is-pii-and-phi-why-is-it-important/#.YNWtyOgzZPY

[4] "What Personal Information Should You Safeguard?," Norton, accessed May 20, 2021. https://us.norton.com/internetsecurity-privacy-what-personal-information-should-you-safeguard.html

the resultant harm that they may have to contend with. Let us examine the common causes breaches of personal cybersecurity.

Stolen passwords are one of the most common causes of data breaches. Passwords are the key to accessing IT systems. Weak passwords make it easier for hackers to steal them and represent one of the biggest threats for personal data protection. The common characteristics of weak passwords are as follows:[5]

- Passwords having few characters (specially less than eight)
- Passwords that are words from an English or language dictionary
- Names of pets, family members, birthdays, phone numbers, etc.
- Computer commands or other terminology
- Using word or number patterns like xxxyyy, qwerty, 123321, etc.

Apart from using weak passwords, users are also prone to making the following common mistakes, which should be avoided:[6]

- Changing passwords frequently or making them complex as you may tend to forget them for another frequently used one.
- Not screening them by comparing your password against lists of commonly used or known compromised ones.
- Recycling or reusing the same passwords across multiple websites is especially dangerous when it comes to email, banking and social media accounts.
- Using passwords or answers to website security questions: names of family and pets, anniversary or birthdays or any such information that could be gathered by doing a bit of online research.
- Using the 'save' or 'remember me' options on a public computer. The next user could easily gain access to your account.
- Using common, easily guessed characters like "123456," "admin" or "password".
- Not protecting mobile devices with passwords or not changing their default passwords.
- Maintaining a password list on your computer.

Users must enhance their awareness on the use of passwords and other means of authentication that are available to them to use. It is of prime importance to use passwords that are difficult to break and make yourself as safe as possible. The key characteristics of strong passwords are as follows:

- They must contain both upper- and lowercase characters (a–z, A–Z).
- They must have digits, special characters and letters.
- The use of long passwords or passphrases are useful as protection.

Wherever the use of multi-factor authentication is available as a means of accessing a system, it must be used. Sharing of passwords is not a healthy practice and, if ever this needs to be done, care must be taken to change the password immediately after.

Phishing is a form of cybercrime where hackers use email, telephone or text messages to pose as legitimate institutions to entice individuals into providing sensitive data such as personal sensitive information, banking and credit card details and passwords. The target is then deceived into clicking a malicious link, which can lead to the installation of malware, the freezing of the system as part

---

[5] "Weak Password - an Overview," ScienceDirect, accessed May 22, 2021. https://www.sciencedirect.com/topics/computer-science/weak-password
[6] "Weak Password - an Overview," ScienceDirect, accessed May 22, 2021. https://www.sciencedirect.com/topics/computer-science/weak-password

of a ransomware attack or the revealing of sensitive information. Victims could suffer from theft of funds, identify theft, etc. Examples of unsolicited phishing emails are shown in Fig. 9.1.

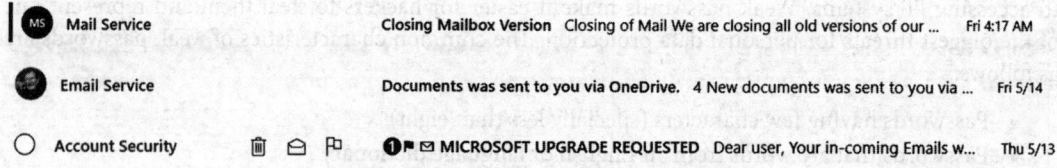

Figure 9.1 Unsolicited phishing emails

Hackers also use a variant of a phishing campaign called vishing (short for voice phishing). Here, the hacker masquerades as someone from a trusted company but uses a phone call instead of an email. Vishing relies on persuading victims that they are doing the right thing by following the instructions of the caller who often pretends to be calling on behalf of the government, tax department, police or the victim's bank or offers credit, insurance and loans, investment opportunities and charitable requests for urgent causes. The objective is to get you to part with your personal information. Another example of a common vishing pretext is a call from tech-support requesting actions such as going to a specific page by clicking on a link sent to them to update user information for updates. Dealing with this requires a high degree of alertness, security consciousness and situational awareness.

Internet scams are a form of cybercrime that make use of the Internet in order to trick victims out of money, property and inheritance. Internet scams comprise the use of multiple manipulative schemes such as phishing emails, social media, SMS/WhatsApp messages, fake tech-support phone calls, scareware and more, which are deployed along with a range of illegal and illicit actions, making it a composite form of crime involving technologies and methodologies. It is distinct from theft in the sense that here the victim is persuaded or lured into parting with sensitive information which can be used against the same person. Awareness of these types of scams is necessary to protect yourself from becoming a victim of these scams. A list of scams is provided in Table 9.2, but it must be remembered that each has its own variants and more types of scams come up every day. A security-first approach in your online interactions is needed to safeguard yourself from these scams.

The list of scams is endless, and it is important to develop the awareness required to recognize the methodologies and be able to identify fake communications, links and websites. Victims of online scams are often reluctant to report these incidents to law enforcement agencies who will have a better chance tracking and shutting down the perpetrators.[7]

There are several types of **malware** that can be used to target individuals. The more common ones are spyware, keyloggers, scareware, adware, screen locking ransomware and trojans. These malware are usually distributed through emails, software apps and malicious links. The use of security software, being aware and alert can help in protection against such malware.

Cyberbullying, cyberstalking, sextortion and online predation are different forms of using electronic means to threaten, harass, intimidate or embarrass victims. The help of law enforcement agencies is required to deal with these forms of cybercrimes and individuals will be well advised to seek their help.

Social media is increasingly used by adults and children alike. The use of platforms like Facebook, LinkedIn, Twitter, Snapchat and Instagram all require the creation of an online profile that involves sharing varying amounts of personal information. They also contain information of your affiliations and

---

[7] Jon Watson, "70+ Common Online Scams Used by Cyber Criminals and Fraudsters," Comparitech, accessed May 22, 2021. https://www.comparitech.com/vpn/avoiding-common-scams-schemes/

Table 9.2 Types of cyber frauds and scams

Email-based scams	Advanced-fee fraud	Nigerian Lottery scam	Charity fraud	Work-at-home job scams
Cancelled account	CEO fraud; business email compromise	Greeting cards infected with malware	Affinity or common interest fraud	Guaranteed bank loan or credit card
Service provider scam	Scam compensation scam	Scams targeted at elderly persons	Investment scams	Insurance schemes
Health scams	Inheritance scam	Bank scam	Tax scams	Fake prizes or contest winnings
Tech-support scams	Covid-related scams	Fake news scams	Job offer scams	Travel and ticketing scams
Free or discounted vacation	Points scheme	Fake audit	Fake refund	Erroneous refund
Bitcoin and cryptocurrency scams	Wallet impersonators	Fake antivirus software pop-up windows	Fake websites	Counterfeit goods sites
Online dating and romance scams	Delivery and invoice-related scams	Buyer scams	Payment scams	Advertising scams

interests, likes and dislikes. While social media platforms try to maintain personal data security (they have also been compromised at times), the threats and risks to personal data comes from hackers who target this information for perpetrating cybercrimes such as identity theft, cyberbullying, cyberstalking etc. Leaving online accounts unattended for long periods of time, using weak passwords and not using privacy controls provided by the platforms can lead to sensitive data landing up in the wrong hands.

Unpatched software and hardware is another common cause for breaches of personal cybersecurity. To secure themselves, users need to ensure that all their software and hardware solutions are fully patched and up to date at all times. Not doing so will make you vulnerable to exploits by hackers. Other causes for security breaches include improper configuration, user errors, not making use of security settings, use of insecure and public Wi-Fi networks, etc.

By and large, cyber threats fall under two categories based on the delivery method deployed by hackers: push and pull.

Push-based threats make use of deceptive techniques like phishing and spamming to attract a user to visit a malicious web page where the attacker can collect an assortment of sensitive information or introduce malware. Spear phishing is an example of a precisely targeted push-based threat. The victim here is carefully selected knowing that he is in a position of power and authority to yield better results for the hacker. Hackers also use social engineering techniques with appealing subject lines designed to grab attention such as holiday offers, current affairs, sports or entertainment news to lure unsuspecting victims into clicking on malicious links or opening malicious attachments that could compromise their security.[8]

---

[8] Trend Micro, "Web Threats: Challenges and Solutions," (2008): 19. http://book.itep.ru/depository/security/web_security/Web_Threats_White_Paper.pdf

Pull-based threats are another form of cyber threats wherein hackers make use of what are called 'drive-by downloads' by introducing malware into legitimate websites and transmitting the same to unsuspecting visitors to the website.[9]

9.3 PERSONAL CYBERSECURITY BEST PRACTICES

When it comes to personal cybersecurity, we are all at different levels of understanding the threats and risks and taking the required actions to make our online activities more secure. As a starting point, whether or not you have the knowledge and background to address your personal cybersecurity needs, you need to know that the risks are for real and that you could be the next target for hackers. We tend to imagine that we have nothing that would interest a hacker, but the truth is that regardless of whether you are a child, adult or elderly person, hackers know how to use information stolen from you in many different ways. A personal commitment to understanding and implementing the available security and privacy controls across the platforms that you use is essential. Users often prefer convenience over security considerations and, due to this predisposition, make security decisions that can jeopardise their personal cybersecurity.

A commitment to personal cybersecurity demands the use of good personal cybersecurity practices as part of our daily online activity. This is the only way to offer the best resistance we can by putting up robust defences in the face of cyber threats. While there is no way to become immune to all types of cyber threats, incorporating personal cybersecurity best practices can help us respond better to threats as and when they occur.

Best practices in personal cybersecurity revolve around the following three areas: awareness, vigilance and protection. Let us examine each in turn.

9.3.1 Awareness

A good starting point is to run a search about yourself to identify what information about you is already available in the public domain. This will help you figure out what information you have put out about yourself through social media platforms, your own/organization website, etc. as well as information about you that has been put out by third parties on the web.

Developing general awareness about cybercrime and methods deployed by cybercriminals is essential to protect yourself. Such information today is widely available on the Internet, and everyone must be capable of identifying social engineering threats such as phishing emails, Internet scams, spoofed emails, malicious links and other types of common threats.

There are several types of malware including those that are deployed to target a user with spyware, keyloggers, scareware, etc. to prise out personal and financial information. Deploying antivirus software on personal systems and mobile phones can help mitigate these threats to a large extent.

Phishing scams are a scourge to personal cybersecurity. A high degree of awareness of techniques used by hackers can help save data from being compromised. Scrutinizing any email or links sent through other messaging platforms must become a part of your online behaviour. Being suspicious of links and attachments involves looking out for giveaways such as poor grammar and spelling, checking with senders on matters of importance especially where urgency or threats are used, detecting spoofed email IDs by hovering over a URL and exercising care when responding to emails seeking personal or sensitive information are steps that can help in detecting phishing activities. Once you are convinced that the email or attachment can cause you harm, it is best to delete it and not leave it on your computer system.

---

[9] Trend Micro, "Web Threats: Challenges and Solutions," (2008): 19. http://book.itep.ru/depository/security/web_security/Web_Threats_White_Paper.pdf

There is no substitute for awareness of the online harms that can be caused by cybercriminals. Trusting only after verification should become the norm that defines your online activity. Every individual is responsible for their own personal cybersecurity, and we also have a responsibility towards the institutions we serve, and hence, we need to take charge of protecting our own information and data from attacks and computer-related crimes. Here are nine ways in which you can stay aware of information security threats:[10]

1. Start by taking responsibility by managing your own information security.
2. Do not use pirated software or downloads.
3. Follow news regarding security threats and equip yourself with the latest knowledge.
4. When in doubt, do not hesitate to seek the advice of experts.
5. Maintain a contact list for assistance, such as public services, application support and Internet Service Provider (ISP) hotlines.
6. Be careful when sharing your geo-location. Turn off when not in use.
7. Be cautious and do not underestimate the impact of security incidents, which can lead to leaks of personal information and other related consequences.
8. Do not make the mistake of presuming that security incidents that could happen to the platforms that you use will not affect you.
9. Implement security measures across all the devices that you use and not just computers and mobile phones.

9.3.2 Vigilance

It is important to understand that hackers do not just steal confidential information, they can also steal network resources. A number of variations of the e-greeting scam have often done the rounds. Here, simple spam messages are used to inform recipients that a friend had sent them an e-greeting card and to follow the link in the email to view the card. If the recipients click on the link, it takes them to a website and results in downloading of malicious code. This code then converts the victim's computer into a 'bot' and enables the hackers to use their computing resources. Hackers target both corporate and consumer computers and create 'botnets' to launch bigger DDoS attacks.[11]

Being vigilant demands that users are conscious of online activity in the applications that they use and their own online behaviour. Ten areas where vigilance can be of help in protecting your personal information are:

1. Not getting distracted when you are online and clicking on a link without thinking.
2. Not being fooled by a spoofed email or opening suspicious emails.
3. Being cautious about attractive online offers for discounts.
4. Not being hurried into taking actions like 'buy before last date' or closing offers which you feel are too good to pass up.
5. Understand that children and elders could be targets too.
6. Always verify requests for private information.
7. Use strong passwords and keep different passwords for different accounts.
8. Secure your debit/credit cards while shopping online.

---

[10] "Keeping Self Awareness for Information Security," InfoDec, accessed June 1, 2021. https://www.infosec.gov.hk/en/best-practices/person/keeping-self-awareness-for-information-security
[11] Trend Micro, "Web Threats: Challenges and Solutions," (2008): 19. http://book.itep.ru/depository/security/web_security/Web_Threats_White_Paper.pdf

9. Even if you think you are safe, regularly check your financial statements and credit reports.
10. Refresh your knowledge of the smart habits to keep you safe online.

9.3.3 Protection

Proactively implementing protection measures can protect your personal information from the machinations of threat actors. Securing what is known as your personal area network (PAN) must also be considered while implementing personal cybersecurity. A PAN is a network concerned with the exchange of information in the vicinity of a person. Typically, these systems are wireless and involve the transmission of data between devices such as smartphones, personal computers, tablet computers, etc.[12] Transmission within a PAN is based on the use of different technologies such as Bluetooth, wireless PANs (WPANs), wireless body area networks (WBANs), sensors and actuators and smart tags. It is important to ensure that all devices connected to your PAN conform to international standards and are from trusted vendors who can offer ongoing support and security updates. Paying attention during the set-up process that all default passwords on the devices are replaced with your own passwords which are complex and unique is essential.

From a personal cybersecurity point of view, there are choices that one has to make, especially in the trade-off between convenience and security. It is useful to follow best practices that have evolved over recent years based on the types of cyber threats that are prevalent. Here are a few personal security tips to ensure better protection of your personal information and systems:

- **Use strong passwords and protect them at all times**: Use different passwords for home and work. Use of weak passwords can lead to undesirable consequences. A compilation of the most common passwords that have been used over the years is shown in Table 9.3. Undoubtedly these are weak passwords and should not be used.

Table 9.3 Top 30 most common passwords over the years

Password	123	login	111111	Hello	iloveu
Qwerty	1234	Welcome	666666	Master	letmein
Abc123	12345	Monkey	000000	Flower	Princes
Admin	123456	Superman	999999	Football	Dragon

A more detailed study of worst passwords will throw up literally thousands of passwords that are easy for hackers to guess and breach security and hence should not be used. It is imperative that you use long, strong, unique passphrases instead of passwords and use multi-factor authentication (MFA) wherever possible. It is also a good practice to not permit apps and websites remember your passwords.

- **Deploying antivirus software** along with a firewall and VPN can provide basic protection against various types of viruses and malware from entering your devices and infecting them. It is recommended that you use antivirus software from trusted vendors and only run one antivirus tool on your device. Windows and Mac OS X come with their native firewalls and routers also should have a firewall built in to prevent attacks on your network.

---

[12] "Personal Area Network - an Overview," ScienceDirect, accessed June 1, 2021. https://www.sciencedirect.com/topics/engineering/personal-area-network

- A **VPN connection** provides a secure connection between your computer or mobile phone and the Internet. All data that passes through the VPN is encrypted, providing protection for data that is in transit. It also conceals your IP address when you use the Internet, making its location hidden to everyone.
- An important habit that will ensure better protection of your systems and data is to **keep your devices, browsers and applications up to date**. This cannot be treated as a one-time activity or even a periodic one as security patches are being released all the time and often vendors prompt you to update your systems. Hence, this must become a part of online hygiene and due priority should be given to timely updating your systems.

Surfing the Internet is great fun and is useful in many ways. However, it is worth noting that the way you surf the Internet can be a safety issue. You need to **beware of suspicious websites at all times**. A simple way of protecting yourself is to verify the security notification that is displayed in the form of a lock. If the display shows a closed lock (HTTPS), it means that the link is secure. The lock symbol and associated URL refers to a secure site where the connection between your web browser and the website server is encrypted. Very often we come across the use of shortened URLs which we have to click to access a web page. This could pose a potential threat in the form of allowing malware or entering sensitive personal data into a form that looks authentic but is illegitimately trying to collect your data for malicious purposes. Hence, before clicking a shortened URL, users need to check for the full URL or use a URL checker like getlinkinfo.com or unshorten.it which enables examination of the full URL.

Protecting your data is another important way to safeguard information that is of value to you and can cause harm to you if it is in the hand of hackers. Good practices to protect your information are encrypting sensitive data, deleting sensitive information when it is no longer needed, securely deleting files from old hard drives and devices, using a VPN to undertake banking and other financial transactions, maintaining offline back-ups of your critical data and purging your digital spaces of clutter.

9.3.4 Phone and Mobile Device Security

Mobile phones are an individual's window to the world. We cannot imagine a day without our phone as we go about our daily activities, be it work, entertainment, shopping, banking or socializing. However, the mobile phone also offers hackers and scamsters a window of opportunity to steal our data and compromise our security.

Threats to our phones and other mobile devices abound in the form of device vulnerabilities, applications that mine personal information, web-based mobile threats, dubious downloads, phishing, network threats and even the physical threat of devices being lost or stolen. Vulnerabilities also exist if patching is not up-to-date or devices are used after jailbreaking.

A good source for referencing issues related to mobile threats is the NIST mobile threats catalogue.[13] Mobile devices are extremely important for cybersecurity to be effective as they are the most widely used type of device today. Threats related to mobile phones must be identified and addressed to ensure security (Table 9.4). This requires a broader view of the entire mobile ecosystem, looking at threats beyond devices to include cloud infrastructure and cellular networks. Notably, devices covered in the catalogue are limited to smartphones, tablets and e-readers and excludes other IoT devices.

---

[13] "Mobile Threat Catalogue," National Institute of Standards and Technology, accessed April 14, 2022. https://pages.nist.gov/mobile-threat-catalogue/background/

Table 9.4 Mobile threat categories

Application	Authentication	Cellular
Ecosystem	Enterprise Mobility Management	Global Positioning Systems
Local Area and Personal Area Networks	Payments	Physical Access
Privacy	Stack	Supply Chain

Today's mobile phones and other devices are more powerful than the desktop computers of yesteryears. While mobile devices have taken our digital activities to another level, they are also a major source of cyber threats. Securing your mobile devices is essential for your personal cybersecurity. According to McAfee Labs, your mobile device is now a target to more than 1.5 million new incidents of mobile malware. Here are 12 good practices for mobile device security:[14]

1. Set up a hard-to-crack mobile passcode. Use two-factor authentication.
2. Lock your phone when not in use.
3. Install apps only from trusted sources.
4. Always update your phone's operating system (OS) when prompted. Keep your mobile devices updated.
5. Install antivirus software on mobile devices.
6. Avoid public charging stations.
7. Audit your apps to see what information they are accessing.
8. Do not send any personal or sensitive information over text message or email.
9. Use the find-my-phone functionality to prevent loss or theft.
10. Connect securely. Do not allow apps to access to your phone contacts and camera without your explicit knowledge.
11. Ensure to back up your data on cloud systems regularly.

9.3.5 Identity Theft

One of the major cyber threats to emerge in recent times is that of identity theft. While the concept of identity theft is not new (the term was coined in 1964), the means of stealing person digital identity and misusing it have evolved rapidly. Identity theft occurs when someone uses another person's personal identifying information, like their name, identifying number or credit card number, without their permission, to commit fraud or other crimes. Victims of identity theft can even find themselves saddled with false criminal records.[15] The four basic forms of identity theft include medical, criminal, financial and child identity theft. A few of the other practical incidences of identity theft are listed in Table 9.5.

Protecting your personal data in a highly charged cyber threat environment is of prime importance. Best practices for protecting data involve being very careful and selective in sharing it on different forums and platforms. Here are five tips for the same:

1. As far as possible, provide the least amount of information that does not completely expose your identity.

---

[14] "10 Personal Cyber Security Tips — #CyberAware," Cipher, accessed June 1, 2021. https://cipher.com/blog/10-personal-cyber-security-tips-cyberaware/

[15] "Identity theft Noun," Oxford Advanced American Dictionary at OxfordLearnersDictionaries.Com, accessed June 1, 2021. https://www.oxfordlearnersdictionaries.com/definition/american_english/identity-theft

Table 9.5 Common forms of identity theft

Existing account identity theft and take-over fraud
New account identity theft
Employment identity theft
Debit card or credit card fraud
Driver's licence identity theft
Mail identity theft
Social security number identify theft
Online shopping fraud
Tax identity theft
Child identity theft

2. Use the privacy configuration settings provided by the platforms in such a way that key data elements are not exposed.
3. Review third-party apps that are connected to your social media platforms and understand the data elements that may be shared with them.
4. Share personal information on social media judiciously and selectively.
5. Refrain from sending sensitive banking and other information by email.

While we cannot possible protect ourselves from every threat in existence, we can mitigate any damage or prevent harmful outcomes by implementing good personal cybersecurity practices.

In the unfortunate circumstance of your personal cybersecurity having been violated, there are at least six key actions that you will need to take:

1. Change all passwords.
2. Keep the virus from spreading.
3. Make the most of your back-ups and buy proper software.
4. Determine what was lost.
5. Report to law enforcement authorities.
6. Inform your bankers and cyber insurance company in case you have a policy.

9.4 PRIVACY REGULATIONS AND CYBERSECURITY

Privacy and data protection have taken centre stage and are hotly being debated around the world. There is growing apprehension among all the stakeholders such as technology companies, social media platforms, governments and civil society as to the direction in which we are headed in terms of privacy protection since any change in present practices will affect them in some way. The use of personal information is an essential component for the provision of various kinds of services by government agencies and private businesses.

Most of us are also confused, apprehensive of how data is being used(misused?) and feel a lack of control over our personal information. Many of us think that our personal data is less secure now, and increasingly believe that data submission presents more risks than benefits. There are also fears that it is not possible to go through daily life without being tracked.[16]

Privacy covers a wide range of technologies and issues; a partial list is shown in Table 9.6.

Table 9.6 Partial list of technologies/processes related to privacy

Biometrics Technologies	Video Surveillance	Online Privacy and E-commerce
Workplace Monitoring	Wireless Communications and Location Tracking	Data Profiling
Biometrics	Virtual Private Networks	AI and Analytical Tools
Criminal Identity Theft	Background Checks	Information Broker Industry
Public Records on the Internet	Financial Privacy	Medical Records Confidentiality
Genetic Privacy	Direct to Consumer (DTC) Genetic Testing	Wiretapping and Electronic Communications
Youth Privacy Issues/Child Protection	Digital Rights Management	Digital Television and Broadband Cable TV
Radio Frequency Identification (RFID)	Real ID	Payment Processing
Behavioural Targeting	Cloud Computing	Internet of Things
Smart Grid	Data Anonymization	Big Data

Each of these technologies and processes gives rise to specific concerns that relate to the collection, storage and use of personal information. Moreover, each stakeholder, such as the agency gathering and processing the information and the individual whose personal information it is, have, more often than not, a conflicting set of interests. Whether it is government or private businesses, individuals are concerned about how this information could be used against them. Hence, around the world, there is a great need to bring in regulations that safeguard the privacy rights of an individual, while permitting the use of personal information subject to certain restrictions and accountability. There have been several privacy and data protection regulations that have been enacted in recent years but are yet to pass the test of striking a balance between the interests of different stakeholders, while providing strong assurance to the individual to whom the data belongs. Any law must be a reflection of our goals and needs as a society and the challenge is sometimes related to the changing needs and goals of society itself as we are quick to embrace new technologies without due consideration of all the implications.

There exists a strong connection between privacy protection and cybersecurity. As greater amounts of personal information are processed or stored online, privacy protection increasingly depends on effective cybersecurity implementation by organizations to secure personal data both when it is in transit and at rest.[17]

---

[16] "Americans and Privacy: Concerned, Confused and Feeling Lack of Control Over Their Personal Information," Pew Research Center, accessed June 2, 2021. https://www.pewresearch.org/internet/2019/11/15/americans-and-privacy-concerned-confused-and-feeling-lack-of-control-over-their-personal-information/

[17] "Privacy and Cyber Security," Office of the Privacy Commissioner of Canada, accessed June 2, 2021. https://www.priv.gc.ca/en/opc-actions-and-decisions/research/explore-privacy-research/2014/cs_201412/

Prof. Bradley Gold of the University of Texas suggests data privacy laws should evolve by looking at five simple principles that everyone can understand:[18]

- They should promote and defend honesty.
- They should promote and defend transparency.
- They should promote and protect the commitments we make to one another.
- They should protect us from harm and punish those that purposely cause harm.
- Evolutions in law should be based upon objective measures of society's goals and needs.

Privacy law means any international, national, federal, provincial, state or local law, code, rule or regulation that regulates the processing of personal information in any way, including data protection laws, laws regulating marketing communications and/or electronic communications, information security regulations and security breach notification rules.[19] Privacy laws also apply to acts such as breach of trade secrets and confidential information violation by employees when handing sensitive information.

The Universal Declaration of Human Rights (UDHR) is an important milestone and reference point for the creation and evolution of privacy laws. Although not a legally binding document, UDHR has been adopted by the United Nations and its statement that everyone enjoys the right to privacy has been incorporated in international treaties and the national laws of many countries.

Info Box 62: Justice Puttaswamy vs Union of India

August 23, 2017 was a very important day in the legal history of India. On this day, the Supreme Court unanimously recognised privacy as a fundamental right guaranteed by the Constitution (subject to certain restrictions) under Articles 14, 19 and 21 of the Constitution of India, in the case of Justice KS Puttaswamy and Anr. vs. Union of India and Ors.[20]

General privacy laws that have an overall bearing on the personal information of individuals and affect the policies that govern many different areas of information include trespass, negligence and fiduciary.[21]

Data protection refers to the set of privacy laws, policies and procedures whose purpose is to protect an individual's data and privacy from intrusion. Currently, India is in the process of bringing in specific laws related to privacy and data protection as the IT Act 2000 is inadequate to deal with all matters related to the subject. With large volumes of personal information being collected, processed and stored by both private and government agencies, there is a dire need for specific laws that address matters of privacy and to specify obligations of organizations towards protection of personal data. Section 43A of the IT Act 2000 that states that corporate bodies who collect, store and process any sensitive personal data or information, and are found to be negligent in implementing and maintaining reasonable security practices resulting in wrongful loss or wrongful gain to any person, will be held accountable for payment of compensation to the victim.[22] This section will be replaced through the forthcoming Personal Data Protection Bill, which will impose more specific obligations related to data protection in India.

---

[18] "5 Golden Rules of Data Privacy Law," Grable Martin Fulton PLLC, accessed June 2, 2021. https://grablemartin.com/rules-of-data-privacy/
[19] "Privacy Laws Definition," Law Insider, accessed June 26, 2021. https://www.lawinsider.com/dictionary/privacy-laws
[20] "Fundamental Right to Privacy," Supreme Court Observer, accessed June 26, 2021. https://www.scobserver.in/court-case/fundamental-right-to-privacy
[21] "Fundamental Right to Privacy," Supreme Court Observer, accessed June 26, 2021. https://www.scobserver.in/court-case/fundamental-right-to-privacy.
[22] "Reasonable Security Practices and Procedures and Sensitive Personal Data or Information Article," Law Articles, accessed June 26, 2021. http://www.legalservicesindia.com/law/article/982/6/Reasonable-security-practices-and-procedures-and-sensitive-personal-data-or-information

The government had also notified the Information Technology (Reasonable Security Practices and Procedures and Sensitive Personal Data or Information) Rules, 2011, which are designed to safeguard the sensitive personal data of an individual which includes financial information, passwords, medical information, sexual orientation, health condition as well as biometric information.

Under the current laws, the government has certain rights when it comes privacy issues in that they could through an order direct any agency to intercept, monitor or decrypt or cause to be intercepted or monitored or decrypted any information generated, transmitted, received or stored in any computer resource even if the information is personal in nature.[23] Further, it can divulge personal information where it has to be done in public interest, which could include matters related to national security and breaches of the law or statutory duty or fraud.

Building digital trust involves organizations providing assurance of protection of a user's privacy as well as their sensitive data. It has become increasingly important for the growth of individual businesses to understand that providing such an assurance should take place not just due to the force of regulations, but to provide a fair, safe, transparent and trusted environment for the conduct of their businesses. By doing so, they can ensure long-term revenue growth and greater customer loyalty.

Organizations have thus far flagrantly used the data of users of their systems in ways that may not be in their best interests. For an extended period in the absence of regulatory requirements or other red lines, these companies have exploited their consumer data to generate massive profits. Now there is pressure both from privacy regulators as well as consumers who have become more aware of privacy violations and exploitation.

To adopt to new privacy regimes like the European Union's General Data Protection Regulation (GDPR) or the California Consumer Privacy Act of 2018 (CCPA), organizations need to give individuals greater control over the personal information that businesses collect about them. Similar regulations have been enacted around the world that clearly define the responsibilities of all parties. Compliance with these standards and regulations can ensure that organizations provide the requisite assurance and develop greater trust among their stakeholders.

The Government of India has released a draft National Data Governance Framework Policy (May 2022) that aims to "transform and modernize Governments data collection and management processes and systems through standardised guidelines, rules and standards for the collection, processing, storage, access and use of Government data – with the objective of improving governance". Among the objectives of this initiative is the need to accelerate the creation of common standards-based public digital platforms while ensuring privacy, safety and trust as well as to promote transparency, accountability and ownership in non-personal data.

Privacy and data protection are multi-sided issues. Privacy regulations and standards around the world are incorporating the following issues, which are designed to provide greater control to individuals over their data:

- Transparency about data usage and protection processes
- Compliance with specific requirements related to privacy and data security. This is based on sectoral regulations such as healthcare data, which demands the implementation of specific security requirements and data protection measures that must be followed not only by primary healthcare entities but also their vendors and service providers.
- Limitations on the purpose of use without consent
- Responsibility to maintain accurate data

---

[23] "Information Technology (Procedure and Safeguards for Interception, Monitoring and Decryption of Information) Rules, 2009," The Centre for Internet & Society, accessed June 26, 2021. https://cis-india.org/internet-governance/resources/it-procedure-and-safeguards-for-interception-monitoring-and-decryption-of-information-rules-2009

- Red lines related to legitimacy, specific purpose of data usage
- Requirement of user consent for using data for any other purposes beyond the original purpose
- Ensuring security and resilience of systems
- Fines and penalties for non-compliance
- Breach reporting and guidelines of notifying victims

It is noteworthy that several large global organizations such as Amazon, WhatsApp, Facebook and Google are among those who have been fined for GDPR violations. In 2019, Google was fined 50 million euros for breaking GDPR rules related to transparency and for not having a valid legal basis when processing people's data for advertising purposes.[24]

9.4.1 OECD Guidelines on the Protection of Privacy and Transborder Flows of Personal Data

The Organisation for Economic Co-operation and Development (OECD) is an intergovernmental economic organization, created with the objective of stimulating economic progress and world trade.

The OECD has issued specific guidelines for the Protection of Privacy and Transborder Flows of Personal Data. These guidelines have been incorporated into the legal systems of member countries and are applicable to personal data, whether in the public or private sectors.[25] The guidelines refer to the manner in which personal data is processed, the context in which the data is used (collected, stored, processed or disseminated) and the threat to privacy and individual liberties. The basic principles covered in the guidelines are shown in Table 9.7.

Table 9.7 Basic principles OECD

Collection Limitation Principle	Suggests that this should be limited to the collection of personal data; such data should be obtained by lawful and fair means and, wherever appropriate, with the knowledge or consent of the data subject (individual).
Data Quality Principle	States that personal data should be collected based on the purposes for which they are to be used; should be accurate, complete and kept up-to-date.
Purpose Specification Principle	States that the purposes for which personal data are collected should be specified not later than at the time of data collection; subsequent use must be limited to the fulfilment of those purposes.
Use Limitation Principle	States that personal data should not be disclosed, made available or used for purposes other than those specified, except with the consent of the individual or by the authority of law.
Security Safeguard Principle	States that personal data must be safeguarded through appropriate security measures against such risks as loss or unauthorized access, destruction, use, modification or disclosure of data.
Openness Principle	Suggests that there must be a general policy of openness about developments, practices and policies with respect to personal data.

(Continued)

---

[24] "What Is GDPR? Everything You Need to Know about the New General Data Protection Regulations," ZDNet, accessed March 10, 2022. https://www.zdnet.com/article/gdpr-an-executive-guide-to-what-you-need-to-know/

[25] "OECD Guidelines on the Protection of Privacy and Transborder Flows of Personal Data," OECD, accessed April 14, 2022. https://www.oecd.org/sti/ieconomy/oecdguidelinesontheprotectionofprivacyandtransborderflowsofpersonaldata.htm

Table 9.7 (*Continued*)

Individual Participation Principle	Deals with individual rights such as obtaining confirmation if data is held by the data controller relating to him/her and related rights.
Accountability Principle	A data controller must be accountable for complying with measures which give effect to the principles stated above.

Other guidelines relate to the free flow of data between countries and the obligation of member countries in relation to the same.

9.5 THE ROLE OF ETHICS IN CYBERSECURITY

It is not possible for laws and regulations only to govern our online conduct. Every individual must own up to the responsibility of not doing anything online which he/she would consider illegal or wrong in everyday life. The four basic rules of ethical conduct for online behaviour are:

- To avoid the use of offensive language.
- Not use someone else's passwords.
- To not cause any type of digital harm or use the digital medium to cause physical harm.
- To respect copyright and use only authorized software, music, games, etc.

When it comes to cybersecurity, ethics plays a critical role in any protection strategy. It is virtually the first line as well as, in some cases, the last line of defence. We all work with a certain degree of trust when it comes to our online behaviour and the use of information systems. The source of this trust is an intrinsic belief that all those who have provided us the information environment to work in such as developers, vendors, system administrators and other IT professionals have played their part honestly, diligently and ethically, keeping our safety and security in mind. Without clear ethical standards and rules, cybersecurity professionals are almost indistinguishable from the black-hat criminals against whom they seek to protect systems and data.[26]

> **Info Box 63: An Ethical Dilemma**
>
> Security research vs endangering people?
> In 2015, Chris Roberts, a security researcher, tweeted that he was considering conducting a live penetration test on a domestic United Airlines flight. While he was commandeering a Boeing aircraft, he was reported to have tinkered with the thrust management computer through its in-flight entertainment system, causing "one of the airplane engines to climb, resulting in a lateral or sideways movement" of the aircraft. While it is highly unlikely that Roberts meant to threaten or cause harm to passengers and staff on board, including himself, the consequences of his decision could have been grave.[27]

---

[26] "Tough Challenges in Cybersecurity Ethics," Security Intelligence, accessed June 25, 2021. https://securityintelligence.com/tough-challenges-cybersecurity-ethics/

[27] "Tough Challenges in Cybersecurity Ethics." Security Intelligence, accessed June 25, 2021. https://securityintelligence.com/tough-challenges-cybersecurity-ethics/

In a cybersecurity landscape which is continuously evolving in the form of new technologies and legal systems, ethics acts as the safety net in terms of security considerations. There is no new technology that does not bring with it new vulnerabilities, and regulation and compliance-based security takes a long time to come into play to be effective. Hence, it is ethical considerations that provide us with the moral compass that is required to ensure security and safety.

Cybersecurity professionals, product developers and other IT professionals face many ethical dilemmas in the course of their work. There is also often a conflict of interest between the demands of the job such as speed of delivery, additional cost of security and expediency which supersede issues of security. Here it becomes imperative that individuals use their own moral compass to determine the right course of action as the wrong approach could cause harm to others, irrespective of all other considerations.

Managements of organizations must take the lead in setting cybersecurity ethical standards and values. This will help them ingrain a cybersecurity culture in their employees and also enhance customer trust. A way to do this is to implement an ethical practice policy, guidelines and/or code of conduct for IT, security staff and users to follow.

Organizations too have social and legal obligations that become more important when they face cyberattacks or data breaches which could potentially affect others. Whether or not the laws of that country or state impose any legal obligation, organizations must from an ethical standpoint notify all those likely to be affected by the security breach as well as all the stakeholders immediately and where necessary.

In various walks of life such as legal, accountancy and medical professions, there are clearly defined and even legally binding codes of conduct. However, IT professionals as a whole are not bound by any ethical code of conduct and must follow the dictates of their own conscience when it comes to the ethical dilemmas they often face.

As a comprehensive code of cybersecurity ethics remains elusive, security professionals must be made aware of the ethical choices that they may face in future in the early stages of their IT education or even induction in a workplace.

QUICK TEST

1. Personal cybersecurity entails the protection of personal information, personal devices and the networks that you use.
   a. True
   b. False
2. Any health information that is individually identifiable and created or received by a provider of healthcare, a health plan operator or health clearing house is known as:
   a. PII
   b. PHI
   c. None of the above
3. Characteristics of weak passwords are:
   a. Passwords having less than eight characters
   b. Passwords which are words found in a dictionary (English or other language)
   c. Using names of family, pets, friends, co-workers, fantasy characters, etc.
   d. Use of computer terms and names, commands, sites, companies, hardware, software
   e. All of the above
   f. a, b, c only
4. When you use the "save" or "remember me" options on a public computer, the next user could easily gain access to your account.
   a. True
   b. False
5. Common forms of identity theft are:
   a. Existing account identity theft and take-over fraud
   b. New account identity theft
   c. Employment identity theft
   d. All of the above
   e. Only b and c
6. In the unfortunate incident of your personal cybersecurity having been violated, there are a few actions that you will need to take:
   a. Change all passwords.
   c. Keep the virus from spreading.
   d. Make the most of your back-ups and buy proper software.
   e. Determine what was lost.
   f. All of the above
   g. a and c only
7. The Universal Declaration of Human Rights (UDHR) is an important milestone and reference point for the creation and evolution of privacy laws, although it is not a legally binding document.
   a. True
   b. False
8. Data protection refers to the set of privacy laws, policies and procedures whose purpose is to protect and individual's data and privacy from intrusion.
   a. True
   b. False
9. The Supreme Court of India recognised privacy as a fundamental right guaranteed by the Constitution (subject to certain restrictions) under which article(s)?
   a. Article 14
   b. Article 17

c. Article 21
   d. All of the above
10. IT professionals as a whole are not bound by any ethical code of conduct and must follow the dictates of their own conscience when it comes to ethical dilemmas they often face.
   a. True
   b. False

QUESTIONS

1. Personal cybersecurity or online safety is a matter of growing concern for all those who are connected to the Internet. Discuss with reasons.
2. What is personal cybersecurity? What is it aimed at protecting?
3. Individuals unlike corporations, who have access to specialist IT skills and resources, have to depend on their own understanding of security issues and the threats that they face. In the light of this statement, discuss the types of threats to personal cybersecurity and the ways in which individuals can safeguard their privacy and data.
4. Discuss with examples the push and pull types of web threats.
5. Best practices in personal cybersecurity revolve around the following three areas: Awareness, Vigilance and Protection. Explain with examples.
6. Threats to our phones and other mobile devices abound in the form of device vulnerabilities and applications. Discuss measures for threat mitigation in mobile devices.
7. Explain with examples the concept of identity theft and the harm that can be caused due to it.
8. What is the difference between privacy and data protection?
9. There exists a strong connection between privacy protection and cybersecurity. Explain this statement.
10. What is an ethical dilemma with respect to cybersecurity? Discuss the importance of ethics in cybersecurity.

ANSWER KEYS

Quick Test

1. (a) 3. (e) 5. (d) 7. (a) 9. (d)
2. (b) 4. (a) 6. (f) 8. (a) 10. (a)

10 Cybersecurity in Evolving Technology and Practice

> **OBJECTIVES**
>
> *At the end of this chapter, you will be able to:*
>
> - ☑ Explain the influence of advances in digital technologies on cybercrime and cybersecurity
> - ☑ Describe the future challenges for cybersecurity and develop an understanding of technologies to address emerging cybersecurity challenges.
> - ☑ List other evolving aspects that are important in boosting cybersecurity

10.0 INTRODUCTION

The surge in cybercrime and data breaches leads us to believe that security systems are still behind the curve when compared to the techniques, tactics and procedures that are being deployed by cybercriminals. The cyber threat landscape represents an active and fertile ground for cybercriminals who have the inherent advantage of finding one vulnerability to cash in on, while the defenders need to protect their systems from thousands of vulnerabilities.

For the defenders to gain the advantage, a revolutionary approach along with associated technologies and procedures are required. Till such time, the scales are tilted in favour of cybercriminals. Thus far, cybersecurity technologies and procedures have been reactionary and evolutionary.

10.1 FUTURE CHALLENGES IN CYBERSECURITY

Cybersecurity challenges are many and varied. The march of digital technology-led transformations is taking place at a frantic pace. More industry sectors, governments and individuals are grabbing opportunities in the digital world to address all kinds of problems such as increasing productivity and operating efficiencies, reducing costs, enhancing speed of transactions and operating non-stop (24x7x365). Table 10.1 shows what we will be up against in terms of cybersecurity challenges in the future.

Table 10.1 Future cybersecurity challenges

Web 3.0	<ul><li>Distributed control</li><li>Immersive technologies</li><li>Metaverse security</li><li>IT+OT integration (Industry 4.0)</li></ul>
Smart everything	<ul><li>Era of smart cars, smart houses, smart cities</li><li>Physical infrastructure hacking</li><li>Use and misuse of AI</li></ul>

(Continued)

Table 10.1 (*Continued*)

The promise of blockchain for cybersecurity	• More use cases • Performance issues • Talent availability
The arrival of quantum computing	• Threat to current encryption schemes • Migration to a quantum-ready architecture
Better equipped cybercriminal gangs	• Threats from APTs • AI and ML usage on both sides of the barricade • Deadlier and more large-scale attacks, even as ransomware attacks continue • New forms of malware • Increased impact of state-sponsored cyberattacks
Crisis of digital trust	• Complex privacy challenges and regulatory compliance • Technology usage increases vulnerabilities • Increased cost of security • Deep fakes • Scams and frauds • The evergreen phishing and social engineering threat • Paradigm shift in identity management approaches
Introduction of 5G technologies	• New set of vulnerabilities • Attacks that exploit device application and endpoint vulnerabilities • 5G will add more devices, which means more vulnerabilities • Reports suggest that by 2030, the Internet will have 91 billion connected devices, which is greater than 10 connected devices per human • Mobile devices, the new target
Adoption of secure-by-design approaches	• More automation and integration • 'Design-in' instead of 'bolt on' security • Minimizing the attack surface
Supply chain, the weak link	• Risk of data leaks, breaches and malware attacks • Enforcement and compliance • SBOM management
A growing cybersecurity skill gap	• The digital divide • Growing shortage of cybersecurity specialists • Skill upgradation • Cybersecurity awareness for everyone

The cyber landscape is an everchanging one in which threats continue to morph and evolve into more potent and dangerous ones. The same technologies that are used for cybersecurity are often used by cybercriminals to launch attacks. Let us examine emerging security concepts and key technologies that will play a crucial role in enhancing cybersecurity in the future and hopefully shift the balance in favour of the defenders.

10.2 WEB 3.0

Web 3.0 is the third generation of the web. To understand what Web 3.0 represents, we need to understand the evolution of the web from Web 1.0 and Web 2.0.

Web 1.0 was characterised by the following:

- Static web pages.
- Content that was served from the server's file system.
- Pages built using server side includes (SSI), a mechanism for employing the web server to perform tasks like displaying files as part of other files or displaying information such as the URL of web pages or dates and times dynamically, or the common gateway interface (CGI), a data-passing specification used when a web server must send or receive data from an application such as a database.
- Tables and frames, which are used to position and align the elements on a page.

Web 2.0 was characterised by the following:

- Dynamic web pages, responsive to user input.
- Ability to sort information for retrieving and classifying it collectively.
- Use of Application Programming Interfaces (APIs).
- Rich web applications, web-oriented architecture and social web.

Web 3.0 is already in use and is characterised by:

- Distributed control.
- Rights over data ownership.
- Decentralised applications.
- Fewer intermediaries through blockchain applications.
- Greater transparency, privacy protection and trust mechanisms.
- Personalised web surfing, searching and information linking.
- Greater use of AI and IoT devices.
- Semantic web, whose goal is to make Internet data machine-readable.
- Read-write-interactive AI-powered web, where users can read, write and interact with content, including 3D. Examples are immersive gaming and metaverse.

Web 3.0 is manifesting itself in many different ways. Concepts like metaverse, a network of 3D virtual worlds focused on social connection and interaction, will bring dramatic changes to the way we live, work and entertain ourselves and, in many respects, will function as a parallel world to the real physical world. Metaverse uses augmented reality (AR), virtual reality (VR), AI and blockchain, along with constructs from social media, to create virtual spaces where rich user interaction imitating the real world can be simulated.

All this calls for revisiting the very architectures that supported Web1.0 and Web 2.0 and the creation of next-generation architecture that can support the needs and requirements of Web 3.0. Security systems too, along with issues related to privacy protection, control over personal data and enhancing digital trust, will need to be designed into the applications rather than 'bolted-on' to old architectures for maximum effectiveness. Since the use of AI is critical in Web 3.0, its responsible and ethical use are an important consideration going forward.

While there is great excitement over the innovations and enhancements to the digital world as the vision of the Web 3.0 is unfolding, there are also several security concerns. A new mix of elements and technologies will have new vulnerabilities that will need to be addressed. Issues like data quality, privacy, data manipulation, device-level vulnerabilities, identity risks and social engineering, which were largely unaddressed in Web 2.0, will continue to haunt us in Web 3.0.

10.3 HARNESSING ARTIFICIAL INTELLIGENCE FOR CYBERSECURITY

Hackers have already begun to use AI in multiple ways to boost their attack capabilities. They have developed the ability to weaponize malware using AI, to control the timing of attacks and trigger the execution of malicious code. AI-powered attacks ensure that even if a particular attack vector or attempt fails, others can be triggered, improving their chances of success in subsequent attempts.

> **Info Box 64: Weaponizing AI**
>
> Hackers are adept at concealing malicious code in benign applications using AI which can be executed at a time of their choosing. By doing so they can weaponize AI models for authenticating a trigger for code execution, enabling them to attack at will as and when they feel that the applications are most vulnerable.[1]

In days to come, hackers will only get better at leveraging AI for creating more intelligent malware with self-propagation capability and in carrying out deeper reconnaissance to gain greater knowledge of IT infrastructure and application vulnerabilities.

To counter this, cybersecurity solutions will also continue to evolve and offer stronger defence capabilities. Cyber defence technologies such as firewalls, IDS, IDPS, endpoint security and antivirus solutions already leverage the use of AI and ML in a big way.

Solutions such as security orchestration automation and response (SOAR) systems enable the integration of orchestration processes, automation, incident management and collaboration, visualization and reporting under a single interface. AI and ML can make SOAR implementations more effective by analyzing large volumes of data in a faster and more accurate way to help detect and remediate impending or ongoing attacks.

The time has come not only for greater security automation, but also developing predictive and adaptive cybersecurity capabilities using three core capabilities: AI, ML and analytics. While these are three distinct fields of expertise, they also have a lot in common; they are all data driven and can generate insights and predictions. The combined power of these three capabilities can take cybersecurity solutions to another level to meet future challenges.

Being forewarned of a cyber threat or even early detection can enable faster and better response. In future, automated detection and response will constitute the bulk of threat management capabilities, and a vital component for cybersecurity will be threat intelligence.

Threat intelligence and response will become more effective by unleashing the full power of AI and ML to detect anomalies in the network, identify threats and leverage the power of analytics to predict imminent adversary actions by correlating data and drawing statistical inferences to understand the nature of attacks and assess network vulnerabilities and risks.

AI and, in some cases, ML is being used by many cybersecurity developers to bolster the capabilities of their systems such as modelling user behaviour, scanning emails, blocking phishing attempts,

---

[1] Julien Legrand, "Artificial Intelligence as Security Solution and Weaponization by Hackers," CISOMAG, accessed August 31, 2021. https://cisomag.com/hackers-using-ai/

enhancing antivirus systems, network defences and endpoint security. For organizations with a large digital footprint, manual analysis is impossible considering the volume of data gathered about security intrusions and other user activity. AI-based systems are the only answer.

We must be careful to understand that AI, ML and analytics are not the answer to all cybersecurity problems and issues. While they can handle routine tasks on a 24x7 basis, and predict imminent threats, they need to be supplemented with other cybersecurity mechanisms and measures as well as human intelligence and interventions to strengthen the security posture.

More cybersecurity applications will continue to use AI in some form or the other, but organizations that use AI for specific purposes, which are a source of concern and risk, can also gain some advantage over adversaries. For example, the use of AI and ML for analyzing disinformation campaigns or fake news against an organization and/or for identifying deep fakes to prevent any malicious activity that can cause harm.

Cybersecurity experts recognize that the use of defensive AI and ML enables organizations to match the speed and innovativeness of attackers and will play a significant role in securing systems from automotive to healthcare. While AI-based cybersecurity solutions have their limitations, the advantages offered by them far offset their drawbacks.

10.4 BLOCKCHAIN FOR CYBERSECURITY

There are many who believe that blockchain technology could be the ultimate solution for cybersecurity. Blockchains are also set to become the cornerstone of Web 3.0. The role of blockchain technology in maintaining distributed ledgers and creating trust in an ecosystem that it is lacking in or needs high levels of trust is crucial. The relative success of blockchain technology in the context of building a secure ecosystem for cryptocurrencies is often cited to illustrate how the technology ensures data integrity, auditability and availability.

The financial services industry was among the early adopters of blockchain technology, but adoption by other industries has been slower than expected. The primary reasons for this are related to the technology's inherent features such as low scalability, complexities in technology design, interoperability, the lack of standardization and talent availability. Nevertheless, other features like immutability, transparency and distributed ledgers all lend themselves to help solve cybersecurity issues. Security experts are optimistic that blockchain technology will redefine the way many business processes, workflows and organizational supply chains function along with addressing regulatory and compliance requirements.

> ### Info Box 65: Leveraging Blockchain for Cybersecurity
> **Blockchain Represents a More Secure Approach**
>
> At the heart of blockchain technology is the guarantee of secure contracts, transactions and business records. These form the foundation of secure economic, legal and political systems. Companies across sectors such as real estate, construction firms, law firms, healthcare providers and entertainment are already leveraging blockchain technology to enable tasks like auditing and verifying the integrity of data.
>
> Walmart, the retail giant, has set up a consortium to trace raw foods and other items through the supply chain using blockchain. The project can track food-borne illnesses and recalls across farmers, brokers, distributors, processors, regulators, retailers and consumers. Also partnering them in this initiative are prominent food companies such as Dole, Nestlé, Unilever and McCormick and Company.[2]

---

[2] Asha Barbaschow, "IBM Blockchain to Help Prevent Contamination in Global Food Supply Chain," ZDNET, accessed October 2, 2022. https://www.zdnet.com/article/ibm-blockchain-to-help-prevent-contamination-in-global-food-supply-chain/

Beyond the hype, it is reasonable to expect that blockchain technology can go mainstream across industries given the overwhelming operating advantages like business continuity, strong cybersecurity and resilience.

10.5 QUANTUM COMPUTING AND CYBERSECURITY

Quantum computing represents a revolutionary change by unleashing computing power of a magnitude that will radically alter the dynamics of information technology as it exists today. The basic unit of quantum computing is the qubit, which can be considered similar to a bit that processes information in traditional computing. A bit can exist in only one (binary) state at a time, either zero or one, a qubit can be in both zero and one at the same time.

> **Info Box 66: Quantum Computing**
>
> A quantum computer with just 30 qubits can perform 10 billion floating-point operations per second, which is about 5.8 billion times more than the most powerful PlayStation video game console.[3]

The characteristic property of a qubit to be in a superposition (the principle which states that a quantum particle can exist in two distinct locations at the same time) gives it the ability to exponentially speed up computing operations, as well as to hold and process enormous amounts of information. It is expected that quantum computing will help solve large and complex problems through a combination of mathematical modelling and phenomenal computing power such as weather forecasting, drug discovery and traffic management and optimization across several fields. The concept of quantum entanglement, which refers to the ability of quantum particles to correlate their measurement results with each other, enhances the time to process between qubits, enabling tasks such as quantum cryptography, superdense coding (a form of secure quantum communication) and teleportation (the transfer of quantum information from a sender at one location to a receiver some distance away).

The battle for achieving quantum supremacy is underway between the world's leading companies such as IBM, Google, Honeywell and Amazon and even some countries which are making their own efforts in this space. Quantum supremacy is said to be the threshold or point where a quantum computer can solve a computational task which a traditional computer cannot complete within a reasonable time. Google's Sycamore, a 54-qubit superconducting processor, achieved this in 2019, by calculating in 200 seconds what could take present-day supercomputers over 10,000 years to complete. The University of Science and Technology of China has also claimed that their quantum processor could complete in 200 seconds a task that would have taken as many as 600 million years to complete with traditional computers.

While these breakthroughs represent an exponential leap in processing power, capabilities to handle and much larger data sets and execute machine AI and ML algorithms at much faster speeds, we are not likely to see quantum computing make a significant impact before the year 2030.

How does all this add up in the context of cybersecurity? Does the entry of quantum computing have an impact on how cybersecurity is implemented today? Cybersecurity experts are concerned that one of the key areas where cybersecurity will be affected by quantum computing is that it could render currently used cryptographic techniques obsolete. This poses a significant threat to cybersecurity, requiring us to effect changes in the way we encrypt data. We may find ourselves in a position where we cannot wait for quantum computers to start breaking our encryption but must move quickly to explore new ways of encrypting data that could withstand the impact of quantum computing. Experts are of the opinion that encryption algorithms such as the Diffie–Hellman key exchange, RSA encryption and elliptic curve

---

[3] "Quantum Computing and Supercomputers will Revolutionize Technology," Iberdrola, accessed September 2, 2021. https://www.iberdrola.com/innovation/what-is-quantum-computing

cryptography are quantum-breakable and other encryption techniques such as lattice-based cryptography, code-based cryptography and multivariate cryptography can be considered quantum-secure.

There is a high degree of excitement and anticipation about the introduction of quantum computing and the benefits it can provide, and companies around the world are building different cybersecurity solutions that leverage quantum technologies for key distribution, quantum random number generation, quantum-resistant cryptography, and more. It is important for organizations to evaluate the potential impact of quantum computing with regard to cybersecurity and incorporate the use of technologies that can boost their cybersecurity in the near term and make them resistant to quantum-technology–leveraged cyberattacks in future.

10.6 COMBATING ADVANCED PERSISTENT THREATS

Advanced persistent threats (APTs) are clandestine attacks against specific targets that are carefully planned and orchestrated by established threat actors to meet different objectives.

These attacks are called 'advanced' as the combination of techniques that the attackers use is not only sophisticated in their construct, but also because of the nature of potential harm that they can cause. Hackers deploy an assortment of intelligence-gathering methods and selected network intrusion techniques combined with multiple types of malware components (both basic and advanced) as required to establish their long-term presence in target networks. In essence, based on their attack objectives, they put together multiple targeting methods, tools and techniques in order to reach and compromise their target and maintain access to it.

The use of the word 'persistent' indicates that once the attacker gains access to a system or network, he is likely to remain there for an extended period of time without arousing suspicion of his presence. Attackers perpetrating APTs are often driven by their strategic target objectives and are not looking at opportunistically cracking into accounts for financial gain or other motives. They are so focused that even if they lose access to a target account after gaining entry, they will reattempt access till they succeed.

The threat factor in APTs represents a high level of danger to target accounts as the attackers have both capability and intent. The attackers not only are committed to specific objectives but are skilled, motivated organized and well-funded. Trained hacker groups have the ability to adapt their tools, techniques and procedures (TTPs) to changing situations in the target environment as the attack progresses.

APTs are generally the handiwork of organized cybercrime groups who use them to steal intellectual property, computer source code, defence secrets, sensitive data as well as for financial gain. Nation states also use these groups as proxies to carry out APTs on their behalf in furtherance of their political and economic agendas. Traditionally, the targets of APTs have been government organizations and agencies and large public and private organizations who hold large amounts of sensitive data or data of strategic value to the attackers.

The anatomy or construct of a typical APT can be broadly divided into the following phases:

Info Box 67: APT Phases

APT phase	Typical activities
Define target	Select target, set attack objectives.
Find and organize accomplices	Identify those who will participate in or carry out the attack.
Build or acquire tools	Identify/Source the methods, tools and techniques to carry out APTs.

APT phase	Typical activities
Research target infrastructure/ employees	Conduct reconnaissance to discover the effective points of attack, assess target vulnerabilities and identify the people within the organization who can expedite security breaches.
Test for detection	APTs can be detected by UEBA, deception technology and network monitoring systems. Check for the presence of these systems.
Deployment	Deploy tools for gaining initial access, penetration and malware deployment.
Initial intrusion	Commonly use techniques for intrusion are spear phishing and various forms of social engineering or exploitation of other vulnerabilities that are discovered when the reconnaissance activity is carried out.
Outbound connection initiation	Often the goal of an APT is to steal data rather than cause damage to the target organization's network. Hence, the APT, after having successfully carried out the intrusion activity, sets up a tunnel through which data exfiltration will take place. Techniques used by hackers exfiltrate data from organizations' networks and systems include anonymizing connections to servers, DNS, HTTP, HTTPS tunnelling and emails.
Expand access and obtain credentials	Hackers set up a 'ghost network' under their control inside the target network, and then move laterally within the network by stealing other credentials.
Strengthen foothold	Staying undetected is important in an APT. In this phase, hackers look to exploit other vulnerabilities to strengthen their presence within the network and extend their access to other valuable locations.
Exfiltrate data	The attacker has found what he is looking for and initiates moving the data to base.
Cover tracks and remain undetected	This is an important phase in the attack as the attacker cleans up his tracks and wants to stay undetected so that he can continue to perform covert attacks.

Info Box 68: The GhostNet APT Attack

GhostNet is the name given by researchers to a large-scale cyber espionage operation which was discovered in March 2009. GhostNet was spread over 103 countries and compromised about 1300 computers belonging mainly to foreign ministries, embassies and the offices of the Dalai Lama and the Tibetan government-in-exile. It was alleged that the control infrastructure of the attackers was located in China; however, the Chinese government denied this.

The initial intrusion was executed through spear phishing emails which carried a downloadable malicious payload that installed a trojan on the user's system, enabling execution from a remote command and control server, which then downloaded more software to take control of the system. The malware could use audio as well as video recording devices to monitor the locations housing the compromised computers.

The impact of this APT was widespread and had among its victims the embassies of India, South Korea, Romania, Indonesia and the Asian Development Bank, and the ministries of foreign affairs of Bangladesh, Brunei, Indonesia, Iran, Latvia and the Philippines.

Also see Chapter 2, for details of the Sony APT attack.

APTs are a matter of growing security concern for organizations, especially those that have not progressed significantly along the cybersecurity maturity curve. When hackers begin to think of long-term strategies to mount attacks, they carry out significant amounts of intelligence gathering combined with a deep assessment of vulnerabilities, and hence, can pose formidable security challenges for organizations to deal with. Fortunately, there are strategies that organizations can adopt apart from regular security measures, which can help in mitigating the impact of APTs, such as:

- Deploying endpoint detection and response tools
- Employing zero trust strategies
- Improving device visibility and network monitoring
- Deploying user behaviour analytical tools
- Improving asset visibility and deploying data loss prevention tools
- Employee training for identifying suspicious files and behaviour
- Timely patching of tools and software
- Using the cyber kill chain

Advanced persistent threats of the future are likely to be more complex and involve the use of more sophisticated technologies and tactics that enable greater deception as well as invisibility and new methods to defeat most contemporary defence mechanisms. Therefore, organizations must not be content with dealing with situational threats and instead use stronger security measures deeply embedded in their systems and infrastructure with defence-in-depth approaches (see Section 10.10.7).

10.7 DIGITAL TRUST AND IDENTITY MANAGEMENT

In the digital world, digital identities are the credentials or set of attributes of an entity such as an individual, organization, application or device that are used to recognize, authenticate and authorize access to a computer network or other IT resource.

Digital identities are used by organizations, governments and individuals to access information, services and other online activities. The crux of the matter from a cybersecurity point of view is that a strong digital identity is effective protection against various kinds of cyberthreats.

The characteristics of a strong digital identity are that it is unique, verifiable with a high degree of assurance, ensures privacy protection and provides user control. Aadhaar, the unique 12-digit identity number that is given to Indian residents, has become the backbone of multiple systems across banking, telecom, government and several other services. It functions as a single, universal digital identity number that any registered entity can use to authenticate an Indian resident. Popular identity management and authentication tools and technologies currently in use are listed in Table 10.2.

We have outgrown the era of simple username and password regimes and are moving towards the adoption of multi-factor authentication schemes to enhance security. The increasing use of biometrics and alternative authentication mechanisms such as certificate or token-based schemes are also gaining ground. The field of biometrics provides multiple means and mechanisms such as fingerprints, retina scans, facial recognition and speech recognition used by personal systems, home security systems, government systems, public utilities and private corporations including airports, educational institutions, military bases and national borders.

Table 10.2 Popular identity management and authentication tools and technologies

Biometrics	Active directory	Digital certificates	Password management
Database authentication methods	Wireless authentication methods	SSO and centralised identity management	Multi-factor authentication
Phone, Captcha codes, OTP and SMS authentication	Web access control: cookie-based, token-based, third-party access, OpenID and SAML	Remote authentication methods such as Challenge Handshake Authentication Protocol (CHAP) and Password Authentication Protocol (PAP)	Payment authentication: 3D secure, card verification value, and address verification
Email authentication	API authentication	Server and network authentication	Password-less authentication

> **Info Box 69: The Aadhaar Platform**
>
> The Aadhaar platform is the world largest online digital identity platform that uses biometric digital ID for the delivery of government schemes, services and programs. Countries all over the world are setting up national digital ID platforms to enable services such as voting, filing tax returns, banking, passports, public transportation and access to health services.

Over time, biometric authentication solutions can form an important part of multi-factor authentication schemes and will gain more widespread adoption and integration into organizational systems. The key driver for the adoption of biometric technologies stems from the high degree of uniqueness they provide, eliminating counterfeiting risks and other weaknesses associated with other forms of identity management, thus making systems more secure.

The critical nature of identity management and authentication with regard to overall cybersecurity cannot be understated. Many other forms of authentication approaches are also emerging which work with other technologies with the basic objective of enhancing cybersecurity, such as:

- Use of embedded/card/cloud-based digital identity technologies in IoT for automotive, home automation, etc.
- Risk-based authentication that use calculations based on factors like geo-location, level of privileges and other compliance requirements to allow access and authentication using multiple identifying factors.
- Use of zero trust models along with micro-segmentation (creating virtual groups based on usage requirements and specific permissions).
- Use of blockchain for identity management to deliver continuous non-repudiation of digital identities and a chain of trust. Traditional approaches of maintaining a central repository of user identities can be a very big security risk if compromised. Blockchain technology, through its decentralized structure, enhances security by enabling users to create their own identities, register authenticating factors and have the information verified by a trusted third party before being stored in the blockchain.

Management of digital identities and their protection from being compromised is one of the biggest challenges we face in the digital world. Several methods and schemes have evolved over the years, but the quest for a perfect and secure solution that balances the two important measures of effectiveness – security and usability – still continues. Digital identity management solutions are evolving in a variety of ways and are combining with other technologies and approaches to ensure greater security and establish trust in digital systems.

10.7.1 Self-Sovereign Identity (SSI)

The concept of self-sovereign identity represents a paradigm shift in the way digital identities are controlled and used. Traditionally, digital identities were issued as a credential by an organization that would allow users to gain access to their services. We were required to enter our credentials each time for every website or online service that we wanted to register in or access. While this generally involved username and password creation for logging in, some sites required more personal information to be entered. Over time, with the proliferation of websites and services, this became cumbersome, and individuals often struggled to remember the information that they had entered, leave alone have any kind of control over the way the information was used.

To make things easier for users, a new 'federated' model came into existence. Here, third parties began issuing credentials and websites and service providers allowed users to "Login with Facebook" or "Login with Google", thereby enabling them to use one ID to access multiple services. While this addressed the problem of maintaining multiple credentials to some extent, it soon began to raise privacy concerns. The companies that were entrusted with your personal data which could be used to access different services such as Facebook, Google and others became repositories of massive amounts of personal information of individuals around the world. While they provided convenience to users, the companies also used the available data for their own profitable purposes and almost enjoyed full control over the data.

The emergence of technologies like blockchain, decentralised identifiers and secure wallets combined with innovative ways to verify credentials has paved the way for a major shift in the way personal information is controlled. Along with these technologies, regulatory bodies are also pushing for the use of SSI so that the rightful owners of the data, that is, the individuals, have control of their digital identities.

The ability to verify credentials in the SSI scheme is an added bonus as it becomes the foundation for establishing digital trust. SSIs can be stored in personal secure wallets and be used for a variety of purposes with complete safety and control by the individual concerned.

Examples of digital verifiable credentials in our daily lives could be driving licences, national IDs, e-passports, educational qualifications, etc. Credential holders can not only share existing selected credentials from their wallets to third parties, but also have them verified by them.

10.8 5G NETWORKS AND CYBERSECURITY

The advent of fifth generation (5G) broadband cellular network telecommunication and its roll out across continents has sparked a debate on the impact it may have on traditional approaches and existing cybersecurity arrangements. The digital world is fascinated by the following advantages that 5G networks offer them when compared to the 4G networks:

- 5G is estimated to deliver peak speeds that are 20 times faster than 4G. This radically alters the dynamics of network data transmission from 10 Mb per second in 4G to up to a theoretical speed of 20 GB per second in 5G networks.
- 5G networks are designed for low latency and improved reliability.
- 4G networks have limitations when it comes to handling a number of devices in an individual location; 5G is designed to handle as many as a million devices per square kilometre.

- 5G is also capable of connecting to many more types of devices and providing differential performance levels depending upon the requirement of each device.
- 4G enabled the use of cloud services on mobile phones, but 5G takes this to another level through its ability to function as a distributed data centre for performing processing tasks, by leveraging the power of centralized computing resources and taking edge computing close to the user.

All these features and more make 5G an attractive proposition for bandwidth-hungry applications and the extensive use of IoT devices. Its flexible design enables it to function as multiple separate networks at the same time. This feature, also known as network slicing, enables optimum use of resources while guaranteeing the performance levels required by each slice.

The influence and impact of 5G on cybersecurity is likely to be significant. On the positive side, 5G offers capabilities such as encrypting identifiers, enhanced privacy through spoofing and anti-tracking features, boosting the use of artificial intelligence (AI), cloud computing and the deployment of IoT to prevent new cybersecurity threats. 5G will also enhance network virtualization capabilities by consolidating hardware and software resources into a single virtual network, enabling better security management and aid in the use of deep packet inspection (DPI) for detection of malicious traffic.

Unfortunately, 5G will also bring in a host of vulnerabilities that hackers can exploit to launch cyberattacks. A major change is that 5G represents a transition to a largely software-based network, making it potentially more susceptible to cyberattacks due to its possibilities and flexibility. As even core networks are virtualized by software, it lends itself to greater security risk. Other ways in which 5G could create greater cyber vulnerabilities is in the form of rapid expansion in attack surface through connectivity of a large number of IoT devices (more devices means more opportunities for hackers). This could lead to breaches that can have an impact on human safety and well-being; for example, attacks involving connected medical devices, smart automobiles, etc. There have also been allegations that companies developing 5G code could insert strategic backdoors that could compromise cybersecurity.

The National Security Agency (NSA), USA, has identified three vectors (along with sub-vectors) in the areas of Policy and Standards, Supply Chain and 5G Systems Architecture that could have an adverse impact on cybersecurity (Table 10.3).[4]

Table 10.3 Important threat vectors – 5G infrastructure

Primary attack vector	Sub-threat vector
Policy and Standards	**Open standards:** Lack of interoperability, untrusted proprietary technologies **Optional controls:** Standards bodies specify protocols and controls that could be mandatory or optional. Where network operators do not implement optional controls, such networks become vulnerable to cyberattacks.
Supply Chain	**Counterfeit components:** These increase the chances of a cyberattack as they are more likely to break because of their poor quality. **Inherited components:** These refer to component vulnerabilities that may come from extended supply chains including third-party suppliers, vendors and service providers. These components could be compromised thorough attacks via their suppliers.

(*Continued*)

---

[4] "Potential Threat Vectors to 5G Infrastructure," National Security Agency, 2021: 1–16. https://www.cisa.gov/sites/default/files/publications/potential-threat-vectors-5G-infrastructure_508_v2_0 %281%29.pdf

Table 10.3 (*Continued*)

Primary attack vector	Sub-threat vector
5G Systems Architecture	**Software/Configuration:** Unauthorized access to software or network components enables a threat actor to alter the configuration and security controls that could allow installation of malware and exploitation of privileged access within a system or network. **Network security:** The large number of connected devices, each with their own capabilities and vulnerabilities along with the 5G infrastructure components such as cellular towers, beamforming transmission, small cells and mobile devices, provide opportunities for threat actors to launch cyberattacks. **Network slicing:** Permits users to get authenticated for only one network area, enabling data and security isolation. Currently, there are no standards defining specifications implementing network slicing. Inappropriate network slice management may enable threat actors to access data from different slices or deny access to prioritized users. **Legacy communications infrastructure:** 4G legacy infrastructure can be supported by 5G networks. This enables threat actors to exploit vulnerabilities inherent in legacy infrastructure. **Multi-access edge computing (MEC):** Takes processing of data closer to the end user at the network edge. The introduction of untrusted 5G components which may have flaws could expose the network elements to cyber threats. **Spectrum sharing:** These could be exploited by threat actors to jam or disturb non-critical communication paths, thereby adversely affecting more critical communications networks. **Software defined networking (SDN):** This enables automatic configuring of routes across a network, mainly using an SDN controller. Threat actors could embed code in SDN controller applications to restrict bandwidth and negatively affect operations.

Fifth-generation networks, while offering several advantages based on inherent capabilities of speed and flexibility, will also be a source of new cyber vulnerabilities. The crucial point here is that network-related cybersecurity measures and controls that have worked well in the past may not be good enough in the 5G era.

5G has challenged our fundamental approaches to network security and the security of its connected devices and applications. Overcoming these challenges will require the following:

- Coordinated efforts among governments, standards bodies, corporates and other stakeholders.
- Implementation of AI- and ML-based protection.
- Monitoring of lead indicators of cyber threats, rather than lag indicators.
- Exercising due care and diligence in the choice of devices that are connected to the network in terms of security capabilities.
- Making security a part of the development and operations cycle.

Cyberattacks in the pre-5G era were focused on hacking databases, stealing intellectual property and extortion, among other forms of threats. The introduction of 5G brings us one level closer to dealing with attacks that can cause physical harm and affect the safety of individuals and communities. The biggest cyber threat to the nation comes through attacks on economic networks, but even more dangerous are those that can cause harm to citizens and other critical systems. Proactively addressing the cybersecurity challenges posed by the introduction of 5G networks is therefore a critical necessity.

10.9 ADOPTING A 'SECURE-BY-DESIGN' APPROACH

Adopting a proactive stance to cybersecurity begins with laying strong emphasis on implementing a 'secure-by-design' approach. This enables the identification and prevention of errors from an early stage and becomes embedded into every subsequent stage and iteration. As IT environments become more complex, with cloud applications and IoT devices increasingly becoming all pervasive, a security by design approach to software and hardware can help in making systems reduce vulnerabilities and put in place safeguards through measures such as continuous testing, authentication safeguards and adherence to best programming practices.

The best practices which help in implementing a secure-by-design approach are as follows (Table 10.4):

Table 10.4 Key actions for implementing a 'secure-by-design' approach

Minimize	The attack surface by deactivating redundant, deactivated, unneeded software programs and system components
Authenticate	As required
Check	Every input for permissible characters
Segment and Segregate	Systems so that even if one is compromised, lateral entry is denied
Encrypt	All confidential and sensitive data
Update	All system components regularly
Test	Security on a continuous basis

A security by design approach provides several benefits, whether you are a product developer or a user organization, including reduction in potential liabilities that could arise in future due to flaws and security weaknesses in a given system. It enables an organization to adopt a confident security posture that reinforces trust while reducing risks. Implementing this approach involves teams working closely and collaboratively on issues such as cyber threats, breach scenarios, business continuity and cyber resilience. To achieve this, the use of a DevSecOps team that ensures the integration of security at every phase of the software development life cycle, from initial design through integration, testing, deployment and software delivery, is an ideal methodology.

10.9.1 Kubernetes Container Security

An increasingly popular approach which supports the key principles of DevSecOps is the use of Kubernetes.

Kubernetes security is an open-source container management system that helps automate the deployment, scaling and management of containerized applications. Containerization is a method of virtualization where applications run in separated user spaces, called containers, while using the same shared operating system (OS). In essence, a container is a wholly packaged and portable computing environment and includes the binaries, libraries, configuration files and dependencies that an application needs to run. Hence, container images are executable software bundles that can run standalone.

Kubernetes API communication is encrypted with Transport Layer Security (TLS) for all API traffic and is considered to be secure by default. It ensures response only to requests that it can properly authenticate and authorize. The use of Kubernetes can speed up application deployment and simplify management and operations. Kubernetes also enables implementation of a comprehensive set of controls that can be used to effectively secure clusters and their applications.

The basic concept of immutable infrastructure, which is enabled by Kubernetes in the form of replacing deployed components entirely rather than updating them, requires standardization and emulation of common infrastructure components to provide consistent and predictable results.

10.10 SUPPLY CHAIN CYBERSECURITY

Organizations are increasingly relying on suppliers and third parties to provide them with cost-effective products and services. While this reliance has brought with it capabilities, efficiencies, innovation and cost effectiveness, it has also become a source of enterprise cyber risk. Cyberattacks through supply chain partners have become commonplace in recent times.

Hackers recognize that supply chains have several vulnerabilities and represent easier targets than their client organizations, who may have better cybersecurity arrangements. Organizations too have begun to recognize that securing their own information systems is not sufficient and that they need to develop an understanding of cyber threats emanating from their supply chain and implement strategies and systems to protect their information. The most common cyber threats through the supply chain are data leaks, supply chain breaches and introduction of malware.

To deal with supply chain cyber threats requires an understanding of the possible threats, assessment of existing controls and implementing controls as required in an evolving threat scenario. Fortunately, technologies and approaches have evolved to help mitigate supply chain threats.

> **Info Box 70: The SolarWinds Supply Chain Attack**
>
> The SolarWinds Orion data breach underlined the devastating potential of supply chain attacks. It also exposed vulnerabilities in current practices related to managing vendor cyber risks.
>
> Hackers introduced malicious code into an update of the SolarWinds Orion IT performance monitoring and management tool used by thousands of enterprises, government agencies and managed services providers worldwide to cause widespread harm.
>
> While some may say that the sophistication of the SolarWinds breach was exceptional, it still demonstrated that greater attention and efforts are required to mitigate the risks associated with an organization's digital supply chain.

There is no single technology that can be used to effectively deal with supply chain cyberattacks. What is required is strong vendor cyber risk policies and procedures that support the implementation and enforcement of policies and security controls. Some of the strategies that organizations have successfully deployed to fend off supply chain risks and make things difficult for hackers are:

- Implementation of zero trust models
- Using honeytokens that keep hackers busy chasing fake resources
- Segmentation and micro-segmentation of networks
- Secure privileged access management

- Data encryption
- Detection of vendor data leaks with the use of AI and ML
- Multi-factor authentication
- Minimizing access to sensitive data
- Sensitizing employees regarding sharing of sensitive and confidential information

While the above strategies can strengthen the supply chain related cyber risks, there is no substitute for ensuring that regular third-party risk assessments are carried out and monitoring of vendor networks for vulnerabilities. The added pressure from regulators for compliance across an organization's supply chain will ensure that technologies and processes related to the management of supply chain cyber risks continue to evolve.

10.10.1 The Importance of SBOMs

Modern software development processes allow for the use of third-party code/open-source components to meet the functionality requirements. This cuts down the overall development time, reduces cost and enables faster implementation cycles, but brings in vulnerabilities inherent in these components.

While the risks associated with using third-party components has been well understood for some time now, it is only the high-profile cyberattacks that exploited the Orion Performance Monitoring Platform from SolarWinds and Log4J, a widely used Java logging framework, that brought to the forefront the risks posed through the software supply chain. In these attacks, hackers exploited vulnerabilities to affect thousands of downstream customers who were using products and services that depended on these software components.

> **Info Box 71: Log4J Software Supply Chain Attack**
>
> Log4J is a widely used piece of open-source software provided by the Apache Software Foundation that is used for logging activities such as errors and routine system operations and also for communicating diagnostic messages to users and system administrators.
>
> Hackers discovered and exploited a vulnerability called Log4J Shell, which is a part of the Log4J framework, to infiltrate thousands of computers around the world and cause panic among its user organizations and service providers. Its widespread impact has earned it the infamy of being one of the biggest software supply chain blunders.

The imperative today from a cybersecurity point of view is to maintain an inventory of third-party software components, also called software bill of materials (SBOM), used across applications and IT infrastructure. The next step is to list the product versions in use, the latest updates available from suppliers, whether it is supported by the vendor, licence information or not and a list of known vulnerabilities in these components.

Without SBOMs, organizations can never fully know how secure and safe their applications are from cyber threats and attacks. Managing SBOMS proactively can help organizations in several ways to enhance cybersecurity, such as:

- Enhance visibility into operational software, components and system relationships
- Help in better vulnerability management
- Ensure timely rollouts and rollback of critical patches and remediation steps

- Support compliance and supply chain integrity through close coordination between vendors and customers
- Provide support to developers, security, risk assessment teams as well as compliance and audit personnel

10.11 OTHER EVOLVING ASPECTS OF CYBERSECURITY

The most serious impediment to the growth of the digital world is 'trust'. The rapidly increasing cybercriminal activity is disturbing the very foundations of digital trust and the scale and sophistication of cyberattacks in recent times has led us to believe that several aspects of cybersecurity such as technologies, practices, standards and legal systems need to evolve at a faster rate than before. Apart from technology, some other aspects of cybersecurity which stakeholders need to focus upon to prevent the continuing erosion of digital trust are discussed in this section.

10.11.1 Combating Disinformation

Digital technologies, electronic media and social media are all being aggressively used to publish and disseminate false information or fake news. Digital technologies can make fake news look more authentic through digital editing and the use of deep fake technology.

False information can be extremely harmful for governments, organizations and individuals, leading to reputational damage, loss of public trust, financial losses, and more. Strategies to combat fake news require the use of AI bots or other risk sensing tools that can monitor digital media platforms and data sources in real time to predict and detect issues before they get out of control. Other response processes and guidelines need to be put in place to ensure that any form of damage is mitigated. Technologies such as natural language processing (NLP) are also being used to identify fake news by examining the nature and tone of the content. Technology alone is not enough to fight the battle against fake news.

Legal systems and regulation of news networks and social media is high on the agenda of governments around the world and needs to evolve quickly to minimize damage from 'information warfare'. Brian Nichiporuk, Senior Political Scientist at RAND Corporation, suggests that there are six components of information warfare: electronic, operations security, deception, physical attack, information attack and psychological.[5]

Does combating disinformation and fake news fall under the realm of cybersecurity? Strictly speaking from an IT point of view, it may not, but if we consider the fact that digital technologies and means are put to use to generate and spread disinformation, then they become an extension of security and protection mechanisms.

A full-fledged disinformation campaign can cause as much or more damage than other forms of cyberattacks. Cybersecurity technologies and processes can not only be effective in identifying disinformation campaigns at an early date, but also in developing responses such as identifying and bringing down false stories and websites, thus preventing their further spread. There are also several technologies that are available and being developed to help in attribution, which could lead to legal recourse and even compensation.

---

[5] Jessica Mason, "What Is Information Warfare and How Is It Different from Traditional Warfare?," Social Media Writings, accessed September 12, 2021. https://medium.com/social-media-writings/what-is-information-warfare-and-how-is-it-different-from-traditional-warfare-a42294ae8c8d

10.11.2 Convergence

The concept of convergence or the integration of various aspects of security such as IT infrastructure, information security, physical and people security, operational technology (OT) systems, business continuity, disaster recovery and other aspects of safety and security management has been debated for some time. Yet many organizations view these activities and manage them in organization silos. This leads to security gaps and vulnerabilities, which offer a window of opportunity for hackers to exploit, leading to increased cost of security and duplication of efforts.

Organizations would do well to leverage different technologies such as identity management and authentication, threat intelligence and other cybersecurity and physical security functions to enhance their security posture and become more resilient and better prepared to identify, prevent, mitigate and respond to threats. The introduction of IoT devices and the integration of IT infrastructure with OT systems that monitor and adjust industrial and other automated systems makes it necessary for organizations to take a holistic view of cybersecurity, safety and resilience.

Organizations must develop unified security policies across all security divisions and with the help of a well-integrated Security Operations Centre (SOC), they can enhance their capabilities to address multiple cybersecurity challenges and move from siloed security to a more holistic security posture.

10.11.3 Confidential Computing

Confidential computing is an emerging technology that is designed to protect data during processing. The technology is being promoted by several industry leaders including Google, IBM/Red Hat, Intel, AMD, Microsoft, Oracle, Swisscom, Tencent and VMware, among others, who have formed the Confidential Computing Consortium.[6]

For some time now, cloud service providers have offered encryption services to enable protection of data at rest and in transit. Confidential computing addresses the other residual data security vulnerability by protecting data in use – that is, during processing or runtime.[7]

For data to be processed by an application, it needs to be unencrypted in memory. This leaves it exposed to threats such as allowing access to memory dumps, root user compromises and other such exploits. Through the use of hardware-based trust execution environment, confidential computing sets up a secure enclave within a central processing unit (CPU) by employing embedded encryption keys which are available to authorised application code only. In simple terms, it is the equivalent of setting up a secure locker within the CPU, where sensitive data is decrypted and processed while remaining invisible to even the OS.

Confidential computing can be used in many areas such as for the protection of intellectual property, ML algorithms, analytic functions and even complete applications which require high security.

10.11.4 Malware Detection through Deep Learning and Binary Visualization

Malware detection methods have for a long time used signatures. Hackers and malware developers have been able to evade such detection mechanisms by obfuscating their code or using techniques like polymorphism which can mutate malicious code at runtime.[8]

---

[6] "Confidential Computing?," IBM, accessed September 22, 2021. https://www.ibm.com/cloud/learn/confidential-computing
[7] "Confidential Computing?," IBM, accessed September 22, 2021. https://www.ibm.com/cloud/learn/confidential-computing
[8] "Computer Vision and Deep Learning Provide New Ways to Detect Cyber Threats," VentureBeat, accessed September 25, 2021. https://venturebeat.com/2021/09/11/computer-vision-and-deep-learning-provide-new-ways-to-detect-cyber-threats/

In recent years, the use of ML has enhanced the effectiveness of antivirus solutions and now researchers have made further advances by combining the use of deep learning with binary visualization to boost malware detection.

Binary visualization used along with deep learning offers a powerful combination as files are run through algorithms that transform binary and ASCII values to colour codes. Using this methodology, malicious files show different patterns that can be examined visually and be used to separate malicious and safe files. These patterns can then be used to train an artificial neural network, which will be able to keep learning and updating the data sets that differentiate between benign files and malicious files.

10.11.5 Threat Intelligence

Cyberattacks have become more sophisticated and can cause more damage than ever before. Threat actors are posing all kinds of challenges to security teams by unleashing a variety of threats, which are a part of the daily flood of data, false alerts and alarms that they need to deal with. Deciphering genuine threats from enormous amounts of extraneous data across multiple systems is a very challenging task. Without the proper tools, security teams struggle to identify indicators of compromise (IOC) and indicators of attack (IOA) to take informed decisions and initiate appropriate response actions.

Threat intelligence refers to the context, information and knowledge that security teams need in order to determine the source of the threat, type of threat, type of threat actors and their possible motivations, and the potential damage that can be caused. All this requires a deeper analysis of threat data on an ongoing basis and cyber threat intelligence tools provide the means to do so.

Threat intelligence must be timely, actionable and provide the required context for security teams to be able to take decisions. It can be at multiple levels: strategic, tactical and operational.

Strategic Threat Intelligence

This is intended for high-level decision-making and offers a broad overview of an organization's threat environment. Sources of strategic intelligence are policy documents, white papers, research reports of governments and other organizations engaged in studying and analyzing cybersecurity trends, related news from national and international media, industry reports, user groups, and so on. In order for strategic threat intelligence to be useful, it must provide insights into the key areas of security concern, threat actor tactics and targets as well as broad trends that can help an organization understand the threat landscape. The output of terms of strategic intelligence is largely non-technical, but still requires analysis of vast amounts of data. Threat intelligence tools can help in data collection through automated means as well as in analysis, thereby enabling security teams to use their expertise in contextualizing the same for their organization.

Tactical Threat Intelligence

This is focused on the tactics, techniques and procedures (TTPs) of threat actors. Tactical threat intelligence is useful in evaluation of existing security controls with respect to existing and emerging threats from threat actors who may be targeting specific industries or vulnerabilities. There is a significant technical aspect to tactical intelligence which can be of use to system architects, administrators and members of security teams to prioritize and take decisions to defend against threats and minimize their impact. Security vendors are a reliable source of tactical threat intelligence as they closely follow the attack vectors and TTPs used by hackers as well as vulnerabilities to strengthen their product offerings in the market. Other ways of gathering tactical threat intelligence include deploying a solution within an organization's network to integrate and analyze data.

> **Info Box 72: What is OSINT?**
>
> The Central Intelligence Agency (CIA) of the USA describes open source intelligence (OSINT) as intelligence "drawn from publicly available material." OSINT can also be explained as information collected concerning an individual, entity or organization through legitimate means from public domain sources.[9]
>
> OSINT can often be gathered without specialist skills or tools, other than those sources that are behind a paywall or other forms of restricted access. While OSINT is often associated with social media and human tools, there are tools such as Shodan that enable users to search for distinct types of servers connected to the Internet using a several types of filters.
>
> Other popular OSINT tools include Maltego (provides a library of transforms for the discovery of data from open sources and its graphic visualization), TinEye (reverse image search), Recon-ng (web-based reconnaissance) and WHOIS (to find out the address, email address and phone number of the person/entity who owns or has registered the website).

Operational Threat Intelligence

Also known as technical threat intelligence, this refers to information about cyberattacks, events or campaigns which can enable incident response teams to understand the kind of attack, motivation and timing of specific attacks. An important source of this information is from threat data feeds which are derived from threat indicators such as malware hashes or suspicious domains.

Threat intelligence solutions are increasingly using ML processes for automated data collection on a large scale and combine data gathered from many different types of sources including open, dark web, security vendor reports and other technical resources which can help construct a comprehensive threat assessment and develop effective operational threat intelligence.

10.11.6 Standards and Regulations

Cybersecurity standards have provided several benefits by developing best practices and conformance requirements by incorporating learnings and experiences pertaining to specific industry sectors as well as across industries and geographies. By following standards and regulations, organizations can raise their cybersecurity standards, build a baseline and strengthen their security posture. Standards like ISO and NIST also enable continuous evaluation and improvement. However, they are not the be-all and end-all of cybersecurity and often in an effort to be a 'one-size-fits-all' model, tend to become non-specific and offer limited guidance for emerging situations. Nevertheless, the importance of standards and regulations cannot be undermined in the overall development of cybersecurity practices.

Standards bodies around the world are engaged in the evolution of existing standards as well as developing new standards as newer technologies and uses emerge. Standards are so important that we have formalized the process of developing standards on both a national and international scale. This formal process, however, is being challenged by the rapid pace of technology development and by the increasingly ad hoc nature of computer technology development. We seem to have reached a key point in the history of standards, and one that will have a profound effect on the user community, which has

---

[9] "OSINT: What Is Open Source Intelligence and How Is It Used?," The Daily Swig, accessed October 11, 2021. https://portswigger.net/daily-swig/osint-what-is-open-source-intelligence-and-how-is-it-used

a strong dependence on standards. Standards have everything to do with change. They hold change in check by fixing certain parts of a technology. They also allow innovation to happen in a controlled way by creating an area of certainty around which change can happen. The process of change, however, is itself changing due to the increased rate of technology development, and this is having a profound effect on how we create and manage standards.

Current-day standards and frameworks like ISO 27001 and NIST allow flexibility and can facilitate adaptation to changing security contexts. Standards are also subjected to constant reviews, reassessment and revision which help organizations evolve their own security systems and mechanisms.

Organizations can follow different approaches to achieve their security objectives. However, standards and best practices are always helpful in giving direction to security initiatives. The Department of Homeland Security and the National Institute of Standards and Technology, both US bodies, have together released category-based goals that classify cybersecurity practices into nine categories as bases for cyber performance goals. It is expected that these goals will help organizations adopt effective cyber practices and controls. The nine category-based goals that have evolved over time are:

- Architecture and Design
- Configuration and Change Management
- Continuous Monitoring and Vulnerability Management
- Incident Response and Recovery
- Physical Security
- Risk Management and Cybersecurity Governance
- Supply Chain Risk Management
- System and Data Integrity, Availability and Confidentiality
- Training and Awareness

These nine goals, which include specific objectives, represent current best practices that support the deployment and operation of secure control systems and are useful pointers for building a cybersecurity program. It is important to note that these nine categories have evolved in response to a recent spate of cyberattacks on critical systems in the USA.

There is unanimity around the world among different stakeholders that cybersecurity regulations have been more of a patchwork of existing and new regulations and have generally fallen short of expectations and requirements. However, like standards, they continue to evolve and place mandatory obligations on organizations which they must follow. While compliance with regulations often increases the cost of doing business, it also enhances cybersecurity and provides additional protection for all stakeholders.

10.11.7 Defence-in-Depth (D-in-D)

Implementing bulletproof security is always an elusive goal. It is often said that there is no silver bullet that can address all the cybersecurity challenges. Hence, a strategy that builds security in layers with no single point of failure is a prudent approach. The defence-in-depth (D-in-D) approach incorporates physical, technical and administrative controls. If one control fails, another one steps up to protect information assets.

While the concept of D-in-D has a long history by virtue of its uses by the military to protect their nations, assets and people, its use or cybersecurity is relatively new. As technologies have evolved and methods used by hackers have become more sophisticated, D-in-D strategies have also undergone changes.

D-in-D strategies span across several security elements, including the following:
- Endpoint security
- Patch management
- Network security
- Intrusion detection
- Identity and access management

An example of the span of security elements that form a part of D-in-D strategies in the context of industrial control systems is shown in Table 10.5.

Table 10.5 Defence-in-depth security elements[10]

Risk Management Program	Identify Threats Characterize Risk Maintaining Asset Inventory
Cybersecurity Architecture	Standards/Recommendations Policy Procedures
Physical Security	Field Electronics Locked Down Control Centre Access Controls Remote Site Video, Access Controls, Barriers
ICS Network Architecture	Common Architectural Zones Demilitarized Zones Virtual LANs
ICS Network Perimeter Security	Firewalls, One-way Diodes Remote Access and Authentication Jump Servers, Hosts
Host Security	Patch and Vulnerability Management Field Devices Virtual Machines
Security Monitoring	Intrusion Detection Systems Security Audit Logging Security Incident and Event Monitoring
Vendor Management	Supply Chain Management Managed Services/Outsourcing Leveraging Cloud Services
The Human Element	Polices Procedures Training and Awareness

---

[10] "Improving Industrial Control Systems Cybersecurity with Defense-In-Depth Strategies," National Cybersecurity and Communications Integration Center. https://www.cisa.gov/uscert/sites/default/files/FactSheets/NCCIC%20ICS_FactSheet_Defense_in_Depth_Strategies_S508C.pdf

The past few years have seen several technological advances that are related to the above elements, such as:

- EDR and XDR solutions to handle perimeter-less security along with intrusion detection and response
- Automated patch management
- Micro-segmentation and zero trust approaches to security
- The use of biometrics and context (geo-location, device, IP address, etc.) along with business rules for identity management
- Deployment of privileged access management solutions to monitor and secure access to privileged accounts such as administrator and superuser accounts by human as well as non-human identities such as applications, bots and scripts
- Next-generation firewalls and next-generation antivirus software

Layering the defences will always give defenders a better chance to survive cyber threats and attacks, and D-in-D offers just that, that is, several layers of security. An area where D-in-D strategies still need greater focus is in managing third-party risks. It is simply not enough to secure the defences of an enterprise without considering vulnerabilities from service providers and other third parties.

10.11.8 Cybersecurity Skills Shortage and the Digital Divide

The skills shortage in the cybersecurity domain is well known and various estimates indicate that the unmet requirement of cybersecurity professionals is of the order of 3.5 million. While this is a great opportunity for students to opt for a career in cybersecurity, the increasing frequency of cyberattacks means that this short supply of cybersecurity talent is proving to be a major hazard. Companies are resorting to increased automation of cybersecurity activities and deploying advanced technologies, but the requirement for trained cybersecurity personnel cannot be adequately substituted by technology only. In the near-term, companies will need to undertake employee training in cybersecurity on a war footing and use specialist cybersecurity skills from an outsourced pool. Cybersecurity must become a part of every employee's job and companies would do well to co-opt them to fight against hackers and criminals. Incentivizing cybersecurity learning and using innovative tools such as simulation and gaming can ensure that employees are ready to become a part of the response mechanism against cyber threats.

The digital divide is another major challenge when it comes to cybersecurity. In every country, there are sections of the population who are not computer literate or even have basic access to modern technologies. This problem has its roots in the economic divide between the rich and the poor as also the demographic composition of the people in a given geographic area, Institutions like the United Nations and the World Economic Forum are working to bridge the digital divide by making technology accessible, available and usable through multi-lateral training and awareness efforts.

10.11.9 Governance, Culture and Ethics

Cybersecurity governance is often not given the importance it deserves even though it serves as the very basis by which organizational security is controlled and operates, and the mechanisms and standards by its employees are held to account. Elements of good governance include risk management practices, compliance, administration, development of a security culture and adopting a code of cyber ethics. Business leaders must first recognize the usefulness of leveraging these elements in the context of cybersecurity and must then turn towards technologies that enable them to enhance the performance of each element in line with organizational objectives. For example, the use of governance, risk management and compliance (GRC) software can enable an organization to effectively meet compliance requirements, manage risk and standardize processes across the enterprise. Similarly, simulation and gamification tools are widely available for cybersecurity training purposes.

It must also be remembered that to evolve company culture in a desired direction a typical analyze-plan-direct process, while useful for operational issues, is inadequate when it comes to embedding a security culture. Cultures also develop with an evolutionary process, that is, in response to the environment, to opportunities – never against resistance.[11] Developing a cybersecurity culture requires the creation of the right learning environment along with strong and continuous leadership support.

> **Info Box 73: Importance of Cybersecurity Culture**
> Company culture evolves if it develops in a direction that is good for people, and good for business. The process mirrors biological evolution, where genetic changes survive because they are advantageous to the species. Similarly, desirable corporate changes (like developing a cybersecurity culture) are those that ensure the health and long-term survival of the company.[12]

Ethics will continue to be an important aspect of cybersecurity. Technological advancements bring with them several ethical choices and dilemmas. By themselves, technologies cannot make moral choices. These decisions will be in the hands of the people and organizations who use them. Confidentiality is a key ethical issue in cybersecurity. Security personnel, due to the nature of their job, are privy to and handle personal, private or proprietary information that should be kept strictly confidential. The many benefits that technologies like AI and ML have to offer are far too many to list here, but the same technology in the wrong hands can cause greater damage through the use of AI-based automatic weapons, unauthorized access and surveillance. The uses of AI in medical science can be numerous, but the same technology can be maliciously used by hackers to contaminate medicines and case harm.

The more powerful technologies become, the greater the chances for their use for unethical activities and illicit purposes. To some extent, technologies have addressed basic issues such as deploying encryption techniques to protect confidentiality, identity management and authentication to prevent unauthorized access, but every day, modern technologies give rise to ethical questions and considerations regarding their use and deployment. Similarly, regulations and laws also help in clarifying what uses of technology are legal and what are not. The evolution of a code of conduct that is widely adopted and accepted by all stakeholders to make the digital world a safer place is essential, but perhaps utopian. Till such time the ethical considerations thrown up by various technologies are addressed by key stakeholders and consensus is reached on a globally acceptable code of conduct, organizations and individuals must create and abide by their own ethical codes and dictates of their conscience. The history of cybersecurity thus far has been one of evolution rather than revolution. The future will likely see the triumphant march of technology, unfortunately with its attendant cybersecurity challenges. Cybercrime is also rampant and on a growth path that will continue to be the scourge of the organizations and individuals who are a part of the digital world. To stay ahead, organizations and cybersecurity professionals must continuously ask themselves if they are sufficiently prepared to protect their information assets and ensure that threat actors do not seize the initiative to perpetrate their nefarious activities.

---

[11] "Evolution and Company Culture", Company Culture, accessed September 14, 2021. https://companyculture.com/123-evolution-of-a-work-culture/

[12] "Evolution and Company Culture", Company Culture, accessed September 14, 2021. https://companyculture.com/123-evolution-of-a-work-culture/

QUICK TEST

1. AI and, in some cases, ML is being used by many cybersecurity developers to bolster the capabilities of their systems such as modelling user behaviour, scanning emails, blocking phishing attempts, and enhancing antivirus systems, network defences and endpoint security.
   a. True
   b. False
2. Which of the following features of blockchain technology are useful in solving cybersecurity problems?
   a. Immutability
   b. Distributed ledgers
   c. Transparency
   d. All of the above
   e. b and c only
3. Slow adoption of blockchain technology across industries is on account of:
   a. Low scalability
   b. Design complexities
   c. Its suitability for only cryptocurrency applications
   d. All of the above
   e. a and b only
4. Cybersecurity experts are concerned that all current approaches will be rendered obsolete with the arrival of quantum computing.
   a. True
   b. False
5. The characteristics of a strong digital identity are:
   a. It is unique
   b. Verifiable with a high degree of assurance
   c. Ensures privacy protection
   d. Provides user control
   e. All of the above
   f. a, b and c only
6. 5G networks, while providing many benefits, will also provide hackers with opportunities due to the following:
   a. 5G is largely software based
   b. Increase in attack surface as more devices can be connected and managed
   c. More potential entry points for attackers
   d. Increased exposure to risks due to reliance of mobile network operators on suppliers
   e. All of the above
   f. a, b and c only
7. A 'security by design' approach provides several benefits whether you are a product developer or a user organization, including reduction in potential liabilities that could arise in future due to flaws and security weaknesses in a given system.
   a. True
   b. False
8. The SolarWinds Orion data breach:
   a. Underlined the devastating potential of supply chain attacks
   b. Exposed vulnerabilities in current practices related to managing vendor cyber risks

c. Could lead to broad changes in the cybersecurity industry
   d. All of the above
   e. a and b only
9. A full-fledged disinformation campaign can cause as much or more damage that other forms of cyberattacks; cybersecurity technologies and processes can not only be effective in identifying disinformation campaigns at an early date, but also in developing responses such as identifying and bringing down false stories and websites, thus preventing their further spread.
   a. True
   b. False
10. The concept of security convergence refers to the integration of various aspects of security, such as:
    a. IT infrastructure
    b. Information security
    c. Physical and people security
    d. Operational technology (OT) systems
    e. Business continuity and disaster recovery
    f. All of the above
    g. a, b and c only

QUESTIONS

1. The cyber landscape is an everchanging one in which threats continue to morph and evolve into more potent and dangerous ones. The same technologies that are used for cybersecurity are often used by cybercriminals to launch attacks. Discuss this statement.
2. To what extent are current technologies adequate to handle future challenges in cybersecurity? What modern technologies and approaches will be required and why?
3. How can AI technology be used for and against information security?
4. Technologies like blockchain and quantum computing are set to change the dynamics of cybersecurity. Explain.
5. How can the use of biometrics enable strong digital identity management and authentication?
6. Cyberattacks in the pre-5G era were focused on hacking databases, stealing intellectual property and extortion, among other forms of threats. The introduction of 5G brings us one level closer to dealing with attacks that can cause physical harm and affect the safety of individuals and communities. Discuss this statement.
7. What are the key technologies that enable supply chain security management?
8. What is an SBOM? Explain its importance in cybersecurity with examples.
9. What are the elements of implementing a defence-in-dept strategy? How is this a better approach to establishing a strong cybersecurity posture?
10. Explain the role of governance, culture and ethics towards better organizational information security.

ANSWER KEYS

Quick Test

1. (a)	3. (e)	5. (e)	7. (a)	9. (a)
2. (d)	4. (b)	6. (e)	8. (d)	10. (f)

11 Cybersecurity in E-commerce and Digital Payments

> **OBJECTIVES** ···
> *At the end of this chapter, you will be able to:*
> - ☑ Describe the cybersecurity issues and challenges that have emerged based on the use of e-commerce platforms and digital payments
> - ☑ State the underlying concepts, legal aspects and best practices for secure use of the above platforms
> - ☑ Explain the different approaches to address related security concerns

11.0 INTRODUCTION

The Internet has evolved over time to not only become a source of information but also a medium of communication that enables us to complete an entire business transaction online. Technologies such as digital payments, mobile phones, supply chain management systems and artificial intelligence have enabled e-commerce businesses to become an important part of our daily lives. The growing popularity and use of these platforms has come about as they provide several benefits like savings in terms of time and cost, availability of services 24 hours x 7 days a week, simplicity of conducting transactions and much more. However, there are also several areas of concern that have emerged such as privacy, safety, security, legality, lack of trust and ethics (all of which are an integral part of cybersecurity) in the way business is conducted online.

In this chapter, we will examine the cybersecurity issues and challenges surrounding e-commerce and digital payments, as well as approaches for enhancing cybersecurity at both individual and organizational levels.

11.1 WHAT IS E-COMMERCE?

For centuries, business has revolved around physical marketplaces where goods and services were exchanged for cash or goods. Other forms of payment instruments and systems such as cheques, cards and letters of credit also came into play to facilitate trade in and beyond the marketplace. E-commerce or online business is a relatively recent development that began in the last decade of the 20th century and has been growing rapidly since.

E-commerce or m-commerce (the use of mobile devices such as phones and tablets for e-commerce) can be described as the buying and selling of goods and services over the Internet. At one end, there are online platforms and websites that enable the sale and purchase of goods and services and at the other end, there are users who interact with them using computers, tablets and smartphones.

The most common example of e-commerce is online shopping, where users are provided with the information required to make a purchase decision, an order placement mechanism, reviews and testimonials, a fulfillment system (online for virtual goods and offline for physical goods) along with the ability to electronically transfer money towards payment to complete the transaction. Amazon and e-Bay are considered the pioneers of e-commerce and their success has prompted many other platforms which are both purely e-commerce platforms or hybrid ones that conduct their business online and have a brick-and-mortar physical presence. E-commerce covers a broad spectrum of economic activities including online auctions, payment gateways, online ticketing and Internet banking. It must be said that today almost every business leverages the e-commerce opportunity in one way or another to promote and conduct their business.

> **Info Box 74: E-commerce Sales in 2022**
> Industry reports indicate that in 2022, e-commerce sales is expected to grow to nearly 20% of all retail sales, with a value close to USD 6 trillion.

The rapid growth and acceptance of e-commerce can be attributed to a combination of technology and innovation, which has helped create a complete ecosystem that spans suppliers and consumers. Factors such as the Covid-19 pandemic have also contributed to more people spending time online and making purchases from the comfort of their homes to meet their daily needs as human mobility was severely curtailed due to prolonged lockdowns. A fast-growing variant of e-commerce, referred to as m-commerce, involves the use of smartphones for online shopping.

11.2 ELEMENTS OF E-COMMERCE SECURITY

E-commerce security comprises the protocols, processes and technological safeguards that ensure trustworthy transactions and provide the requisite security for all stakeholders. Important aspects of e-commerce security are discussed below:

- **Authenticity**: Given that the Internet allows for anonymity, it is important for a customer and user to establish a level of basic trust to ensure that transactions can take place securely between them. Hence, proper authentication of each of the transacting entities is a basic requisite. E-commerce platforms uses authenticity as a means of ensuring that the identity of the person they are dealing with is not a fraudulent one. At the same time, the customer also wants to be sure that the platform she is dealing with is genuine.
- **Integrity**: Maintaining integrity ensures that information on the Internet has not been modified or altered in any way by an unauthorized party and that the consistency, accuracy and trustworthiness of the information is guaranteed over its entire life cycle. For example, bills for items ordered and payments made should not be altered in any way that could impact the trustworthiness of a transaction.
- **Confidentiality**: Ensuring confidentiality of online transactions is an important consideration in e-commerce security. Information shared between the transacting parties should not be accessed by any unauthorized person on the Internet. Simply put, only the people who are authorized to access, view, modify or use the sensitive data of any customer or merchant should be able to do so.
- **Non-repudiation**: Non-repudiation is a legal principle that ensures that parties to a transaction do not deny the actions, facts that they have stated or rules that they have accepted. Non-repudiation provides an assurance that the parties cannot deny the validity of a transaction that they have performed. It also provides an additional layer of security for e-commerce transactions and confirms that any communication such as a signature, email, purchase or payment that occurred between the two parties has indeed reached the recipients.

- **Privacy**: Issues related to privacy have been receiving the global attention of governments, consumers and activists. Legal systems for privacy rights and obligations of custodians of personal information are still evolving. Hence, privacy can be considered as a major threat even when it comes to online transactions. There is no way that sensitive personal information once revealed to an unauthorized person can be prevented from being misused, sold or exploited. Other than the online seller that a customer has chosen to deal with, no one else should be able to access their personal information and account details. Any e-commerce business must therefore put in place at least a basic minimum of security measures such as an antivirus, firewall, encryption, secure payment gateway and other data protection measures.
- **Availability**: Availability of data on a continuous basis is key to providing a 24 × 7 customer experience. It not only increases online visibility and improves search engine rankings, but also boosts site traffic. Data availability must be ensured without downtime, which enhances customer confidence and becomes a means of competitive advantage. Availability also ensures prevention of data delays and removal.

11.2.1 Common E-commerce Security Issues

Even as e-commerce platforms have improved their security measures and mechanisms, cybercriminals have found new ways of breaching security for their malicious acts. Studies reveal that the e-commerce industry is among the most vulnerable ones when it comes to cybercrimes.

> **Info Box 75: Statistics on E-commerce Security**
>
> About 32.4% of all attacks are targeted at the e-commerce industry. Half of all small e-commerce store owners are increasingly becoming concerned about the severity of the cyberattacks. Reports also indicate that around a third of traffic accessing a website consists of malicious requests. The impact of such attacks has led to significant financial loss, drop in market share and reputational damage. Furthermore, nearly 60% of small e-commerce stores that suffer cybercrimes do not survive more than six months.[1]

In a rapidly developing cyber threat landscape, e-commerce platforms and users need to be aware and proactively engage in enhancing cybersecurity on an ongoing basis. Table 11.1 lists the main threats to e-commerce security.

Table 11.1 Threats to e-commerce security

Type of threat	Tactics, techniques and procedures
Fake or counterfeit websites	Cybercriminals are adept at creating lookalike websites that can pass off as genuine ones and which can lead to financial loss, loss of trust and reputation damage.
Fake returns and refund scams	Creating fake returns and refunds by initiating a fraudulent chargeback or disputing a legitimate transaction.

(Continued)

---

[1] Jinson Varghese, "Ecommerce Security: Importance, Issues & Protection Measures," Astra Security, accessed October 11, 2022. https://www.getastra.com/blog/knowledge-base/ecommerce-security

Table 11.1 (*Continued*)

Type of threat	Tactics, techniques and procedures
Unauthorized transactions	Conducting unauthorized transactions through account takeover by stealing credentials using brute force attacks. Attackers can also gain access to inventory information and steal, destroy or change it, creating problems between consumers and suppliers.
Theft of client information and credit card data	Cybercriminals use methods such as e-skimming to steal credit card information and personal data from payment card processing pages on e-commerce platforms.
Malware attacks	Malicious programs like ransomware, spyware, adware, trojans, bots and worms can be used to cause damage to e-commerce platforms by erasing data and causing malfunctions in performance.
Exploiting vulnerabilities	Exploiting vulnerabilities to launch SQL injection and cross-site scripting attacks.
Denial of service attacks	Shutting down of websites by flooding them with junk traffic, thereby preventing users from accessing the websites.
Uncertainty in transaction completion	When faced with uncertainty about completing critical transaction activities, consumers may fall into the hands of cybercriminals while trying to resolve issues related to payment, dispute resolution and delivery.

11.3 E-COMMERCE SECURITY BEST PRACTICES

Cybersecurity is extremely important for the long-term success of any e-commerce platform. Cyberattacks can result in loss of revenue and data that could adversely impact the business and even lead to its closure. E-commerce platform owners not only need to protect their own systems and data but also safeguard their customers' data. Any failure to do so could harm the trust and customer confidence that takes years to build. Here are nine best practices in e-commerce security that can prevent and mitigate the impact of cyberattacks.

- **Have a cybersecurity policy**: A cybersecurity policy ensures that all stakeholders including employees, customers, suppliers and regulators are on the same page as far as the cybersecurity posture is concerned. A cybersecurity policy outlines the security rules for everyone to follow and provides guidance and clarity on various aspects of security.
- **Deploy multiple layers of security**: Layered security is essential for an e-commerce platform as it is prone to different kinds of cyber threats. Such a security approach deploys multiple security controls to protect the most vulnerable areas of the platform environment where a breach or cyberattack could occur. For example, the use of multi-factor authentication can help in preventing fraudsters from breaking into user accounts. By implementing additional authentication factors which may be cumbersome for users at times, 2-step verification, 2-factor authentication or multi-factor authentication provides further assurance that only authorized users can log into a website. Multiple layers of an effective security system could include further layers such as perimeter intrusion detection, home exterior intrusion detection and home interior intrusion detection.
- **Implement HTTPS and Secure Server Layer (SSL) certificates**: SSL certificates are used to encrypt sensitive data shared across the Internet. It ensures that the information reaches only the

intended recipient. In the absence of an SSL certificate, data is unencrypted between the user and the e-commerce platform and any electronic device or person between the sender and the server could access sensitive details. Cybercriminals can exploit this weakness to get hold of a user's passwords, usernames, credit card numbers and other information.

- **Deploy firewalls**: Deployment of firewalls is a basic requirement to stop unwanted traffic such as spam, cross-site scripting, malware, cross-site request forgery, SQL injections and other potentially harmful traffic from entering. Web application firewalls (WAFs) can be deployed to help to differentiate between DDoS attacks and genuine traffic. A WAF can protect a website from DDoS attacks and ensure that customers enjoy uninterrupted access to the site. Another measure to make it difficult for hackers to find and attack the main server is to use a content delivery network (CDN). Since this approach uses a group of servers to deliver content online, it becomes difficult for an attacker to identify the main server.
- **Deploy anti-malware software**: Specialized malware protection software must be deployed that not only detects but also blocks different types of malicious software, neutralizes cyber threats and prevents cyberattacks. A malware scanner is useful for scanning the web system for all malicious software on a round-the-clock basis.
- **Implement a secure payment gateway**: Secure payments are a crucial part of an e-commerce transaction. E-commerce platforms use various electronic payment methods to receive money in exchange for their products or services. Digital or electronic payment systems have completely revolutionized the online business process and made it convenient for both the business and customers. There are various ways in which electronic payments are made, such as credit cards, debit cards, e-wallets, smart cards and net banking. Online payment systems work by connecting an e-commerce platform to the payment processing network through a payment gateway. This in turn is connected to the designated bank account for clearance of funds. Payment systems around the world are mostly regulated by the central banks of the respective countries and prescribe specific guidelines regarding security of transactions and data. There are also industry groups such as the Payment Card Industry that prescribe standards which regulators adopt, such as credit and debit card processing standards. Payment Card Industry Data Security Standard (PCI DSS) is widely accepted and used around the world. Using trusted payment systems which conform to standards such as PCI DSS or a Unified Payment Interface ensures compliance with regulations and can be trusted by both consumers and business owners.
- **Regularly review all plug-ins and third-party integrations**: Third-party solutions and plug-ins are an integral part of an e-commerce platform. Maintaining an inventory of all the third-party solutions that have been deployed and ensuring regular updates as well as removing them when they are no longer in use is necessary to prevent any cyberattacks through them.
- **Implement privacy and data protection measures**: Privacy and data protection are important legal obligations that e-commerce platforms must comply with. Apart from basic data protection measures like maintaining secure and up-to-date backups, e-commerce platforms must ensure the privacy and confidentiality of customer data. Customer privacy violations can lead to legal and regulatory action as well as the imposition of fines and penalties. To ensure compliance from data collection to storage, sharing and usage, e-commerce organizations must comply with existing laws and regulations. Other important regulatory issues that must be complied with are protection of trademarks, patents and copyrights, shipping restrictions, age restrictions, licences and permits and taxation.
- **Security training of staff and consumer education**: For security to be effective and fool-proof, security training of all staff of an e-commerce platform as well as educating customers regarding common threats to look out for when transacting online is absolutely necessary. A formal process

and programme must be drawn up and implemented to not only act as a safeguard against threats but also prevent operational mistakes that could lead to compromising data and systems.

11.4 DIGITAL PAYMENTS

Digital payments have transformed the way transactions between a payer and a payee are conducted. Digital payment transactions can take place online or in person using electronic payment systems but do not involve the use of cash. Instead, payments are transferred from the payer's bank, credit card or e-wallet account to the payee's account electronically. Governments around the world are encouraging citizens and businesses to use digital payments as it eliminates the need for managing physical cash, which is both expensive and hard to store, secure and track. On the other hand, digital payments are fast, convenient and have a clear audit trail for accounting. They also enable making payments 24x7 without the drudgery of standing in queues or waiting for bill payment and ticketing counters to open. Digital payments have been a key facilitator of e-commerce, enabling consumers to make payments for goods and services purchased online at any time and from anywhere.

> **Info Box 76: Digital Payments in India**
>
> Digital payments in India have been growing rapidly. *The Economic Times* cited an Accenture report that estimated that transactions worth USD 7 trillion are expected to shift from cash to cards and digital payments by 2023, and increase to USD 48 trillion by 2030.[2]

Cryptocurrency is also a form of digital payment system but does not depend on the banking system to verify transactions. It functions as a peer-to-peer system that can enable anyone anywhere to send and receive payments. Currently, regulators are grappling with security and other issues related to cryptocurrency and in many countries have not accorded it the status of legal tender money.

11.4.1 Components of Digital Payments and Stakeholders

The smooth flow of digital payment transactions requires the setting up and management of several components. Some of these components operate at the frontend, while others work at the backend to ensure safety, security, integrity and availability. As digital payments are a vital part of the economy, all these components must work in unison following predetermined rules and procedures.

Broadly speaking, we can look at digital payment system components under the following heads:

- **Major components**, which include the payment application (website/mobile app), the payment initiation mechanisms and the interfaces between front-facing and backend systems.
- **The backend infrastructure components** that provide the hardware, software and networks for secure payment transfer facilities, accounting and settlement mechanisms.
- **The security mechanisms** that ensure that transactions are carried out in a secure fashion, protecting the integrity and confidentiality of payment transaction information.
- **The stakeholders** of the digital payment transaction would include the application user, payment brokers including banks, credit card companies and merchants, and other service providers.

---

[2] "Nearly 7,000 Crore Payments Transactions to Move Digital by 2023: Report", *The Economic Times*, accessed October 12, 2022. https://economictimes.indiatimes.com/tech/tech-bytes/nearly-7000-crore-payments-transactions-to-move-digital-by-2023-report/articleshow/79428898.cms

The Reserve Bank of India (RBI) has been proactive in introducing digital payment systems and has been encouraging their use. Deploying technology, the RBI has transited from old systems to newer ones: Electronic Clearing Service (Credit) and Electronic Clearing Service (Debit) have been replaced with the National Automated Clearing House run by National Payments Corporation of India (NPCI). The RBI has also migrated its old Electronic Funds Transfer (EFT) system to the modern and feature-rich National Electronic Funds Transfer (NEFT) system.

11.4.2 Modes of Digital Payments in India

Under the aegis of the Digital India programme, the Government of India is implementing its vision to transform India into a digitally empowered society and knowledge economy through 'faceless, paperless, cashless' means. While becoming a totally cashless society is difficult considering the 'digital divide' that exists between the people who are capable of operating digital systems and those who cannot, we are moving towards a 'less cash' economy. To facilitate this, several modes of digital payments are available, as listed in Table 11.2.

Table 11.2 Digital payment systems in India[3]

Banking cards	Credit, debit and prepaid cards are issued by banks which offer greater security and convenience to consumers. They are governed by PCI DSS security standards. Other security features include two-factor authentication for secure payments such as PIN and OTP. Visa, MasterCard and RuPay are some of the examples of card payment systems.
USSD	This is an innovative payment service that uses the Unstructured Supplementary Service Data (USSD) channel. This service allows mobile banking transactions using a basic-feature mobile phone and is aimed at providing services to unbanked sections of society, even where Internet services are not available.
UPI	Unified Payments Interface (UPI) is a digital payment system that provides access to multiple bank accounts through a single mobile application (of any participating bank), incorporating multiple banking features, enabling funds transfer and merchant payments.
Mobile wallets	Mobile wallets are a popular way of making digital payments. A mobile wallet is linked to a bank account and enables the loading of money into the wallet to make small retail payments and money transfers.
Point-of-sale terminals	Point-of-sale terminals are installed at checkout counters (points-of-purchase) and bill payment facilities to enable consumers to make payments digitally using credit, debit and prepaid cards.
Mobile banking	Mobile banking is a service like net banking but conducted through a mobile phone or tablet instead of a regular desktop computer or laptop.
AEPS/Micro ATMs	Aadhaar-Enabled Payment System (AEPS) is a bank-led model which allows online interoperable financial transactions at points-of-sale or micro ATMs through a Business Correspondent (BC) of any bank using Aadhaar authentication.

---

[3] "Cashless India," Government of India, accessed October 12, 2022. http://cashlessindia.gov.in/digital_payment_methods.html

11.4.3 Digital Payments-Related Common Frauds and Preventive Measures

Digital payment systems are not immune to cyber threats as cybercriminals find new and innovative ways to deceive unsuspecting consumers. The following are common frauds that are related to digital payments along with some preventive steps:

- **Fake UPI-based payment links**: Here, the fraudster tries to deceive the victim by sending fake payment links through which he can get access to the victim's UPI ID and One-Time Password (OTP) and use the information to transfer money to accounts controlled by him. Prevention involves the use of official bank UPI apps or BHIM and not making payments through links sent by unknown entities.
- **Vishing and smishing KYC update fraud**: In this type of fraud, cybercriminals use emails, SMS and phone calls stating that your bank account will be frozen if you do not update your KYC (know-your-customer) details. By providing the details on the phone or through links sent by the cybercriminals, you can compromise the security of your bank account. Preventive measures are that you must interact only with the bank's official website and not provide any details on phone or through suspicious links.
- **Bill payment scam**: Another common method used by scamsters is to send messages supposedly from electricity supply companies stating that if you do not make payment of a pending bill by that evening, your electricity will be cut off. Any response to this message (usually sent by SMS) will lead to the scamster sending a fake payment link. On initiation of payment through this link, your bank details and OTP will be compromised. Situational awareness is required to deal with this type of fraud. Any payment that you may want to make must be made through the official website of the company.
- **Fake UPI apps and helpline numbers**: There are several Twitter handles that position themselves as official helpline for the National Payments Corporation of India or BHIM apps which are aimed at deceiving customers seeking help to reveal their account, wallet or card details.
- **SIM swap/identity theft/impersonation/account take over**: Here, the fraudsters use social engineering tactics such as phishing, vishing or smishing to obtain a victim's bank account details along with the registered mobile number. They then proceed to get a new SIM issued against the registered mobile number using fake identity proof and to get the original SIM deactivated. This enables the fraudster to gain access to OTPs and conduct fraudulent transactions. Preventive measures including being careful of social engineering attempts, registering for SMS alerts as well as email alerts for banking transactions and checking bank statement details regularly. In case you observe any suspicious activity in your account, you can use phone banking to block the account.
- **Refund frauds**: The proposition of getting a refund is always attractive and hard to resist. Knowing this, fraudsters send messages to potential victims stating that they are eligible for a refund and that they must enter the details of their bank accounts to receive the refund. Once they have elicited these account access details, they proceed to siphon off money. It is important to know that all bank details are already available in your tax returns and no additional details or forms are required to be filled for getting a refund if you are eligible for the same.
- **Web skimming**: Skimming happens through illegally installed devices on POS terminals and ATMs to capture cardholder information including Personal Identification Number (PIN). This data is then used to create fake credit and debit cards to steal money from the victim's account.

Similarly, cybercriminals use web skimming through form jacking or a Magecart attack. In a Magecart attack, the attacker injects malicious code into a website and extracts data from an HTML form that a user has filled in. An important preventive measure is to regularly update the OS and software.

- **QR code fraud**: Using QR codes is very convenient but can be dicey as well. Fraudsters send QR codes under the pretext of crediting an account, but on scanning, they deduct funds from the account. This type of fraud has become extremely common in recent times. To stay safe, you need to be careful while sharing your bank account or UPI ID details and if you receive a QR code from an unknown source, never scan it. Other measures include not sharing PINs or OTPs under any circumstances.
- **Remote access assistance**: Here, the fraudster approaches the victim through a phone or pop-up advertisement posing as an employee of a legitimate company like an Internet service provider or cable network provider and requests that remote access be given to install some updates or new software. This could lead to your credentials being compromised and could further result in the fraudsters hacking into bank accounts and e-wallets and stealing money.
- **Social engineering and data breaches**: Social engineering comprises a range of malicious activities that use psychological manipulation to convince the victims to part with their personal data, passwords, bank information, card numbers and more. Social engineering attacks are a multi-step process. Firstly, a hacker investigates the intended victim to gather background information, such as potential points of entry, weak security protocols and the person's interests to proceed with the attack. He/She would then use this information to lay the bait in the form of a tempting time-bound offer, thereby luring you into revealing your personal information. Social engineering could also lead to large-scale data breaches at an organizational level, and over time, compromise the information of several people, which could result in financial loss for them. The use of multi-factor authentication, keeping systems updated and being aware of such fraudulent practices can help in preventing such frauds.

We must remember that payment-related frauds are the most rewarding for fraudsters and they are constantly finding new ways to trick people into revealing personal information that can be used for stealing money. It is important that individuals are aware and alert to such attempts and, in the worst case, if their credentials are compromised, they must intimate their bankers immediately so that their accounts can be temporarily frozen as well as lodge a complaint with the cyber police.

11.5 RBI GUIDELINES ON DIGITAL PAYMENTS AND CUSTOMER PROTECTION

The Reserve Bank of India (RBI) has played an active role and been the driving force behind the development of national payment systems. RBI's objective has been to ensure that payment systems are operated in a safe, secure, sound, efficient and accessible manner. The Board for Regulation and Supervision of Payment and Settlement Systems (BPSS) is a sub-committee of the Central Board of the RBI and the Department of Payment and Settlement Systems of the RBI functions as the Secretariat to the Board and executes its directions. The BPSS mandate is to regulate, supervise, authorize and set standards and policies for all the payment and settlement systems in the country.[4]

---

[4] "Payment and Settlement Systems," Reserve Bank of India, accessed October 13, 2022. https://www.rbi.org.in/scripts/Payment-Systems_UM.aspx

All payment and settlement systems are governed by the Payment and Settlement Systems Act, 2007 (PSS Act). The PSS Act as well as the Payment and Settlement Systems Regulations, 2008 prescribe that no person other than the RBI can commence or operate a payment in India unless authorized by the RBI. Under the Act, the RBI has authorized payment system operators of pre-paid payment instruments, card schemes, cross-border in-bound money transfers, Automated Teller Machine (ATM) networks and centralized clearing arrangements. Salient features of the PSS Act and Master directions (issued from time to time) which act as guidelines and also provide for consumer protection are enumerated in Table 11.3.[5]

Table 11.3 Excerpts from Payment and Settlement Systems Act and related guidelines

Coverage	Entities covered under the Act are Scheduled Commercial Banks (excluding Regional Rural Banks), Small Finance Banks, Payments Banks and credit card-issuing Non-Banking Finance Companies. These are known as regulated entities (REs).
General Controls: Governance and Management of Risks	• REs should formulate policies for digital payment products covering risk management/mitigation measures, compliance with regulatory instructions, customer experience, etc., and should explicitly discuss the payment security requirements. • REs should implement necessary controls to protect the confidentiality of customer data and integrity of data and ensure availability of requisite infrastructure such as human resources, technology, etc. with necessary back-up. • REs should provide assurance that the payment product has been developed taking into account security considerations and that it offers robust performance ensuring safety and consistency and has been rolled out after necessary testing.
Other Generic Security Controls	• REs should conduct risk assessments with regard to the safety and security of digital payment products and associated processes. • It is necessary that any risks arising from integration of the digital payment platform (both internal and external to REs) must be a part of risk assessment. • REs are required to develop and implement internal control systems to mitigate consequences of operational risks before introducing their digital payment products and services. • The storage of sensitive information in HTML hidden fields, cookies or any other client-side storage is prohibited in web applications that provide digital payment products and services to prevent data integrity compromise. • International standards must be followed in determining the key length for various purposes such as encryption, exchange of keys, digital certificates, authentication, etc. • REs are duty bound to renew their digital certificates used in the digital payment ecosystem before expiry of such certificates.

(*Continued*)

---

[5] "Master Directions," Reserve Bank of India, accessed October 12, 2022. https://rbi.org.in/Scripts/BS_ViewMasDirections.aspx?id=12032

Table 11.3 (*Continued*)

Application Security Life Cycle (ASLC)	• A secure-by-design approach must be followed by REs in developing the digital payment offerings. • REs should clearly articulate security objectives (including customer data protection) throughout the design, development and testing stages as well as the implementation, maintenance, monitoring and retiring of the digital payment applications. • Vulnerability assessments (VA) should be conducted at least on a half-yearly basis and as and when new infrastructure is added or a major change in the application is carried out. Penetration Testing (PT) should be conducted at least annually. • Testing related to review of source code/certification should be conducted/ obtained. To ensure compliance by third-party applications, contracts must have in-built penalties for non-compliance.
Authentication Framework	• REs are required to implement multi-factor authentication for payments through digital modes, fund transfers and cash withdrawals through ATMs, except for those areas where relaxations to this have been given. • At least one of the authentication methodologies should be generally dynamic or non-replicable such as the use of One-Time Passwords, hardware tokens, etc. with server-side verification that could be termed dynamic or which use non-replicable methodologies.
Fraud Risk Management	• REs are required to document and implement configuration aspects for identifying suspect transactional behaviour in relation to rules, prevention and detection types of controls, and a mechanism to alert customers about failed authentication or other anomalies. • RE employees, especially in the fraud control function, should be educated about frauds.
Reconciliation Mechanism	• REs must implement a reconciliation framework for all digital transactions between the RE and all other stakeholders. Reconciliation should be completed in real time/near-real time (not later than 24 hours from the time of receipt of settlement file(s)).
Customer Protection, Awareness and Grievance Redressal Mechanism	• REs should incorporate secure, safe and responsible usage guidelines and training materials for end users within the digital payment applications, on-boarding procedures as well as first use after each update/major updates of the payment application. • REs must educate customers regarding the importance of maintaining the security of their devices (both physical and logical security) through which they access digital payment products and services. Customer education should include using anti-malware software, secure/regular installation of operating systems, downloading applications from authorized sources and updating them as and when updates are made available. • REs are required to create public awareness on the different types of threats and attacks used against the consumers of digital payment products as well as preventive measures to protect themselves from any harm.

(*Continued*)

Table 11.3 (*Continued*)

	• Customers should be made aware about commonly known threats like phishing, vishing, reverse-phishing, remote access of mobile devices and educated to secure and safeguard their account details, credentials, PIN, card details, devices, etc.
Internet Banking Security Controls	• Based on the RE's individual risk/vulnerability assessment on authentication-related attacks such as brute force/DoS attacks, REs should implement additional levels of authentication to Internet banking websites such as adaptive authentication, strong CAPTCHA (preferably with anti-bot features) with server-side validation, etc. • An online session should be automatically terminated after a fixed period of inactivity. • Secure delivery of password for log-in purpose should be ensured.

Mobile Payments Application Security Controls	• REs should be able to verify the version of the mobile application before the transactions are enabled.
	• Specific controls for mobile applications include:
	  • Device policy enforcement (allowing app installation/ execution after baseline requirements are met)
	  • Application secure download/install
	  • Deactivating older application versions in a phased but time-bound manner
	  • Storage of customer data
	  • Device or application encryption
	  • Ensuring minimal data collection/app permissions
	  • Application sandbox/containerization
	• Considering that the additional factor of authentication and mobile application may reside on the same mobile device in the case of mobile banking and mobile payments, REs may consider implementing alternatives to SMS-based OTP authentication mechanisms.

Card Payments	• REs shall follow various payment card standards (over and above PCI DSS and PA DSS6) as per the Payment Card Industry. • REs should ensure robust surveillance/monitoring of card transactions (especially overseas cash withdrawals) and setting up of rules and limits commensurate with their risk appetites.

These are only the key provisions. A complete set of master directions for payments systems can be accessed at: https://rbi.org.in/Scripts/BS_ViewMasDirections.aspx?id=12032

11.6 LAWS ON PRIVACY AND DATA PROTECTION FOR E-COMMERCE COMPANIES

E-commerce companies gather, store and use large amounts personal information which calls for the creation of new cyber laws to ensure that they are responsible for maintaining consumer privacy and personal data protection. The European Union has been among the foremost champions of privacy and protection of personal information and through a comprehensive regulation (GDPR) have shown the way of the rest of the world. Many countries outside the European Union have used the GDPR as a template to frame their own laws regarding privacy and personal data protection.

India has been on the verge of passing similar legislation, first through the Personal Data Protection Bill 2019, which was withdrawn from parliament before it became law, and now with the Digital Personal Data Protection Bill (DPDPB), 2022, which is still in the draft stage. However, it is important to understand some of the key aspects of the proposed bill and its impact on e-commerce companies. The bill imposes obligations on e-commerce companies in the way they deal with consumer data. The following seven principles highlight the focus of the new bill:

- Usage of personal data of consumers by companies should be done in a way that is lawful, fair and transparent.
- Personal data cannot be used for any purpose beyond that for which it was collected.
- Companies should restrict the collection of personal information to what is directly relevant and necessary for a specified purpose.
- Companies are responsible for ensuring and maintaining the accuracy of the data collected.
- The personal data collected cannot be stored perpetually by default and must be limited to a fixed duration.
- Companies must implement reasonable safeguards to ensure that there is no unauthorized collection or processing of personal data.
- The person who determines the purpose and means of processing of personal data should be held accountable for such processing.

The bill, once passed, will establish a new legal regime governing digital personal data protection in India and have a major impact on all companies handling digital personal data. E-commerce companies too will need to make changes and implement various measures and systems in the way they handle personal data to ensure compliance, including the appointment of a Data Protection Officer when the organization handles high volumes of personal data.

The draft bill also seeks to impose significant penalties on businesses that undergo data breaches or fail to notify users when breaches happen. Entities that fail to take reasonable security safeguards to prevent personal data breaches can face fines as high as Rs 500 crore, which will be imposed by the Data Protection Board, a new regulatory body which the government proposes to set up.

QUICK TEST

1. E-commerce covers a broad range of activities conducted on the Internet, such as:
   a. Online ticketing
   b. Payment gateways
   c. Buying and selling of goods and services over the Internet
   d. All of the above
   e. b and c only
2. E-commerce _____ refers to the principles which ensure safe electronic transactions:
   a. Transactions
   b. Authorization
   c. Security
   d. Authority
3. Which of the following describes non-repudiation?
   a. Verification of identity
   b. Assurance that someone cannot deny the validity of something
   c. The action of remedying something
   d. None of the above
4. What best describes data privacy in cybersecurity?
   a. Protection of organizational data
   b. Protection of intellectual property
   c. Defines who has access to data
   d. None of the above
5. Major threats to e-commerce cybersecurity include:
   a. Theft of client information and credit card data
   b. Denial of service attacks
   c. Malware attacks
   d. All of the above
6. Digital payment transactions can take place online or in person through electronic payment systems but do not involve the use of cash.
   a. True
   b. False
7. Digital payment systems include payments made through credit and debit cards and through point-of-sale terminals.
   a. True
   b. False
8. Cybersecurity requirements for card systems are covered by:
   a. Indian IT Act
   b. Card Regulation Act
   c. PCI DSS
   d. None of the above

9. _____ is a bank-led model which allows online interoperable financial transactions at the point-of-sale or micro ATMs through a Business Correspondent (BC) of any bank using Aadhaar authentication:
   a. UPI
   b. SWIFT
   c. AEPS
   d. USSD
10. Which of the following are not considered a mode of digital payment?
    a. Mobile wallets
    b. Internet banking
    c. Bank pre-paid cards
    d. None of the above

QUESTIONS

1. Why is e-commerce security important? What are the main threats to e-commerce security?
2. Describe the various protection mechanisms and technologies that can be deployed to enhance e-commerce cybersecurity.
3. What is privacy in e-commerce? Why is it important?
4. Explain the relevance and importance of authentication and authorization for e-commerce.
5. Non-repudiation is a legal principle that gives e-commerce another security layer. Explain this statement.
6. List and describe the various technologies that have enabled the growth of e-commerce.
7. How are digital payments better than cash? What are the objectives of digital transactions?
8. What are the different components of a digital payment system? Describe the different modes of digital payments.
9. What are the main security threats to digital payment systems?
10. How effective have the consumer and fraud protection guidelines prescribed under the Payment and Settlement Systems Act been in preventing cybercrimes related to digital payments?

ANSWER KEYS

Quick Test

1. (d)
2. (c)
3. (b)
4. (c)
5. (d)
6. (a)
7. (a)
8. (c)
9. (c)
10. (d)

12 Overview of Social Media and Security

> **OBJECTIVES**
> *At the end of this chapter, you will be able to:*
> - ☑ Identify the threats and cybersecurity issues that have arisen from the increasing usage of social media platforms
> - ☑ Understand how threat actors are exploiting new routes to gain access to target both individuals and organizations
> - ☑ Describe the challenges in collating threat information across social media platforms
> - ☑ List the legal recourses and cybersecurity best practices for security concerns related to social media

12.0 INTRODUCTION TO SOCIAL NETWORKS

The term social media refers to Internet-based platforms that enable users to share ideas, thoughts and various types of content (text, images, audio and video) across a user group or community or with people at large. Users can engage with social media platforms using computers, tablets and smart phones. According to the latest reports, about 4.5 billion people around the world use social media. Among the largest social media networks are platforms like Facebook, Instagram, Twitter, YouTube, LinkedIn and TikTok.

Social media has become a major target for cybercrime. Everyone shares a certain amount of personal information on social media platforms. Once a person creates his/her profile on a social media platform, it is there for anyone to see. The more information people share about their background, everyday activities, interests, locations and preferences, the greater the security risk. Threat actors have become adept at collecting information across social media platforms and use this information for malicious activities. The risk that emanates from such malicious activities not only affects individuals but could extend to the organizations in which they are employed.

Social media is a veritable treasure trove of easily available personal information for cybercriminals, thereby offering them the basic ingredients required for launching social engineering attacks. Data privacy is a primary concern on social media, involving issues related to personal data collection, storage, re-purposing and sharing with third parties. The tendency of people to overshare information on social media provides many opportunities for cybercriminals to use it to conduct an attack.

12.1 TYPES OF SOCIAL MEDIA AND POPULAR PLATFORMS

Social media has brought with it a variety of benefits and its own lexicon, such as hashtags and going viral. A hashtag (represented by the # symbol) is used for indexing keywords or topics, making it easier for people to follow their interests. Viral content is any online content that is widely circulated because of shares and exposure on social media networks, news websites, aggregators, email newsletters and search engines.

The key benefits offered to users of social media are:

- Building and maintaining relationships with friends, associates, people with similar interests and customers
- Sharing experiences and expertise
- Increasing visibility and brand awareness
- Marketing and promotions
- Educating and participating in interest groups
- Connecting (through text, audio and video) anytime and from anywhere

The different types of social media platforms that enable users to enlist and use them based on their purpose and interests are listed in Table 12.1.

Table 12.1 Types of social media platforms

Type of platform	Purpose	Popular platforms
Traditional social networking sites	To connect with friends, family and brands for sharing personal experiences, views, expertise and other person-to-person interactions as well as brand promotion.	Facebook, LinkedIn, Twitter, TikTok
Social review sites	To share experiences and views about products, travel, etc.	Tripadvisor, Yelp, Angie, Choice (choice.com.au)
Image and video sharing sites	To share visual content such as images, infographics and illustrations.	Instagram, Imgur, Snapchat
Video hosting sites	To host video content for sharing and streaming.	YouTube, Vimeo
Discussion forums/ Microblogging sites	Posting thoughts and questions which can be answered by anyone. This attracts people with shared interests and curiosities to comment or post their responses.	Reddit, Quora
Sharing economy networks	To share information with people who may need it. Trading or exchanging goods and services.	Uber, e-Bay, Airbnb
Messaging apps	To connect, communicate and share.	WhatsApp, Telegram
Bookmarking and content sharing	To discover, save and share content.	Twitter, Pinterest
Interest-based networks	To explore hobbies and interests.	Centre for Environmental Research and Conservation (Facebook)
Audio-only networks	To have audio-only conversations.	Clubhouse, Twitter Spaces

12.2 SOCIAL MEDIA MARKETING

Social media marketing is the leveraging of social media platforms and websites to promote a product or service. Given the vast number of benefits that social media marketing offers, more organizations are increasing its usage. The main benefits of using social media marketing are listed in Table 12.2.

Table 12.2 Benefits of social media marketing

Increased brand awareness	Means of customer feedback
Generating inbound traffic	Business insights
Improved search engine rankings	User-generated content and testimonials
Better conversion rates	Building customer loyalty
Low cost of reach	Forum for customer care
Global reach	Opportunity to assess new ideas

Social media, if used intelligently and securely, can bring tremendous success, both at an individual and at an organization level. It represents the best way to address, engage and remain in direct contact with the target audience.

12.3 SOCIAL MEDIA MONITORING

Social media monitoring involves tracking hashtags, keywords and mentions relevant to an organization's posts/brand which helps it stay informed of any developments that may concern the organization, its audience or its industry. Through monitoring social media, organizations can gain insights from both quantitative information in the form of metrics and analytics as well as qualitative aspects of the posts and marketing strategies. The analytics listed in Table 12.3 can help in planning better social media campaigns for promoting a brand, product or service.

Table 12.3 Social media metrics

Content reach	Impressions	Audience growth rate
Engagement rate	Amplification rate	Virality rate
Social media share of voice	Relevant hashtags and keywords	Trends

From a cybersecurity point of view, collecting threat information across platforms is a challenging task given the number of platforms, and the large volume and frequency of posts. Extending the monitoring to messaging platforms is also complicated, as is analyzing the data for threat information. However, organizations must use social media monitoring as part of any comprehensive cybersecurity strategy. Fortunately, there are tools available that enable social media monitoring. While different monitoring tools provide their own functionalities, the following is a list of important tasks performed by them:

- Searching for any subject, topic or keyword
- Filtering search by date, demographics, location, and more
- Identifying brand perception and in raising alerts for good and bad posts or mentions
- Visualization of data and heat maps
- Tracking popular keywords of interest and most active accounts across multiple languages
- Using multiple filters to monitor conversations across millions of data sources, such as blogs, forums, videos, news and review sites, and social networks

Social media monitoring can help in increased security and situational awareness, but can be a daunting task without the use of the right tools. Social media activity happens 24 × 7 and is forever growing in volume in terms of the number of posts, tweets and other forms of information sharing. It is almost impossible to effectively monitor these multiple channels. Security teams can learn about various events that may adversely impact their organization through social media monitoring such as spreading false information concerning an organization and identifying discussions on social media which can be potentially dangerous or harmful even before they become a tangible risk.

Apart from wider threat intelligence gathering, given the fact that there is an enormous amount of data to analyze, security teams can focus their social media monitoring efforts on the following key cybersecurity areas:

- Fake accounts
- Executive impersonation
- Account takeovers
- Inactive company social media accounts
- Tracking threats and trends
- Adverse reviews and mentions

12.4 SOCIAL MEDIA PRIVACY

One of the biggest concerns while using social media is privacy. With close to half the world's population connecting to social media networks, the opportunity for threat actors to perpetrate fraud by using social media is growing by the day. Social media platforms store enormous amounts of personal information and have not been very successful in preventing this information from being compromised. Platforms like Facebook, Twitter and LinkedIn have faced multiple data breaches and are prime targets of threat actors who want to steal personal information for furthering their malicious activities. There is a lengthy list of threats that can emerge from the violation and exploitation of personal information that hackers can access or steal from social media platforms. Table 12.4 lists a few types of social media threats.

Table 12.4 Social media privacy threats

Objective of cybercriminals
Building fake profiles, impersonation, opening credit cards and bank accounts
Cyber bullying, extortion, physical threats
Spreading malware, spam and viruses
Data mining
Social engineering and phishing attempts
Business fraud
Launching botnet attacks

Social media platforms are also intrusive and leverage personal information and usage of the platform to promote various products, services and other content. Privacy agreements on social media apps tend to be intrusive and often state that the content and messages uploaded by the users are owned by the platform, even if the user decides to delete his or her account. Each social media platform also has its own policies for sharing user information with other platforms. Cambridge Analytica, a British firm, harvested the data of at least 87 million users without their knowledge through a loophole on Facebook, which allowed them to conduct a quiz for Facebook users, and then sell the information to the Donald Trump campaign.

> **Info Box 77: Social Media Threats are Rising**
>
> Social media platforms have become a treasure trove for mining personal information for scammers and cybercriminals.
>
> In April 2021, *The Hindu* reported that 533 million Facebook records were leaked on the Internet and were available for free.[1]
>
> A Bromium report titled 'Into the Web of Profit' indicates that around 30–40% of social media platforms feature accounts offering some form of hacking activities and that at least one-fifth of social media infections emerge from add-ons or plug-ins for social media platforms.[2]
>
> An ENISA Threat Landscape report reveals that social media phishing is on the rise, with social channels accounting for 8% of attacks.[3]

Another privacy threat can be from location applications. Though extremely useful in locating places, they hold information about a person's past and current whereabouts. This information in the wrong hands can be dangerous. Hence, these apps are targeted by thieves or stalkers for the geo-location information and can have harmful consequences.

12.5 SOCIAL MEDIA PRIVACY LAWS AND PERSONAL DATA PROTECTION

In India, the Digital Personal Data Protection Bill (DPDPB), 2022 proposes to bring in governmental controls which include monitoring of social media platforms and imposition of penalties for non-compliance. Other proposals such as treating social media platforms such as Meta as publishers and setting up a watchdog to oversee them will have far-reaching implications for social media companies. According to the provisions of the Information Technology Act, 2000, an intermediary (such as a social media platform) is not liable for any third-party information, data or communication link that is made available or hosted by them. This is a legal principle that is known as giving such companies safe harbour and is conditional in that an intermediary must not initiate the transmission, choose the receiver of the communication and select or alter the information contained in the transmission. Social media firms will be subject to a new regime which calls for content moderation and compliance with the new social media and intermediary guidelines.

The draft bill also places obligations of parent entities of social media platforms to provide a consent management mechanism which enables users to give, manage, review and withdraw consent. It is also noteworthy that it proposes that the personal data of children cannot be obtained or processed without parental consent. Social media companies will be permitted to store the collected data only for specified periods and can transfer data to countries and territories to be notified by the government.

Under the DPDBP, certain legal rights will be given to the natural person to whom the personal data relates (also referred to as data principal), which can be exercised through the digital fiduciary (the entity: individual, company, firm, state, etc.), which decides the purpose and means of processing of an individual's personal data and with whom their data has been shared. These rights are as follows:

---

[1] "Explained | How Facebook's Recent Data Breach Affects Its Users," The Hindu, accessed December 1, 2022. https://www.thehindu.com/sci-tech/technology/internet/explainer-how-facebooks-recent-data-breach-affect-its-users/article34324019.ece

[2] Andra Zaharia, "300+ Terrifying Cybercrime and Cybersecurity Statistics (2022 Edition)," Comparitech, accessed December 1, 2022. https://www.comparitech.com/vpn/cybersecurity-cyber-crime-statistics-facts-trends/

[3] Andra Zaharia, "300+ Terrifying Cybercrime and Cybersecurity Statistics (2022 Edition)," Comparitech, accessed December 1, 2022. https://www.comparitech.com/vpn/cybersecurity-cyber-crime-statistics-facts-trends/

- Right to obtain information on the personal data that is being processed, the processing activities and identities of all the data fiduciaries
- Right to correction and erasure of the data
- Right to nominate an individual to exercise rights on their behalf in the event of their death or incapacitation
- Right to grievance redressal

Once the bill is enacted, it will have an over-riding effect on other laws in case of conflicting provisions. It will also be applicable to existing sectoral laws/regulations on data governance.

12.6 FLAGGING AND REPORTING OF INAPPROPRIATE CONTENT

Flagging and reporting of inappropriate content is a means by which any user can inform the social media platform that he or she finds some content on their platform objectionable since they find that it is hateful, sexually inappropriate, spam or has the potential to incite violence. Every platform has its own way of flagging and reporting inappropriate content. For example on Facebook, if a user goes to the post and taps on the top-right corner, he/she is provided a way by which they can articulate the reason why they find a post objectionable. The user can also block the person who has posted the content. Similarly, other social media platforms provide ways for flagging and reporting inappropriate content. Once the user flags and reports his objections to any post, the platform is obliged to review it and remove the content if they find that it is indeed offensive or objectionable.

12.7 LAWS REGARDING POSTING OF INAPPROPRIATE CONTENT

The state of California in the US was among the first to enact a law (California Age-Appropriate Design Code Act) for the online protection of children. The new privacy rules under this law would apply to social media applications like Meta, Instagram, TikTok, and YouTube, who have often been criticized for not doing enough for online protection of children. The bill covers online services, products or features that are likely to be accessed by children and could extend to education and gaming platforms as well.

The United Kingdom too has proposed what is known as the Online Safety Bill, which is meant to improve Internet safety. This bill will also create a new obligation for online platforms towards their users, requiring them to act against illegal as well as legal but harmful content.

Social networking platforms around the world have in the past played a significant role in social movements such as 'Arab Spring', 'Black Lives Matter', etc. Social media has the power to shape public opinion and there is a thin line between being a passive platform for information sharing and promoting propaganda and activism. Hence, social media platforms are increasingly coming under government and public scrutiny and have faced severe criticism whether or not they have played a role in specific instances of violations of social norms.

In India too there have been concerns regarding the extent of freedom of speech on social media platforms, where issues like scrapping of Article 370 and the farmers' agitation have been extensively debated. Freedom of expression is the right of every individual to hold opinions and express the same on various forums including social media. In a landmark judgement, the Supreme Court of India in the case of *Shreya Singhal v. Union of India* held that a citizen's right to freedom of speech and expression over the Internet is constitutionally protected. However, as per Article 19(2) of the Indian constitution, freedom of speech can be subject to certain restrictions on sensitive matters through legislation, such as:

- Sovereignty and integrity of India
- Security of the state
- Friendly relations with foreign states
- Public order
- Decency or morality
- Contempt of court
- Defamatory posts
- Incitement to an offence

Thus far in India, there is no legislation that is specifically directed at the use and control of social media, even though the Information Technology Act, 2000 does have legal provisions, listed in Table 12.5, that can be invoked if social media posts are objectionable and offensive.

Table 12.5 Sections of law related to inappropriate content

Sections 67, 67A of the IT Act, 2000	This section deals with punishment for sharing obscene or sexually explicit material in electronic form. The punishment can be jail for seven years and a fine of Rs 10 lakhs.
Section 66E of the IT Act, 2000	Under this section, any person who intentionally or knowingly captures, publishes or transmits the image of a private area of any person without his or her consent, under circumstances violating the privacy of that person, shall be punished with imprisonment which may extend to three years or with fine not exceeding Rupees 2 lakhs or with both.
Section 67B of the IT Act, 2000	Transmitting material depicting children, including nude or sexually explicit pictures of self, if a child.

Most users are not fully aware of these legal provisions, nor do they fully understand the impact or possible consequences of their online activities on social media. It is important for individuals and organizations to be careful with the content that they are sharing on social media platforms lest it offend other users. If it is flagged and reported as inappropriate, it is advisable for platform providers and intermediaries to remove it immediately on notification.

12.8 DATA HARVESTING AND PERSONAL DATA PROTECTION

The issue of harvesting of data by social platforms and related violations of privacy is a matter of growing concern for governments and citizens around the world. Experts estimate that social media platforms harvest information and sell the attention of over a billion people every single day. However, there are security issues associated with data harvesting. LocalBlox a social media aggregator and customer intelligence platform, gathered the data of millions of individuals including their names, addresses, birth dates and other personal data from platforms like LinkedIn, Facebook and Twitter. The platform enables professionals and businesses to search, combine and validate business and people profiles. This data was left without protection, leading to the exposure of 48 million records containing personal information.

It is important to note that most forms of data harvesting as such are legal, but the individuals whose personal data was compromised were put to great personal risk.[4]

Large technology companies and social media platforms have been accused of leveraging the personal data of their customers for their own benefit by using the data for purposes beyond the original purpose for which the data was collected. The Cambridge Analytica case, which involved the firm using their access to Facebook accounts to harvest the personal information of millions of users by conducting their own quizzes and questionnaires and then using the same for political advertising, highlights the need for specific legislation and enforcement mechanisms that ensure that such actions cannot happen without the knowledge and consent of users. Laws such as GDPR have helped in giving citizens of the European Union more control over their personal data by ensuring that it can be used only with the consent of the individual concerned. Similar laws are required around the world to provide greater control for users over their personal data, which is best for all stakeholders in the long term.

12.9 BEST PRACTICES FOR THE USE OF SOCIAL MEDIA

There are several issues and challenges from a cybersecurity point of view when it comes to the use of social media. Social media has been evolving rapidly and has become an integral part of the daily lives of people around the world. In the context of social media, people need to constantly exercise trade-offs between how much personal information to share and how much to keep private. There are, however, several best practices which can be used to ensure that user interests and data are well protected to enable them to leverage the advantages that social media offers.

12.9.1 Personal Security and Social Media

Social media has become ubiquitous, and people are spending more time online on various platforms. Over time, social media platforms have enhanced the user's experience by offering features and functionality that they find interesting and engaging. Users are quick to sign up since most services are available for free, though some platforms do charge for providing additional or advanced services. What users seldom realize is that for the free use of social media, they are trading their right to privacy by sharing personal information.

Pre–sign-up: Social media companies profit from harvesting personal data and using the same for promoting products and services. To protect personal security, users must pay attention to the following aspects before they sign up for on a particular social media platform:

- Be aware of what personal data you are sharing
- Read the fine print of the terms of use
- Examine clauses for closure of user accounts
- Understand how a privacy breach can be reported
- Verify if any third parties will have access to personal information

Post–sign-up: The following is a list of cybersecurity practices that individuals can use for maintaining good social media security hygiene after sign-up:

- Use a different password/paraphrase (hard to guess) for each social media account
- Use multi-factor authentication wherever available
- Think before sharing any post

---

[4] "Block Buster: How A Private Intelligence Platform Leaked 48 Million Personal Data Records," *UpGuard* (blog), accessed December 1, 2022. https://www.upguard.com/breaches/s3-localblox

- Do not post any pictures that show an employee ID, driving licence and similar personal identifiable information
- Shut down any accounts not in use
- Keep corporate accounts secure
- Review friend list/connections regularly
- Check account security settings
- Ensure that social media apps are kept updated
- Beware of phishing scams
- Remember to log out after every session
- Configure privacy settings
- Use the block button for unsolicited messages
- Manage third-party application permissions
- Use a VPN
- Stay alert and vigilant and beware of fake news and propaganda

12.9.2 Enterprise Cybersecurity and Social Media

The reach and influence of social media continues to expand. From being a means of connecting with friends and co-workers, it has become an important means for corporate communication, marketing and brand building. One of the implications of this is that the lines between personal and professional usage of social media have blurred.

From an enterprise perspective, social media has provided a wonderful way for them to engage with prospective and existing customers at low cost. While the advantages are many, security challenges like vulnerability to social engineering attacks such as spear phishing, exposure to malware, spread of disinformation or fake news and privacy risks are all much more pronounced.

Securing social media usage starts with having a clear idea of how the organization uses social media. This is far more difficult than it appears, as often there is no central co-ordinator for social media and hence pinpointing the people and platforms being used is a difficult task.

Organizations often have multiple corporate social media accounts as they find it an effective way of communicating and engaging with consumers. Collating threat information across multiple platforms and users on an ongoing basis poses a major challenge for security teams. Cybersecurity measures at an organizational level for the use of social media are also more difficult to enforce, but given the risks involved must be prioritized.

Organizations can implement the following best practices to enhance social media security:

- Publish and communicate a social media security policy to all employees, particularly to those who are directly responsible for posting on social media accounts.
- Implement a least-privilege administrative model to restrict social media access.
- Nominate a member of the senior management to oversee social media issues to ensure that security, reputational aspects and legal compliance are enforced as per corporate guidelines.
- Sensitize employees to be alert to and watch out for phishing and social engineering attempts, friend requests, dubious messages and more while using social media.
- Request employees to use different passwords for different social media accounts and implement two-factor or multi-factor authentication wherever available.
- Make use of Single Sign-on (SSO) for corporate social media accounts, which allows any application access through the organization's identity management platform.

- Closely monitor posts for fake news regarding the organization and social media accounts for security risks.
- Shut down corporate social media accounts if they are not in use.
- Conduct regular training on the secure use of social media.

Each form of new Internet technology comes with its own set of security concerns and challenges. This is true of social media too. One major issue with social media is that it can place individuals and organizations at risk by opening pathways that are insecure or enable threat actors to bypass traditional cybersecurity mechanisms and controls.

12.9.3 Metaverse and Cybersecurity

Metaverse is an amalgamation of technologies that comprises virtual reality, augmented reality, social media and e-commerce. It brings to users graphic-rich experiences which take social media to another level, popularly called 'immersive social media.' Cybersecurity in the metaverse is already a key concern which involves securing the host platform, the property (renters on the platform) and the users of the property. Further, the metaverse ecosystem also involves the use of IoT devices, various types of sensors and wearables, all of which call for the implementation of additional security measures. Metaverse is still in its infancy and security approaches in the form of standards and frameworks for the same are still evolving. Meanwhile, apart from the regular set of social media security measures that must be used in the context of the metaverse, one fundamental problem that needs to be addressed is related to identity authentication, theft and impersonation, where concepts like zero-trust and continuous authentication are required to ensure personal security.

QUICK TEST

1. What is a good security practice to follow when you step away from using a social media platform?
   a. Sign-in
   b. Log-out
   c. Sign-up
   d. Log-in
2. Social media monitoring involves tracking:
   a. Hashtags
   b. Keywords
   c. Mentions
   d. All of the above
3. Cybercriminals use personal information from social media for which of the following purposes?
   a. Spear phishing
   b. Building fake profiles
   c. Both a and b
   d. None of the above
4. Which of the following is the most common means that social media sites use for authentication?
   a. Face recognition
   b. Fingerprints
   c. CAPTCHA codes
   d. Two-step verification
5. On receiving a friend request from an unknown person on social media, what is the best course of action from a security viewpoint?
   a. Block them
   b. Ignore/Decline
   c. Add them to expand your friend list
   d. a or b
6. Securing your social media account involves:
   a. Configuring privacy settings
   b. Monitoring your account regularly
   c. Being aware of who you are connecting with
   d. All of the above
7. Which of the following is not a social media platform?
   a. Instagram
   b. LinkedIn
   c. Amazon
   d. WeChat
8. Which of the following is not a threat associated with social media?
   a. Identity theft
   b. Hardware failure
   c. Social engineering
   d. Cyber bullying

9. Which of the following are social media threats to look out for?
   a. Likejacking/Clickjacking
   b. Unbelievable news that is really malware
   c. Fake friends or followers
   d. All of the above
10. Social media platforms include:
    a. Blogs
    b. News portals
    c. E-commerce sites
    d. None of the above

QUESTIONS

1. Explain the benefits of social media monitoring from an organizational perspective.
2. One of the biggest concerns about the use of social media is privacy protection. Discuss this statement.
3. Describe the best practices that could help an individual in making the use of social media more secure.
4. What are the measures that organizations can take to enhance social media security?
5. Explain the possible negative repercussions of restricting access to social media sites for employee morale and company culture.
6. What are the security risks for individuals that are associated with the use of social media?
7. What are the important legal issues involved with using social media?
8. What are the legal and other remedies available for reporting and flagging inappropriate content on social media?
9. What are the risks associated with answering quizzes on social media?
10. What are the restrictions on freedom of speech in the context of social media?

ANSWER KEYS

Quick Test

1. (b)
2. (d)
3. (c)
4. (d)
5. (d)
6. (d)
7. (c)
8. (b)
9. (d)
10. (a)

Annexure A: Cybercrime and Cyberattack Reporting in India

REPORTING CYBERCRIMES

The Government of India has established the National Cyber Crime Reporting Portal (www.cybercrime.gov.in) to enable people to report incidents pertaining to all types of cybercrimes. Complaints on this portal can be logged online and they will be sent to local cyber cells for investigation as required.

FILING A CYBERCRIME COMPLAINT

The portal provides two options for reporting cybercrimes:[1]

- **Report Crime related to Women/ Children:** Under this section, you can report complaints pertaining to online child pornography (CP), child sexual abuse material (CSAM) or sexually explicit content such as rape/gang rape (CP/RGR) content.
- **Report Other Cybercrimes:** Under this option, you can report complaints pertaining to cybercrimes such as mobile crimes, online and social media crimes, online financial frauds, ransomware, hacking, cryptocurrency crimes and online cyber trafficking.

REPORTING CYBERATTACKS

CERT-IN (the Indian Computer Emergency Response Team) is a government-mandated information technology (IT) security organization. On 28 April 2022, CERT-IN issued a directive (No. 20(3)/2022-CERT-IN) mandating that all organizations that come under the purview of the IT Act, 2000, must report 20 specified types of cybersecurity incidents listed below within six hours from incident identification/notification.

- Targeted scanning/probing of critical networks/systems
- Compromise of critical systems/information
- Unauthorized access of IT systems/data
- Defacement of website or intrusion into a website and unauthorized changes such as inserting malicious code, links to external websites, etc.
- Malicious code attacks such as spreading of virus/worm/trojan/bots/spyware/ransomware/crypto miners
- Attacks on servers such as database, mail and DNS and network devices such as routers
- Identity theft, spoofing and phishing attacks
- Denial of Service (DoS) and Distributed Denial of Service (DDoS) attacks
- Attacks on critical infrastructure, SCADA and operational technology systems and wireless networks

---

[1] "National Cyber Crime Portal," Government of India, Minstry of Home Affairs, accessed October 17, 2022. https://www.cybercrime.gov.in/Webform/FAQ.aspx

- Attacks on applications such as e-governance, e-commerce, etc
- Data breach
- Data leak
- Attacks on Internet of Things (IoT) devices and associated systems, networks, software, servers
- Attacks or incidents affecting digital payment systems
- Attacks through malicious mobile apps
- Fake mobile apps
- Unauthorized access to social media accounts
- Attacks or malicious/suspicious activities affecting cloud computing systems/servers/software/applications
- Attacks or malicious/suspicious activities affecting systems/servers/networks/software/applications related to Big Data, blockchain, virtual assets, virtual asset exchanges, custodian wallets, robotics, 3D and 4D printing, additive manufacturing, drones
- Attacks or malicious/suspicious activities affecting systems/servers/software/applications related to artificial intelligence and machine learning

Annexure B

50 Significant Cyberattacks/Data Breaches: 2011–2021

Year	Organization Attacked	Type of Cyberattack	Impact
2011	Epsilon	Data Breach	The email services company hosts over 2,500 customer email lists from Capital One to Walmart and said about 50 of its clients were affected.
2011	Sony PlayStation	Data Breach	Hackers gained access to 70 million user accounts. Credit card data may also have been compromised.
2011	Citi	Data Breach	200,000 accounts were compromised by a cyberattack.
2011	International Monetary Fund	Spear Phishing	Degree of compromise not publicly known.
2012	LinkedIn, Last.fm, Dropbox and Gamigo	Password Leaks	LinkedIn was among those hacked by unknown persons and the password hashes of more than 6.4 million people were leaked on the Internet.
2012	Apple Mac	Malware	More than 700,000 Macs were infected by Mac OS X Trojan FlashBack/Fakeflash.
2012	Aramco	Shamoon Virus	Over 30,000 computers were permanently destroyed by the malware.
2103	Target Corporation	Hacking of Point-of-Sale Terminals	One of the biggest security breaches in history. Target had to pay an $18.5 million settlement after hackers stole 40 million credit and debit records.
2013	Adobe Systems Inc	Data Breach	152,000,000 records compromised.
2013	New York Times	Domain Redirection	The NYT website went offline for almost two hours as its domain was redirected to Syrian Electronic Army servers.
2013	Spamhaus	DDoS	Started as a 10–80 Gbps DDoS attack that grew to 100 Gbps over a few days and peaked at 309 Gbps. This is the world's largest cyberattack.

Year	Organization Attacked	Type of Cyberattack	Impact
2013–14	Yahoo	Data Breach	Information related to three billion accounts was stolen, making it one of the biggest data breaches in history.
2014	Home Depot	Data Breach	56 million credit and debit cards were affected by a data breach.
2014	eBay	Data Breach	233 million users' data were exposed to cybercriminals.
2014	JP Morgan Chase	Data Breach	Affected 76 million households and 7 million small businesses.
2014	Sony	APT	Hackers leaked five unreleased movies online and exposed over 47,000 Social Security numbers.
2015	Premera	Data Breach	Health records and personal identifiable information (PII) of 11 million were exposed.
2015	Experian, T-Mobile	Data Breach	Information on 15 million customers of T-Mobile were exposed.
2015	Ashley Madison	Data Breach	Information pertaining to 37 million users was stolen.
2015	Anthem	Data Breach	80 million patient and employee records were compromised.
2016	MySpace	Data Breach	427 million passwords of 360 million users of social networking site Myspace were stolen and sold by a hacker on the dark web.
2016	Mossack Fonseca/The Panama Papers	Data Breach	Exposed 2.6 TB of sensitive data totalling 11.5 million files. The leaked data contained 4.8 million emails, 2.2 million PDF documents, 1.1 million image files, 3 million database records, and 320,000 other text files.
2016	Dyn	DDoS Attack using the Mirai Botnet	This DDoS attack resulted in widespread outages across Dyn's systems, leaving various Internet platforms temporarily unavailable to users throughout North America and Europe.
2016	21st Century Oncology	Data Breach	Exposed the information of 2.2 million patients based across all 50 states and internationally.
2017	Equifax	Data Breach	Affected 145.5 million consumers whose records were compromised.

Year	Organization Attacked	Type of Cyberattack	Impact
2017	Uber	Ransomware	Personal information of more than 57 million Uber drivers and riders was exposed.
2017	WannaCry	Ransomware	Infected an estimated 300,000 computer systems in just four days.
2017	About 60 Universities and US Federal Agencies	SQL Injection Attack by Rasputin	Web applications hosted by the victims were targeted and the hacker attempted to sell access to the databases.
2017	Maersk	NotPetya Malware	3500 servers, all end-user devices comprising 49,000 laptops were destroyed. A total of 1,200 applications were inaccessible and approximately 1,000 were destroyed.
2017	HBO	Ransomware	1.5 TB of data including unreleased episodes and scripts were stolen.
2017	MongoDB	Unprotected Database (also called the MongoDB Apocalypse)	System administrators had left databases exposed online without a password for years.
2018	British Airways	Magecart Breach	Credit card details of around 380,000 customers were compromised.
2018	Marriott	Data Breach	Up to 500 million hotel guests' information were stolen.
2018	MyFitnessPal	Data Breach	Hackers gained access to over 150 million usernames, emails and passwords.
2018	Facebook	Data Breach	Hackers gained access to over 30 million users' records.
2018	Exactis	Data Breach	Over 400 categories of information, such as phone numbers, email and physical addresses, interests, ages, religions, pet ownership, etc. of 340 million victims (230M consumers, 110M businesses).
2018	Aadhaar	Data Breach	Aadhaar numbers, names, emails and physical addresses were exposed.
2019	Facebook	User Data Leak	540 million records of Facebook users were compromised and were published on Amazon's cloud computing service.
2019	Capital One	Data Breach SSRF Vulnerability Exploited	Compromised approximately 140,000 Social Security numbers and approximately 80,000 bank account numbers of U.S. customers.

Year	Organization Attacked	Type of Cyberattack	Impact
2019	First American Corporation	Data Leak-Insecure Direct Object Reference	Exposed over 800 million title and escrow document images.
2019-20	EasyJet	Data Breach	Nearly 9,000,000 basic booking and 2208 credit card details were compromised.
2020	SolarWinds	Software Supply Chain Attack	Potentially impacted thousands of customers and service providers around the world who used their Orion software.
2020	Twitter	Hacking	Some of the most recognized and highly regarded global Twitter handles were compromised and used to fraudulently tweet about Bitcoin.
2020	Zoom	Data Breach	Approximately 500,000 user accounts emerged for sale on a dark web forum.
2021	Domino's India	Data Leak	Customers' personal data related to 18 crore orders were exposed.
2021	Microsoft Exchange	Mass Cyberattack	Exploited the four zero-day vulnerabilities in Microsoft's Exchange Server, affecting 9 government agencies and over 60,000 private companies in the U.S. alone.
2021	Acer	Ransomware	Hackers breached company servers and stole 60 GB of company information.
2020	Zoom	Credential Compromise	More than half a million Zoom account credentials, usernames and passwords were made available in dark web crime forums.
2021	Colonial Pipeline	Ransomware	Forced the company to shut down the East Coast fuel pipeline for a long period of time.
2021	Pegasus Spyware	Zero-Click Mobile Exploit	Surveillance of a large number of phones around the world.

Annexure C

Self-Assessment Questions

1. What is the strategic role of an information system?
2. How can security issues become an integral part of the software development cycle?
3. Cybersecurity is a journey and not a destination. Explain this statement.
4. Is information security the same as cybersecurity. Discuss.
5. What is a cybersecurity threat? List and explain common cybersecurity threats faced by an organization.
6. From a cybersecurity viewpoint, which is the most important element of the CIA triad and why? What are some other security elements that could be added to the CIA triad to make it more comprehensive?
7. What are CIS Critical Security Controls? What are they useful for?
8. What is scamming in cybercrime?
9. A successful cyberattack can cause major damage to a business. It can affect the bottom line, as well as its reputation and consumer trust. Explain the statement.
10. What are the issues in Internet governance?
11. Describe the efforts being made at international and national levels towards controlling cybercrime.
12. Explain with examples how cyberattacks can affect citizens and communities.
13. What is the cyber kill chain? How is it useful?
14. Describe the different phases of an advanced persistent threat (APT)?
15. Describe the ways in which organizations can protect themselves against insider threats.
16. What is a zero-day vulnerability? How can organizations protect themselves against zero-day attacks?
17. What is Common Weakness Enumeration (CWE)? How is it useful for securing applications?
18. Explain DNS spoofing with an example.
19. What are the five types of steganography?
20. What is social engineering? Explain with examples.
21. List and explain the different types of cyber offenders.
22. What is the difference between cyber espionage and cyberwarfare?
23. Describe the various forms of cybercrimes.
24. List and describe important security issues and challenges faced by organizations today.
25. Institutional mechanisms and user communities play an important role in vulnerability management. Discuss this statement.
26. Explain some of the major challenges faced in securing cyber-physical systems and IoT devices.
27. How does the use of social media cause security issues?
28. What are the benefits of using a VPN in the context of remote working?
29. Explain the role of policies, standards, benchmarks and procedures in cybersecurity.
30. List and explain the different types of security controls that can be deployed by an organization.
31. What are the major concerns that must be addressed in a business continuity plan?
32. Explain the importance and mechanisms of communication during incident response.

33. What is Business Impact Analysis used for?
34. How can organizations prepare their security teams for developing secure information systems?
35. Explain with examples the different types of critical systems and their relative importance from a cybersecurity perspective.
36. Explain the various security issues involved in digital file sharing and ways to address related risks.
37. What is pseudonymization? How is it useful in securing data?
38. What is cryptography? How is it important for data protection? What exactly are encryption and decryption?
39. Explain the importance of access control in a security program.
40. List and explain some of the best practices for ensuring database security.
41. Why is the OSI model important to cybersecurity?
42. Why should you merge physical security and cybersecurity?
43. What are the basic principles of data protection and data security? What is the focus of data protection and data security strategies?
44. List and explain key actions that organizations can take to enhance their security posture.
45. What are some of the challenges that organizations face in establishing a cybersecurity program?
46. The cyber risk management process is not a one-time activity but must be carefully monitored, reviewed and evaluated to check if existing controls are still fit for the purpose for which they were originally deployed. Explain this statement.
47. How can organizations benefit from adopting a cybersecurity framework?
48. What is required to ensure effective implementation of the ISO standard for cybersecurity?
49. The NIST framework is organized around five core functions. What are they and what is their relevance in enhancing cybersecurity?
50. What are the key actions involved in shaping a cyber resilience program?
51. What are the five primary rules of HIPAA?
52. List the key compliance requirements of the PCI DSS standard.
53. List the six lawful bases for processing of personal data under GDPR.
54. What are the human factors that affect cybersecurity?
55. What are the key elements of a SETA program?
56. What are the key considerations for implementing cybersecurity technologies?
57. There is no single piece of software that can provide comprehensive cybersecurity to an organization. Organizations must figure out what technologies can help them execute their cybersecurity plans and programs. Discuss this statement.
58. Describe the steps involved in configuring a firewall.
59. What is a honeypot? How is it useful?
60. What is the role of UEBA software in cybersecurity?
61. Artificial intelligence is emerging as a key cybersecurity tool for both attackers and defenders. Discuss this statement.
62. What are the advantages and disadvantages of virtual currencies?
63. What is a smart contract? What are its disadvantages?
64. What is the use of Identity and Access Management (IAM) systems in the context of cybersecurity?
65. Explain how antivirus solutions work.
66. What is a DMZ in a network? How does it work?

67. Cyber laws are still evolving. What are some of the emerging challenges that need to be addressed?
68. Explain the difference between laws and regulations. Do they have the same effect in practice?
69. What is the purpose of cyber laws?
70. What is the role of treaties and conventions in the enforcement of cyber laws?
71. What are the main objectives of the Indian IT Act, 2000?
72. What is prescribed under Section 43A of the Information Technology Act, 2000 for the protection of personal information?
73. What are the challenges faced by enforcement agencies in enforcing cyber laws?
74. What is CERT-IN? What are its functions?
75. What are the factors to be considered while handling and presenting digital evidence?
76. List and describe the cyber forensic tools used in the investigation of cybercrimes.
77. Who are the stakeholders in the prevention of and protection from cybercrime?
78. What are the goals and benefits of GDPR?
79. What is PII and PHI? Why do they need to be protected?
80. What are the actions you must take in the event your personal cybersecurity has been compromised?
81. What is identity theft? What are the most common categories of identity theft?
82. What are best practices related to password creation and protection?
83. Describe various types of cybercrimes that target individuals.
84. What is cyberbullying? What are the effects of cyberbullying?
85. What are the steps you can take to improve your personal cybersecurity?
86. What is a personal area network (PAN)? What security concerns does a PAN have?
87. List some of the dos and don'ts related to mobile security.
88. What are the biggest future challenges in cybersecurity?
89. Explain the role and importance of ethics in cybersecurity.
90. What is the defence-in-depth cybersecurity approach? How does it enhance cybersecurity?
91. What is OSINT? Why is cyber threat intelligence important for a business?
92. What is disinformation? How can organizations combat it?
93. How can cybersecurity culture be improved?
94. What sections of the Information Technology Act, 2000 deal with posting of inappropriate content?
95. What are the features and functions of social media monitoring tools?
96. What are the modes of digital payments operating in India?
97. What are key focus areas for social media monitoring?
98. What are the social media trends that security professionals must be aware of?
99. Why is Web 3.0 expected to be more secure?
100. What are the types of digital identities? How can we secure each of them?

Annexure D: List of Abbreviations and Acronyms

AD	Active Directory
AES	Advanced Encryption Standard
AI	Artificial intelligence. Refers to computer programs that can perform intelligent functions by mimicking the human brain.
ALG	Application layer gateway
API	Application programming interface
APT	Advanced persistent threat
Asymmetric key	The foundation of public key infrastructure (PKI)
ATM	Automated teller machine
B2B	Business to Business
B2C	Business to Consumer
BAN	Body area networks
BCE	Before the Common Era
BC and DR	Business continuity and disaster recovery
BEC	Business email compromise
BIA	Business impact analysis
BLP	Bell–LaPadula
BSIMM	Building Security in Maturity Model
BYOD	Bring your own device
C&C	Command and Control
CA	Certificate Authorities
CASB	Cloud Access Security Broker
CCPA	California Consumer Privacy Act
CEO	Chief Executive Officer
CERN	Conseil Européen pour la Recherche Nucléaire or European Council for Nuclear Research
CERT	Computer Emergency Response Team

CHAP	Challenge Handshake Authentication Protocol
CIO	Chief Information Officer
CIA	Confidentiality, Integrity and Availability
CIS	Center for Internet Security
CISA	Cybersecurity and Infrastructure Security Agency
CISO	Chief Information Security Officer
COSO	Committee of Sponsoring Organizations
CPS	Cyber-physical system. An integrated system that combines computation, networking and physical processes.
CPU	Central processing unit
CRC	Cyclic redundancy check
CRR	Cyber Resilience Review
Cryptography	A broader term that refers to the study of methods/techniques such as encryption for secure communication in the presence of third parties.
CSIRT	Cybersecurity Incident Response Team
CSMA	Cybersecurity Mesh Architecture
CSRF	Cross-Site Request Forgery
CTO	Chief Technical Officer
CVE	Common Vulnerabilities and Exposures
CWE	Common Weakness Enumeration
Cyber kill chain	A framework developed by Lockheed Martin for identification and prevention of cyber intrusions.
Cyberspace	A symbolic and conceptual representation of the virtual space that exists within the scope of the Internet.
DAST	Dynamic Application Security Testing. Tools to test running code by simulating web application threats and attacks for identifying vulnerabilities.
DDoS	Distributed Denial of Service
DES	Data Encryption Standard
DevOps	A concept that promotes members of the Development and Operations teams working together collaboratively and iteratively to ensure that aspects of operational issues are addressed.
DL	Deep learning. A category of ML based on neural networks that can correct itself.
DLP	Data Loss Prevention. A set of technologies and solutions that provides protection against loss of sensitive data from organizational systems.

DMZ	Demilitarised Zone. A kind of subnetwork that is placed between private networks and the public Internet and provides an extra layer of security for data stored on internal networks.
DNS	Domain Name System
DoS	Denial of Service
DPI	Deep packet inspection
DSA	Digital Signature Algorithm
DSS	Decision support system
DTC	Direct to Consumer
DVR	Digital video recorder
ECDSA	Elliptic Curve Digital Signature Algorithm
EDP	Electronic data processing
EDR	Endpoint detection and response. Technologies focused on preventing malicious threat actors and exploits from targeting endpoints or entry points.
EEA	European Economic Area
EIS	Executive information system
EMV	Europay, MasterCard and Visa
ERP	Enterprise resource planning
EU	European Union
EXIF	Exchangeable image file format
Firewall	A network security device (software or hardware) that filters data packets which attempt to enter a computer or network.
FISMA	Federal Information Security Management Act
FTP	File Transfer Protocol
5G	The fifth generation of cellular mobile network technology that offers greater speed, lower latency, higher bandwidth and the ability to connect a larger number of devices, among other advantages.
GLBA	Gramm–Leach–Bliley Act
GPS	Global Positioning System
GRC	Governance, Risk and Compliance
Hacker	A person who uses computer programming, technical and manipulative skills to intentionally violate computer security for a variety of reasons, such as theft, fraud, corporate espionage and even revenge.
HIPAA	Health Insurance Portability and Accountability Act

HLD	High-level design
HTML	HyperText Markup Language
HTTP	HyperText Transfer Protocol
HTTPS	HyperText Transfer Protocol Secure
IAM	Identity and access management
IASME	Information Assurance for Small and Medium Enterprises
IAST	Interactive Application Security Testing. Tools that combine both SAST and DAST capabilities. A few of them also include open-source security analysis.
IC	Integrated circuit
ICANN	Internet Corporation for Assigned Names and Numbers
ID	Identity
IDPS	Intrusion detection and prevention system
IDS	Intrusion detection system
IEEE	Institute of Electrical and Electronics Engineers
IETF	Internet Engineering Task Force
IoT	Internet of Things
IP	Internet Protocol
IPC	Indian Penal Code
ISACA	Information Systems Audit and Control Association
ISO/IEC	International Organization for Standardization / International Electrotechnical Commission
ISP	Internet Service Provider
IT	Information Technology
JSON	JavaScript Object Notation
LAN	Local area network
LDAP	Lightweight Directory Access Protocol
LLD	Low-level design
LSD	Lean software development
MAC	Media access control
Malware	Malicious software aimed at causing harm or exploiting a computer system, device, service or network to extract data and/or cause other types of harm.
MAST	Mobile Application Security Testing. Tools to identify and analyze vulnerabilities in applications used with mobile platforms.

MD5	Message-Digest Algorithm 5
MEC	Multi-Access Edge Computing
MFA	Multi-factor authentication
MIS	Management information system
MITM	Man in the middle
ML	Machine learning. An extension to the science of artificial intelligence. Systems that support ML are capable of 'learning' from data and with the help of algorithms can adapt to and apply learning to accomplish tasks.
MVP	Minimum viable product
NGFW	Next-generation firewall. It provides a range of functionality that includes deep packet inspection features, stateful inspection as well as capabilities like intrusion detection, intrusion prevention, malware filtering and antivirus.
NFT	Non-fungible token
NIS	Network Information System
NIST	National Institute of Standards and Technology
NOC	Network operations center
NY CRR 500	New York State Department of Financial Services Cybersecurity Requirements Regulation for Financial Services Companies Part 500
NYDFS	New York State Department of Financial Services
OIDC	OpenID Connect
OS	Operating system
OSA	Open Security Architecture
OSB	Online Safety Bill
OSI	Open Systems Interconnection
OSINT	Open-source intelligence
OT	Operational technology
OWASP	Open Web Application Security Project
PAN	Personal area network. A network involved with the exchange of information in the vicinity of a person.
PAP	Password Authentication Protocol
PC	Personal computer
PCI DSS	Payment Card Industry Data Security Standard
PDCA	Plan, Do, Check, Act
PGP	Pretty Good Privacy

PHI	Protected or personal health information
PII	Personal identifiable information
PIN	Personal Identification Number
PKI	Public key infrastructure. It plays a key role in modern-day enterprise cybersecurity. It serves as an effective way of managing public key encryption and using digital certificates through a set of roles, policies, hardware, software and procedures that enable the creation, management, distribution, storage and use of the same.
POP	Post Office Protocol
POS	Point of sale
R&D	Research and Development
RAD	Rapid application development
RAID	Redundant array of independent disks
RASP	Runtime application self-protection
RC4	Rivest Cipher 4
RFID	Radio-frequency identification
RSA	Rivest–Shamir–Adleman
SABSA	Sherwood Applied Business Security Architecture
SAE	Simultaneous Authentication of Equals
SAML	Security Access Markup Language
SAMM	Software Assurance Maturity Model
SASE	Secure Access Service Edge
SAST	Static Application Security Testing. Tools to enable developers to analyze code during the development process for security flaws and issues.
SBOM	Software bill of materials
SCIM	System for Cross-domain Identity Management
SDLC	Software development life cycle. Consists of several stages of the development process that is used for activities like design, build, test and deploy information systems as per pre-specified requirements and as per cost and time estimates.
SDN	Software-defined networking
SD-WAN	Software-defined wide area network
SETA	Security education, training and awareness
SHA2	Secure Hash Algorithm 2
SHA3	Secure Hash Algorithm 3

SIEM		Security information and event management. Enables organizations to detect security incidents and manage security by filtering copious amounts of security data from across different systems and raising security alerts.
SME		Small and medium-sized enterprises
SMS		Short message service
SMTP		Simple Mail Transfer Protocol
S/MIME		Secure/Multipurpose Internet Mail Extension
SOAR		Security orchestration, automation and response. Systems that enable the integration of orchestration processes, automation, incident management and collaboration, visualization and reporting under a single interface.
SOC		Security operations centre
SQL		Structured Query Language
SRD		System Requirements Document
SSID		Service Set Identifier
SSL		Security Socket Layer
SSO		Single Sign-On
Symmetric key		Secret key for encryption.
TCP		Transmission Control Protocol
TCP/IP		Transmission Control Protocol/Internet Protocol
TEE		Trusted Execution Environment
TKIP		Temporal Key Integrity Protocol
TLS		Transport Security Layer. Used for encrypting data sent over the Internet.
TOGAF		The Open Group Architecture Framework
TOR		The Onion Router
TPM		Trusted Platform Module
TPS		Transaction processing system
TSP		Trust service provider
TTPs		Tactics, techniques and procedures
UDHR		Universal Declaration of Human Rights
UDP		User Datagram Protocol
UEBA		User and entity behaviour analytics. A class of software that enables organizations to understand and monitor actions of users to determine deviations from 'normal behaviour' such as oddities, outliers and anomalies.

UK	United Kingdom
UNCITRAL	United Nations Commission on International Trade Law
URL	Uniform Resource Locator
US	United States
USB	Universal Serial Bus
USD	United States Dollar
VOIP	Voice over Internet Protocol
VPN	Virtual private network
WEF	World Economic Forum
WEP	Wireless Equivalent Privacy. A wireless security protocol which uses an encryption scheme that employs a combination of user and system generated keys.
WPA	Wi-Fi Protected Access
WPA2	Wi-Fi Protected Access 2
WPAN	Wireless personal area network

Index

#

5G networks
   about 234, 243
   advantages 243
   important threat vectors 244
   steps to overcome challenges 245

A

Aadhaar 241, 242, 265
advanced persistent threat (APT)
   about 32, 44
   combating 239
   phases 239
   steps to mitigate impact 241
Alibaba 1
agile methodologies 8, 95, 97
Amazon 4, 6, 16, 112, 227, 238, 259
antivirus solution
   about 35, 47, 84, 94, 108, 157
   how it works 157
   next generation 158
application security
   about 51, 95, 96
   DevOps 97
   DevSecOps 97
   secure development methodologies 97
   tools 96
   vulnerability 60
artificial intelligence (AI) 141, 171, 236
attack surface
   about 30, 56, 246
   monitoring 180

B

behavioural analytics 172
best practices
   data protection 94
   database security 110
   e-commerce security 262
   personal cybersecurity 218
   social media use 282

bitcoin
   about 166, 217
   components 166
black hat hacker 28
blockchain
   about 165, 173, 234
   basics 176
   components 174
   how it works 174
   advantages for cybersecurity 176, 237, 242
bot 34, 219
business continuity (BC) 51, 87, 129, 134
business email compromise (BEC) 25, 140, 217

C

CIA triad 16, 161
cloud access security broker (CASB) 181
Common Vulnerabilities and Exposures (CVEs)
   about 70, 95
   history 70
   process 70
cross-site scripting 39, 41, 95, 104
cryptography
   about 129, 161, 166
   applications 164
   hardware security module 163
   how asymmetric cryptography works 162
   objectives 161
   techniques 162
   types and uses of cryptographic keys 163
cryptocurrency 165, 204, 264
cryptojacking 25
cyber espionage 25, 29, 240
cyber forensics
   about 200, 205
   order of evidence collection 201
   phases 201
   types 200
cyber kill chain 44, 45, 85, 241
cyber law
   about 58, 191
   challenges 198

cybersecurity regulations 199
   need for 191
   role of international law and governments 192
cyber offender
   about 30, 205
   kinds of 31
cyber risk management
   about 122, 123
   identification of risk 124
   risk categorization 124
   risk treatment 125
cyber resilience
   about 132, 145, 246
   benefits 133
   criteria for incident classification 133
   key actions 134
   key elements 134
   schema for incident classification 133
cyber scam 27, 31
cyber terrorism 29, 192
cyberattack
   advanced persistent threat (APT) 44
   cross-site scripting 41
   cyber kill chain 45
   definition 38
   denial of service (DoS) 42
   distributed denial of service (DoS) 42
   domain name system (DNS) spoofing 42
   drive-by 43
   impacting citizens and community 46
   insider threat 43
   international efforts 48
   man-in-the-middle (MITM) 42
   organizational implication 45
   password 40
   phishing 40
   prevention of 47
   ransomware 39
   responding to 44
   session hijacking 42
   SQL injection 41
   types 39
      active 39
      passive 39
   uniform resource locator (URL) interpretation 42
   web 40
   zero-day 43
cybercrime
   classification 25
   cyber kill chain 45
   cyber offenders 30
   definition 24
   evidence collection and analysis 206
   execution 35
   forms 25
   impacting citizens and community 46
   international efforts 48
   introduction 23
   investigation 205
   motive of cybercriminals 24
   organizational implication 45
   prevention of 47, 204
   responding to 44
   sources of threat 28
   techniques 202
   tools and methods 32
cybercrime execution
   about 35
   code injection 37
   keylogger 37
   pharming 36
   phishing 35
   smishing 36
   social engineering 35
   steganography 36
cybercrime tools and methods
   malware 33
   reconnaissance 32
cyberextortion 25
cyber-physical system (CPS) 4, 66
cybersecurity
   5G networks 243
   algorithms and techniques 140
   and privacy regulations 223
   basic principles 12
   blockchain 237
   definition 11
   digital trust and identity management 241
   framework 125
   future challenges 233
   governance 17
   harnessing artificial intelligence 236
   human factor 139
   importance of 11
   management 73
   national policy 49
   online code of conduct 51
   organization 17
   other evolving aspects 249
   personal 213
   quantum computing 238
   regulations 199
   role of ethics in 228
   role of internet 18

secure-by-design approach 246
skills shortage 255
strategies and approaches 121
supply chain 247
technologies 145
vulnerabilities 59
cybersecurity advanced technologies and approaches
  about 171
  artificial intelligence (AI) 171
  attack surface monitoring 180
  behavioural analytics 172
  blockchain 173
  cloud access security broker (CASB) 181
  data loss prevention 179
  deep learning (DL) 171
  embedded hardware security and
    authentication 173
  endpoint detection and response (EDR) 181
  extended detection and response (XDR) 181
  machine learning (ML) 171
  platforms 180
  secure access service edge (SASE) 181
  zero trust model 177
cybersecurity and privacy regulations
  about 223
  OECD guidelines 227
    basic principles 227
  principles 225
  related technologies 224
cybersecurity framework
  about 125
  definition 126
  industry-specific
    about 135
    GDPR 137
    HIPAA 135
    NYDFS 136
    PCI DSS 135
    PDPB 138
    region-specific 137
  ISO/IEC 127
  NIST 130
cybersecurity in e-commerce
  best practices 262
  definition 259
  digital payments 264
  elements of security 260
    common issues 261
  introduction 259
  laws on privacy 270
cybersecurity management
  business continuity (BC) 86

controls 77
disaster recovery (DR) 86
incident response 81
information classification 74
overview 73
security organization 79
security policies 75
security procedures and guidelines 76
cybersecurity mesh architecture (CSMA) 178
cybersecurity, other evolving aspects
  about 249
  combating disinformation 249
  confidential computing 250
  convergence 250
  culture 255
    importance of 256
  defence-in-depth 253
  digital divide 255
  ethics 255
  governance 255
  malware detection 250
  skills shortage 255
  standards and regulations 252
  threat intelligence 251
cybersecurity technologies
  advanced technologies and approaches 171
  antivirus 157
  authentication 160
  considerations for implementing 146
  cryptography 161
  digital money, cyptocurrency and NFT 165
  digital signature 167
  email security 155
  firewalls 146
  identity and access management (IAM) 158
  internet protocols and ports 182
  introduction 145
  intrusion detection and prevention (IDP) 150
  network segmentation 152
  security information and event monitoring
    (SIEM) 152
cybersecurity vulnerabilities
  assessment 67
  authentication and authorization 63
  cloud system 61
  Common Vulnerabilities and Exposures (CVEs) 70
  cyber-physical system (CPS) 66
  firmware 61
  hardware 61
  internet of things (IoT) 66
  introduction 55
  network 64

password management 63
Project OWASP 66
remote working 64
social media 65
software application 59
software deployment 62
supply chain 62
system administration 63
third party 62
cyberspace 10, 31, 50, 192, 208
cyberspace piracy
    about 208
    modes of 208
cyberwarfare 24, 29

D

dark web 26, 27, 37
data loss prevention 94, 115, 179
data security/protection techniques
    about 112
    access control 113
    back-up, snapshot, replication 115
    data loss prevention 115
    encryption 113
    firewall 114
    intrusion detection system 114
    pseudonymization 115
    remote access security 115
    storage with built-in protection 115
deep learning (DL) 141, 171
deep web 27, 30
defence-in-depth
    about 182, 241, 253
    security elements 254
denial of service (DoS) 16, 26, 41, 105, 154, 262
decision support system (DSS) 3
DevOps 10, 97
DevSecOps 10, 97
digital money 165
digital payment
    about 264
    common frauds 266
    components 264
    modes of payment in India 265
    preventive measures 266
    RBI guidelines 267
Digital Personal Data Protection Bill (DPDPB), 2022 271
digital trust and identity management
    Aadhaar 242
    about 241
    authentication approaches 242
    self-sovereign identity (SSI) 243
digital signature
    about 97, 148, 167
    benefits 170
    block cipher
        about 168
        mode of operation 169
    classes 168
    digital certificate 167
    features to enhance security 167
    purposes 167
    public key infrastructure (PKI)
        about 170
        components 170
        required elements 170
    stream cipher
        about 169
        types 170
    use case 168
disaster recovery (DR) 86, 94, 134
distributed denial of service (DDoS) 16, 26, 41, 103, 112, 219, 263
domain name system (DNS)
    about 5, 17, 240, 102
    spoofing 38, 42
dynamic application security testing (DAST) 96

E

eBay 1, 4, 6, 259
electronic data processing (EDP) system 3
employee security education, training and awareness (SETA) program 140
encryption 37, 42, 113, 204, 234, 238, 250
endpoint detection and response (EDR) 181, 255
executive information system (EIS) 4
extended detection and response (XDR) 94, 181

F

Facebook 1, 65, 216, 275
firewall
    about 17, 39, 114, 146, 220, 255, 263
    configuring 148
    deployment 148
    how it works 147
firmware 61, 70, 100, 177

G

grey hat hacker 28

General Data Protection Regulation (GDPR) 12, 16, 126, 137, 196, 199, 227
Google 1, 6

H

hacker
  about 40, 42, 49, 57, 65
  black hat 28
  definition 28
  grey hat 28
  white hat 28
hacking 15, 24, 26, 30, 32, 112, 233, 245
Health Insurance Portability and Accountability Act (HIPAA), 1996 126, 135
honeypot 153, 205
HyperText Markup Language (HTML) 5, 18
HyperText Transfer Protocol (HTTP) 5, 159, 186
HyperText Transfer Protocol Secure (HTTPS) 165, 221
human factor in cybersecurity
  about 139
  common errors 140
  employee security education, training and awareness (SETA) program 140

I

ICANN 17
identity and access management (IAM)
  about 158
  criteria 158
  how it works 159
identity theft 25, 197, 222
inappropriate content
  flagging and reporting 280
  laws regarding posting 280
incident response
  about 81
  constituting the team 82
  criteria to trigger 82
  investigation 84
  planning 83
  preparation 83
  response 84
  triage 85
information age 3
information security
  about 12
  fundamental concepts 15
  governance 122
  models 19
  need for 13

  principles 15
  risk management 122
  threats to 13
  types 16
    administrative 16
    physical 17
    technical 17
  versus cybersecurity 13
information systems
  definition 2
  development 6
    agile methodologies 8
    change management 9
    rapid application development 8
    software development life cycle (SDLC) 7
  evolution of 3
  introduction to 1
  maintenance 6
  secure system development 91
  types 3
information system, secure development
  application security 95
  data protection 93
    best practices 94
    techniques 112
  data security 93
    techniques 112
  database security 109
  file sharing issues 116
  introduction 91
  network security 100
  OS security 105
    comparison 106
  physical security 111
  securing information assets 92
  security architecture 98
  security design 98
  security issues 99
  user management 110
Information Technology Act, 2000 196, 225
intellectual property (IP)
  about 26, 51, 92, 113, 174, 192
  issues in cyberspace 208
  steps for protection 209
interactive application security testing (IAST) 96
international law and governments, role of
  about 192
  important cyber laws and regulations
    1970–1990 194
    1990–1999 194
    2000–2010 195

        2011–2020 195
        about 194
        Information Technology Act, 2000 196, 225
    treaties and conventions 193
internet
    evolution of 5
    governance 17
    growth of 5
    organization 17
internet engineering task force (IETF) 17
internet of things (IoT) 4, 66, 99
Internet Protocol (IP) 5, 17, 42, 167, 182
intrusion detection and prevention system (IDPS)
    about 115, 150
    categories 150
    how it works 151
    ways 150
intrusion detection system (IDS)
    about 47, 94, 114, 115, 150
    categories 150
    how it works 151
    ways 150
ISO/IEC 13, 126, 127

J

JSON 158

K

Kubernetes container security 246

L

LinkedIn 1, 65, 216, 275

M

m-commerce 259, 260
machine learning (ML) 115, 141, 151, 171
malware
    about 33, 172, 207, 216, 262
    forensics 201
    types 34
        characterized by action and behaviour 34
        for infecting a system 34
    malware for infecting a system
        about 34
        bot 34
        fileless 34
        trojan 34
        virus 34
        worm 34

malware characterized by action and behaviour
    about 34
    adware 34
    ransomware 34
    spyware 34
    rootkit 35
mainframe era 3
man-in-the-middle (MITM) 42, 154
manufacturing resource planning (MRP) system 3
management information system (MIS) 3
metaverse 233, 235, 284
mobile application security testing (MAST) 96

N

National Institute of Standards and Technology (NIST) 2, 125, 130, 221
National Security Policy 50
network security
    about 100
    challenges 101
    OSI model 103
    techniques and tools 102
network segmentation
    about 152
    demilitarized zone (DMZ) 152
    honeypot
        about 153
        how it works 153
    wireless security and VPNs 154
        how it works 154, 155
network vulnerabilities 64, 79
non-fungible token (NFT) 166
New York State Department of Financial Services (NYDFS) 127, 136

O

OSI model 103, 182
OSINT 252

P

Payment and Settlement Systems Act, 2007 268
Payment Card Industry Data Security Standard (PCI DSS) 127, 135, 199, 26
payment fraud 25
personal cybersecurity
    best practices 218
        awareness 218
        identity theft 222
        phone and mobile device security 221

protection 220
vigilance 219
causes of breaches 214
definition 213
  personal identifiable information (PII) 214
  protected or personal health information (PHI) 214
introduction 213
personal identifiable information (PII) 136, 214
Personal Data Protection Bill (PDPB) 138, 196, 225
pharming 36
phishing
  about 35, 40
  deceptive 36
  malware-based 36
  methods 36
  spear 34
Project OWASP 66
protected or personal health information (PHI) 135, 214
pseudonymization 115
public key infrastructure (PKI) 164, 170

Q

quantum computing 234, 238

R

ransomware attack 39, 64, 133
rapid application development 8
reconnaissance
  about 32
  active 32
  passive 32
remote working 12, 56, 64, 76, 117
REST 96

S

SCRUM 9
secure access service edge (SASE) 181
secure-by-design approach
  about 246
  benefits 248
  importance of 248
  key actions for implementing 246
  Kubernetes container security 246
securing information assets
  about 92
  business critical 92
  mission critical 92
  safety critical 92

security considerations and challenges
  being unmindful of vulnerabilities 58
  dissolving of perimeter 56
  evolving law and regulations 59
  importance of prevention 60
  increase in attack surface 56
  limited awareness 57
  more complex 55
  safeguarding credentials 56
  third-party dependence 58
security information and event monitoring (SIEM)
  about 81, 102, 152
  how it works 152
self-sovereign identity (SSI) 243
session hijacking 42, 104
Simple Mail Transfer Protocol (SMTP) 5, 104, 186
smishing 36
SOAP 97
social engineering 14, 25, 35, 40, 57, 267
social media and security
  benefits 276
  best practices 282
    enterprise cybersecurity 283
    metaverse 284
    personal security 282
  data harvesting 281
  flagging and reporting content 280
    laws 280
  introduction 275
  marketing 276
  monitoring 277
  personal data protection 279, 281
  privacy 278
  privacy laws 279
  types 275
software bill of materials (SBOM) 234, 248
software development life cycle (SDLC) 7, 97
SQL injection 39, 41, 95
static application security testing (SAST) 96
steganography 36, 204
surface web 27

T

threat intelligence
  about 124, 141, 157, 251
  operational 252
  OSINT 252
  strategic 251
  tactical 251
Transmission Control Protocol (TCP) 5, 147, 185

transaction processing system (TPS) 3
trojan 34, 149, 203, 240

U

user and entity behaviour analytics (UEBA) 172

V

virus 34, 65, 101, 149
vulnerabilities assessment
    about 67, 269
    analysis 69
    evaluation 69
    methods 68
    planning 67
    remediation 69
    repetition 69
    scanning 68

W

Web 3.0 233, 235
web skimming 266
white hat hacker 28
Wi-Fi Protected Access (WPA)
    about 154
    how it works 154
    WPA2 155
    WPA3 155
Wired Equivalent Privacy (WEP) 154
World Wide Web (WWW) 4
worm 34, 201

Y

Yahoo 1, 6

Z

zero-day attack 43
zero trust model
    about 114, 177
    challenges 178
    enforcement requirements 177
    implementation 178
    key principles 178